SECURITY POLICY OF INDIA

Modi Doctrine

The primary purpose of any country's security policy is to promote its national interest- to ensure security, safeguard its sovereignty, and contribute to its growth and prosperity.

SECURITY POLICY OF INDIA

Modi Doctrine

Col Dr Narendar Singh (Retd)

PENTAGON PRESS

Security Policy of India: Modi Doctrine
Col Dr Narendar Singh (Retd)

ISBN 978-81-8274-939-9

First Published in 2017

Published by
PENTAGON PRESS
206, Peacock Lane, Shahpur Jat,
New Delhi-110049
Phones: 011-64706243, 26491568
Telefax: 011-26490600
email: rajan@pentagonpress.in
website: www.pentagonpress.in

Printed at Aegean Offset Printers, Greater Noida, U.P.

The Book is dedicated to gallant Indian Soldier, especially Infantrymen who ask nothing.

My wife Beena,

sons

Lieutenant Colonel Ravi Raja an infantryman,
Major Tarun Singh, AMC,

Daughters-in-Law

Tapasya and Veena

&

Grandson Sankalp and Granddaughter Sanskriti

CONTENTS

जनरल (डा.) विजय सिंह
पीवीएसएम, एवीएसएम, वाईएसएम (से.नि.)

GEN. (DR) VIJAY KUMAR SINGH
PVSM, AVSM, YSM (Retd)

सत्यमेव जयते

विदेश राज्य मंत्री
भारत सरकार, नई दिल्ली
Minister of State for External Affairs
Government of India, New Delhi

FOREWORD

This Book by Col Narendar Singh, with a fascinating title *Security Policy of India: Modi Doctrine* is focused on India's Security Policy. The author investigates the underlying principles of India's foreign policy from 1947 until the present day.

India's Foreign Policy has been a constant matter of speculations and debate on what approach India should take in the emerging Global Order. There is no denying the fact that India, one of the largest democracies and vibrant economy in the world, has a pivotal role in shaping up the Global Order. After sixty years of independence, India's foreign policy in early 21st Century created certain doubts. The reason for this is the acceptance of old definitions rather than an appreciation of the country's background and its human resource potential. The word "neutrality or non-alignment" as applied to India's foreign policy has little meaning as explained by the writer. Like a hundred other often-repeated words, it appears to have been blunted with use, and can be related to India only in the context of her past and present policies. What does neutrality—or, as we prefer to call it, non-alignment—mean, and why does India follow this path? The writer has dealt with this lucidly.

India, since Independence, did not carry out an assessment of its security needs and lived in a Utopian World. India has a cherished history of collaboration with several countries as the leader of the developing world. India was one of the founding members of several international organisations, most notably the United Nations, the Non-Aligned Movement, the Asian Development Bank and the G-20 industrial nations. India also played an important role in international organisations like the East Asia Summit, World Trade Organisation, International Monetary Fund G8+5, IBSA Dialogue Forum and regional organisations which include SAARC, BIMSTEC, etc., but it never ensured that her vital Security interests are more important than being a preacher of peace. No policy can ensure security unless it is backed by economic and military power. India ignored her defence forces to her peril. This is a vital lesson that flows out of the book.

I commend the writer for his forthrightness and logic of views expressed. I wish him many more successful books to his credit.

ACKNOWLEDGEMENTS

I have long been convinced that students of strategic studies especially in India know too little Security Policy. A book should explain what happened and not advance authors, so that the reader can judge for themselves where the balance of probability lies. All that I can say is that I tried to be neutral on the more controversial topics. However, the assertive habits of being a professional soldier cannot easily be set aside.

Since independence, security has taken a back seat. The irony is that today the nation has not provided its forces with the wherewithal necessary to ensure security. The last 10 years were the worst, A chief was haunted when he spoke of the deficiencies.

A professional soldier not only plays his part as executant of the policies of the government but also thinks how the policies of the government can be put into effect in the environment in which he operates. The criticism in the parliament, media and society at large, although healthy at large in a democracy, impairs the functioning of the personnel executing the task or administering the policy. It is during the execution, that we really come to know the efficacy of the policy. Controversies around Indian Defence Forces hurt the morale of the men who faces death at every minute. It is best avoided. It is because of his dedication that we sleep peacefully.

The book is benefitted greatly from what I have learnt teaching, and from numerous discussions and arguments with seniors, peers and colleagues. I know from experience—that reader's experience—that this melding of history, international relations and strategy works well. I would like to thank my peers for their feedback, cooperation and of course friendship. In addition I would like to express my gratitude to them for last minute favours.

My principal debt is to Mr Rajan Arya and the staff at Pentagon Press. I am amazed by his patience. His advice has been sound.

I would like to put on record my gratitude to Honourable Gen VK Singh, PVSM, AVSM, YSM, ADC for having been a guide and at times expressing his view loudly at forums on strategic issues.

Last, but not the least, my ever suffering family deserve the most sincere thanks for tolerating, usually with good humour, my protracted distraction with the challenges of book creation supporting me spiritually throughout writing this thesis and my life in general. I put on record my sincere thanks to my wife Beena for her patience, especially bearing the typing. I would like to thank Lieutenant Colonel Ravi Raja, Major Tarun Singh, AMC, for their candid opinions. I place on record my gratitude to Tapasya and Squadron Leader Veena for their patience in reading the script and suggesting changes. I would be unjust if I do not thank Sankalp and Sanskriti, without their presence nothing could have been possible. They both inspire me daily to do something new.

Col Dr Narendar Singh (Retd)

PREFACE

Philosophies the world over are 'society centred,' or 'this-world-centred' and direct man to find fulfillment here in this world through socio-political activities, whereas Indian Philosophy looks upon the world as fleeting, transitory and 'unreal' and encourages human beings to seek spiritual realisation of the 'Absolute'. Indian philosophers in olden days never concerned themselves with theories of kingship and nature of government, but were grappling with the problem of transmigration of souls and underplaying the importance of life in this world. Religious and no politics dominated Indian social life. In spite of periodic invasions and few eras of internal breakdown. India never oriented her thoughts to military power, or the socio-politically oriented ideology of a unitary, humane government, and lacked a strong unifying credo. The only book worth mention is the Kautilya's Arthashastra. It is believed that Kautilya, the author of the tremendously influential manual on statecraft, engineered the rise of the Mauryas. Kautilya rose to be the Chief Political Advisor of the first Maurya Emperor.

Another work of importance appeared just as India was about to achieve Independence by Anand Coomaraswamy. In his work *Spiritual Authority and Temporal Power in The Indian Theory of Government*, Anand Coomaraswamy has drawn extensively from texts like the *Vajasneyi Samhita*, and the *Satpatha Brahmana* to arrive at an alternative understanding of kingship, its responsibilities and goals. According to Coomaraswamy, 'the only royal road to power is to become one's own master; the mastery of whatever else follows', this is the traditional secret of government.

Publications and commentaries world over continue to proclaim India has potential. But NO ONE really took India seriously at the high table. The world continues to speak that India will be a power in future. The analyst evinces passion by elucidating the many limits to India's great power ambitions. Fewer still take account of the unique circumstances that India land borders 8 countries (Pakistan Occupied Kashmir abuts Afghanistan) and are at the centre of the Indian Ocean through which 80 per cent of world's energy requirement flows. India has perhaps the world's most strategically complex geography.

India has made significant progress in forging diplomatic and economic links with its neighbour and in resolving many territorial disputes, but India and its neighbours disagree over a significant number of overlapping, economic, territorial and maritime disputes.

This book is hardly the first to discuss the Modi Doctrine. However, in this book we confront the impact of Modi on Security. The conciliatory behaviour of India reflects a supposed internalisation of international norms, a favourite notion of those who see India bending to the American-Centric global order.

The present volume of 12 essays addresses India's security issues and how the advent of Modi on the scene has impacted the Nation and its standing globally.

Chapter 1 gives the background to the What is Strategy and the strategic culture in India. Strategic culture in India is an indigenous construct over millennia, modified considerably by our experience in the last two centuries. For instance, war and peace are continuing themes in a Indian strategic culture. While not celebrating war, the culture treats it as acceptable when good fights evil. The primary purpose of any country's security policy is to promote its national interest and core values. However, the successive Governments have had a lackadaisical attitude towards National Security.

Chapter 2 primarily deals with Notions of Security. The principle of sovereignty appears to be the hallmark of 'Modi Doctrine'; it underlies the contemporary international system in which state as the main entity may be seen as a major source of instability. Consider 'external sovereignty' in particular – no entity can dictate to a state what it should do; hence, there is anarchy as there is no central law that governs relations amongst the nations and the laws that exist are for the states to accept or reject. Hence, the present system is of 'self-help'. The incipient Modi doctrine has five key elements. First, and most important, is the idea that a strong, self-reliant and self-confident India will pursue a foreign policy of "enlightened national interest". Enlightened national interest adds a moral prism to the policy.

In Chapter 3: Security Environment as existing today is discussed. For strategic leaders of the 21st Century primarily concerned with the issues of national security policy, the international system with which they will be dealing is likely to reflect only partially the traditional international system as seen few years back. The change is primarily due to a combination of relationship of nation states at the international level with the transnational threats posed by some of the failed or failing states, ungoverned regions, terror, the proliferation of weapons of mass destruction (WMDs), crime, drugs, pandemics, and environmental degradation, as well as by elements of the system that also have potentially positive impacts such as globalisation and the information revolution. Threats, challenges, and opportunities can come in many shapes and sizes. A traditional threat might take the shape of a nation-state in possession of WMD and a hostile attitude. India suffers from internal and external threat. The permeability of India's borders with several of its immediate neighbours combined with India's constitutionally guaranteed freedoms and the free flow of potential security threats of various sorts across these boundaries continues to preoccupy Indian policymakers. Regional insecurities are exacerbated to a great extent by the persistence of domestic challenges to India's national security and foreign policy. India today represents a fascinating coalescence of caste, ethnic, religious and regional groupings, often cutting across each other, that has produced arguably the world's oldest and, during many centuries, and most successful, pluralistic society. The vibrancy of its democratic experiment combined with its heterogeneous society and rapidly growing economy has caught the attention of observers around the world.

Chapter 4: Centrality of India. History of India has been profoundly influenced by its geographical location and physical features. India lies amongst politically assertive and dynamic states. All the historical pretenders to global power originated in the vicinity of India or aimed to reach India. The world's most populous aspirant to power, as also, the entire potential—economic and political challengers—lie in her vicinity. The geo-strategic importance of India cannot be overemphasised, due to its interrelationship with large part of the world, in terms of its location, trade orientation, cultural and ideological bonds. India meets five of the six critical elements as advocated by Admiral Mahan for a country to be a great sea power viz. geographical position, physical conformation, and extent of territory, population and national character; lastly, the direction from the government. The region is world's axial super subcontinent. A power that dominates the vicinity and India would exercise decisive influence of worlds two of the three most economically productive regions, Europe and East Asia. A glance at the map also suggests that the dominant power would almost automatically control the Middle East and Africa.

Chapter 5: Traditionally great powers have played a dominant role in shaping international society. Great powers, the main actors, pay careful attention to how much economic and military power they have relative to each other. It is important not only to have substantial amount of power, but also to make sure that no other state sharply shifts the balance of power in its favour. That role can be either responsible or predatory Classical History was confined to three distinct areas of China, India and the Mesopotamia with little awareness of events in the rest of the world viz. Greece etc. In the Middle Ages, the policy of the European Powers was conducted in isolation from that of Asian Empires. With modern technologies, and in the face of the contemporary intellectual ferment, there is no longer any isolated area; any diplomatic or military move involves worldwide consequences. History indicates that a prominent power cannot long maintain its global leadership without the support and the cooperation of other nations in the pursuit of mutual interests. Modi understood that is power the currency of international/ world politics. Modi cosseted with the US; he did not leave Russia, China and Japan behind. India's partnership with Japan has witnessed the most dynamic growth. Several historic decisions have been taken, the most telling being the decision by Japan, the only country to have suffered a nuclear attack, to sign a civilian nuclear deal with India. Modi just changed the game with China; he was candid and forthcoming. 'Panchsheel' was out. Look East Policy (LEP), initiated by Prime Minister Narasimha Rao in 1992; Prime Minister Narendra Modi, renamed and advocated Act East Policy (AEP), which was launched at the East Asia Summit in Myanmar in November 2014. India Modi accorded a new focus to promoting connectivity through Myanmar and Thailand with other ASEAN states

Chapter 6: The ongoing power shifts in the world are primarily linked to Asia's phenomenal economic rise. One of the most striking things about the larger Asian strategic landscape is the arc of failing or troubled states around India. This harsh geographical reality is India's most-glaring weaknesses—one that weighs it down regionally. Its neighbourhood is so chronically troubled that India confronts what can be called a tyranny of geography. The root cause of these manifold failures, in many minds, is the very artificiality of Pakistan itself: a cartographic puzzle piece sandwiched between India and Central Asia. Pakistan is the most dangerous nation in the world, hub of all terrorism. The ongoing power shifts in the world are primarily linked to Asia's phenomenal economic rise. Modi clearly enunciated 'Neighbourhood First Policy', 'Act East policy'; 'Link West Policy', entered into Defence Agreement with Qatar, 'Connect Central Asia', held an African Conclave and for Indian Ocean region went if for SAGAR and 'Indian Ocean out Reach'.

Chapter 7: Modi clearly followed the policy to create web of allies as stated in the Bhartiya Janta Party manifesto. In the short-term Modi has new international initiative to bring structural reform in the world's financial system with more effective regulation and stronger systems of multilateral consultations and surveillance as well as a collaborative and cooperative global effort for successfully overcoming various challenges. India has to confront with well entrenched powers like US, Russia, European Union, Japan and China in getting the institutions to be more responsive to new needs.

Chapter 8: India's soft power worked its magic before without much government support. India had been able to use Bollywood, Buddhism and other spiritual forays to promote the country. Modi has taken on to promote India. He has gone on to promote soft power of the nation. Yoga, Sanskrit Conference in Bangkok, Buddhism Circuit etc are some of the initiatives.

Chapter 9: Technology has been his favourite. Modi has taken on to reduce dependence of India on imports. Modi Government for the first time accepted to export weapons. Modi's policy changes include fewer curbs on foreign investment in defence, looser export controls and a reworked procurement policy that's set to encourage domestic output

One of the major failures has been to keep the Defence Forces in good stead. There has been a general resentment in the Armed Forces against the Modi Government. This has been covered in Chapter 10.

From the strength of the treasury the army is born', said Kautilya. Traditionally, the economy has entered into the national security debate through its impact on the nation's hard power: the funding of defence. 'Make in India' has become Narendra Modi's signature programme as he aspires to convert India into a global manufacturing hub. His foreign policy mantra therefore is strongly driven by geo-economics—especially attracting foreign direct investment (FDI)—and at the same time seeks to consolidate India's leadership role in South Asia covered in Chapter 11.

The Modi Doctrine is about projecting India's soft economic power along with military might for strategic initiatives in the region and across the globe. the Modi Doctrine does not seek to confine itself to the old set rules of international diplomacy and relations. Modi seems to be redefining the terms on which India is likely to engage with the world in the coming years. Pragmatism coupled with a more confident assertion of Indian interests is likely to be the hallmark.

The Modi Doctrine about "Strategic Autonomy" with Deterrence.

1

INTRODUCTION

Here's what Kautilya told the King of Magadha

"The Mauryan soldier does not himself the Royal treasuries enrich, nor does he the Royal granaries fill. He does not himself carry out trade and commerce nor produce scholars, thinkers, littérateurs, artists, artisans, sculptors, architects, craftsmen, doctors and administrators. He does not himself build roads and ramparts, nor dig wells and reservoirs. He does not himself write poetry and plays, paint or sculpt, nor delve in metaphysics, arts and sciences. He does not do any of this directly as he is neither gifted and trained, nor mandated to do so.

The soldier only and merely ensures that:

The tax, tribute and revenue collectors travel far and wide unharmed and return safely; the farmer tills, grows, harvests, stores and markets his produce unafraid of pillage and plunder; the trader, merchant and moneylender function and travel across the length and breadth of the realm unmolested.

The savant, sculptor, painter, maestro and master create works of art, literature, philosophy, astronomy and astrology in peace and quiet; the architect designs and builds his *Vaastus* without tension; the tutor (*acharya*), the mentor (*guru*) and the priest (*purohita*) teach and preach in tranquility.

The sages (*rishis, munis,* and *tapaswees*) meditate and undertake penance in wordless silence; the doctor (*vaidyaraja*) tends to the ill and the infirm well, adds to the pharmacopoeia, discovers new herbs and invents new medical formulations undisturbed.

The mason, the bricklayer, the artisan, the weaver, the tailor, the jeweller, the potter, the carpenter, the cobbler, the cowherd (*gopaala*) and the smith work unhindered; the mother, wife and governess go about their chores and bring up children in harmony and tranquility.

The aged and the disabled are well taken care of, tended to and are able to fade away gracefully and with dignity; cattle graze freely without being lifted or harmed by miscreants.

He is thus the **very basis** and silent, barely visible **cornerstone** of our fame, culture, physical well-being and prosperity; in short, of the entire nation building activity. He **does not** perform any of these chores himself directly. He **enables** the rest of us to perform these without letting hindrance or worry (*nirbhheek* and *nishchinta*) affecting us.

Our military sinews, on the other hand, lending credibility to our pronouncements of adherence to good *Dharma*, goodwill, amiability and peaceful intentions towards all our neighbouring nations (*sarve bhavantu sukhinaha, sarve santu niramayaha...*) as also those far away and beyond. These also serve as a ***powerful deterrent against military misadventure by any one of them against us.***

If Pataliputra reposes each night in peaceful comfort, O King, it is so because she is secure in the belief that the distant borders of Magadha are inviolate and the interiors are safe and secure, thanks to the mighty Mauryan Army constantly patrolling and standing vigil with naked swords and eyes peeled for action (*animish netre*) day and night (*ratrau-divase*), in weather fair and foul, dawn-to-dusk-to-dawn (*ashtau prahare*). And they do so, quite unmindful of personal discomfort and hardship, loss of life and limb, separation from their families all through the year, year after year (*varsha nu varshe*).

While the Magadha citizenry endeavours to make the State prosper and flourish, the Mauryan soldier guarantees that the State continues to exist! He is the silent 'sine qua non' of our very being!"

—***Kautilya***

India's Foreign Policy has been a constant matter of intrigue and debate as to what approach New Delhi should take in the emerging Global Order in the 21st century. There is no denying that India, one of the largest democracies and economy in the world, plays a pivotal role in shaping up the Global Order. There are various schools of thought on India's Foreign Policy; first is the classic old school of thought that advocates India maintaining its strong friendship with Russia, ironing out differences with China and creating a Pan-Asian Bloc, somewhat on the lines of Brazil-Russia-India-China-South Africa (BRICS). Then there is the other school of thought, which calls for a shift in India's Foreign Policy from the Classical Asian One to a Global One, suggesting New Delhi to embrace Washington, Tokyo and Canberra more openly in Asia-Pacific. These two schools of thought on India's Foreign Policy are advocated by various intellectuals and backed by vested interest, lobbies etc. It is in this context that one needs a clear view of India's aggressive Foreign Policy, which has been the hallmark of Prime Minister Narendra Modi.

Unlike the above-mentioned schools of thought, the 'Modi Doctrine', as it is being referred to now, is about maintaining India's "strategic autonomy" vis-à-vis Global Powers while furthering and protecting its national interest. This is a sea change in the Foreign Policy of India, which over the decades, had been mostly confined regionally—Pakistan, Sri Lanka and the extended SAARC region. The Modi Doctrine is about projecting India's soft economic power along with military might for strategic initiatives in the region and across the globe. The Modi Doctrine does not seek to confine itself to the old set rules of international diplomacy and relations. It also does not believe in the traditional way of thinking about the Cold War era, i.e. Soviets vs. West or Russia vs. USA, Russia vs. China or China vs. US. India, under Modi's governance, has sought to re-define its foreign policy by interacting with all players in the international arena, with the sole purpose of forwarding national interest—be it geopolitics or geo-economics.

Every day, newspapers, television news channels and internet sites inform us of the many countries that Mr Modi has visited around the world thus far for a variety of political, economic and military developments. Given this vast volume and variety of information, it can be difficult to determine which events and trends are most likely to affect the national security of India; but one thing stands out: Mr Modi has broken away from the past of Non-Alignment and Socialism.

Modi Doctrine of "Strategic Autonomy" is perceivable through India's engagement with Russia in the defence sector from Sukhois for the Indian Air Force, Brahmos missiles and leasing nuclear submarines to aircraft carriers or the latest helicopter deal with Reliance under the flagship scheme of 'Make in India'. India has been in consultation with Russia regarding the joint venture of Fifth Generation Fighter Aircraft (stealth technology). Russia has been a time-tested friend of India for decades. Although the United States has, in the last few years, become the largest supplier of arms to India, it has been able to ward off pressure from the US when it comes to sanctions against Russia vis-à-vis the Ukraine conflict. India has refused to be drawn in into the US vs. Russia tug-of-war, asserting its policy of Strategic Autonomy, which is determined by India's national interest, not blocs of world powers.

We are witnessing a dramatic shift in the locus of global power with the relative decline of the United States and the spectacular rise of China, with India now getting out of the cocoon. The rise of China and India will alter the geopolitical landscape and the nature of the global system in the coming two decades. We are in a time of a great geopolitical transformation. Our assumptions, theories and paradigms need to be revaluated in light of the technological, social, economic and political developments in the emerging world. Despite growing economic interdependency between China and the United States, trends suggest a potential for great power conflict in the Asia-Pacific region, which will have consequences for our security.

Historically, Indian leaders have demonstrated competence in combining strength with humility, and power with purpose. Our strengths are derived from history, culture, people and our democratic institutions. The Indian Defence Forces and our diplomatic apparatus are manifestations of our national purpose of defence and development. Also, historically, our defence and security policies have sought to combine strength with restraint. We should continue the policy of restraint while bolstering our military capabilities.

In the past two decades, India has undergone dramatic transformations in the economic, social and political spheres. The country has radically transformed its economy, and is now projected to be on course to become the third largest economy in the world by 2030. Besides this spectacular economic growth, Indian democracy has steadily consolidated and expanded its scope and remit in the post-independence era. The recent successes of civil society groups in mobilising public support for various causes are testimony to the power and resilience of democratic India's ability to negotiate conflicts within the society through peaceful methods. However, despite its numerous successes, India faces enormous challenges at the domestic, regional and global levels.

However, to maintain its cherished democracy, India must learn lessons from history and not repeat the same patterns. India, till date, is groping in to find its rightful place in the international order. To look at Indian needs, there is need to articulate What security is, What security needs, What methods it can adopt et al. And above all, what all of this means for India.

Security is 'the condition of being protected from or not exposed to danger; [...] a feeling of safety or freedom from or absence of danger'.[1] Also described as 'freedom from fear', security clearly contains a subjective element—perception. The latter part of the statement can also be expressed as 'confidence in the future', which has a more positive ring to it. Since there are many kinds of danger, security is by nature a very broad concept that comprises several dimensions. Security policy can be defined as a policy aiming to keep an object, in this case the values and interests of the India, safe. Traditionally, security policy was associated only with the use of politico-military instruments.[2] Hence, defence policy is the aspect of security policy that has to do with self-defence against acts of aggression.

The term 'national security' refers to the safeguarding of a people, territory and way of life. It includes protection from physical assault, and in that sense, is similar to the term 'defence'. National security in the umbrella term security also implies protection, through a variety of means, of a broad array of interests and values. It implies providing 'physical security'.

Physical security implies providing protection against attack on the territory and the people of India in order to ensure survival with fundamental values and institutions intact, promotion of values and economic prosperity. Preserving the national security of India requires safeguarding individual freedoms and other Indian values, as well as upholding the Indian Constitution and the institutions established under it to protect them. In essence, national security encompasses the protection of the fundamental values, and core interests necessary to the continued existence and vitality of the state.

Strategic Studies: Assumptions and Approaches

Strategic studies was a phrase that developed after World War II, signifying the general study of military power in international politics. Strategic studies became an umbrella term for the study of defence and security issues.

The traditional conception of national security, which focuses on preserving the state from threats, is being challenged from several directions. Advocates seek to focus on broader security agenda to encompass human security, degradation of the environment, energy security, narcotics, transnational crimes, terrorism, etc.

The term 'national security' is an elastic one; its meaning and implications have shifted over time. National security has at times been invoked/used to justify/conceal illegal acts. National security issues involve high stakes; hence, it is important to critically examine and analyse arguments invoking national security as a justification for a position or action. It is useful to understand that India's national security policy should serve both, material interests and non-material (soft power)[3] values. Hence, while analysing, if a particular policy furthers India's security and economic interests while preserving Indian Constitution and the framework it has established for Indian ethos and way of life, then if the answer is uncertain, so may be the grounds on which a particular policy rests.

> **INTERNATIONAL SECURITY STUDIES**
>
> Buzan observed 'like International Relations itself, International Security Studies is mainly a Western subject, largely done with all of the Western-centrism's that this entail'.[1]
>
> [1]Buzan, Barry (2009) **The Middle East through English school theory** In: Buzan, Barry and Gonzalez-Pelaez, Ana, (eds.) *International society and the Middle East: English school theory at the regional level.* Palgrave Studies in International Relations, (Basingstoke, UK. Palgrave Macmillan), p.2. ISBN 9780230537644

The Indian National Security Council has been in existence since 1999. Yet, the government has not put out an official document outlining a National Security Strategy for India. This is despite the fact that India faces numerous formidable challenges to its national security. Why is it that India does not have a well-articulated National Security Strategy document? There is, after all, an active debate on national security issues in the media, think tanks and numerous forums. The leaders make statements on national security inside and outside the Parliament quite regularly, but the government hesitates from spelling out a national security strategy.

Four reasons can be adduced for this state of affairs.

First, there is no political consensus in the country on national security issues. For instance, there is no consensus on how to treat challenges from Pakistan and China. The government's policies on these issues have fluctuated. To give another example, there is little agreement on how to deal with Maoist insurgency. Similarly, the views of political parties on Kashmir and insurgencies in the North-East differ widely. In the aftermath of the Mumbai terror attacks, there was an acute debate on how India should have responded to the attacks. The government used restraint. Many appreciated the restraint while others saw the government's response as weak. Even today, there is no clarity how the government will deal with such terror attacks in the future.

Secondly, the government has not been able to address the crucial issue of coordination required to formulate and address the issues of national security. The Indian National Security Council has been a useful invention, but it is anaemic in terms of resources. More importantly, it lacks the power to enforce anything. The departmental interests are very strong and it becomes difficult to synchronise them. There is no

> While the word 'strategy' has its roots in the Greek language, it was a Frenchman, Lt Col Gideon Joly de Maizeroy, who, in 1777, identified a second level in the art of war that he referred to as strategy and defined it as, "what happened off the battlefield and what happened on it."[1] It was JFC Fuller and his contemporaries who developed this further to differentiate between strategy and grand strategy. It was seen "to coordinate and direct all the resources of the nation towards the attainment of the political object of the war".[2] By the middle of the twentieth century, the advent of nuclear weapons and the concept of total war grand strategy came to be concerned with politics as well and involved "basically in the mobilisation and deployment of national resources of wealth, manpower and industrial capacity...for the purpose of achieving the goals of national policy in wartime."[3]
>
> [1]Strachan, Hew (2013) *The Direction of War: Contemporary Strategy in Historical Perspective* (Cambridge (UK): Cambridge University Press), p. 28.
>
> [2]Ibid p.33.
>
> [3]Ibid p.34.

common understanding among various segments of the government of what national security constitutes.

Thirdly, politics within the confines of the nation state, whether at the neighbours, local or national levels, cannot be insulated from powerful international forces and the ramifications of events in distant countries. To talk of global politics is to acknowledge that political activity and the political process, embracing the exercise of power and authority, are no longer primarily defined by national legal and territorial boundaries.[4]

Fourthly, Indian polity has not been able to decide the role for the country in 'global politics'. It is not sure whether it wants to be a global player, or just wants to reconcile to the idea of just being a regional player. There is no 'strategic thinking' or independent assessment of what the nation wants. It is not sure how to tackle 'globalisation' or even 'the nuances of the strategy of sovereign states'. This may be primarily due to ignorance of our political elites in the nuances of statecraft on matters related to security. Look at the way political mileage was being taken by Congress, National Conference from the issue of an intelligence unit of an army employed in covert operations to defeat terrorism to settle scores with the former Chief of Army Staff Gen. VK Singh (Retd.) PVSM, AVSM, YSM, ADC; while the United States gave a long sentence to one of its soldiers for leaking documents to Wiki. In fact, all who raised this issue, including editors of the *Indian Express*, should be tried for high treason in strategic and security interest of the nation.

> Richard Ullman, a revisionist scholar, writes: *'A threat to national security is an action or sequence of events that:*
>
> (1) *Threatens drastically and even over a relatively brief span of time to degrade the quality of life for inhabitants of a state, or;*
>
> (2) *Threatens significantly to narrow the range of policy choices available to the government of a state or to private non-governmental entities within the state'*.

The discipline which goes under security deals with all relations between states, all processes of intercourses—political, economic, social and cultural, etc. which take place across the boundaries of the state or within the boundaries of the state. It is concerned with only those relations that pertain to the maintenance of peace in the world, and to the establishment of a condition in which wars do not pose a threat to the survival of barriers such as seas and mountain ranges. The way the protection organises, the resources available and their ability to exploit them and the nature of their beliefs, fears and aspirations still provide the basic raw material of international politics.[5] The subject matter of this analysis is an aspect of security.

Strategy

The term 'strategy'[6] must be one of the most commonly used terms in public discourse. It is employed to refer to anything from state policy to personal choices. Yet, few appreciate what this term really is, and what it implies as a system of inquiry. In fact, I have rarely been called upon to state what it is that explicitly underpins a strategic theory approach to the study of social phenomena.

Clausewitz defines Strategy as 'the employment of battle as the means towards attainment of an end'.

However, today, purely military definitions of strategy have virtually disappeared because strategy today is an employment of value system, thought-process, and ideas which straddle the spectrum of war and peace, politics and economics, culture and psychology. Yes, it still **remains a 'means' towards an end of peace and mutually beneficial existence.**

The entire 'industry' of strategic thinking and studies is today geared towards maintaining peace. A herculean task, given the complexities of the human society today! It is not only complex in different silos, but the complexity also runs within the silos itself.

The Assumptions of Strategic Theory

There are seven assumptions for strategic theories:

1. ***The study of ends and means.*** The term strategy denotes the endeavour to relate ends to means. The strategic analysis thus refers to the study, in Michael Howard's words, of the 'use of available resources to gain any objective'.[7] Here, the term 'resources' or the 'means' refers not simply to the tangibles of power that may be employed to gain objectives but also to the many intangible factors that may impose themselves on any decision-maker, most notably the degree of political will that an actor may exert to attain its goals.
2. ***The study of the political actor as the central unit of analysis.*** What do strategic theorists study? Principally, they examine the calculations of the individual social actor, be it a state, a sub-state entity, or any other social grouping. Hence, strategic theory analysis is interested in describing the choices available to an actor and evaluating the quality of decision making.
3. ***Understanding the political actor's value system and preferences.*** What specifically do strategic theorists wish to understand in their examination of political actors? They want to comprehend the actor's value system. What motivates them? How do actors construct their interests, which, thereby, inform the objectives they strive for and the manner in which they seek to attain them?

4. ***An actor's interest will be influenced by the wider strategic environment.*** Integral to the endeavour to understand the actor's values and preferences is an appreciation of the wider social environment in which it functions. Lyndsey Harris puts it well when she argues that the strategic environment is the crucial 'determinant of the information that is available to an actor and the structure within which actors operate. The environment determines what the actors think they know for sure and what they have to infer, if possible, from the behaviour of others'.[8]
5. ***The actor is behaving rationally in pursuit of its aims.*** It is sometimes said that strategic theorists assume rationality on the part of those whom they study because they cannot assume anything else.[9] To pass judgment on whether anyone is rational or irrational in political life is to assume that one exists in Olympian detachment with a unique insight into what constitutes supreme powers of reasoning (a self-evidently delusional position). The assumption of rationality, however, does not suppose that the actor is functioning with perfect efficiency or 'that all rational decisions are right ones merely that an actor's decisions are made after careful cost–benefits calculation and the means chosen seem optimal to accomplish the desired end.'[10]
6. ***The acceptance of clashing interests.*** An individual actor has to function in an environment full of other actors all trying to pursue their interests and objectives. It is a constantly reactive condition in which, according to Schelling, the 'ability of one participant to gain his ends is dependent to an important degree on the choices or decisions the other participant [or participants] will make'.[11] The strategic theory thus accepts that clashes of interest are liable to occur among actors and that in some instances this will lead to the resort to war as a means of obtaining objectives.
7. ***The observance moral neutrality.*** Strategic theory is intellectually disinterested in the moral validity of the means and ends of any actor. The commentary is confined to evaluating how effectively chosen means are in attaining stated objectives. This understanding includes and applies to all acts of violence which are viewed as politically instrumental; that is undertaken with the conscious purpose of securing goals and interests. This may seem clinical, even cold-blooded, but it is a logical extension of any dispassionate understanding of the wider political environment and vital to sustaining coherent evaluation. As Schelling again elucidates, this is for two reasons. First, strategic 'analysis is usually about the situation, not the individuals—about the structure of incentives, of information and communication, the choices available, and the tactics that can be employed'.[12] Second, strategic theory 'cannot proceed from the point of

view of a single favored participant. It deals with situations in which one party has to think about how the others are going to reach their decisions'.[13]

These seven assumptions comprise the core of the strategic theory. It is a precise and economical method because it applies the principle of Occam's Razor.[14] That is to say, it incorporates as few postulates as possible in its understanding. In essence, strategic theory is the study of correlations between ends and means, including the use, or threat of use, of armed force as a conscious choice of political actors who are intent on rationally pursuing their objectives.[15] It is as simple as that (Merriam-Webster states Occam's Razor is as a scientific and philosophic rule that entities should not be multiplied unnecessarily which is interpreted as requiring that the simplest of competing theories be preferred to the more complex or that explanations of unknown phenomena be sought first in terms of known quantities).

India and Strategic Culture

Strategic thinking is a challenge, but it is particularly problematic in India. We often hear statements alleging that India lacks a strategic culture. Sadly, this is more often heard from Indians than foreigners. One sometimes wonders whether the idea that India lacks a strategic culture was not useful in the past to those who did not wish to see India's weight translate into the effective exercise of power on the international stage. While one can understand foreigners spreading this idea, it is incomprehensible to me that some Indians should also believe this and still propagate this idea. In fact, the mission of Indian Armed Forces to defend India from external and internal threats depends on the ability to make a good strategic assessment, derived from sound strategic thought.

What is strategic culture? *Strategic culture is that set of shared beliefs, assumptions and modes of behaviour, derived from common experience and accepted narratives (both oral and written) that shape collective identity and relationships to other groups, and which determine appropriate ends and means for achieving security objectives.*

> **STRATEGIC CULTURE**
>
> *Strategic culture is that set of shared beliefs, assumptions and modes of behaviour, derived from common experience and accepted narratives (both oral and written) that shape collective identity and relationships to other groups, and which determine appropriate ends and means for achieving security objectives.*
>
> Or, it can be just said as:
>
> *Strategic culture is an identifiable set of basic assumptions about the nature of international and military issues. This would involve both a central strategic paradigm (about the role of war in human affairs, the efficacy of force, the nature of the adversary, and so on), and a grand strategy or secondary assumptions about operational policy that flow from the assumptions.*

By this definition, of course, we in India have a strategic culture. It is an indigenous construct over millennia, modified considerably by our experience in the last two centuries. For instance, war and peace are continuing themes in the Indian strategic culture. While not celebrating war, the culture treats it as acceptable when good fights evil. The Indian strategic culture has been comfortable with this contradiction. Both the major Indian epics deal with wars and treat rivalries as natural and normal. Kautilya addressed the use of force in detail. *While Gandhi shunned the use of force and opposed violence in politics, he was politically steely and unyielding and accepted appropriate violence as unavoidable in certain circumstances.*

Philosophies the world over are 'society-centred,' or 'this-world-centred' and directs man to find fulfillment here in this world through socio-political activities, whereas Indian Philosophy looks upon the world as *fleeting, transitory* and *'unreal'* and encourages human beings to seek the spiritual realisation of the 'Absolute'.[16]

Indian philosophers in the olden days never concerned themselves with theories of kingship and nature of government, but were grappling with the problem of transmigration of souls and underplaying the importance of life in *this* world. Religion and not politics dominated Indian social life. In spite of periodic invasions and few eras of internal breakdown, India never oriented her thoughts to military power, or the socio-politically oriented ideology of a unitary, humane government, and lacked a strong unifying credo.[17]

India was never unified; it had no unified organisation or cause. Indian through the ages could fight only uncoordinated local skirmishes. The early Indians, lacking a concept of unitary political state, never desired a single name for this sub-continent. By the fourth century CE, the term **'Bharatvarsha'** (homeland of the mythical King Bharat) may have been used to refer to the subcontinent.[18] The word **'Hindustan'** which became current during the Mughal period technically applied only to the Northern Indo-Gangetic Plains area and excluded the area of the Deccan.

It is on the plains of Northern India that major war-affecting destinies of India were fought. On the plains to the west of Yamuna more than twenty cities have been built one over the other for good reasons in Delhi; it is laid at the most dominating area before the outsiders cross into the plains of India. It was on the plains around it that the wars were fought for over 5000 years. The art of war in India has existed at all times. War was the same under Porus as under Chandragupta, Tipu Sultan or in modern times. But the theory/treatise, confined to the understanding of the Great Captains, does not exist in the number of warriors India boasts about.

The only book worth mention is the Kautilya's **Arthashastra.**[19] It is believed that Kautilya, the author of the tremendously influential manual on statecraft engineered the rise of the Indian's times past; an Indian ruler met an invading army not at the frontiers of his kingdom but close to the seat of power. He remained well entrenched with his army within a fort or a fortified location. The enemy had a free run of the rest of the territory, winning half the battle without firing a single shot. He then reached the seat of governance. Here, he was met by the king's army on the outskirts or a king capitulated. In the alternative, he laid siege to the fort. Expecting a long siege, the fortifications of the defending king were well stocked. Meanwhile, the enemy looted and plundered the surroundings for sustenance, labour, riches and pleasures.

Barring perhaps the Mauryas and to some extent the Cholas, the history of Hindu Kingdoms of India brings forth a frustrating chronology of defeats, nay, meek capitulation.[20] It is necessary to study and analyse correctly so that lessons from historical lapses and mistakes are not repeated.

The geographical factor is widely accepted as a paramount determinant in foreign policymaking. India occupies a strategic geopolitical position in Asia, on a subcontinent jutting southward deep into the Indian Ocean, sitting astride major sea lines of communication linking the Persian Gulf with the Asia-Pacific, thus providing a kind of connecting link between East and West. It is obvious that the country's unique geographical location has significantly shaped the Indian elite's worldview and strategic outlook. There is a clear notion that because of its strategic location in South Asia, the sheer geographical size and large population, India is a geopolitically important player that is entitled and, therefore, should play a central role in solving major world problems. As Jawaharlal Nehru earlier asserted, "India is too big a country herself to be bound down to any country, however, big it may be. India is going to be and is bound to be a big country that counts in world affairs."[21] Accordingly, India's central and dominant position in South Asia and the Indian Ocean has and will increasingly affect the foreign, economic and military policies of the European Union, the United States, China and other major powers—and vice versa.

Last twenty years have been years of conflict between 'sovereignty of states' on one hand and 'globalisation' on the other. India while formulating policies have yet to reconcile these two.

Sovereign States

The most important feature of the present-day world community is that the chief participant in its value processes is the sovereign state. ***Nations and states are not the same*** as codified by the Treaty of Westphalia. Nations today represent groupings of a people that claim certain common bonds, such as descent, language, history, or culture. Collectively, such an aggregation would constitute a national entity.[22] States, also known as nation-states, have a legal character and possess certain rights and duties under the tenets of international law. The 1933 Montevideo Convention on Rights and Duties of States considered the classic legal definition for states, which indicates that states possess the following characteristics: a permanent population, defined territory, and a government capable of maintaining effective control over its territory and conducting international relations with other states.[23]

Sovereignty implies a high degree of control over the people, resources and institutions within the state, and absence of control by any external authority over the internal acts of the state or its external behavior. The concept of sovereignty came into existence with the 1648 Treaty of Westphalia ending the Thirty Years War in Europe, when, for the first time, the authority of state governments became officially recognised as greater than the authority of organised religion in formal state affairs. Modern recognition of sovereignty can be found in the United Nations Carter. This document recognises the "sovereign equality" of all the member states of the United Nations and affirms that "nothing contained in the present Charter shall authorize the United Nations to intervene in the matters which are essentially within domestic jurisdiction of any state." In contemporary international law, sovereign states are treated as equals; every recognised state can participate in the international system on the same plane. This sovereign equality possesses the following elements:

1. States are legally equal.
2. Every state enjoys the rights inherent in full sovereignty.
3. Every state is obligated to respect the fact of the legal entity of other states.
4. The territorial integrity and political independence of a state are inviolable.
5. Each state has the right to freely choose and develop its own political, social, economic, and cultural systems.
6. Each state is obligated to carry out its international obligations fully and conscientiously and to live in peace with other states.[24]

There is, however, a limit on sovereignty, although in United Nations all states are equal and all states get one vote, the limit of the idea can be recognised in the United Nations Security Council, where five permanent members (great powers) get a veto. The second is the Convention on the Prevention and Punishment of the Crime of Genocide went into force in 1951. This act commits the 'contracting states to "undertake to prevent and to punish" acts of genocide. This agreement justifies the intervention of states in each other's affairs.

The world is organised in approximately 195 sovereign nations each jealously guarding its national independence. Hence, insecurity is a universal and permanent feature of the international order, due to the latter's abiding anarchic character,[25] leading to international instability.[26] *War and permanent preparation for war, political fragmentation, cultural diversity and the immense gap between the advanced states and the poorest state remains the central feature of the contemporary global system.*[27] There are other factors that contribute to a state's propensity to engage in international violence, not least of which is traditional *raison d'état* and power politics. These *make it difficult to compare* in the Indian context.[28] In addition, the government must possess a monopoly on the legitimate use of force in the state, and other states in the international system must recognise the sovereignty of that government.[29] Each state is obligated to carry out its international obligations fully and conscientiously and to live in peace with other states.[30]

The primary purpose of any country's security policy is to promote its national interest and core values.[31] It is achieved by ensuring its security, safeguarding sovereignty, contributing to growth and prosperity, and generally by enhancing stature, influence, and a role in the comity of nations. Indian defence policy should also be able to serve the broader purpose of promoting peace, disarmament and development, and of establishing a stable, fair and equitable global order.

National Power

Despite the central importance of National Power, there is no universally accepted definition. The main reason for this situation is that power is ***dynamic***. New instruments of power have appeared over the centuries. Even a seemingly a backward society with strong political leadership that is willing to engender sacrifice and a sense of purpose among its people can defeat the mightiest of nations. The defeat of French and subsequent failure of United States intervention in Vietnam are a classic cases. In addition to being dynamic, power is also *relative, situational,* and at least partially *subjective.* Power is relative because its utility depends upon comparison with whatever opposes it, and it is situational because what may generate power in a particular set of circumstance may not in another. Finally, power is subjective in that a reputation for being powerful may be sufficient to achieve results without power actually having to be applied.

Morgenthau's in *Politics Among Nations* defines power as **consisting of geography, natural resources, industrial capacity, military preparedness, technology and innovations, leadership, quantity and quality of armed forces, population, national character, national morale, quality of diplomacy, and quality of government.**

Globalisation

In the 21st Century, the era of conflict and rivalry seems to be replaced by the expanding awareness of ***global inter-dependence***. This is reflected in the language of the contemporary politics, which is increasingly suffused with references to global problems, appeals to universal values and visions of global community. Certainly the fact that no modern nation-state can insulate itself from the vagaries of the world market, or transnational movements of capital, ideas, beliefs, crime, knowledge and news seems to evidence enough of the emergence of a truly global society.[32] As Machuhan remarked many years ago, one of the defining characteristics of the modern age is developing realisation that we live in a *'global village'*.[33] In identifying the globalisation of the political arena, as a distinctive feature of the contemporary world, Rosenau articulated what can be observed almost daily, namely the declining significance of territorial boundaries and place as the definitive parameters of political life. Rosenau observed that, in the modern era, *'Politics everywhere, it would seem, are related to politics everywhere else.... Now the roots... political life can be traced to remote corners of globe'*.[34]

Globalisation's security implications have led to a number of attempts at "Redefining Security".[35] Jessica Mathews argued in 1989 the "global development now suggests the need for a broadening definition of national security to include resource, environmental and demographic issues."[36]

Globalisation did not inevitably mean 'homogenization', but rather a fragmentation as pointed out by Agnew.[37] The world of cultural and economic flows is concomitantly also a world of structural transformation, uneven regional development, and spatial differentiation. In many cases, the increased interdependence and integration among nations have changed the meanings of state boundaries. Territories have different relations with each other through their border areas, along a continuum stretching from alienated borderlands (India-Pakistan) through to completely integrated borderlands (US-Canada). As far as the effects of interdependence and integration inside states are concerned, this means that new voices will arise to articulate their interests. Most recent troubles be it Iraq, Kosovo, Libya, Syria, Pashtuns in Pakistan or Turkey has concentrated on the need to identify the political identities and social groupings which have been previously effectively suppressed by the hegemony of states.

Globalisation, however, offered alternatives.[38]

(1) First, worldwide economic progress would overcome national barriers and knit the world closer together;

(2) Second, military force, if it had to be used at all, would be launched by international coalitions under the banner of humanitarian intervention free of selfish national interests; and

(3) Third, the only super power the USA was able to use its unique military asset, precise air power, would reach remote places without the risks of expeditionary forces or massive casualties without fear of Soviet support or veto in UN Security Council.

(4) The method of the conduct of warfare, the combined arms operation that laid the Taliban low relied upon careful coordination between infantry and precision air power. The Special Forces were key to success.

On balance, these ideas had many merits; but these ideas did not work. Globalisation as an economic phenomenon began well and lasted the better part of the decade. Astonishing flows of capital moved abroad, nourishing newly emerging markets, especially in Asia. Countries such as China, India, and the whole swath of ASEAN suddenly became the "tigers" of a region long thought invulnerable to economic progress because of lack of resources, excessive population, or just bad government. The gross domestic product (GDP) growth of eight or twelve or even twenty percent per year doubled per capita incomes in a decade. Then the bubble burst: debt, corruption, and other accumulated ills suddenly spooked capital in Asia,—the Asia of the coming Pacific Century, and the scene of globalisations greatest successes. Global players led by IMF arrived, prescribing tight money and other financial virtues. Amidst all the tumult, an untidy little fact emerged. The private capital that knew no borders suddenly rediscovered them. Capital fled back to within the borders of Western Europe and the United States, places where laws and governments gave investors reasonable protection and what has been called "transparency." In other words, money moved to those places, an investor could see what was being done with his money and he had legal recourse in the event of dishonesty. To use a metaphor, *the capitalists grazed in far-flung pastures during the 1990s, but when they got skittish, they remembered the location of the barn.*

War was another subject where geopolitics was supposedly passé. A world led by US Administration believed that the security could be lifted out of the rut of geopolitics with the use of the UN. The Security Council, freed of a Soviet veto, would take up conflicts around the world and settle them in the general interest. Boutros-Ghali, the Secretary General, had advanced with American support a plan for a permanent UN force.[39] In a fulsome report to the Security Council, he saw the UN as the leading international peacemaker, not only a peacekeeper. This project could not take off a due ambush in Mogadishu, the derelict capital of Somalia, a country which had become a "geographic expression" rather than a state. The project was finally abandoned, few years later, after several disasters in the Balkans and a successful anti-UN campaign in the US led by Madeleine Albright and Jesse Helms, the Security Council was clearly sidelined.

That left the US to deal with distressing bouts of violence in Haiti, Bosnia, and Kosovo, often at the head of reluctant coalitions. US actions, however, could not be easily justified in the old terms of national interest to which the American people were largely attached. So a new idea surfaced, given a name by British Prime Minister Tony Blair: **humanitarian war**.

In humanitarian war the United States and its allies would act to rescue at-risk populations unsullied by any motive of self-interest (however, national self-interest was the prime motive of all actions by the United States and its allies), and they would not be limited by geography in doing so. The trigger of humanitarian war proved to be the CNN effect: horrors brought into the living room convinced the American public that action was necessary, thereby rallying popular support the President could ride to war. However, humanitarian war was highly selective, and political geography, not fashionable labels, determined that selection.

This brings us to the third great shibboleth of the post-Cold War era, the unhindered use of air power to meet the foreign policy and security goals of United States. The revival of air power as a strategic weapon enabled the US to fight wars while avoiding the trouble and casualties of the infantry.

The 1991 Gulf War with its highly dramatic scenes of continuous bombardment broadcast in every American home promised a new era of warfare.

It was too easy to overlook that in **Desert Storm and succeeding campaigns in the Balkans, ground action—or the threat of it—was vital to carrying the day**. And in 1999, the air campaign over Kosovo made its greatest impression when NATO's armored columns, supported by the Russian finally forced capitulation of Milosevic's. **In short, a ground campaign, or at least the threat of one, was still fundamental to military success.** American military forces are even waging war today in defence of the US national security interests in Afghanistan, not to secure the freedom of Afghanis. Humanitarian warfare as a doctrine has come and gone.

War, while inhumane by definition, may still have human consequences. The enslaved are freed, the oppressed relieved. This alone is rarely enough to reconstruct a decent social order or an effective state. Yet the record of post-war "nation-building" in last few years is a study in frustration. Does anyone seriously believe, for example, that NATO's expeditions in the Balkans or US actions in Afghanistan will implant multicultural democracies? The choice is between social and political engineering. Social reformers work from the bottom up, and their favorite devices are schools, institutions, and the like—a new civil society. Political reformers work from the top down, for without sound government civil society cannot flourish. Outside of a long military occupation, can we really hope to change Afghan ways? Or is our best bet to get a decent government, i.e., one respective of our interests, give it some security and money, and let the Afghans do it their way?

In either case, the US will be picking up, with its coalition partners, in South Asia amongst the failed and failing states of Afghanistan and Pakistan for some

> The ideal factor for determining the likelihood of war is not the aggressive behaviour of certain states, but rather whether power is balanced or not within the system of states. If it is, then aggression is not likely to pay; if it is not, then states will be tempted to take advantage of their neighbours. In its purest form, the **'distribution of power'** *is single most important determinant of war and peace.*

time to come. Surely, it is unwelcome in the region but at this point unavoidable consequence of the war on terrorism. Washington will need great skill to pass off the nation-sustaining burden on its allies while retaining political leadership. It is betting that new regional power balances rather than new nations will be the way to secure the future.

The combined arms operation that laid the Taliban low relied upon careful coordination between infantry and precision air power. The Special Forces were key to success. The US recruited the Northern Alliance to supply the ground elements. Once again, the US waged a victorious war with advanced weaponry and communications, using air and infantry in a way that minimised American casualties while maximising enemy losses.

The world is today grappling with the downsides of globalisation, including difficult civil liberties and cultural issues in a war where the front is everywhere. The campaign and its targets, especially the state sponsors of terrorism, have an identifiable geography. The war against terrorism is a classic protracted conflict that will probably defy a single decisive campaign, as illustrated by the tricky endgame in Afghanistan where the US forces are still fighting small-scale but deadly encounters and India is waging its own counter-terrorism operations in Kashmir.

Militarisation

Whether the war is a necessary factor in the evolution of mankind, but a fact which cannot be questioned is that; from the earliest record of man to the present, war has been his dominant occupation. There has never been a period in human history altogether free from war, and seldom one or more of a generation which has not witnessed a major conflict: great wars flow and ebb almost as regularly as the tides.[40] Will and Ariel Durant, two humanists reviewing the lessons of history in the epilogue of their life work, *The Story of Civilisation* wrote: '*War is one of the constants of history, and has not diminished with civilisation or democracy. In the last 3,421 years of recorded history, only 268 have seen no war.*' Indeed, advances of civilisation could cynically be identified with man's growing capacity to kill ever increasing numbers of people by single, less intensive efforts, and primitiveness with man's inability to kill except at very close quarters or in hand to hand fight.

The ideal factor for determining the likelihood of war in international order is not the aggressive behaviour of certain states, but rather whether power is balanced or not within the system of states. If it is, then aggression is not likely to pay; if it is not, then states will be tempted to take advantage of their neighbours. In its purest form, the **'distribution of power'** *is a single most important determinant of war and peace.* Therefore, the art of war is of vital importance to the State.[41] Nation state[42] is a legal and geographical entity. In terms of the later, a central authority empowered[43] to make and enforce laws, rules and decisions anywhere within the established boundaries governs the state.[44]

At the same time the use of power, and possibly the use of force, is inseparable from the *beneesse* of politics, inseparable from politics'. Power acts for politics and is inseparable from the human pursuit of the national and international common good by political means. You never have good politics without the use of power, possibly armed forces.[45]

> **SOFT POWER**
> Originally coined by Nye, soft power refers "the ability to achieve desired outcomes in international affairs through attraction rather than coercion."

Power is the ability to influence the behaviour of others. In international relations, as the Harvard academic Joseph Nye reminds us, power can be exercised in three ways: by threatening or actually using military force, by offering economic incentives or imposing economic sanctions, or by building what Nye famously dubbed "soft power". That is, the soft power of nations to persuade others based on the attractiveness of their technology, politics, culture, ideas or ideals.

Twenty-First Century Challenges to National Security

The challenge of the 21st Century is to adapt India's policy to account for how the world has changed. These changes can be highlighted by reviewing some traditional perceptions that helped shape India's security policy. During the latter half of the twentieth century, five large ideas seemed to have permeated politics in the Western world writ large:

- Peaceful settlement of issues was better than going to war;
- Countries tolerated U.S. hegemony in exchange for keeping the peace;
- United States and Europe could determine policy on most major international issues; China says, "We care about rules. US just set the rules. This is not an issue between China and India but (about) the pillar for non-proliferation system," Chinese Foreign Ministry Spokesperson Hua Chunying said to reporters in a media briefing on Tuesday, when asked to comment on the US backing India's NSG bid.[46]
- United States could assist countries to democratise because democracies

were more likely than dictatorships to have shared values and to keep the peace; and

- Western culture was appealing and more universal than any other. Mickey Mouse, the number of kids in jeans and education excellence. (Soft Power)

ENDNOTES

1. Oxford English Dictionary.
2. Politico-military instruments comprise, *inter alia,* mechanisms for early warning and peaceful settlement of disputes; confidence and security-building measures (CSBMs), political dialogue and military cooperation; non-proliferation, arms control and disarmament; preventive diplomacy; sanction regimes; observer, humanitarian, peacekeeping, police and peace enforcement operations (which can be summarised under the general heading of peace support operations and which include a civil dimension) and defence operations.
3. Originally coined by Nye, soft power refers to "the ability to achieve desired outcomes in international affairs through attraction rather than coercion." He explains:

   'It works in convincing others to follow, or getting them to agree to, norms and institutions that produce the desired behavior...... If a state can make its power legitimate in the perception of others and establish international institutions that encourage them to channel or limit their activities, it may not need to expend many of its costly traditional economic or military resources."
4. George Modelski has devised a useful analogy for thinking through some distinctions and connections between different levels of political interaction and activity in the contemporary world. His layer cake model provides a powerful heuristic device for easing the complex patterns of political interaction, which define global politics. There are, he suggests, three distinct layers of political activity, from the local through the national to the global. To this might be added a fourth, the regional, which sits between the global and the national. Each layer, he argues, constitutes a defined political community with its own particular aspirations and needs. Each also embraces an identifiable set of political processes and institutions, which exist to facilitate the taking of the authoritative decisions. Whilst there are discontinuities, Modelski's model points to the systematic interdependencies between them; they are porous membranes.

   Isolating the global layer in Modelski's model requires us to distinguish between two particular forms of political interaction: inter-state or international relations, and transnational relations. Since, nation states are the predominant form of political and legal organisations in the modern world, the first step towards understanding the dynamics of global politics brings into focus the interactions and relations between sovereign nation-states, or simply put **international relations.** In effect, since nation-states are taken to be synonymous with the government or regimes which rule them, international relations and diplomatic interactions between national governments, (including relations between governments and intergovernmental organisations such as the United Nations) leads us to understanding of international relations. This is the domain of on foreign and defence policy. It is the domain which is inherently political because it involves exercise of influence, power, and force governments in the pursuit of their own national interests.
5. National Power. India has all the means to project power. National strategy is defined by the United States Department of Defense as the '*art and science of developing and using political, economic and psychological powers of a nation state, together with its armed forces during peace and war, to serve national objectives*' {Jablonsky, David (1992) 'National Power', *In the United*

States Army War College Selected Readings AY 93, Course 2, War, National Policy and Strategy', Vol. 3 (Carlisle Barracks, PA: US Army War College, 1992), p. 1}.

6. The term 'strategy' can be traced back to one thousand years in ancient Greece and had been used as a way to train 'generalship' (See Mclean, Ian (1996), *Oxford Concise dictionary of Politics* (Oxford: Oxford University Press) p. 480). The Byzantine Emperor Maurice has been regarded as the first one using 'strategy' (*Strategicon)* for guiding high-ranking generals in order to win battles. See Palmer, Jr., Bruce (1978) 'Strategic Guidelines for thew United States in the 1980s', in Palmer, Jr., Bruce (ed.) *Grand Strategy for the 1980s,* (Washington DC.: American Enterprise Institute for Public Policy Research), p. 73). In ancient China strategy was generally referred to the 'Sun Ze Doctrine' that has become a textbook to many military academies.
7. Howard, Michael (1983), *The Causes of War* (London: Counterpoint, 1983), p. 86.
8. Harris, Lyndsey (2006), 'Introducing the Strategic Approach: An Examination of Loyalist Paramilitaries in Northern Ireland', *British Journal of Politics and International Relations*', Vol. 8, No. 4, p. 542.
9. Smith, M.L.R. (1995), *Fighting For Ireland? The Military Strategy of the Irish Republican Movement* (London: Routledge), p. 3.
10. Lopez-Alvez, F. (1989), "Political Crises, Strategic Choices and Terrorism: The Rise and Fall of the Uruguayan Tupamaros," *Terrorism and Political Violence*, Vol. 1, No. 2, p. 204.
11. Schelling, Thomas (1980), *The Strategy of Conflict* (Cambridge, MA: Harvard University Press), p. 5.
12. Schelling, Thomas (1984), *Choice and Consequence: Perspectives of an Errant Economist* (Cambridge, MA: Harvard University Press), pp. 198-199.
13. Ibid., p. 199.
14. ***Occam's Razor***, also spelled Ockham's razor, also called law of economy or law of parsimony, principle stated by William of Ockham (1285–1347/49), a Scholastic, that *Pluralitas non est ponenda sine necessitate*, "Plurality should not be posited without necessity." The principle gives precedence to simplicity; of two competing theories, the simpler explanation of an entity is to be preferred. The principle is also expressed as "Entities are not to be multiplied beyond necessity." Ockham's razor is an idea that, in trying to understand something, getting unnecessary information out of the way is the fastest way to the truth or to the best explanation. He used it, for instance, to dispense with relations, which he held to be nothing distinct from their foundation in things; with efficient causality, which he tended to view merely as regular succession; with motion, which is merely the reappearance of a thing in a different place; with psychological powers distinct for each mode of sense; and with the presence of ideas in the mind of the Creator, which are merely the creatures themselves.
15. Smith, M.L.R. (2008), 'William of Ockham, Where Are You When We Need You? Reviewing Modern Terrorism Studies', *Journal of Contemporary History*, Vol. 44, No. 2, p. 322.
16. **Hinduism** is in many ways a confusing and a nebulous term which relates to the manner in which Vedic Brahmanical values have influenced Indian Society. According to Dr Radhakrishnan, '*The term* '**Hindu**' *had originally a territorial and not creedal significance. It implied residence in a well defined geographical area. Aboriginal tribes, savage and half-savage people, the cultured Dravidians and the Vedic Aryans were all Hindus as they were the sons of the same mother*" [Dr Sarvepalli Radhakrishnan, *the Hindu View of Life* (London: Uncoin Books, 1927) p. 12.]. Others have said term **Hindu** is of non-Indian origin and was initially used by the Persians to denote the region of the Sindhu River (Sind); later Persians, Greeks and Arabs extended the region to include the whole of the Northern India. The term may even have referred to the people of the Area, but after the entry of Islam into the subcontinent;

it was distinctly used to distinguish people who practiced Hinduism from the followers of Islam.

Jawaharlal Nehru declared it was *'incorrect and undesirable to use* **Hindu** *or* **Hinduism** *for Indian Culture, even with reference to distant past'.* Nehru suggested that, "the correct word for **'Indian'** as applied to country or culture or the historical continuity of varying traditions, is **'Hindi'**, from **'Hind'**, a shortened form of **"Hindustan"** [Land of Hindus].

17. Indian civilisation is noted for its historical continuity and for the fact that elements of Indian tradition so firmly imbedded in the country's culture that they persists in influencing contemporary social and political behaviour. The vitality of Indian tradition lies in the **socio-religious** developments identified with the ideas and practices connected with **Hinduism.** India never developed a strong sense of political and social unity, and Indians are not homogeneous people, but Hinduism contributed to the making of a social system that has held together by the strength of religious philosophy. In India, even today like in many other parts of the world especially Africa separatist's tendencies are widely manifested in demands by several sections of the population for independent homelands.

18. *Vishnu Purana*, II.3.1. It would be wrong to think, as many do, that the conception of the fundamental unity of India is only of recent growth. This idea can be traced to ancient periods by the use of common name, **Bharatvarsha,** for the whole country, and the designation **Bharati Santati** applied to the people of India. Thus we read in the *Vishnu Purana* that *"the country lying to the north of the Ocean and to the south of* **himaadri** *(Himalaya) is called Bharata-varsha (land of Bharata), for there live the descendants of Bharat (Bharat santatih)."*

Similarly the conception of political unity of India appears from references to *"thousand* **Yojanas** *of land that stretch from the Himalayas to the sea as the proper domain of a single universal emperor,"* and the conventional description in literature and epigraphic records of imperial domain stretching from Brahmaputra (on the Eastern Ocean) to the seven mouths of the Indus (or the Western Ocean). As regards cultural unity, the find-spots of Asoka's records prove that one language and one script were used, or at least understood by common people all over India in the third century BC. Since then, the Sanskrit language and literature have throughout been a common bond of culture in addition to religious and social ideas and institutions.

19. Composed as primer for kings, the **Arthashastra** is a masterpiece of tough-minded real-politick. It makes no concessions to the gentler sensibilities in its understanding of how the business of government is to be conducted. Kautilya urges the King to use the sovereignty to its fullest: not only must he control his subjects by means of an intricate surveillance system, but he must constantly destabilize rival kingdoms by means of intrigues and war. Kautilya was not in the least disturbed by the use of force, deception or conspiracy in the interest of the state. Indeed, he advocated extreme measures as routine policy.

20. For Details see, **'The History of Hindu's: A Saga of Defeats Part 2'**, *Alive,* January 1998, No. 183, Vishwanath (ed.), pp. 72-74.

21. Bandyopadhyaya, J., (1970), *The Making of India's Foreign Policy: Determinants, Institutions, Processes and Personalities* (Bombay: Allied Publishers), pp. 30-31.

22. Berridge G.R. and James, Alan (2003), *A Dictionary of Diplomacy,* (Hampshire, UK: Palgrave Macmillan), p. 180; Griffiths, Martin and O'Callaghan, Terry (2002) International Relations: The Key Concepts, (London: Routledge), p. 209.

23. Evans, Graham and Newnham, Jeffrey (1988), *The Penguin Dictionary of International Relations,* London: Penguin Books), p. 512.

24. Griffiths, Martin and O'Callaghan, Terry (2002), *International Relations: The Key Concepts* (London: Routledge), p. 209.

25. Waltz, Kenneth (1959), *Man, the State, and War* (New York: Columbia University Press, 1959).
26. International instability is used here to mean international conflict involving the use or projection of forces across the borders. Note that this is much broader use of the term than its use by many system theorists. See Waltz, K.N., (1979), *'The Theory of International Politics'*, Reading: Addison-Wesley, pp. 161-2.
27. THE ANATOMY OF GLOBAL POLITICS

To simply identify the important features of global politics requires some implicit and explicit conceptual framework of inquiry. One strategy for managing, although by no means resolving, this dilemma is to explicate the theoretical traditions which frame the study of global politics. For pedagogic reasons this is the strategy followed here. It is important to voice few caveats of the three traditions—namely realism, liberal-pluralism and neo-Marxism.

Realism and Neo-Realism: Realism asserts the primacy of the state in global politics. Although realism acknowledges the existence of other actors in the global system, such as international organisations, multinational corporations and individuals, it posits that states are the dominant actors. The reason for this is simply that realists attach great importance to sovereignty, the ultimate legal authority which a state exercises over a defined territory and the people within it. The international organisations are regarded as subservient to states, since they are the creatures of the state. Realism places great stress upon the significance of **military power** in shaping global politics.

Neo-Realism, which has emerged recently as an attempt to update classic realism, gives particular weight to the role of hegemonic powers *(dominating powers such as the United States and Russia)* in establishing and maintaining order in the global system. Neo-realism stresses the significance of the structure of power in the global system in shaping the character of the political order than a world in which there are three or more powers. The structure of power is thus important to the durability of the political order.

Liberal-Pluralism: A rather different concept of global politics is proffered from within the liberal-pluralist paradigm. Although not as coherent a body of theory as realism and neo-realism, liberal-pluralism starts from the assumption that the state is no longer the primary actor on the world stage. Rather the growth of the transnational relations points to the significance of non-actors, such as multi-national corporations, and a myriad of other transnational associations.

Rather than viewing the global political process as one which only embraces states, liberal-pluralists argue that it involves processes of bargaining and exertion of influence amongst the variety of actors, each pursuing its own interests. For liberal-pluralists the order is maintained in the global system not through states or the balance of power, but through a complex web of criss-crossing governing arrangements which bind states and societies together.

Finally, liberal pluralism identifies technological and economic forces as the most important harbingers of global interdependence. Technology, particularly the revolution in communications and transport technologies is regarded as being responsible for the growing insignificance of territorial boundaries. For liberal-pluralists, therefore economic and technological power are regarded as primarily responsible for bringing about increasingly higher levels of global political interdependence.

Neo-Marxism: Whilst neo-Marxism, as an explanation of global politics, shares some common ground with realism and liberal-pluralism, it also has many quite significant points of divergence. Neo-Marxists conceive global politics as constrained by the needs of transnational capitalism, with the consequence that the dominant **'political process'** at the global level are viewed essentially as expressions of underlying class conflicts on a world scale.

Although a brief of each paradigm has been given above in an impressionistic manner, nonetheless it should be evident that each delivers a quite distinct account of global politics. See Table Below.

Table: A Summary of Three Paradigms

	Realism and Neo-Realism	Liberal-Pluralism	Neo-Marxism
Dominant Actors	States	Mixed Actor System, e.g. stets, corporations, international organisations.	States, classes, transnational corporations. International economic organisations.
Political Process	Competition, conflict, bargaining, negotiation and diplomacy between states.	Polyarchy, issue areas, global policy processes, and consensual and authoritative decision making.	Class conflict mediated through stets. Conflict between national and transnational capital.
Global Order	Balance of Power. Hegemonic Power. Structure of Power. Society of states.	Global management. International organisation and regimes.	Global structure of production and exchange. Rule of capital.
Dominant forms of power and processes of globalisation.	Military Power. Struggle of hegemony between great powers.	Technological and economic progress. Technological and economic power.	Economic power and ideological power. Transnational capital. Capitalist modernization.

28. The appropriate counterfactual in making comparisons, is thus that same state with legitimating institutions, not other states with a variety of other characteristics. Similarly, this argument does not suggest that India or any other state with no problem of legitimisation will suffer no international violence. It simply implies that it is less prone to such violence than a similar system with greater problems of state legitimisation.

Table: Sources of Legitimisation and Dominant Norms in Five Historical Eras

Era	Legitimisation	Norms
Post Treaty of Westphalia (1648-1789)	**Absolutist**	*Prince absolute functional embodiment of the state.*
Congress of Vienna (1815-48)	**Monarchicalist**	*State required legitimate monarch to be internationally acceptable.*
Two World Wars (1870-1939)	**Nationalist**	*Nation seen as a source of legitimacy for the state.*
Cold War (1945-1989)	**Territorial**	*State legitimised by control of a previously defined set of borders.*
Post Cold War (1990-	**Human Rights**	*State seen as a legitimate one in as much as it respects the civil rights of its citizens.*

29. Baylis, John and Smith, Steve (2001), *The Globalisation of World Politics: An Introduction to International Relations*, (Oxford: Oxford University Press), p. 158.

30. Griffiths, Martin and O' Callaghan, Terry (2002) *International Relations: The Key Concepts* (London: Routledge), pp. 296-97.

31. Ullman, Richard H. (1983), 'Redefining Security', *International Security*, 8 (1), pp. 129-153. See also Kenneth H. Keller (1997), 'Unpackaging the Environment', in *Environment Change and Security Project Report* (Washington D.C.: Woodrow Wilson Centre), Issue 3, spring, pp. 11-12.

32. International Political System's, are comprised of agents and structure. What is more, agency and structure are inter-related. This basic tenet of social theory is shared by the three most

widely acclaimed modern social theorists—Durkheim, Weber, and Marx. Durkheim recognises that social facts *'consists of manners of acting, thinking and feeling external to the individual, which are invested with a coercive power by virtue of which they exercise control over him'.* But concomitantly social facts **'are the beliefs, tendencies and practices of the group taken collectively'**. [See Durkheim, Emile, *The Rules of Sociological Method,* translated and edited by WD Halls and Steven Lukes (New York: The Free Press, 1982), p. 52 and 54].

33. Machuhan, M. (1969), *Understanding Media: The Extension of Man,* New York, New American Library,, p. 302.
34. Mansbach, R.W., Ferguson, Y.H. and Lampert, D.E., (1976), *The Web of World Politics,* New York: Prentice-Hall, p. 22.
35. Mathews, Jessica (1989), 'Redefining Secutiry', *Foreign Affairs*, Spring, p. 162.
36. Ibid., p. 162.
37. Agnew, J. (1994), 'The Territorial Trap: The geographical assumption of international relations theory', *Reviews of International Political Economy*, Vol. I, pp. 53-80.
38. Sicherman, Harvey, (2002), 'The Revival of Geopolitics', *The Intercollegiate Review*, Spring 2002, pp. 16-23.
39. This powerful idea needed as its corollary an international military force. No less a figure than Winston Churchill, in the oft quoted but rarely read Iron Curtain speech, endorsed such a force. He noted, however, that in the absence of such a force, the only recourse would be regional coalitions. The creation of a UN military run by the Security Council had been a victim of the Cold War.
40. Fuller, J.F.C., *A Military History of the Western World* (New York: Funk & Wagnalls Company, 1955), I, p. xi.
41. The Cold War post-World War II saw a standoff between United States and its allies and erstwhile Union of Soviet Socialist Republics (USSR) for approximately forty years till the collapse of the USSR. Both nations were involved in a proxy war and supported various factions during the period but avoided direct confrontation with each other.
42. In national sates:
    (a) The state has assumed a monopoly over all instruments of force and has prohibited private individuals and associations from possessing weapons except to the limited extent permitted by it.
    (b) It has undertaken the task of policing the community and of securing redress to all individuals whose rights be violated by others. It has permitted measures of self help only in extremely rare cases.
    (c) It has established institutions to settle disputes amongst the members of the community when they arise, and also to take measures to reduce their occurrence.
43. Op. cit., at 14.
44. Jablonsky, *National Power.*
45. Ramsay, Paul (1968), *The Just War* (New York: Charles Scribners), p. 5.
46. Neelakantani, Shailaja (2016), About NPT and India, China says it 'cares about rules' but US 'just sets rules', *Times of India,* Jun 21, 2016, (New Delhi), timesofindia.indiatimes.com accessed on 23 Jun 2016.

2

NOTIONS OF SECURITY

Modi must have studied or have been briefed well on Security. He embarked on the very first day to secure the nation. Security[1] has long been by and large a matter of the ***state***,[2] executed in the formulation of foreign and defence policies. The **principle of sovereignty appears to be the hallmark of the 'Modi Doctrine'**; it underlies the contemporary international system in which state is the main entity may be seen as a major source of instability. Consider **'external sovereignty'** in particular, no entity can dictate to a state what it should do; hence, there is **anarchy** as there is no central law that governs relations amongst the nations and the laws that exist are for the states to accept or reject. Hence, the present system is of **'self-help'**. A concept clearly understood by Mr Modi.

Under conditions of anarchy which are prevalent today, the use of force is always a distinct possibility. This means that each sovereign state must ensure that he has enough capabilities to meet possible threats. All states hence, strive to maximise their power relative to other states because only the most powerful states can guarantee their survival. Sovereign states pursue expansionist policies when and where the benefits of doing so outweigh the costs. Modi understood the India has been ignoring its defence capabilities for long. On accession as Prime Minister, Modi brought Mr Parrikar from Goa to head the Ministry of Defence. He also appointed Mr Ajit Doval as National Security Advisor.

> **ANARCHY**
>
> Anarchy involves two features that make up the self-help system of the states:
>
> (a) No authority to enforce agreements, and
>
> (b) Possible recourse to force by actors if the agreement is not followed/implemented.

The state to increase its strength could seek the assistance of allies or friends, but there is no guarantee that they would help. In fact, help if called upon may be acted upon, but this is normally based upon their narrow self-interest. There is however, nothing to compel them to uphold any promises they may have made. The international system thus is self-help and self-help means that each actor must provide for his own security (defence). Hence, each actor would seek to acquire the means to maintain enough power to meet it security needs.

This does not extend equally to all the states; because some states are more equal than others. Such states are normally referred to as the 'Great Powers'. By definition, **a state is a Great Power if it is able to protect its external sovereignty from encroachments by other great powers.** In last over two decades, however, many security issues have become increasingly transnational; e.g. terrorism is commonly perceived as one of the new challenges that cannot be countered effectively at the level of the nation-state alone, as its roots, causes and effects are cross-border.[3]

Regulating the Use of Military Force

Modi understood the need of regulating the use of military force in international relations. Regulating the use of military force in international relations has been a perennial challenge since distinct human communities began pursuing regularised contacts amongst each other. In the modern era—when the notion of international relations emerged in the European context—the historic landmarks of diplomacy and international politics primarily focused upon issues of territory and restraint in the use of force amongst the great powers, based upon an intentional balance of power.

However, since international politics became formalised, the use of force has been something that has been regulated amongst the leading powers, but generally reserved as a tool for dealing with lesser states and colonial territories, and not prohibited as a matter of moral repugnance. Indeed, the use of military force has generally been accepted in international relations, until the 21st Century, for maintaining stability amongst great powers, responding to challenges to hegemons or balance of power systems, or putting down rebellions inside states which might threaten the order (North Korea, Iraq, and many Central American/African Nations).

Making the Sovereign State Insecure

Charles Glaser posits three ways through which making one's adversaries insecure can prove self-defeating. First, even security-seeking policies can set in motion a process that reduces the state's own military capabilities—the ability to perform particular military missions. Second, self-help strategies may increase the value an adversary places on expansion as a means of self-defence, which in turn makes deterrence harder. Third, both military build-ups and alliances can change the adversary's beliefs about the state's motives, thus convincing the adversary that the state is inherently more dangerous than previously thought. An adversary may conclude that a state harbors "greedy" motives—that is, a desire to expand for reasons other than security. Arms build-ups may simply be a waste of a state's finite resources, because others may be able to meet or exceed its level of armament. In short, a state that initiates a military buildup to increase its security may inadvertently set in motion a chain of events that leaves it less secure.[4]

What does Security mean?[5]

Security or the national security as it is commonly known is arguably one of the least understood and most contested concepts to enter the lexicon and discourse of international relations. Security is an elusive term. Like peace, honour or justice, it denotes a quality of relationship which resists definition. It has an active verbal form which seems to take it out of the realm of the abstruse, and a hard tangibility in its nominal form which promises something solid and measurable. But it eludes the attempt to capture it, to enclose it.

The ambiguity it should be noted is not confined to the modern era. In the early 1960s, British historian Michael Howard bemoaned 'the appalling crude conceptual standards',[6] which applied to the national security; while a decade earlier, American academic Arnold Wolfers thought the concept might 'not have any precise meaning at all'.[7] Arnold Wolfers, in the classic essay titled National Security as an Ambiguous Symbol, published more than 50 years ago did not dismiss the concept as meaningless or hopelessly ambiguous. He was, however, concerned about the ambiguity of 'national security', as the following passage indicates:

> **NATIONAL SECURITY**
>
> The term 'national security' implies much of the traditional thinking and theorising about security cast in terms of the nation state. At the systematic or structural level, the debate has tended to concentrate on the most effective means of preserving the integrity and balance of the system of states itself (Bull, 1971, p.18). The concerns are typically expressed in terms of defending the sovereignty and territoriality of individual states from the hostile or predatory intentions of others. Survival of the state as a political, cultural and social entity, and freedom from war or external aggression, is usually considered to be the key measures of security. The other element most commonly mentioned is the protection of core values and the assurance of future well-being (Buzan, 1983, pp. 16-17).

> It would be an exaggeration to claim that the symbol of national security is nothing but a stimulus to semantic confusion, though closer analysis will show that if used without specifications it leaves room for more confusion than sound political counsel or scientific usage can afford.[8]

Others have compared the difficulty of defining national security with attempting to encapsulate a human emotion like anger—it is an '**uncertain quality: it is relative not absolute: it is largely subjective and takes countless forms**'.[9]

Security is a complex construct. Essentially, there are two schools of thought. One tends to view it from the military angle, both external and internal.[10] The others find the epicentre of the source of threat in the environmental, demographic, ecological and economic variables. These variables, according to the second school have become the part and parcel of security analysis. Richard Ullman, a revisionist scholar, writes: '*A threat to national security is an action or sequence of events that: (1) threatens drastically and even over a relatively brief span of*

> **THE SECURITY DILEMMA DEFINED**
>
> The security dilemma is a two-level strategic predicament in relations between states and other actors, with each level consisting of two related dilemmas which force decision-makers to choose between them. The first and basic level consists of a dilemma of interpretation about the motives, intentions and capabilities of others; the second and derivative level consists of a dilemma of response about the most rational way of responding.
>
> *First level* dilemma of interpretation is the predicament facing decision makers when they are confronted, on matters affecting security, with a choice between two significant and usually (but not always) undesirable alternatives about the military policies and political postures of other entities. This dilemma of interpretation is the result of the perceived need to make a decision in the existential condition of unresolvable uncertainty, about the motives, intentions and capabilities of others. Those responsible have to decide whether perceived military developments are for defensive or self-protection purposes only (to enhance security in an uncertain world) or whether they are for offensive purposes (to seek to change the status quo to their advantage).
>
> *Second level* dilemma of response logically begins when the dilemma of interpretation has been settled. Decision-makers then need to determine how to react. Responses are based on misplaced suspicion regarding the motives and intentions of others, and decision-makers react in a militarily confrontational manner, then they risk creating a significant level of mutual hostility when none was originally intended by either party. If the response is based on misplaced trust, there is a risk they will be exposed to coercion by those with hostile intentions. When leaders resolve their dilemma of response in a manner that creates a spiral of mutual hostility, when neither wanted it, a situation has developed which we call the security paradox.

time to degrade the quality of life for inhabitants of a state, or (2) threatens significantly to narrow the range of policy choices available to the government of a state or to private non-governmental entities within the state'.[11]

There are two images that come to mind when we use the word "security". First is to defend against the indeterminate actions of others by guarding the house, policing the street, or saving for the rainy day; then we feel safe. Second, our display of security also displays our vulnerability and makes us feel unsafe. It serves to condition attitudes in those undefined 'others' who may perceive our actions to protect/ secure as a threat, as an incitement, or some may read it as a 'deterrent'. In other words it may limit actions of others, but it leaves their intentions unclear. Our efforts to protect/ secure against perceived threat have yielded insecurity to other. Thus our action to make ourselves secure may lead to escalation. This "vicious circle of security and power accumulation" is called the '***security dilemma***', and it means that in a self-help system one cannot simultaneously improve one's own security without reducing that of others.

> **FACTORS FUELING THE SECURITY DILEMMA**
>
> First, **anarchy**—each state must fend for itself and has only itself to depend on for its survival.
>
> Second, the **lack of trust**—one could not depend on the benevolence of a rival.
>
> Third, **misperception**—capabilities matter more than intentions and increasing capabilities produces apprehension in the opponent.
>
> Fourth, **offense/defence** ambiguity—forces that can be used for defence can also be used for offense.
>
> **THE SECURITY PARADOX**
>
> A security paradox is a situation in which two or more actors, seeking only to improve their own security, provoke through their words or actions an increase in mutual tension, resulting in less security all round.
>
> (From Booth, Ken and Wheeler, Nicholas J. (2008), *The Security Dilemma: Fear, Cooperation and Trust in World Politics* (Basingstoke: Palgrave), p. 9)

This predicament arises from the mistrust which underlies 'security'. The state's perception of the intentions of its regional rivals causes it to escalate 'security'; which results in the sequential interaction of interaction of this misperception, with the consequence of greater insecurity which no one intended. If the response is based on misplaced trust, there is a risk they will be exposed to coercion by those with hostile intentions. When leaders resolve their dilemma of response in a manner that creates a spiral of mutual hostility, when neither wanted it, a situation has developed which we call the '***security paradox***'.

> This evokes security as a negative freedom—'the absence of threat'. Even Arnold Wolfers saw it thus, '*security after all is nothing but the absence of the evil of insecurity, a negative value so to speak*'.[12]

In the late seventies an international commission headed by the former West German Chancellor, Mr Willy Brandt, called for new, more inclusive approach to security, which would incorporate the non-military agenda of complex interdependence.[13] The Palme Commission in 1982, which developed some of the themes of the earlier Brandt Commission and formulated the notion of Common Security, followed this.[14] The common security represented a significant departure from the realist security paradigm because it eschewed competitive, zero-sum notion of deterrence and power, and emphasised instead cooperation, dialogue and confidence building, averring that genuine security could never be achieved unless all states recognised and accepted the legitimate security concerns of others, in essence, '**achieving security with others,** civilisation and the mankind,[15] not relations **against them**'.[16] While common security recognised the need for a multidimensional definition of security, its primary concern was still the military realm.

Security problems arise due to the geographical position of a nation. A landlocked country may feel more threatened and at risk than whose potential enemies are across the sea. Nations dependent on external raw materials has to be concerned about the nations supplying materials to it, as also sea lanes over which the supplies are being transported. On the other hand landlocked countries are concerned about threats from more than one front. Similarly ideological, the religious difference can cause severe security problems.

The Concept of Security

In a world of sovereign nation-states, the predominant concept of security has been '***unilateral competitive national military security***, (UCNMS)' a term in which each of the italicised words is important. "Unilateral" means "put into effect without consulting others." "Competitive" means "striving to win while others lose." "National" means protecting one's own nation-state only. "Military" means by using military threats or force. "Security" means protection from danger by the continuation of the existing international system. The concept has been so well ingrained in our consciousness that we equate "security" to UCNMS without considering other meanings of "security," or other means for achieving it.

> **Unilateral Competitive National Military Security (UCNMS)**
>
> A term in which each of the italicised words is important. "**Unilateral**" means "put into effect without consulting others." "**Competitive**" means "striving to win while others lose." "**National**" means protecting one's own nation-state only. "**Military**" means by using military threats or force. "**Security**" means protection from danger by continuation of the existing international system.

Concepts of security are the different bases on which States and the international community relies for their security. Examples of concepts are the "balance of power", "deterrence", "peaceful coexistence" and "collective security". Security policies, on the other hand, are meant to promote security, such as disarmament and arms limitation arrangements or the maintenance and development of military capabilities.

Balance of Power

The Balance of power theory posits that because states have an interest in maximising their long-term odds on survival, they will coordinate to check dangerous concentrations of power. This will also be the case in a system based on "collective self-help" where states form alliances against each other. The main principle of order in such a system, according to Realism, is the ***balance of power***. A system based exclusively on national self-help will inevitably be anarchical,[17] if only because of the workings of the "security dilemma", implying that a state's pursuit of security generates insecurity for its adversaries, who then respond in ways that make the first stateless secure, etc.

The concept of 'balance of power' is complex and multifaceted.[18] Waltz has noted that, 'if there is any distinctively political theory of international politics, balance-of-power theory is it. And yet one cannot find a statement of the theory that is generally accepted'.[19] Balance of power may be understood in several ways;[20] it may describe the general character of an international system where states, in the absence of a higher authority regulating relations between them, seek security by creating power arrangements that reduce the risk of attack upon them, a process that has tended to produce offsetting coalitions against emerging concentrations of power anywhere in the system. The basic notion of the concept of balance of power in international relations is **'the relationship between the number of actors and the stability of the system'**.[21]

It may refer to a situation in which equivalent power is held by two or more nations or groups of nations and to a policy of promoting the creation or preservation of such equivalence in power. Also, it is sometimes understood as a system of international relations in which agreed arrangements are made by States concerning the operation and adjustment of their power relationships, which may be reflected either in a lower or higher level of armaments.

There is, however, also a theoretical component of the concept which acts as a guide for policymakers with the intention to avoid the dominance of one particular state in the system. Such a system may take on various forms, either with two or more dominant players, possibly accompanied by a balancer, a state who keeps the balance even.

Ultimately, the balance of power concept fulfills three functions in the international system:

1. It prevents the system from being transformed by conquest into a universal empire.
2. Localised balances of power serve to protect actors from absorption by a dominant regional actor.
3. Most important, the balance of power has helped create the conditions in which other elements or characteristics of the international system can develop (i.e., diplomacy, stability, anarchy, war).[22]

If the security threat to others inheres in power potential alone, as Kenneth Waltz maintains, then there is nothing India can do to affect the probability and rate of counterbalancing. If, however, other states assess India's intentions as well as its capabilities when deciding whether to balance, as Stephen Walt and many other realists argue, then Indian policy makers can use support for international institutions to demonstrate their satisfaction with the status quo and dampen other states' security fears, thus forestalling the emergence of a counterbalancing coalition.[23]

Pakistan historically has been trying to balance power with India. From the early 1950s, Pakistan government sought Western diplomatic and military ties initially with the UK, and then with the US, to protect identity and its territoriality, and to widen its diplomatic and military influence in the sub-continent and in the world politics, especially in Middle Eastern Affairs. The UK/US-Pakistan vis-à-vis India triangularity had an ideological and strategic basis because Pakistan was judged to be part of the inner circle of Western Defence against Soviet expansionism during the Cold war, and Indian nonalignment made it an unreliable element in Cold War politics. US military and diplomatic aid to Pakistan commenced in 1954, it affected the Indo-Pakistan military balance and it polarised the political relations between India and Pakistan and India and the United States of America.[24]

Soft Balancing

International Relation scholars are increasingly coming to recognise the absence of traditional great-power balancing since the end of the cold war.[25] In response, realists have shifted their argument, claiming that under unipolarity, balancing dynamics emerges more subtly in the form of "soft balancing," as it is typically called. T.V. Paul provides a concise definition of this concept:

> Soft balancing involves tacit balancing short of formal alliances. It occurs when states generally develop ententes or limited security understandings with one another to balance a potentially threatening state or a rising power. Soft

> balancing is often based on a limited arms build-up, ad hoc cooperative exercises, or collaboration in regional or international institutions; these policies may be converted to open, hard-balancing strategies if and when security competition becomes intense and the powerful state becomes threatening.[26]

Three of the four key cases could be cited as soft-balancing; (i) Russian assistance to Iranian nuclear efforts; (ii) European military coordination; (iii) Russia's strategic partnerships with India and China. Russia's nuclear sales to Iran are driven by economic concerns. Profit is also a key motive in Russia's relationships with its Asian partners; through mutual efforts to enhance security on local and regional issues such as drug trafficking and terrorism also figure. And the European Union's efforts to beef up its joint military capability are almost entirely a response to a perceived need to be able to address regional security. In India cases of soft balancing that could be cited are: (i) opposition to Sanctions against Iran by the US; (ii) Military and technological agreements with Vietnam; (iii) Strategic partnership with central Asian countries and Japan. Again profit and energy security is a chief motive; though mutual efforts to enhance security in local and regional issues also figure.

TYPES OF STATES/ACTORS IN THE INTERNATIONAL ARENA

India faces three types of states/ actors in the international arena.

First, the ***friendly satisfied powers.*** These are actors whose general interests are so aligned with one's own that they present no military threat and do not perceive one as threatening in turn; Russia, South Africa, etc.

The second group of ***implacable enemies*** includes actors who cannot be satisfied with concessions, and who cannot be deterred. This group would include entities like ULFA, LeT, whose political goals are so irreconcilably opposed to those of the India that there is nothing India can offer them that would be acceptable to a degree that would cause them to abandon their attempts at revisionism.

The third, and perhaps most interesting, group comprises the ***potential revisionists.*** These are states who are dissatisfied with the status quo but that could be deterred from challenging it with a combination of coercive strategies and reassurance. Pakistan falls in this category.

Containment

The notion of containment[27] was first conceived by the American diplomat George Kennan. As a Charge d'affaires in the Moscow embassy, Kennan disagreed with US policy on the basis that it did not deal with the nature of 'Russia'. Kennan was pessimistic about a peaceful relation with Moscow due to the fundamental differences between capitalism and socialism.

Kennan pointed out the complete destruction of capitalism and any official, organised form of opposition within the country, leaving the Soviet leaders in absolute control of every aspect of Soviet life. Kennan further notes that these two factors are not to be understood unless a third factor is taken into account, namely the Soviet leadership's monopoly on truth claims. This means that truth is not a constant but is actually created, for all intents and purposes, by the Soviet leaders themselves'.[28]

The appropriate strategy, therefore, was containment. "It is clear that the main element of any United States policy toward the Soviet Union must be that of a long-term, patient but firm and vigilant containment of Russian expansive tendencies." Kennan argued that the Soviet regime is far weaker than the Western world and:

> *'this would of itself warrant the United States entering with reasonable confidence upon a policy of firm containment, designed to confront the Russians with unalterable counter-force at every point where they show signs of encroaching upon the interests of a peaceful and stable world.'*[29]

The Soviet assault on the free institutions of the Western world, Kennan emphasised, could "be contained by the adroit and vigilant application of counter-force at a series of constantly shifting geographical and political points, corresponding to the shifts and maneuvers of Soviet policy, but which cannot be charmed or talked out of existence."

Herein lay the basis of what became the policy of containment. Other parts of Kennan's article express the nature of his idea's concerning containment. The main element of any United States policy toward the Soviet Union must be that of a long-term, patient but firm and vigilant containment of Russian expansive tendencies and:

> *'that the Soviet pressure against the free institutions of the Western world is something that can be contained by the adroit and vigilant application of counter-force at a series of constantly shifting geographical and political points, corresponding to the shifts and maneuvers of Soviet policy'.*[30]

Although occasionally contested by other strategies, containment remained part of US foreign policy for a long time. It became the preferred strategy of US foreign policy from the 1950s onwards, lasting through the Vietnam War and the Cold War.[31] China today is actively following the policy of containment vis-à-vis India. We shall discuss this subsequently under threats to India.

Containment thus demands tough choices about where to extend commitments. Military capabilities constitute the "indispensable backdrop." Containment, after all, is a "policy of calculated and gradual coercion." Without superior military power, it was no more than "a policy of bluff." Containment is real war involving covert actions and psychological warfare throughout the world. Still the real war prudently avoids direct confrontation with the real adversary. China lately has been following this policy with India.

Deterrence

Deterrence is seen as the leading concept for stability during the Cold War. The concept rests on the notion that the parties involved do not dare to attack in fear of a retaliatory strike by the other. In the case of the US and the Soviet Union, both parties deterred each other from launching an attack. Critics of the concept claimed that deterrence raised unnecessary tensions between the superpowers and caused an arms race unprecedented in the history of mankind. Different types of deterrence can be identified, notably finite deterrence, Mutual Assured Destruction (MAD) and war-fighting deterrence. Finite deterrence was based on the premise that leaders on both sides feared the prospect of nuclear war so much, that only a limited amount of nuclear weapons would be sufficient to deter the adversary. MAD was adopted as the official US strategic doctrine in the 1960s. Its main proposition was that the United States should be able to retaliate and destroy at least 50 percent of the Soviet population and industry in the case of a Soviet attack.[32] War-fighting deterrence was the most aggressive of the different types of deterrence. It was based on the idea that the nation should be able to win any confrontation, requiring a much larger nuclear arsenal and highly accurate missiles.[33] During the Reagan administration war-fighting deterrence was part of the official doctrine; as a result, the American defence budget rose to immense proportions. This led some commentators to note that it contributed to a faster ending of the Cold War because the Soviet Union could not keep up with the arms race.

TYPES OF COMPLEX—DETERRENCE RELATIONSHIPS

As the 21st Century dawn, deterrence had become complex because of changes along several dimensions of the international system:

(a) An increase in the importance of multiple states and non-state actors;
(b) The distribution of power; with United States having a very large edge over all other states in the system, but the system is not unipolar;
(c) Power relationships are evolving although great powers are in a state of relative peace;
(d) Goals, ideals, and issues, asymmetric challengers want to alter regional and international status quo.

Paul, T.V. (2009) 'Complex Deterrence: An Introduction' in Paul, T.V., Morgan, Patrick M., and Wirtz, James J., (Eds.) *Complex Deterrence: Strategy in the Global Age,* (Chicago: The University of Chicago Press)

Several points of critique have been made in relation to deterrence theory and the study of security. The fact that it emerged from East-West issues and focused on military capabilities led Nye and Lynn-Jones[34] to point out that 'deterrence theory and game theory provided a powerful unifying framework for those central issues, but often at the cost of losing sight of the political and historical context.' Jervis[35] contended that the concept of deterrence was 'so vague as to accommodate almost all behavior' and that it 'merely summarised what statesmen and even casual observers already knew'.

Despite being elegant and parsimonious, deterrence theory has received considerable criticism for its weaknesses when examined in the light of case studies of actual decision situations.

India and Pakistan, actively began building nuclear weapons in the 1980's, conducted underground weapons tests in May 1998. Soon afterward, the two rivals entered into an intense phase of adversarial relationship characterised by a **"stability-instability paradox"**. The two nations fought a war in the Kargil Region of Kashmir in 1999; thereby raising questions about deterrence in an intense conflict environment involving the nuclear dyad. Yet some observers argue that because the Kargil war did not escalate and the subsequent mobilisation crisis in 2002-2003 did not prompt a full-scale war across the entire region, largely because of the fear of nuclear escalation by the leaders of the two countries, the recent history demonstrates that deterrence can work even in a theatre of active enduring rivalry such as India-Pakistan in South Asia.

The attack at the Indian Parliament House, Mumbai, and in Baramullah seems to sound a death knell for deterrence. The history of deterrence, however, shows that recent doubts about the efficacy of deterrence are hardly unique. In both the political arena and academic research, deterrence has always had critics but has still often emerged as policy compromise around most people's second choices. In a changing strategic environment, it is unlikely that deterrence would remain as central security concept as it was during some years back. At the same time, the continued existence of security threats made it unlikely deterrence would go away completely. The complex nature of the contemporary security environment makes it desirable to broaden our understanding of deterrence to see if there are new ways to achieve deterrence that might prove more effective that the traditional deterrent strategies.

Coalitions/Alliances[36]

States can opt to form or join existing alliances or coalitions. An alliance is a formal security agreement between two or more states. Typically, states enter into alliances to protect themselves against a common threat. By consolidating resources and acting in unison, members of an alliance believe they can improve their overall position in the international system and their security relative to states that are not members of their alliance. Additional benefits to alliance membership might include the ability to offset the cost of defence.

Wartime alliances are formal or informal agreements between two or more states intended to further (militarily) the national security of the participating states, usually in the form of joint consultation and cooperation to prevail in the war against a common enemy or enemies. Such alliances are usually concluded in peacetime in order to prevent or prevail in war, but continue to operate under wartime conditions. States augment their joint planning, consultation, and sometimes integrate their forces as their plans for war unfold and are implemented. Member states usually expect the alliance will endure beyond any specific war or crisis.

There is a range of commitment levels that alliances may provide. Six can be identified:

1. A promise to maintain benevolent neutrality in the event of war;
2. A promise to consult in the event of military hostilities with an implication of aid;
3. Promises of military assistance and other aid in event of war, but unilateral and without pre prepared or explicit conditions specified;
4. A promise to come to the active assistance of an ally under specific circumstances; and
5. An unconditional promise of mutual assistance, short of joint planning, with division of forces;
6. An unconditional promise of mutual assistance in the event of an attack with preplanned command and control and the integration of forces and strategy.[37]

Coalitions are normally less formal than alliances. Normally, they represent a broad grouping of often very diverse states temporarily united for a specific purpose, typically military action. About 20 states often agree to participate in a coalition, strictly as a matter of convenience. Coalitions are likely to be temporary, while alliances frequently can endure for lengthy periods. Examples would be the American-led coalitions during the first Persian Gulf War (Operations DESERT SHIELD/STORM) and the second conflict (Operation IRAQI FREEDOM).

Collective Security[38]

Collective security implies an acknowledgment that security is indivisible. It provides protection of national interests and sovereignty in a collective manner and leads to the strengthening of international security. As a concept it aims at a broader objective by taking into account the wider requirements of peace and security. The concept of collective security is based on a commitment to the peaceful settlement of disputes and obligation to support collective measures, both military and non-military, to defeat aggression.

> **COLLECTIVE SECURITY**
>
> The theory of collective security deals with the issue of how to cause peace. The key to enhancing stability in this world of armed states is the proper management of military power, which is best achieved through institutions.

Two principles underline 'collective security'. In the first place, collective security is a product of law: the power of collective security organs exists because, and to the extent that, they are delegated to these organs by the state party to their constituent instruments. Collective security action has to fit within the consensual limits of delegation. It is the consensual approach that holds the key to identifying the extent of jurisdiction and operational capabilities vested in institutions.

The second principal refers to the process by which collective security institutions multiply.

Collective security is premised on general interests shared by all states and aims to protect those interests by concentrating force. Collective security is a matter of interpreting and applying legal framework consisting of constituent treaties, summit communiqués and declarations, and institutional decisions of binding or recommendatory character.[39] Collective security thus understood imposes universal concepts on national policies;[40] it is, then, about an international compromise on permissible limits to how states perceive security, and means by which they can maximise security.

Collective security operates against the background that governments lack a strong sense that they are part of larger (political, economic, social, cultural) entity in international politics with overreaching interests, goals, perspectives and values they share.[41] Furthermore, 'although States might engage in the occasional act of security cooperation, anarchy ultimately and decisively causes them to seek advantage over their neighbours, and to act in self-interested and self-help manner.[42]

A number of questions need to be addressed viz. does a legal, or rule-based, framework regulate the use of military force? Was the concept undermined by the war against Iraq of 2003 and the doctrine of the preventive use of military force? In 2003 French President Jacques Chirac demanded, it is the role of the Council to set the bounds to the use of force. No one is entitled to assume the right to utilise it unilaterally and preventively."[43]

It comes as little surprise that a renowned realist such as Michael Glennon would argue that "no rational state will be deluded into believing that the UN Charter protects its security",[44] or that Richard Perle would proclaim "the intellectual wreckage of the liberal conceit of safety through international law administered by international institutions."[45]

The League, at least in theory, sought to prohibit aggression by international law; members states committed themselves to respect "the territorial integrity and existing political independence of all Members of the League" against "external aggression" (Article 10). Article 16 stated that, "should any Member of the League resort to war in disregard of its covenants .... it shall so facto be deemed to have committed an act of war against all other Members of the League." This was an attempted embodiment of Woodrow Wilson's "fourteen points" for world peace; point 14 suggests: "A general association of nations should be formed on the basis of covenants designed to create mutual guarantees of the political independence and territorial integrity of States, large and small equally."

The major difficulty with the concept of collective security is that on a number of occasions States have been reluctant to fulfill their obligations, which is the basic condition for the functioning of the system. Another reason why the collective security system has not always functioned as effectively as expected is the lack of political will to co-operate amongst the member states.

The League of Nations is best known for its failures, however. The Japanese aggression in China, the Italian aggression in North Africa, the German aggression in Europe, and finally the Second World War occurred in violation of the League Covenant. The failure was due to lack of political will; aggravated by the absence of an effective enforcement mechanism; and by the lack of universality in the League. The interpretations of most historians are that Britain, France and to a lesser extent the United States, were attempting to operate an unrealistic hegemony-concert and keep Germany, Italy, Japan and the Soviet Union under control.

The UN regime for international peace and security was, in principle, a continuation of earlier ideas of collective security: the use of military force would be prohibited unless in cases of self-defence, collective self-defence, or under the authorisation of the UN Security Council. The UN would take effective collective measures for the prevention and removal of threats to the peace, and for the suppression of acts of aggression or other breaches of the peace. As the Charter states, it would also bring about by peaceful means, and in conformity with the principles of justice and international law, the settlement of international disputes which might lead to a breach of the peace. Yet, the UN Charter was not a completely liberal internationalist treaty. Its structure clearly reflects power in international relations, most obviously in the form of the Permanent Five Security Council concert.

The special voting powers have been accorded to five States as permanent members of the UN Security Council. Collective security action by the United

Nations requires the concurrence of the five permanent members of the Council; a negative vote by anyone of the five States "vetoes" the proposed action. The "veto" provision reflects the original assumption that the great Powers would maintain a cooperative working relationship among them and, therefore, only use the veto in exceptional circumstances. In practice, however, disagreements between the permanent members have in a number of cases led to the use of the veto, which, in turn, has prevented collective security action. The view has been expressed that the veto power has been abused. India has been able to retain a hold on Kashmir after Pakistan joined the SEATO and CENTO alliances only due to 'veto' exercised by erstwhile USSR and Russia.

SECURITY AND GLOBALISATION

Globalisation is best understood as a spatial phenomenon. It is not an 'event', but a gradual and ongoing expansion of interaction processes, forms of organisation, and forms of cooperation outside the traditional spaces defined by sovereignty. Activity takes place in a less localised, less insulated way as transcontinental and interregional patterns criss-cross and overlap one and another.

Globalisation processes are not just about linkages but about interpenetration. As Guehenno noted, globalisation is defined not just by ever expanding connections between states measured in terms of movement of goods and capital but the circulation and interpenetration of people and ideas (Guehenno, 1999, p. 7).

Globalisation is a spatial reorganisation of production, industry, finance, and other areas which causes local decisions to have global repercussions and daily life to be affected by global events.

It is perhaps more meaningful when such John Ruggie[46] would state that the UN "lacks the capacity to act predictably on its core mission: to save succeeding generations from the scourge of war". Ziring, Riggs and Plano argue that, "When one country dominates world events and holds a monopoly of world power, the system of collective security is doomed to failure".[47] The 2003 Iraq war was the epitome of this; although the US was not the only country which supported the conflict diplomatically or militarily, the coalition of the willing would not have existed without US leadership and the US was not reliant upon any such assistance.

Common Security

The idea of common security was put forward in the report of the Independent Commission on Disarmament and Security Issues (Palme Commission in 1982). The Commission stated that "a doctrine of common security must replace the present expedient of deterrence through armaments. International Peace must rest on a commitment to joint survival rather than a threat of mutual destruction". When it was first promulgated by the Palme Commission in its 1982 report, Common Security was conceived as simply a novel means to the traditional end of national security. It was presumably preferable to a unilateral quest for security which would almost inevitably be at the expense of one's adversaries. Common Security was thus conceived as an escape route from the 'security dilemma', implying that states could only make themselves more secure by making their adversaries less so.[48] By thus placing the security of their adversaries in jeopardy, states tended to provoke a response that detracted from their own security so that, at the end of each interactive cycle, both sides found themselves less secure. This security dilemma manifested itself in, at least, three different dynamics:

- An action-reaction pattern in arms acquisitions, where one state armed out of fear of its opponent's armaments, yet by so doing made the latter reciprocate, resulting in an arms race.[49]
- A risk of preventive war (one state attacking another in the belief that its opponent would otherwise do so at a later stage when force ratios were less favourable), or of pre-emptive attack resulting from crisis instability.[50]
- Competitive alliance-building, where one world power sought allies (in a specific region or worldwide) in order to prevent its adversary from gaining a foothold, yet by so doing tended to push remaining states into the opposing camp.[51]

The Commission began with the premise that threats to security—the conventional and nuclear arms races, resource shortages, environmental degradation, under development—are threats that nations increasingly have in common, and that solutions should therefore be sought in common. As the Commission reported the key to security lies in the willingness of nations to organise their security policies in co-operation with each other.

Common security as a concept is based on two preferences: for international over national means of achieving security, and for means that are peaceful over those that rely on the use or the threatened use of force. These extremely venerable preferences are interpreted in the light of modern destructive technologies, principally nuclear but also 'conventional', chemical and biological weapons. On the other hand, the existence of modern weapons makes it likely that the costs of resorting to military force (certainly to nuclear force) would exceed the benefits; no one would win a nuclear war. On the other hand, the effects of the use of modern weapons would cross international frontiers. No country would be secure from the consequences of nuclear war: 'national' and 'international' interests coincide in the need to prevent war.

Even though there were competing interpretations of the actual implications of Common Security, as a minimum it entailed taking the security of one's respective opponent into consideration. Security was only obtainable for either side of an adversarial dyad if both sides enjoyed it simultaneously. In the words of the Palme Commission:[52]

> 'In the absence of a world authority with the right and power to police international relations, states have to protect themselves. Unless they show mutual restraint and proper appreciation of the realities of the nuclear age, however, the pursuit of security can cause intensified competition and more tense political relations and, at the end of the day, a reduction in security for all concerned. ... Restraint should be the watchword of all states; restraint, out of respect for the right of others to security, but also in selfish recognition that security can be attained only by common action.'

The South Asian Region is 'anarchic' in the sense of having no political authority over and above the states. On a spectrum of "maturity"[53] the Gulf also clearly ranks quite low, inter alia reflecting state weakness. India-China competition is going to overspill.

Non-Alignment

The concept of 'non-alignment' was first introduced by the Indian Prime Minister Jawaharlal Nehru in 1954 as part of his five principles of restraint, which formed the basic tenets of India's foreign policy. Non-alignment is not merely a policy of Governments but also a movement of the peoples of non-aligned countries. Non-aligned countries did not wish to take sides in a conflict from which they had little to gain and much to lose. Non-aligned countries reacted against the dangers inherent in great Power struggles, military alliances and the arms race, voiced their opposition to colonialism and expressed a reaffirmation of the principle of the equality of all nations in the international system. The Bandung Conference of Asian and African countries, held at Bandung, Indonesia, in 1955, was an important milestone in Afro-Asian history and some of the ideas were later taken up by non-aligned nations. Nehru's principles

FIVE PRINCIPLES OF PEACEFUL COEXISTENCE

Premier Zhou Enlai met with members of the Indian Government Delegation on 31 December 1953 where he put forward for the first time the Five Principles of Peaceful Coexistence, namely, mutual respect for each other's territorial integrity and sovereignty (changed to mutual respect for each other's sovereignty and territorial integrity at the Asian-African Conference), mutual non-aggression, non-interference in each other's internal affairs, equality and mutual benefit (changed to equality and mutual benefit in the Sino-Indian Joint Statement and Sino-Burmese Joint Statement), and peaceful coexistence.

gathered momentum here at the Bandung, where 29 governments discussed the role of the 'Third World' in the Cold War era, and strengthened cooperation towards peace, development and decolonisation.

Non-alignment concept has basic elements as: (a) staying out of military blocs or other forms of great Power entanglements; (b) working towards defusing international tensions and promoting peace; (c) peaceful coexistence and peaceful co-operation among States irrespective of their social or political systems; (d) support for people struggling for freedom from colonialism, opposition to racism, apartheid, etc.; (e) support for disarmament, especially nuclear disarmament; (f) working towards a more just and equitable international order. These elements formed the core of the non-aligned policies in the 1950s and 1960s and constituted rallying posts for the non-aligned movement as a whole.

Non-alignment has remained an object of immense applause as well as ruthless criticism throughout its existence. The US dubbed it as 'immoral' and 'non sense'.[54] Even Stalin felt that 'Those who were not with us were against us'. The Chinese Communist Supremo Mao declared that a country must 'learn to be on one side or the other and a third path does not exist'. They despised the Non-alignment ever since the latter was reckoned as an important factor in international politics. Notwithstanding this criticism Non-alignment remained a potent and powerful force in the cold war era. It took bold stands on issues affecting the newly independent and developing countries and was decidedly, a force that neither of the two super powers could afford to ignore. The Non-alignment as a movement of the small, newly-independent and developing countries has been determined to carve out an independent path of development and not to remain an appendage of any colonising power or superpower. This objective helped Non-alignment in making a significant headway throughout the cold war era. The crusade against imperialism and racism met with greater success with large number of colonies the list of the UN and Non-alignment as sovereign and Independent nation states. The economic concerns were related to the North-South great economic divide, dubious role of the International Financial bodies, poverty and above all the vitality for a strong South-South cooperation.

Strategic Partnership

The concept of strategic partnership emerged from the post-Cold War era.[55] Countries, particularly in Eurasia and in Asia, reacted to the demise of the bipolar order by developing new "hedging" strategies to deal in a flexible manner with the "lone superpower" and with other regional powers at the same time, without committing to new forms of the alliance in troubled and uncertain times. For a former superpower like Russia and for emerging powers like China and India, the international environment was simply too uncertain and evolving too rapidly to opt for a definitive bandwagoning or balancing posture at the global (vis-à-vis the US) and regional (vis-à-vis other regional powers) levels.[56]

The cost has been immense of such vicarious diplomacy. Not least successive Indian Governments have subordinated long-term defence interests to those of immediate advantage in dealings with great powers A decision on procurement, or an alliance strategy, favoring the view of stronger partners, has for long been preferable to any viewpoint based on narrow domestic considerations. In some ways, these decisions were well-fitted to early years of post-independent India. In those years, India was influential enough to effect on the world scene by being on-aligned. The coming of *détente* and end of cold war has placed all that in doubt.

STRATEGIC PARTNERSHIP

What makes a partnership "strategic"? First, a strategic partnership must be comprehensive, in order to allow linkages and tradeoffs between various policies. Second, it must be built upon reciprocity, short of which it cannot be deemed a partnership at all. Third, a strategic partnership has a strong empathic dimension, which means that both partners share a common understanding of their mutual values and objectives. Fourth, a strategic partnership must be oriented towards the long-term, which is to say that it is not put into question by casual disputes. Finally, a strategic partnership must go beyond bilateral issues to tackle (with the potential to solve) regional and global challenges, because that is its true raison d'être.

Based on those standards, how strategic are the EU's "strategic partnerships"? Among the current ten strategic partnerships (with Brazil, Canada, China, India, Japan, Mexico, Russia, South Africa, South Korea and the United States) probably only the US-relationship qualifies as a true strategic partnership. The others are, among other things, not comprehensive (e.g. India and Japan), not oriented towards global issues (e.g. South Africa) or not based on reciprocity and empathy (e.g. Russia and China).

Renard, Thomas (2011) *The Treachery of Strategies: A Call for True EU Strategic Partnerships,* (Gent: Academia Press) p. 6.

Institutional Cooperation

Institutional Cooperation builds on the observation that global problems beyond the control of individual countries cannot be managed in the absence of institutional structures that establish standards for state action and monitor compliance. United States derives significant efficiency gains from the web of international institutions in the world today, much of which was created at the behest of US policy makers in the decades following World War II.[57]

Who are the Actors?

Since the 17th century, the nation-state has been the dominant entity in the international system, in part because of the power the concept of sovereignty gave the recognised states—both in terms of absolute domestic control and independence on the international level. But nation-states have never been alone in the international system. A variety of non-state actors always has challenged their influence. The term non-state actor typically refers to any participant in the international system that is not a government. It is an entity or group that may have an impact on the internationally related decisions or policies of one or more states. Examples of no-state actors would be International Organisations, Non-Government Organisations, Multi-National Companies, the international media, armed elements attempting to free their territory from external rule, or terrorist groups. An individual may also be a non-state actor.[58]

An international organisation is a formal institutional structure that transcends national boundaries. States create them by multilateral agreement or treaty. International organisations normally function as an association of states that wields state like power through governmental-like organs. The founding treaty defines the limits of the international organisation's legal competence. This is the primary difference between a state and an international organisation. The international organisation only possesses the powers granted to it in its originating document by the states that created it, and cannot legally act beyond those powers. A state possesses the rights and duties recognised by international law, subject to the provisions of that law, and can involve itself in almost any activity of its choosing. International organisations are completely dependent on member states for support and resources, both political and practical (like money and personnel). The result is that every international organisation is dependent on a sufficient number of member states believing that it is in their national interest to support the organisation and its activities. Without member state support, the International organisations will not be able to function. Examples of international organisations include the United Nations Organisation, South Asian Association for Regional Cooperation, and the European Union.[59]

NGOs are voluntary organisations of private individuals, both paid and unpaid, who are committed to a wide range of issues not on the behalf of any specific state government. Owing to increased interconnectedness partly associated with improvements in communications technology and transportation, specialized NGO organisations, agencies, and groups have risen around the globe, and have an unprecedented level of influence in the modern international system. NGOs typically fall in one of two categories: those that have a universal noncommercial (nonprofit), and nonpartisan focus; and those that are primarily motivated by self-interest. The former are likely to involve humanitarian aid organisations, human rights groups, environmentalists, or new social movements. Representative organisations of this first type are Amnesty International, Greenpeace, the Red Cross, and Save the Children.[60]

To combat violations of the world order, the international community has created a number of regimes to ensure that widely accepted principles, procedures, norms, and rules are in place to govern particular issues in the international system. The intent is to create an opportunity for states to use these regimes as fora to cooperate to achieve beneficial outcomes. Membership in these special purpose organisations generally is open to all relevant state actors. The success or failure of regimes is based on the level of coordination and cooperation of policies among the member states.[61]

International regimes can take the form of legal conventions, international agreements, treaties, or international institutions. Special issue areas that they occupy include economics, the environment, human rights, policing, and arms control. Contemporary regimes like the World Trade Organisation (WTO), General Agreement on Tariffs and Trade (GATT), World Bank, International Monetary Fund (IMF), Kyoto Protocol on the Environment, Geneva Conventions, International Criminal Court (ICC), UN Convention on the Law of the Sea, and the Strategic Arms Reduction Treaties (START) I and II are all intended to specify general standards of behavior and identify the rights and obligations of signatory states.[62]

Transnational threats are threats to the international system that cross state borders. Such threats emerged or increased dramatically in the latter part of the last century. While the term transnational relates to any activity that cross state boundaries, transnational threats is a technical term that usually refers to activities with minimal or no governmental control. Three types of movement can be associated with transnational behavior: movement of physical objects, to include human beings; movement of information and ideas; and movement of money and credit.[63]

The combination of the cross-border movement with illicit or dangerous activities has resulted in the identification of an emerging set of threats to human security, the ability of states to govern themselves, and ultimately the stability of the international system at large. These transnational threats fall into two broad categories:

1. Direct threats from human beings (terrorism, organised crime, drug trafficking, illegal alien smuggling, and smuggling of WMD), and
2. Threats from impersonal forces (disease and international pandemics, population growth and migration, resource shortages, global environmental degradation and climate change).[64]

Transnational threats have been expanding since the end of the Cold War for a number of reasons. These include the premise that many emerging democracies are the vestiges of former authoritarian states where there has been a long tradition of coercion, violence, and corruption. Such states relied more on roles and relations than on rules and regulations. Thus, many governments have been constrained by political norms that place factional loyalties above commitment to public policies. Also, as was the case with failing states and ungoverned spaces, diminished assistance from the developed world helped reduce the ability of governments to police their borders.[65]

How does the International System function?

Players on the international stage, both state and non-state actors prefer to work alone or attempt to work with other elements of the system to meet their national aspirations/security needs. One has just to go back to the Mahabharata and see some of the actions undertaken by both Kauravas as well as Pandavas to meet their respective aspirations. First and foremost was building relationships to augment their respective strengths. Such relationships might be with other states or non-state actors on a bilateral basis; formal groupings of states, International Organisations, Non-Government Organisations, or other non-state actors; or informal, even unacknowledged cooperation with other system members. The state might decide to go alone, opt for an alliance, and form a coalition or bandwagon against his adversary. However, any approach taken is a decision by a state, conscious or subconscious, about relations with other members of the international system. Actors on the global stage, both state and non-state, decide to participate in alliances and coalitions and to conduct policies in support of balancing and bandwagoning based on their assessment of their relative power in the international system.

States enter into alliances to protect themselves against a common threat. By consolidating resources and acting in unison, members of an alliance believe they can improve their overall position in the international system and their security relative to states that are not members of their alliance. Additional benefits to alliance membership might include the ability to offset the cost of defence. The alliance is thus, at least theoretically, less expensive than a unilateral approach to security. Also, economically related alliances can provide expanded economic benefits through increased trade, assistance, and loans between allies.[66]

A state is balancing when it joins a weaker alliance or coalition to counter the influence or power of a stronger state or group of states. "Balancing happens when weaker states decide that the dominance and influence of a stronger state are unacceptable, and that the cost of allowing the stronger state to continue their policies unchecked is greater than the cost of action against the stronger state."[67]

Bandwagoning occurs when weaker states determine that the cost of opposing a stronger state exceeds the benefits to be gained from supporting it. The stronger power may offer incentives like territorial gain or trade agreements to entice the weaker actor to join with it. An example is of US bulldozing it way during Desert Shield.[68]

Theoretically, the international system works to prevent any actor from dictating to any other actor—that is, the balance of power concept actually works to maintain the system of independent and sovereign states.[69] In effect, the balance of power describes the distribution of power in the international system in both equal and unequal portions. Given an assumption that unbalanced power is dangerous for the maintenance of stability, actors attempt to conduct policy that produces equilibrium of power in the system. This helps form the rationale for actors to bandwagon or balance as they form alliances or coalitions against potentially dominant competitors.[70]

The belief that equilibrium protects the sovereignty of the states, perceived inequality of power, and the threat of violence combine to give both dominant and subordinate actors a shared (if unequal) interest in maintaining order in the international system. The balance of power becomes a type of compromise among actors that find stability preferable to anarchy, although it results in a system that favors the strong and wealthy over the weak and poor. More powerful actors, like the great power states, play leading roles in a balance of power international system because they have the superior military force and the ability to wield key technology.[71]

What should India do?

How the nation-states and other actors in the international system choose to interpret the concept of security helps determine participation in alliances or coalitions, involvement in collective security frameworks or institutions, and balancing or bandwagoning behaviors. In all cases, the actors consider their ability to wield all the elements of power they have available, whether or not to use force, and—most significantly—what interests their ultimate policies will support.

The security dilemma should be at the heart of security policies not only because its significance pervades the "very geometry" of human conflict, as Butterfield put it, but also because it speaks directly and urgently to some of the main challenges of our time. There are strong grounds for thinking that world politics has entered a period of unprecedented insecurity – a "Great Reckoning", when human society locally and globally will increasingly come face-to-face with its most fundamental self-created difficulties.[72] The coming decades will see a potentially disastrous convergence of dangers unless sensible collective action is quickly taken to head them off. In a new era of uncertainty India will be challenged by a novel combination of old and new security predicaments in relation to such issue areas as nuclear proliferation, terrorism, "climate chaos", competition for non-renewable (especially traditional energy) resources, mass migration, great power rivalry, cultural/religious/civilisational clashes, and the growing gap between haves and have-nots.

In most of these key risk areas security dilemma dynamics threaten to heighten fear, provoke mistrust, and close down possibilities for building cooperation and trust.

First: ***the danger of a new cold war with China***. An imminent threat exists of Sino–India competition developing in dangerous ways.

Second: ***the danger of new arms races***. The post-Cold War peace dividend never materialised, and in a period of intensifying international tension it would not be a surprise to see the revival of competitive arms-building. New arms races might be global (Russia versus the United States) or regional (South versus North Korea), and they might be conventional (Pakistan versus India) or nuclear (Turkey versus Iran) The South China Sea... In these cases, security dilemma dynamics work in well-understood ways, with future uncertainty about motives and intentions feeding existing mistrust, and resulting in a contagion of security paradoxes.

Three: ***the danger of a world of many nuclear powers***. The threat here is of the breakdown of the Nuclear Non-proliferation Treaty (NPT) regime, and with it the spread of nuclear weapons technology to an increasing number of states

Four: ***the danger of terrorism***. When, faced with perceived threats from other states, India has two distinct set of options available to her:

(a) ***First Option***. Under the self-help mechanism action would be taken at the national level (which is most prominent in the present anarchical system); India can either take action unilaterally viz. Eviction of Pakistani troops from Kargil–Batalik area; or take multilateral action like the one taken by India prior to Dec 1971 when India entered into a treaty with the erstwhile Soviet Union.

(b) ***Second Option***. Using the existing structure like the United Nations. However, India has not got a fair hearing from the established institutions. The Kashmir issue was never resolved and The Indo-Pakistan Western Boundary (Rann of Kutch) between India and Pakistan (India, Pakistan) was not fair to India.

Five: ***Internal Threat*** from Naxalities, Unauthorised Immigration, communists.

The options available have been set out in Table 1, which distinguishes between unilateral action ("self-help") and multilateral action in the sense of joining up with others. The latter may be subdivided into alignment and collective action, the former referring to the teaming up with a group of states and the latter to the resort to whatever universal (regional or global) means may be at hand. The choices India, as the unit of international politics, make in this respect determine the structure and the various institutions of the system—which, of course, also define the options available to states.

In the contemporary era, India faces an 'existential threat' from a transnational network enterprise rather than from states organised along similar lines as in the past.[73] This development represents a break with putative histories of world politics as about great power struggles. Al-Qaeda, LeT, ULFA are neither a state nor a great power; it is a transnational network and more importantly an idea around which resistance is organised globally and locally.[74]

The Modi Foreign Policy Doctrine: India as a Smart Power

If President Pranab Mukherjee's opening address to the Indian parliament is anything to go by, the foreign policy of the new Indian government under Prime Minister Narendra Modi will likely employ a nuanced combination of all three of Nye's instruments of international influence. All those who had expected the Modi foreign policy doctrine to be defined by a new muscularity

Table 1: India's Security Strategies

Strategies at National Level					
	Unilateral Actions		Multilateral Actions		
Military Means	Deterrence or Security through strength		Alignment or entering into treaties		Collective Security or Intervention
	Offensive Capability	Defensive Capability	Against a power	Against threats	
Non-Military means	Diplomacy		Containment trade		Arbitration
Strategies using Structures and Institutions					
	Anarchy		International Society		World Order
Military	Deterrence/Balance of Power		Alliances Confidence Building Measures Arms Control Security Regimes		Collective Security
Means	Offensive Capability	Defensive Capability			
Non-Military Means	Common Security		Cooperative Security Institutional		International Law Integration

or even match-politik—the wielding of the conventional stick—will probably be disappointed.

Instead, there will be a renewed emphasis on using the carrots of economic levers and soft power. This suggests a thoughtful understanding of the importance of what Nye terms "smart power": a clever combination of the tools of conventional hard, or military and economic, power and soft power. It is this integrated approach that will best serve India in a complex interdependent world, which is defined as much by conflict and competition as it is by cooperation and the need for greater coordination in confronting common global threats.

The incipient Modi doctrine has five key elements. First, and most important, is the idea that a *strong, self-reliant and self-confident India will pursue a foreign policy of "enlightened national interest".*

National interest is a contested term; enlightened national interest even more so. Often, national interest is defined as a *raison d'etat*, or "reason of state", and can be viewed as the selfish pursuit of national ambitions, mostly as defined by the government of the day.

Enlightened national interest adds a moral prism to the policy. When Alexis de Tocqueville wrote his masterly Democracy in America, in the early 19th Century, he described enlightened self-interest as that which made the United States unique: the ability of its citizens to work for the common good because the pursuit of a better life for everyone serves the self-interest of all.

In international diplomacy, *enlightened national interest is arguably the recognition that the narrow pursuit of self-interest in an interdependent world can lead to sub-optimal policy outcomes.* Japan—a nation Modi clearly admires—has used the term enlightened national-interest to define many of its policies, including those steering its overseas development assistance. Through supporting other nations via giving and via attractive development funding and loans, Japan has greatly increased its regional influence. The concept opens up the possibilities of creating cooperative outcomes for many issues, even those traditionally seen as difficult, zero-sum conflicts by realists in the establishment.

Within the Indian tradition, this sense of enlightened national-interest is captured in this verse from Hindu scripture, the Mahaupinishad, "Only small men discriminate by saying 'one is a relative, the other is a stranger'. For those who live magnanimously the entire world constitutes but a family." Its essence, it may be recalled, can be found in the BJP's manifesto as well.

And while Mr Modi may not be comfortable with this notion, his idea of enlightened national interest sits at ease with Nehruvian thinking. After all, it was Jawaharlal Nehru who believed that while foreign policy must be rooted in a spirit of realism, it should not be stymied by the narrow realism that lets you look only at the tip of the nose and little beyond.

Second, is the idea that *India will help to build and strengthen a democratic, peaceful, stable and economically interlinked neighbourhood.* This, of course, is not particularly new thinking. In the past, the Gujral Doctrine was perhaps the strongest articulation of a policy of reaching out to the neighbourhood, even though gestures that did not demand reciprocity. What was both novel and encouraging, however, was the presence of heads of government or senior representatives from all the South Asian countries at the swearing in of Prime Minister Modi and his Cabinet, effectively turning the ceremony into a regional celebration of democracy.

In the recent past, India has not been explicitly seen as a champion of democracy in the region. Whether or not the strong links in other parts of the world between mature democracies—and absence of conflict—are mirrored in South Asia, it is clear that the strengthening of democracy in the region is the first step towards building what the political scientist, Karl Deutsch, described as a security community. That is, a region in which the large scale use of violence has become unthinkable.

That said, it must be recognised that only a strong and economically resurgent India can lead the process of South Asia integration and so much will now depend on how quickly India's economy can be revived. Meanwhile, however, enlightened national interest will demand India considers making unilateral gestures to serve longer-term self-interest.

Third is Modi's *emphasis on soft-power, explained through yet another Modi alliteration of five Ts: tradition, talent, tourism, trade and technology.* For this to translate into reality, India will require real effort. For a start, the Ministry of External Affairs will need to be restructured and every major mission abroad would need to include a trade, scientific and cultural counsellor knowledgeable in the relevant domains.

In addition, the *role of the Diaspora in the future development of India has been emphasised.* One clear step that would ensure deeper engagement between India and the Diaspora would be to allow Non Resident Indians to carry dual passports. For many Indians continuing to hold an Indian passport is a badge of honour which they will not give up for any convenience, glory or money. Allowing dual citizenship for NRIs carries virtually no additional risk; and indeed most countries in the world allow their citizens this privilege.

Fourth, the incipient Modi doctrine moves beyond the former delineation between "non-alignment", "non-alignment 2.0", and "alignment" to suggest that India could follow a policy of what MP Shashi Tharoor may describe as *"multi-*

track alignment" with all the great powers. This was emphasised in the President's address that explicitly stated the government will work with China to develop a strategic and cooperative partnership, work with Japan to build modern infrastructure, build on the firm foundations of the relations with Russia, pursue the relationship with the United States with renewed vigour and make concerted efforts to achieve progress in key areas with the European Union.

Finally, there was only about 50 words of the address devoted to what may have been seen, pre-election, as the most vital part of a future Modi government's foreign policy: *the willingness to raise issues of concern at a bilateral level (read Pakistan) and the uncontroversial claim that stability can only be built in the region if there is an end of the export of terrorism.* Clearly, concerns about Pakistan have deliberately not been emphasised as this may still be a work in progress. Or perhaps the Modi government recognises that there is much merit in the adage: carry a big stick, but speak with a soft voice. Ashok Guha once remarked: "India has carried a tooth pick, and shouted from the roof top and from television studios".

In last two years Modi has acted like Indian Deng, it is well worth recalling the great Chinese leader's 24 Character Strategy:

> Observe calmly; secure our position; cope with affairs calmly; hide our capacities and bide our time; be good at maintaining a low profile; and never claim leadership.

In other words, India requires stability within and peace in our neighbourhood and beyond for at least the next decade to emerge as great power of some standing. During that period it is best not to get dragged in external conflicts, assume leadership or prominence on the international stage, or attract attention.

ENDNOTES

1. Singh, Col (Retd) Narendar, (2007), *Conduct of War* (New Delhi: Manas Publications), pp. 7-8.
2. Michael Oakeshott described the state in the Western constitutional tradition as a "civil association"—the sole purpose of which is to enable other, more circumscribed social, political, and economic activities to take place and which is necessary (but not sufficient) for the pursuit of those other activities. The existence of such a civil association enables socially legitimate collective action to be undertaken in the first place. Oakeshott distinguishes this from an "enterprise association," which has particular ends and can be dissolved when those ends are no longer or are unsatisfactorily pursued. [See Auspitz, Josiah Lee (1976) "Individuality, Civility, and Theory: The Philosophical Imagination of Michael Oakeshott," *Political Theory* 4 (August), pp. 261-352]. In the modern study of international relations, the state has constituted the key unit of collective action, while the interaction of states has been the very object of inquiry; similarly, in the domestic arena, the state has both encompassed the political system and constituted a potentially autonomous collective agent within that field. (These issues are examined at more length in Cerny, P.G. (1990), *The Changing Architecture of Politics: Structure, Agency, and the Future of the State* (London: Sage Publications), especially chap. 4).

3. Singh, Major Narendar (1982), Terrorism, Dissertation for MSc, Madras University, at Defence Services Staff College Wellington (Unpublished).
4. Glaser, Charles L. (1971), "The Security Dilemma Revisited," *World Politics,* Vol. 50, No. 1 (October 1997), pp. 171–201.
5. Singh, Col (Retd) Narendar (2007), *Conduct of War* (New Delhi: Manas Publications), pp. 7-8.
6. Howard, Michael, 'Military Power and International Order', *International Affairs,* Vol. 40, No. 3, 1964, p.407.
7. Wolfers, Arnold, "National Security as an Ambiguous Symbol', *Political Science Quarterly,* Vol. LXVII, No. 4, December 1952, p. 481.
8. Wolfers, Arnold (1952), '"National Security" as an Ambiguous Symbol', *Political Science Quarterly,* 67, p. 483.
9. Robert Osgood. Cited in E. Azar and Chung in Moon (eds.), *National Security in The Third World: The Management of Internal and External Threats* (University Press, Cambridge 1988), p. 279.
10. Ney, J.S., and S.M. Lynn-Jones, 'International Security Studies: A Report of the Conference on the State of the Field', *International Security,* 12 (4), 1988, pp. 5-27.
11. Ullman, Richard. H. (1983) 'Redefining Security', *International Security,* 8 (1), pp. 129-153. See also Keller, Kenneth H. (1997), 'Unpackaging the Environment', in *Environment Change and Security Project Report* (Washington D.C.: Woodrow Wilson Centre), Issue 3, spring 1997, pp. 11-12.
12. Wolfers, Arnold (1962), *Discord and Collaboration: Essays on International Politics,* (Baltimore: John Hopkins Press), p. 153.
13. *'North South: A Programme For Survival',* Report of the Brandt Commission (London: Pan, 1980).
14. There is no agreed definition of Common Security, but a comprehensive summation of its features can be found in Geoffrey Wiseman, 'Common Security in The Asia Pacific Region', *The Pacific Review,* Vol. 5, No. 1, 1989, pp. 42-3, which remains the best analysis of the concept.
15. **The Concept of Power**

    Power can be exercised by the under-mentioned methodologies.

    Techniques of Influence

    (a) Persuasion
    (b) Offer of Rewards
    (c) Granting of Rewards
    (d) Threat of Punishments
    (e) Force
    (f) Infliction of Non-violent punishments

    Patterns of Influence

    (a) Relations of Consensus-few disagreements
    (b) Relations of Overt Manipulation
    (c) Relations of Coercion
    (d) Relations of Force

    Dynamic and Contextual Aspects

    (a) Dynamic
    (b) **Contextual.** Power can be measured only in relation to the adversary and the situation in which it is being exercised.

Assessment of Power: Assessment of power is difficult. The basic problem is that all elements of power are inter-related. Where people live will affect what they possess; how many they are will affect how much they possess; what their historical experience has been will influence how they look at life; how they look at life will influence how they organise and govern themselves; and all these elements weighed against the problem of national security will influence the nature; size and effectiveness of the armed forces. As a consequence, not only must each separate element be weighed and analysed, but their effect on one and another is considered.

A related problem is the measurement, best illustrated in an attempt by Ray Clarke, to develop a rough of the **'perceived power'** that a country has at its disposal:

$$P = \{C+E+M\} \times \{S+W\}$$

where: P = Perceived Power; C = Critical Mass: Population and Territory; E = Economic Capability; M = Military Capability; S = Strategic Purpose; W = Will to pursue National Strategy.

The first three elements of power {C+E+M} may be described as tangible elements that can be objectively quantified. The last two elements are intangible and may be only subjectively quantified.

16. Garth, Evans (1993), *Cooperating For Peace: The Global Agenda for the 1990's and Beyond* (St Leonard's, NSW: Allen & Unwin), p. 15.
17. Waltz, Kenneth N. (1979), *Theory of International Politics* (Reading: Addison-Wesley), pp. 102-127; for an "English School perspective" see also Bull, Hedley (1995), *The Anarchical Society. A Study of Order in World Politics.* 2nd edn. (Houndsmills: Macmillan); and for a social constructivist one Wendt, Alexander (1992), "Anarchy is What States Make of It: The Social Construction of Power Politics", *International Organisation*, vol. 46, no. 2 (Spring), pp. 391-425.
18. Deutsch, K.W., D. Singer (1964), "Multipolar Power Systems and International Stability" *World Politics,* Vol. 16, No. 3. (April), pp. 390-406.

    Rosecrance, R. (1966), Bipolarity, Multipolarity, and the Future, *The Journal of Conflict Resolution, 10*(3), 314-327. Retrieved from http://www.jstor.org/stable/173003

    Chatterjee, P. (1972), The Classical Balance of Power Theory, *Journal of Peace Research,* March 9:51-61.

    Healy, Brian, and Arthur Stein (1973), "The Balance of Power in International History Theory and Reality" *Journal of Conflict Resolution* 17.1: 33-61.

    Wagner, R. Harrison (1986), "The theory of games and the balance of power," *World Politics* 38.04 : 546-576.
19. Waltz, Kenneth N. (1979), *Theory of International Politics* (Reading: Addison-Wesley), pp. 102-127, p. 117.
20. Haas, Earnest B. (1953), The *Balance of Power: Prescription, Concept, or Propaganda,* (Cambridge University Press) (Source World Politics, Vol. 5, No. 4 (Jul., 1953), pp. 442-477) also states that the concept of balance of power has various meanings, 'one of the more common is a mere factual description of the distribution of political power in the international scene at any one time.'
21. Deutsch, K.W., D. Singer (1964), "Multipolar Power Systems and International Stability" *World Politics,* Vol. 16, No. 3. (April), pp. 390-406, p. 390.
22. Evans, Graham and Newnham, Jeffrey (1988), *The Penguin Dictionary of International Relations,* London: Penguin Books), p. 43.
23. Walt, Stephen M.

___ (1987), *The origins of alliances* (Ithaca: Cornell University Press).

___ (2002), 'Keeping the world "off balance": Self-restraint in U.S. foreign policy' in *America unrivaled: The future of the balance of power,* (ed.) G.J. Ikenberry (Ithaca: Cornell University Press), pp. 121–54.

____ (2004), 'Can the United States be balanced? If so, how?' American Political Science Association Annual Convention, Chicago, September 2–4, 2004.

24. Kapur, Ashok (2011), *India and the South Asian Strategic Triangle,* (Abingdon, Oxon, OX14 4RN).
25. Ikenberry, G. John, (ed.) (2002), *America unrivaled: The future of the balance of power* (Ithaca: Cornell University Press).
    Paul, T.V. (2004), 'The enduring axioms of balance of power theory' in *Balance of power theory and practice in the twenty-first century* (eds.) T.V. Paul, James Wirtz, and Michel Fortmann, (Stanford: Stanford University Press).
26. Paul, T.V. (2004), 'The enduring axioms of balance of power theory' in *Balance of power theory and practice in the twenty-first century,* (eds.) T.V. Paul, James Wirtz, and Michel Fortmann, (Stanford: Stanford University Press), p.14.
27. Shapiro, I., (2007), *Containment: Rebuilding a Strategy against Global Terror,* (Princeton).
28. Ibid., p.573.
29. Ibid., p.581.
30. Ibid., p.576.
31. Ibid.
32. Lebow, Richard Ned and Stein, Janice Gross (1995), *We all Lost the Cold War* (Princeton: Princeton University Press), p. 159.
33. Ibid., p.160.
34. Ney, J.S., and S.M. Lynn-Jones (1988), 'International Security Studies: A Report of the Conference on the State of the Field', *International Security,* 12 (4), p. 6.
35. Jervis, Robert (1979), 'Deterrence theory revisited', *World Politics* 31.02: 289-290.
36. Singh, Col Dr Narendar (2007), *Conduct of War* (New Delhi: Manas Publications), p. 35.
37. Weitsman, P.A. (2004) *Dangerous Alliances: Proponents of Peace, Weapons of War* (Stanford University Press, Palo Alto), p. 35.
38. The first attempt this century at collective security was made in the League of Nations in 1919, and later the United Nations in 1945. The concept of "collective security" was still military, but international rather than national. It was a legal, even legalistic, concept, modelled on the criminal-justice system of domestic law. Nations would form a "society" (league) of law-abiding peace-loving citizens, and any one of them that broke the social contract would be punished by the collective force of all the others, and deprived of "the fruits of aggression." As in any such criminal-law system and any contractarian society, the definitions of "aggressor" and "victim" are formulated "behind the veil of ignorance," i.e. they are anonymous at the time of writing the contract. This is an advance on earlier conceptions, since the league's military force is not directed against a particular "enemy," but against any law-breaker, even one's close friend or ally. However, identifying the "aggressor" is particularly difficult. In domestic criminal law, a trial (with judge *and* jury in important cases) must determine guilt; but in interstate wars there would be no time for this. The "criminal" state would have to be punished before its guilt was established "beyond a reasonable doubt" i.e. the presumption of innocence (until proved guilty) could not exist. And yet, the attack, deemed aggressive on the surface, might be a response to unbeaiable provocation.
39. Nincic, D. (1970), *The Problem of Sovereignty in the Charter and in the Practice of the United Nations,* (Leiden: Nijhof), pp. 81-82.

40. Johnson, H.C. and Niemeyer, (1954), 'Collective Security: The Validity of an Ideal', *International Organisation,* 8, pp. 19, 20 and 35.
41. Morgan, P. (2007), 'Security in International Politics: Traditional Approaches', in Collins, A. (ed.) *Contemporary Security Studies,* (New York: Oxford University Press), p.17.
42. Adler, E., Nad Barnett, M. (1998), 'Security Communities in Theoretical Perspective', in Adler and Barnett (Eds.) *Security Communities* (Cambridge: Cambridge University Press), p.3.
43. Speech of President Chirac to the General Assembly, 23 September 2003.
44. Glennon, Michael J., (2003), "Why the Security Council Failed," *Foreign Affairs* 82, No. 3, p.23.
45. Perle, Richard, (2003), "United They Fall," *The Spectator* (22 March 2003), p. 22.
46. Ruggie, John Gerard (2003), "The United Nations and Globalization: Patterns and Limits of Institutional Adaptation." *Global Governance* 9.3: 301-321.
47. Ziring, Lawrence, and Riggs, Robert E., and Plano, Jack C., (2005), *The United Nations: International Organisation and World Politics*, 4th Edition (Belmont CA: Thomas Wadsworth), p. 173.
48. Herz, J. (1950), "Idealist Internationalism and the Security Dilemma", in *World Politics,* Vol. 2, No.2 (Cambridge University Press), pp. 171-201, at p.157.
    Jervis, Robert (1976), *Perception and Misperception in International Politics (*Princeton, NJ: Princeton University Press), pp. 58-93.
    Buzan, B. (1991), *People, States and Fear. An agenda for International Security Studies in the Post-Cold War Era,* Second Edition, (New York: Harvester Wheatsheaf), pp. 294-327.
49. Rathjens, G.W. (1974), "Flexible Response Options," *Orbits,* Fall 1974, pp. 683 & 687-8
    Hammond, Grant T. (1993), *Plowshares Into Swords: Arms Races in International Politics, 1840-1991* (Columbia, SC: University of South Carolina Press).
    Gleditsch, N.P. & Njølstad, O. (eds.), (1990), *Arms race: Technological and Political Dynamics,* (London: Sage Publications).
50. Schelling, Thomas (1960), *The Strategy of Conflict* (Cambridge, MA: Harvard University Press), pp. 207-248.
    Vázquez-Gómez, José de J. (1993), "Modelling multidomain security," *Proceedings on the 1992-1993 workshop on New security paradigms.* ACM, 1993.
    Levy, Marc A. (1995) "Is the Environment a National Security Issue?" *International Security* 20.2 : 35-62. Web.
51. Snyder, Glenn H. (1984), "The security dilemma in alliance politics." *World Politics* 36(4): 461-495.
52. Palme, Olof (1982), "Common Security: A Programme For Disarmament" Report of the Independent Commission on Disarmament and Security Issues under the Chairmanship of Olof Palme, (London: Pan Books), pp. 138. 9.
53. Buzan, Barry (1991), *People, States and Fear. An Agenda for International Security Studies in the Post-Cold War Era,* 2nd edn. (Boulder, CO: Lynne Rienner).
    Buzan, Barry (1996), "International Society and International Security", in Rick Fawn & Jeremy Larkins (eds.) *International Society after the Cold War. Anarchy and Order Reconsidered* (Houndsmills: Macmillan), pp. 261-287.
54. Rakove, Rob (2012), 'Taking Nonalignment Seriously', foreignpolicy.com/2012/08/27/taking-**nonalignment**-seriously/
56. Kay, Sean (2000), "What is a strategic partnership?", *Problems of Post-Communism,* n°47, pp. 15-24.

57. Nadkarni, Vidya (2010), *Strategic partnerships in Asia: Balancing without alliances* (Abingdon: Routledge).

57. Ikenberry, G. John (2001), *After victory: Institutions, strategic restraint and the rebuilding of order after major wars* (Princeton: Princeton University Press).

58. Berridge G.R. and James, Alan (2003), *A Dictionary of Diplomacy*, (Hampshire, UK: Palgrave Macmillan), p. 189.
Griffiths, Martin and O'Callaghan, Terry (2002), *International Relations: The Key Concepts*, (London: Routledge), p. 209.

59. Baylis, John and Smith, Steve (2001), *The Globalization of World Politics: An Introduction to International Relations*, (Oxford: Oxford University Press), pp.145-146.
Evans, Graham and Newnham, Jeffrey (1988), *The Penguin Dictionary of International Relations*, London: Penguin Books), p. 270.

60. Griffiths, Martin and O'Callaghan, Terry (2002), *International Relations: The Key Concepts*, (London: Routledge), pp. 215-216.
Baylis, John and Smith, Steve (2001), *The Globalization of World Politics: An Introduction to International Relations*, (Oxford: Oxford University Press), pp.362-363.

61. Evans, Graham and Newnham, Jeffrey (1988), *The Penguin Dictionary of International Relations*, London: Penguin Books), pp. 471-472.
Griffiths, Martin and O'Callaghan, Terry (2002), *International Relations: The Key Concepts*, (London: Routledge), pp. 272-273.

62. Griffiths, Martin and O'Callaghan, Terry (2002), *International Relations: The Key Concepts*, (London: Routledge), p. 272.
Baylis, John and Smith, Steve (2001), *The Globalization of World Politics: An Introduction to International Relations*, (Oxford: Oxford University Press), p.303.

63. Evans, Graham and Newnham, Jeffrey (1988), *The Penguin Dictionary of International Relations*, London: Penguin Books), pp. 541-542.

64. Institute for National Strategic Studies, *Strategic Assessment 1995: U.S. Security Challenges in Transition*, Washington, DC: National Defence University, 1995, online at http://www.ndu.edu/inss/Strategic%20Assessments/sa95/sach14co.html
Institute for National Strategic Studies, *Strategic Assessment 1999: Priorities for a Turbulent World*, Washington, DC: National Defence University, 1999, p. 245.
Paul J. Smith, "Transnational Security Threats and State Survival: A Role for the Military," *Parameters*, Autumn 2000, p. 79.

65. Institute for National Strategic Studies, *Strategic Assessment 1999*, pp. 246-247.

66. Evans, Graham and Newnham, Jeffrey (1988), *The Penguin Dictionary of International Relations*, London: Penguin Books), p. 15.
Griffiths, Martin and O'Callaghan, Terry (2002), *International Relations: The Key Concepts*, (London: Routledge), p. 1.

67. Wikipedia, *http://en.wikipedia.org/wiki/Balancing*, accessed December 6, 20013.

68. Wikipedia, *http://en.wikipedia.org/wiki/Bandwagoning*, accessed December 3, 2013.

69. Evans, Graham and Newnham, Jeffrey (1988), *The Penguin Dictionary of International Relations*, London: Penguin Books), p. 42.

70. Singh, Col Dr Narendar (2007), *Conduct of War* (New Delhi: Manas Publications), p.35.
Griffiths, Martin and O'Callaghan, Terry (2002), *International Relations: The Key Concepts*, (London: Routledge), p. 12.

71. Singh, Col Dr Narendar (2007), *Conduct of War* (New Delhi: Manas Publications), p.35.
Griffiths, Martin and O'Callaghan, Terry (2002), *International Relations: The Key Concepts*, (London: Routledge), p. 13.

72. Booth, Ken (2007), *Theory of World Security* (Cambridge: Cambridge University Press), Ch. 9.
73. Condoleezza Rice, 'A balance of power that favors freedom', 1 October 2002, [http://www.manhattaninstitute.org/html/w12002.htm], accessed 17 Jun 2012.
    See also Graham Allison (2004), *Nuclear Terrorism: The Ultimate Preventable Catastrophe* (New York: Times Books).
74. Anonymous (2004), *Imperial Hubris: Why the West is Losing the War on Terror* (Washington, DC: Brassey's); Burke, Jason (2003), *Al-Qaeda: Casting a Shadow of Terror* (London: I.B. Tauris).

3

SECURITY ENVIRONMENT

To determine the Security Environment of the 21st Century in which India has to operate one must understand the international system. As stated earlier in Chapters 1 and 2, nation states, first codified by the Treaty of Westphalia in 1648, remains the dominant political body in international politics. The international system refers to the structure of relationships that exist between the nation states at international level. For strategic leaders of the 21st Century primarily concerned with the issues of national security policy, the international system with which they will be dealing is likely to reflect only partially the traditional international system as seen few years back. The change is primarily due to combination of relationship of nation states at international level with the transnational threats posed by some of the failed or failing states, ungoverned regions, terror, the proliferation of weapons of mass destruction (WMDs), crime, drugs, pandemics, and environmental degradation, as well as by elements of the system that also have potentially positive impacts such as globalisation and the information revolution.

The changes in modern international system frame; the forces and trends in the global environment; creates the workspace for strategy makers of national security policy. Strategy makers work through the formulation process, with an understanding for the interests and objectives of all actors in a given situation. While formulating the strategy, national security strategy makers must be able to account for the associated state and non-state actors present in the international system. In addition, it has become particularly important that they be able to assess the competing values associated with the

> When it is not in the throes of war, trade reshapes the international order.

global actors, both state and non-state, especially in relation with fight on Terror. Given the criticality of being supported by other nation states and international or multinational organisations, the strategist or policymaker must know which alliances and coalitions are stakeholders in the issue in question.

International systems and organisations ability to influence events and people has been challenged by an assortment of non-state actors throughout the history. Thus national security planners have to include the roles and interaction of both state and non-state actors, along with international organisations, multinational corporations (MNC), and nongovernment organisations (NGO) etc.[1] States have to make foreign and national security policy against this external environment. Opportunities for both conflict and cooperation arise within this framework. The international community has tried for years to maintain order and prevent conflict using international institutions like the United Nations (UN) and international legal regimes like the Geneva Conventions.[2]

Another related element of the international system is the economic condition, as influenced by both the positive and negative components of globalisation that helps determine the amount of power actors can wield in the system. It is also important to be able to identify the international legal tenets and regimes that bear on the situation. The 21st Century policy and strategy maker must be able to understand the threats to order in the international system represented by both conventional and transnational entities. If the policymaker or strategist can accurately assess all these factors, he might be able to determine friends and enemies, threats and opportunities, and capabilities and constraints inherent in the contemporary world.

Threats, challenges, and opportunities can come in many shapes and sizes. A traditional threat might take the shape of a nation-state in possession of WMD and a hostile attitude. This is also true for a non-state actor, potentially going down to the individual level, if he is willing to fly an airplane into a building or launch an attack on unsuspected people in Taj Hotel, Mumbai.

Non-traditional and asymmetrical challenges can be very real and very much a part of our broader security environment. Many of those challenges are, needless to say, still with us. The increasing pace of globalisation and its consequences, in terms ranging from terrorism and proliferation of weapons of mass destruction to cyber-threats and organised crime are still highly relevant. The world is becoming interconnected, for good and bad. *When it is not in the throes of war, trade reshapes the international order.*

Less direct but also significant in the 21st Century world are the threats that can be made to the successful execution of a nation-state's policies, if other nation-states are unwilling to provide support in a given situation. This lack of support can manifest itself in an opposing vote in an international organisation like the United Nations (UN), a multinational organisation like the Association of South East Asian Nations (ASEAN), or an international regime such as the International Atomic Energy Agency (IAEA). It can equally be demonstrated by the refusal of a state to grant transit or over flight rights to the forces of another state.

This is not the whole story, however, geopolitics[3] is back. The fundamental structure of the international system is again in flux. The short, unipolar moment is already over, and the global center of gravity is moving eastwards. The combined thrust of the relative decline of the West and the return of geopolitics is actually a strong argument for India to strengthen partnership based on common values, norms and principles.

> "Geopolitics is, definitionally, the art and process of managing global rivalry."
>
> Jay P. (1979), "Regionalism as geopolitics," *Foreign Affairs 58*, p. 486.

India tends to agree on the importance of state sovereignty and the need to reform global governance institutions to reflect the new balance of power. India also shares a strong commitment to the open economic order that has allowed nations to flourish in the global marketplace. But India diverges on many details of the international system, such as the future viability of the Non-Proliferation Treaty and the role of state owned enterprises in fostering globalisation, food security, human rights etc.

China is emerging as an increasingly important global player, and the steady rise of regional powers like India and Brazil is also an important part of this picture. The relative economic and political power and influence of "the West" is declining in favour of emerging powers, particularly in Asia. The current global financial crisis is likely to further strengthen, not weaken, this trend.

> "India has never considered military might as the ultimate measure of national strength. It is a necessary component of overall national strength. I would, therefore, say that the greatest meaning of the tests is that they have given India *shakti* they have given India strength, they have given India self-confidence."[1]
>
> Vajpayee, interviewed in *India Today*, 25 May 1998, www.india-today.com /itoday/25051998/vajint.html.

We begin this overview with some tenets about global trends in the next two to three decades. The propositions are as follows:

(a) Revival of geopolitics,[4] due to the changing political and economic environment.
(b) The geostrategy around Eurasia due to energy needs, the revival of the nationalist agenda in Central Asia Republic and the areas around Caspian Sea.
(c) The Unipolar World, or world dominated by US and its policies. The rise of any other global contender or competitor is uncertain in the near future.

(d) Great Power relationships would be in a flux.
(e) Asymmetric threats, terrorism and unconventional threats leaving India more exposed to attacks.
(f) Spread of technology including military, and weapons of mass destruction (NBC).
(g) The international institutions, role would grow. With growing Indian economy India would have to play a role in International Organisations.
(h) The political fissures would continue to grow in India, bringing strain on the Union and State relationship.
(i) Rise of internal insurgencies or actions by anti-national elements supported by external agencies are going to exist within the country.
(j) Globalisation and migration.

Broadly the above challenges could be grouped as; the first challenge is based on geopolitics and international relations; will India be able to maintain a substantially autonomous foreign policy in the new world order? The second is the Western-style economic globalisation and whether India can, within this context, maintain its unique millennium culture or be subjected to the cultural levelling which is already evident internationally. The third problem pertains to India's internal economic, political and social obstacles that it faces on the chosen path of development and whether or not it will be able to achieve superpower status and provide security and uphold ideals as enshrined in the Indian Constitution.

WHY DO STATES WANT POWER?[1]

There is a simple structural realist explanation for why states compete among themselves for power. It is based on five assumptions about the international system.

1. The great powers are the main actors in world politics and they operate in an anarchic system.
2. All states possess some offensive capability, and can inflict some harm to its adversaries. This capability varies among states and for any state it can change over time.
3. State can never be certain of the intention of the other state. Unlike capabilities, intentions cannot be empirically verified. Intentions are in the minds of decision-makers and they are especially difficult to discern.
4. Main goal of all states is to survive. States seek to maintain their territorial integrity and the autonomy of their domestic political order. All other aims take back seat to survival, because if state does not survive, it cannot pursue other goals.
5. States are rational actors, which is to say they are capable of coming up with sound strategies' that maximize their prospects for survival.

[1]Mearsheimer, John J. (2001), *The Tragedy of Great Power Politics* (New York: W.W. Norton), pp. 79-80.

The Revival of Geopolitics

The roots of revival in geopolitics and writing on it lie in the changing international political and economic environment. The collapse of a bipolar world brought the end to all the associated policy of containment. The rise of Third World nationalism, growth of revolutionary movements and rise of Islamic fundamentalism, all these and many others pointed to growing multipolarity and complexity international politics during the end of 20th century and beginning of 21st Century. This is paralleled by a growth in China's economic and military power, and is also reflected in declining relative US power in world economy. The revival of geopolitics lies in the response by the policy makers to these changing international circumstances and to the increasingly apparent cracks in existing United States and its ally's strategy.

> Actor George Clooney recalls in an interview in the December 2012 issue of *Esquire* magazine: "I talked with the President (Obama) at one of those fundraisers some months back, and I asked him, 'What keeps you up at night?
>
> And he said, 'Everything. Everything that gets to my desk is a critical mass. If it gets to my desk, then no one else could have handled it.' So I said, 'So what's the one that keeps you up at night?' He goes, 'There are quite a few.' So I go, 'What's the one? Period.'
>
> And he says, 'Pakistan. 'Do Indian leaders lose any sleep because of Pakistan? There is nothing in the public domain to suggest that they do. However, one thing is certain, and it is this that Indian leaders lose no opportunity in convincing the world at large that they have no ill-will towards Pakistan, and that a prosperous and stable Pakistan is in India's interest. They also go on to say that they would do all they can to help promote stability in Pakistan."

Post-Cold War geopolitics has been characterised by uni-polar military power (particularly under the aegis of United States) and global economic tri-polarity (North America, the European Union and East Asia). There has been competition over access to natural resources and foreign policy has been moulded to discover new strategies to secure energy supplies. The Central Asian Republics (CAR) and the Caspian region are home to vast oil and gas reserves. This has turned the region into an intersection of interstate rivalry, enterprise competition, and intervention by major powers and non-state actors.[5] *What has complicated the competition is the emergence of Afghanistan and Pakistan as the hub of international terrorism and religious extremism under the Taliban.*

The return of geopolitics does not imply that we by implication will see more inter-state conflicts. While the world is becoming multipolar, international institutions are stronger than ever before and many shared norms and regimes already exists that may help to soften this global systemic change. The return of geopolitics does suggest, however, that we cannot simply go on assuming that all future conflicts that we might get involved in, will continue to be asymmetric or against non-state actors, or for that sake, against odd and isolated "states". We do have to take a critical look both at the key assumption of the 1990s: that all contemporary conflicts were transitional.

Indian geopolitical reasoning remains rooted in fears that the borders of the state must be protected against all perceived 'threats', regardless of any human costs. India lies at the periphery of Eurasia. Eurasia is the home of the world's politically assertive and dynamic states. All the historical pretenders of global power originated in Eurasia. After United States, the next six largest economies and military spenders are here, as are all but one of the world's overt and all but one covert nuclear power. Eurasia accounts for seventy per cent of the world's population, 60 per cent of its GNP, and 75 per cent of its energy resources. Collectively, Eurasia's virtual/potential overshadows even America. All of the potential political and/or economic challengers to American primacy are Eurasian. Cumulatively, Eurasia's power vastly overshadows America's. Fortunately for America, *Eurasia is too big to be politically one.*

However, the major uncertainty looms in the large and geopolitically fluid space of Central Eurasia, maximised by the potential vulnerability of the Turkish-Iranian pivots. In the area from Crimea in the Black Sea directly eastward along the new southern frontiers of Russia, all the way to the Chinese province of Xinjiang, then down to the Indian Ocean and then westward to the Red Sea, then northward to the eastern Mediterranean Sea and back to Crimea, live about 400 million people, located in some 25 states, almost all of them ethnically as well as religiously heterogeneous and practically none of them politically stable.

This huge region, torn by volatile hatreds and surrounded by competing powerful neighbors, is likely to be a major battlefield both for wars among nation-states and, more likely, for protracted ethnic and religious violence. Whether India acts as a restraint or whether it takes advantage of some opportunity to impose its will on Pakistan and in region around Afghanistan will greatly affect the regional scope of the likely conflicts. The internal strains within Turkey and Iran are likely not only to get worse but to greatly reduce the stabilizing role these states are capable of playing within this volcanic region.

Tensions over nuclear testing in May 1998 highlight the persistence of these geopolitical imaginations in the Indian subcontinent, and point to the challenges of formulating more inclusive political communities. The perspective is, however, based on the need to derive a balance of power in an increasingly multi-polar world.

The Unipolar World

The author is convinced that United States will remain engaged as a major player on the global scene through the next three decades of the 21st Century. Indeed, despite the occasional eruption of isolationist sentiments, the author believes that the United States simply has little choice in the matter. The sheer magnitude of the US economy; the country's dense and increasing web of commercial, cultural, political, and security ties to other nations and actors; and its sheer pervasiveness and prominence make the United States the globe's "500-pound gorilla" whether we like it or not.

We would do well not to underestimate the degree to which the United States remains culturally dominant even when its economic and political preeminence is seen by some to be fading. Wander the streets of Delhi, Bangalore, Calcutta, Manipur or remote villages of Uttrakhand, or in Kashmir, or world cities like Paris, Tel Aviv, or Tokyo and note the number of blue jeans clad girls and boys, Michael Jordan, or some university logo jerseys being worn by teenagers, the number of US films being shown in cinemas, and the explosion of Pizza Huts and McDonald's or Mickey Mouse. China has overtaken India by sheer number of students studying in United States. These linkages are not trivial; in some ways they may be deeper and more lasting than political ties. Recall that Levis blue jeans were a status symbol in the pre-perestroika (USSR). And this enmeshing—which seems likely to endure so long as kids worship sports stars and Hollywood remains synonymous with "entertainment"—makes the United States a threat and a target for regimes and creeds that wish to resist our influence, either out of insular motives or a desire to supplant our message with their own.

Should the United States withdraw from the world stage, the implications would be staggering. Just withdrawal from Iraq has brought near crisis in the areas around, the staggering effect of withdrawal from Afghanistan have yet to be felt. It has already made China lose sleep. Globally, the competition to fill the vacuum left behind by the retreat of American power could lead to widespread instability and conflict, endangering former friends and emboldening former adversaries. Within the United States, the military establishment would undoubtedly shrink dramatically as budgets declined.[6]

Great Power Relationships would be in a Flux

Although United States is the lone, comprehensive superpower, it is being challenged by radical ideologies—particularly the jihadist vision of ridding the Muslim world of Western influence, corrupt regimes, and restoring the caliphate—dissenting views of global order—such as the notion of "sovereign democracy" embraced by Russia, China, and other nations who see vigorous US promotion of democracy and human rights as representing unwarranted interference in the internal affairs of sovereign states. With these conditions, volatility will likely be the dominant feature for the foreseeable future.

Interestingly, much of the qualitative re-arrangement of power now underway is not attributed to military capabilities or 'hard power', but to a factor unique to the modern world: rapid economic growth and the related quest for growing energy security. The power shifts towards Asia can be linked to its phenomenal economic rise. The rise of China, as also India, in the global economic arena is the most visible manifestation of the forces of globalisation, which are also resulting in a number of related socioeconomic and security challenges within the region. On the other side, it is also a fact that the fountainhead of global and regional terrorism also lies in this region.

In part because of the changing centers of political and economic gravity, relations among the great powers—membership in the somewhat self-defined coterie of "great powers"—will be quite dynamic through the next two decades. Simply put, great uncertainty prevails.

The single largest variable might be China. How will China carry her rapidly growing weight on the global scene? Will economic security make Beijing a status quo power or whet her appetite for power and influence? The recent renaissance of China and India is owed in large measure to their productive integration into the liberal economic order built and sustained by American hegemony in the postwar period. As a result of that integration, both of these giants have experienced dramatic levels of economic growth in recent decades. China's economic performance, for example, has been simply meteoric, exceeding even the impressive record set by the first generation of Asian tigers between 1960 and 1990. During the last thirty years, China has demonstrated average real growth in excess of 9 per cent annually, with growth rates touching 13–14 per cent in peak years.

A second key actor is Russia. Russia's location, its vastness, and its potential economic and military prowess mean that Moscow's eventual destiny is tightly intertwined with the fates of her neighbours in Europe, Asia, and the Middle East. Whether Russia emerges from her present painful transition as a stable, democratic, and economically strong power—a "Russian miracle" analogous to those seen in postwar West Germany and Japan—or as a new "sick man of Eurasia", the impact will be felt globally.

Asymmetric Challenges/International Terrorism/Unconventional Threats

Asymmetric Warfare concept is popular and much discussed issue. It has drawn attention during Army Commanders Conferences. Understandably, during Air

Force Commanders Conference the phenomenon was the central theme.

> **ASYMMETRIC WARFARE**
>
> We define *asymmetric warfare* as leveraging inferior tactical or operational strength against the vulnerabilities of a superior opponent to achieve disproportionate effect with the aim of undermining the opponent's will in order to achieve the asymmetric actor's strategic objective.[1]
>
> In broad terms it simply means warfare that seeks to avoid an opponent's strengths; it is an approach that tries to focus whatever may be one side's comparative advantage against it enemy's relative weakness.
>
> [1]McKenzie, Jr., Kenneth F., p.76.

However, the concept of asymmetric warfare is not as new as it is sometimes made out to be. Perhaps it is the first time that asymmetric warfare has captured the attention of the American public, the media, and the administration. It is now understood that security sector reforms are needed to tackle asymmetric warfare.

Put simply, "asymmetric threats or techniques are a version of not 'fighting fair,' which can include the use of surprise in all its operational and strategic dimensions and the use of weapons in ways unplanned by regular military forces. Not fighting fair also includes the prospect of an opponent designing a strategy that fundamentally alters the terrain on which a conflict is fought."[7] Therefore, based on one's perception, asymmetric warfare includes terrorism, threat of use of weapons of mass destruction, unconventional and innovative warfare approaches as cyber-attacks and information warfare.

Kautilya in his work, the Arthashastra, states that "a single assassin can achieve, with weapons, fire or poison, more than a fully mobilised army."[8] While Kautilya's tactics of subversion is certainly different from modern day asymmetric warfare, the idea and philosophy of asymmetry behind the use of assassins and guerrillas in past and the present is the same. In both cases, the 'have-nots, be it states or non-state actors can have profound effects by employing asymmetric tactics irrespective of their strengths and weaknesses.

Asymmetric threats target unappreciated vulnerabilities, and they tend to result in surprise. Attacking at unexpected times or in unexpected ways heightens the surprise; so does hiding the preparations or misleading the victim about one's objectives, strategy, capabilities, and deployments. Adversaries that avoid having attacks attributed to them may achieve many objectives *and* avoid retaliation. According to CIA Director George Tenet, "More than ever we risk substantial surprise. This is not for a lack of effort on the part of the Intelligence Community; it results from significant effort on the part of proliferators."[9]

Asymmetric challenges are key India vulnerabilities, Low Intensity Conflicts, Low Intensity maritime Operations, Terrorism including at Sea, Piracy, Maoists

Movements etc., could significantly hamper the military's—and the country's—ability to carry out key missions.

International Terrorism. The rise of international terrorism indeed shows that the information age is both an integrating and a dividing force. Terrorism remains the principal challenge to liberal and democratic societies and now occupies centrestage in the international security matrix. The scourge of terrorism will continue to invite the focus of global attention in the foreseeable future, which will require earnest international cooperation to deal with it effectively.

Other Drivers shaping the Global Security Environment

Let us take a look at other major trends emerging in the global and regional security environment:

(a) ***Proliferation of WMDs***: The efforts of various renegade state and non-state actors to gain access to WMDs have highlighted the dangers of proliferation of WMD material and their delivery means, especially if it reaches the hands of terrorists. India remains as concerned on this count as the other global powers.

(b) ***Energy Security***: India is an energy-deficient country. Ensuring the reliable flow of energy resources from producers to consumers has long been a cornerstone of India's national security strategy, particularly in the Middle East, but changes in energy production and distribution patterns have already called into question many of the traditional ways in which the India has understood the energy security problem. Future changes, both foreseen and unforeseeable, promise to transform the challenge of ensuring energy security even more dramatically. The quest for control of energy resources of West Asia and search for alternate routes for trans-shipment of oil and gas from the Caspian Region has brought the West and Central Asian Regions under sharp focus, thereby enhancing the chances of competition and potential conflict. It is no coincidence that most of the ongoing conflicts are centred in and on the regions that are rich in energy resources.

(c) ***Undermining of the UN:*** In the recent past, we have also witnessed increased undermining of the UN in providing the lead role for resolution of conflicts and stabilisation. There is an urgent need to re-structure the UN for it to remain relevant to the emerging realities. The reality is that the five unelected yet permanent members of the Security Council need to share executive authority with new and emerging powers; India being amongst the most prominent.

(d) ***Radicalisation in the Islamic World***: Wars in Iraq and Afghanistan combined with lack of progress in resolving the Palestinian problem are causing an increasing cross-current of disaffection resulting in radicalisation within the Islamic world and isolation of moderate forces. Relatively, a large yet benign Muslim population has added to India's strengths.

(e) ***Changing Nature of Conflicts***: The wars in Iraq and Afghanistan appear to be at critical crossroads and their outcomes will have a major bearing on future security contours of our region, in particular and the world, in general. These wars, and the one in Lebanon in July-August 2006, have thrown up new political and sectarian equations and emphasised once again that the era of "all out wars" is slowly being replaced by "war by other means"—unconventional, asymmetrical and across a wide range in the spectrum of conflict.

> Dr Rod Thornton, a lecturer at King's College's War Studies Department, states that "asymmetric warfare is violent action undertaken by the 'have-nots' against the 'haves' whereby the have-nots, be it state or sub-state actors, seek to generate profound effects – at all levels of warfare (however defined), from the tactical to the strategic – by employing their own specific relative advantages against the vulnerabilities of a much stronger opponents."[1]
>
> [1] Thornton, Rod (2007), *Asymmetric Warfare* (Polity Press), p. 1.

Multilateralism vs. Unilateralism vs. Non-Aligned

At the beginning of the 21st century, India enjoys an unprecedented accumulation of national power. The Indian economy is the fourth largest in the world and, even in a slowdown, far outstrips that of many nations, especially on the periphery. During Mr PV Narsimha Rao tenure as Prime Minister and post his tenure one of the central debates in India has been the degree to which India should be involved in the affairs of the world. Mr PV Narsimha Rao was the first Prime Minister to articulate the National Security Policy in Parliament. Transnational threats seemed to settle the question of non-alignment or engagement in favour of the latter. After the Kargil Operations, the issue of non-alignment rose again, but only briefly. The real post-Kargil Operations War debate was, and remains, over the degree to which the India should pursue its foreign policy alone or in partnership with other states. The debate can be analysed in terms of multilateralism versus unilateralism and is heavily influenced by competing views on what should India do with its position of preeminent regional power and a nation with international influence. In one sense, "the differences [between the two views] are a matter of degree, and there are few pure unilateralists or multilateralists." Joseph Nye Jr in his work *The Paradox of American Power: Why the World's Only Superpower Can't Go it Alone*,[10] clearly states that multilateralism is the order of the day and United States the sole Super Power has to work with others. However, there are clear differences between the two schools of thought on when and to what extent the India should work with others. We should keep in mind that unilateralism and multilateralism are not strategies. **Strategy is about matching ends, means and ways.** Unilateralism and multilateralism are competing ways to approach problems. The goal is to identify those conditions under which it is better to work with others through coalitions and alliances and when it is might be best go it alone.

The rhetoric in the dispute between followers of Nehru and his non-alignment, multilateralist and unilateralist approaches obscures that there are few foreign policy decisions that are purely one or the other. Advocates for above positions agree that it is better to have allies in support of a cause than to go it alone. National political parties and people disagree over that India should be willing to give up recruiting partners. Unilateralists favour staking out one's position and moving forward with whomever is willing to go along. Multilateralists favour rallying other nations to our cause and are more willing to accept trade-offs in building coalitions like the effort at World Trade Organisation on food subsidies. Unilateralists and multilateralists agree that there is little room for compromise on such fundamental issues as survival interests. Time constraints also may limit the ability of the India to drum up support for a cause dear to its survival and may have to take a unilateral decision. Threats that are immediate and pose a serious threat to survival or vital interests may force India's hand.

Finally, nation agrees irrespective of political affiliations that the India should seek to build an international order that will favour India preserve its values and independence. India by its size and influence has a unique opportunity to work for establishment of international rules and standards that protect Indian and a peaceful world interests. National political parties may differ on what role India should play to build that order. Some tend to favour more assertive, even coercive approaches. They fall more into the realist school of international relations theory and argue that ultimately power is what matters, and reliance on agreements or treaties in lieu of real power is dangerous. On the other hand, some favour moving ahead in a framework of international institutions and treaties that will bind all states, India included, to rules and commitments.

The perceptions and reality of the extent to which the India pursues unilateralist policies undoubtedly will affect India's strategic choices in the future. There are clear trade-offs between sacrificing freedom of action and lowering costs and adding the capabilities of other nations. Considering these trade-offs should be part of the strategic decisionmaking process for the India as it wages a war on terrorism and confronts a range of critical global interests and issues, and safeguards its national values. India cannot limit its options by clinging to notions about whether it should act unilaterally or multilaterally, or be non-aligned. There are times and circumstances for all three approaches. The art is to recognise them and select the proper tool.

Globalisation

Globalisation, defined as a dynamic process of rapidly growing, if uneven, cross-border flows of goods, services, money, people, technology, ideas, cultures, values, crime, and weapons throughout the world, will continue to be a dominant influence on the evolving security order by deepening interdependence and empowering certain actors while alienating and marginalising others. The spiralling inflationary trends, soaring oil prices, fear of food shortages and upheavals in the financial markets driven by global cues, reinforce the fact that no nation today can remain insulated from events related to economic and security trends—in any corner of the globe. The intertwining of economies, as a consequence of globalisation, has resulted in geo-economics supplanting geo-politics. It would be debatable, however, to believe that greater economic interdependence alone would lead to improved geo-political stability. While the benefits of increased global connectivity and technological advances are enormous, its negativities in terms of increasing social and economic disparities, which can be exploited by inimical elements, need to be taken note of. There is also a fear that the ill-effects of globalisation could reinforce tendencies towards competitive 'Protectionism' and regionalism. Globalisation is not bringing geopolitics or ideological struggles to an end. Rather, globalisation's influences interact with traditional regional and ethnic rivalries and are exacerbating many transnational threats. While most futurists describe the inevitability of a globalised society, some point out that catastrophic events or a major global recession could intervene to slow or reverse its course.

Spread of Technology

Technologically, the watchword for the coming years is "diffusion." As commercial needs and standards increasingly dominate, dual-use technology—with both civilian and military applications—will proliferate widely, with important security implications. This will be true on the large scale—where pharmaceutical knowhow can be equally applicable to chemical weapons or aspirin, to biological warfare toxins or antibiotics—and the small—where the realtor's cellular modem becomes the terrorist's remote detonator. The next 20 years will also witness a revolution in the nature and extent of access to space-based capabilities. High-resolution multispectral imagery from space, once the province of superpowers alone, is widely available at low cost.[11] The pictures thus acquired speeds around the globe on a world-girdling information network. The Global Positioning System (GPS)—or a successor family of satellite navigation aids—and satellite communications are just two high technology common-user utilities available to one and all. Military-specific technology will also spread quickly and widely. As the global arms market becomes ever more competitive, profit making pressures will likely allow advanced weapons and weapon technologies to get into more and more hands. Highly lethal "fire-and-forget" beyond visual-range air-to-air missiles could turn even a poorly trained enemy into a deadly opponent for India. To visualise the implications, imagine Anti National Elements "technicals" with SA-18s and laser guided mortar shells in addition to AK-47s, or Naxalites with stealthy ground-launched cruise missiles having GPS guidance and chemical warheads.

India's Internal Situation

India has never been a united country but a federal state of many small kingdoms and states. The internal security situation of the country has become very fragile. Terrorism, trans-national and domestic, poses a very formidable threat. The terrorists are opposed to the very idea of India and they want to destroy the country politically, economically and culturally. Government of India must come out with a clear policy on how the terrorist threat is to be dealt with. The policy will have to have components dealing with terrorists across the border, terrorists within the country, organisations harbouring and sheltering or supporting them.

Maoist problem is another major threat on the internal security front. Here also, the government must come up with a long-term strategic plan to deal with the insurgency. It will have to be a whole of government approach.

These sources of insecurity sometimes flow across its international borders, in both directions. And yet, India presents to the world, altogether credibly, the face of a rising economic and geostrategic power. It is today, well into India's seventh decade, hard to question its overall national cohesion as an international actor.

Indeed, its pluralism, diversity, democratic practices (however chaotic at times), and multicultural make-up are all seen internationally globally as elements of strength rather than weakness, as proof of resilience rather than fragility. But viewed through a regional lens, the permeability of India's borders with several of its immediate neighbours combined with India's constitutionally guaranteed freedoms and the free flow of potential security threats of various sorts across these boundaries continues to preoccupy Indian policy-makers. Regional insecurities are exacerbated to a great extent by the persistence of domestic challenges to India's national security and foreign policy.

India today represents a fascinating coalescence of caste, ethnic, religious and regional groupings, often cutting across each other, that has produced arguably the world's oldest and, during many centuries, and most successful, pluralistic society. The vibrancy of its democratic experiment combined with its heterogeneous society and rapidly growing economy has caught the attention of observers around the world.

ENDNOTES

1. Berridge G. R. and James, Alan (2003), *A Dictionary of Diplomacy*, (Hampshire, UK: Palgrave Macmillan), p. 148.
2. Evans, Graham and Newnham, Jeffrey (1988), *The Penguin Dictionary of International Relations*, London: Penguin Books), p. 277.
3. "Geopolitics—human, realistic science whose goal is to determine, beyond appearances, which are the objective features of human and physical geography that condition the strategic decisions of the players of world ideological, political and economical life" in Silviu Negu Ñ, "Introducere în Geopolitica" *The Romanian Economic Journal Tempus* 15, no. 1 (2005). p.3.
4. Geopolitics teaches us how to identify and assess the compulsions and constraints on nations and their principal actors—the driving forces and limiters that shape the behaviour and direction of nations and their interactions. The balance between "compulsions" (what must be done) and "constraints" (what cannot be done)—a tension that induces or restricts certain behaviours, actions and directions — changes with differing "circumstances," or the current state of being domestically, regionally or internationally at a given moment in time. Thus, some compulsions may exist for years or decades, but only in a very special set of circumstances do they really induce action.

   By identifying these constraints and compulsions, the limitations on options become more apparent, allowing predictions of patterns and actions. If history explains the past with an eye on the present, geopolitics explains the present with an eye on the future. The purpose is not only understanding the pressures on nations, but also predicting future responses — and thus providing time to prepare for, dissuade or counter the actions of others.

   At a certain level, geopolitics eliminates the impact of the individual human element: Each individual is diluted in the totality, subsumed in some sense by the forces at work, namely, the broader constraints and compulsions that compel and limit options and decisions. Individuals by their very nature are highly variable, being affected by numerous unseen elements at any given moment. Consider, for example, John Lewis Gaddis' musing in *The Landscape of History* on the potential that an unrecorded flea may have given Napoleon itchy underwear, and leading to his loss at Waterloo. While individuals are relatively unpredictable on a short timeframe, their collective behaviour, their decisions as they shape the directions of nations, are less variable and more compelled or constrained. Thus, in rising above the individual, geopolitics presents a framework for forecasting and a method that can be taught and tested. The relationship between the constraints and the compulsions is in a constant state of flux and influenced by circumstances. Assessing these three factors presents a picture of fairly limited options and, in reducing possibilities, leaves a very small number of likely directions for future action. This allows geopolitics to serve as the starting point for forecasting. Frequently, however, a directional pattern that appears obvious from a geopolitical assessment and forecast will not come to pass within the expected timeframe, or a dynamic that may appear highly constrained will suddenly break forth far ahead of the forecast.
5. Goo, Xuedong and Mehdi P. Amine (2007), The "Great Game Continued: Central Eurasia and Caspian Region Fossil Fuels", *International Institute for Asian Studies (IIAS)* Newsletter, No. 45, Autumn.

6. Khalilzad, Zalmay, (1995) "Losing the Moment? The United States and the World After the Cold War," *The Washington Quarterly*, Spring 1995, pp. 87–107.
7. This is the classic definition of "asymmetry" by the US National Defense University's Institute for National Strategic Studies in their 1998 Strategic Assessment available at http://www.ndu.edu/inss/ sa98/sa98ch11.html.
8. Kautilya. *Kautilya: The Arthashastra* (ed.) Rangarajan, (1992) (L.N. Penguin Books), p. 498
9. "Text: DIA Director Tenet Outlines Threats to National Security," US Department of State, International Information Programs Internet Site, Washington File, 21 March 2000. Tenet then cited four reasons why: "First and most important, proliferators are showing greater proficiency in the use of denial and deception. Second, the growing availability of dual-use technologies is making it easier for proliferators to obtain the materials they need. Third, the potential for surprise is exacerbated by the growing capacity of countries seeking WMD to import talent that can help them make dramatic leaps on things like new chemical and biological agents and delivery systems.... Finally, the accelerating pace of technological progress makes information and technology easier to obtain and in more advanced forms than when the weapons were initially developed."
10. Nye, Jr., Joseph S. (2002), *The Paradox of American Power: Why the World's Only Superpower Can't Go it Alone*, (New York: Oxford University Press), p. 40.
11. See, for example, "Public Eye," *Scientific American*, August 1996, p. 18; and Charles Lane (1996), "The Satellite Revolution," *The New Republic*, Vol. 215, No. 7, August 12, p. 22.

4

CENTRALITY OF INDIA: GEOGRAPHICAL LOCATION AND GEOPOLITICAL–GEO-STRATEGIC IMPORTANCE

Studies in international conflict frequently disagree on the causes of war. However, one factor consistently found to enhance a war's likelihood is the *geographic* proximity of the adversaries.[1] The Review of literature on conflict brings out one thing very clearly that there is a direct relationship between territory and conflict. Territory reflects the spatial location of the states, including their proximity. Diehls[2] breaks empirical geography and war into two groups:

(a) *"Geography as a facilitating condition"* for conflict, and
(b) *"Geography as a source"* of conflict.

> "Who rules East Europe commands the Heartland; who rules the Heartland commands the World Island; who rules the World Island commands the World."
>
> Mackinder, H.J. (1904), "The geographical pivot of history." *The Geographical Journal*, 1904, 23, pp. 421–37.

It has been observed that proximity of states as measured by borders and contiguity, creates the possibility for conflict through increased interaction (both positive and negative), leading to more conflict, rather than cooperative behavioural though interaction need not necessarily lead to conflict. The geographers Zipfs 'Law of least effort'[3] applies to interaction in general leading to increased conflictual interaction. Borders also have an impact on the willingness of decision makers to choose certain policy options, in that they act as indicators of areas of great importance or salience. Because other states are close, having greater ease of interaction and the ability to bring military capabilities to bear, they are also key areas of external cues (or diffusion). Accordingly, activities in these areas are particularly worrisome, can create uncertainty, and thus deserve attention.

Indian history and geography since pre historic times constitutes the genetic code for how the world looks from the vantage point of New Delhi. India is located at the southern extremity of the Eurasian continent. Continental access is mainly from the West through passes such as the Khyber and Bolan (On international Border between Afghanistan and Pakistan) which are difficult but not impossible to cross. Most foreign invasions and infiltrations from the West took place through these routes. Some came with the purpose of settlement and some to plunder and conquer. South Asia's location bordering the Indian Ocean opened it to maritime trade over 3000 years ago. It was the European traders such as the French, the Dutch, the Portuguese and later the Britishers who took the greatest advantage of such maritime linkages.

> "We are of Asia and the people of Asia are nearer and closer to us than others. India is so situated that she is pivot of Western, Southern and South East Asia. In the past her culture flowed to all these countries and they came to her in many ways. Those contacts are being renewed and the future is bound to see closer union between India and South East Asia on the one side and Afghanistan, Iran and the Arab world on the West. To the furtherance of that close association of free countries, we must devote ourselves. India has followed with anxious interest the struggle of Indonesians for freedom and to them we send our good wishes."[1]
>
> [1]Asians Relations Report of the proceedings and Documentation of the First Asian Relations Conference, New Delhi, March 1947. Jawaharlal Nehru, *Speeches,* Vol. 1 (1946-49) and Vol. 2 (1949-53), Publications Division, Government of India. (Delhi: Government of India 1949 and 1953).

One of the major characteristics features of the region are its **Indo-centric** nature. India is central to the entire region, with a huge territory and population.[4] This is not only in terms of India's geographic location and contiguous boundaries with neighbours, but also with respect to socio-cultural identities and the experiences of the historical and political evolution. The commonalties in South Asia are mostly bi-lateral between India and each of the neighbouring countries, separately and individually. **There is a bit of India in every other country of South Asia.**[5] Thus the geo-strategic importance of India cannot be overemphasised, due to its interrelationship with large part of the world, in terms of its location, trade orientation, cultural and ideological bonds.[6]

The Republic of India is possessed by geographical logic, framed by the Arabian Sea to the West and South West, Bay of Bengal to the East and South East, by the mountainous jungles to the East, and by the Himalayas and the knot of

Karakoram and Hindu Kush to the North and North West. India has a land frontier of 15,200 km and a coastline of 5700 km.[7] With the North-South and East-West extent of 3200 km and 3000 km respectively and an overall coverage of 3,267,500 square kilometers it ranks seventh amongst the countries of the world and holds second and third position respectively in respect of population of over a billion and a cultivable land of 1,362,440 square km. As a geographical unit it can hardly afford to exclude Afghanistan, Pakistan, Nepal, Bhutan and Bangladesh, emerging as they do out of the foundering of the sub-continent.[8] Giving up of Afghanistan would carry momentous geopolitical implications for India. The future directions that Afghanistan takes will affect how successful India is in overcoming the problems on its borders in order to emerge as a world class power.

The key to understanding India is the realisation that while as a sub-continent India makes eminent geographic sense its natural boundaries[9] are, nevertheless quite weak at places. In fact, India and South Asia have dangerously misunderstood geography. Understanding geography delivers to the core of South Asia's political dilemma, which is about borders. India also unlike China lacks a singular nursery of demographic organisation like the Wei Valley or the lower Yellow River, from which polity could expand. Even the Ganges River Valley could not provide enough of a platform for the expansion of unitary Indian State unto the subcontinents, peninsular south. The sub continents other river systems beside the Ganges—the Brahamputra, Narmada, Tungbhadra, Kaveri, Godaveri, and so on—further divide it. There is no change in post-independence era also, with fissures in polity observable everywhere. Moreover India has the hottest climate and most abundant and luxurious landscape of all the Eurasian population hubs. Therefore, as Fairgrive[10] tells us, India lacked the need to build political structures for the organisation of resources, at least to the degree that the temperate-zone Chinese and Europeans did. Thus being open to concentrated invasion from its north west, the least defined and least protected of its frontier regions, where India is dangerously close to the Eurasian Heartland. Indeed, it is the infiltration and invasions from the West that has disrupted the quest for unity and stability in the Indian subcontinent well into the modern era. So central to India's geopolitical fortunes over the course of near and distant history is Afghanistan.

Another Geographical fact is that, India and China sit at the headwaters of several of Asia's most important rivers. Although India has entered into water sharing treaties with Pakistan, Nepal and Bangladesh with whom it shares important trans-boundary river systems, it doesn't have one with China which is the source country of the Yangtze, Mekong, Yarlung-Tsangpo, Indus, Irrawaddy, Sutlej and the Salween River, thereby exercising a degree of hydro-hegemony.[11] In recent years, many in India have warned that China use its upstream position to reroute the Yarlung-Tsangpo. China also dominates one of the largest sources of fresh water in Tibet.

India forms a vast geographical and political system,[12] which, if it cannot boast of strictly *scientific frontier* everywhere, enjoys nonetheless at many points the advantage of the grandest natural boundaries of any region in the globe. India presents a picture of immense geographical diversity. The India peninsula has been conveniently divided into three[13] regions.[14] First the Himalayas Mountain Range in the North and its offshoots on the North-West and North-East; which separate the subcontinent from Central Asia, Iran and Burma respectively, second, the Indo-Gangetic-Brahamputra plains, which stretches from the Arabian Sea to the Bay of Bengal, third, the Deccan Plateau, which is separated from the great river plains by the Vindhya Mountains, is separated from the great river Plain.

IDEA OF PLACE

The first approach—"*space*"—is the one with which...students of conflict are most familiar, emphasizing the *'location of things'* in relationship to other things, and how things are distributed. This idea of spatial contingency is picked up in Kirby and Ward's (1987, p.3) definition of *"spatiality"* as *"a contingent factor within the operation of any social formation,"* in which society's *"components are themselves dependent upon their spatial setting"* (see also O'Loughlin and Anselin 1992:12).... This view of spatiality or location matches the two basic ways to think about location, as presented by Abler, Adams, and Gould in their classic text, *Spatial Organisation* (1997, p. 59)—*"absolute location"* and *"relative location."* According to Abler et al., "absolute location is position in relation to a conventional grid system designed solely for locative purposes." In this view, location is provided by such things as latitude and longitude or a street address. The concept becomes much more rich and trickier in the second way to think about location: "Relative location is position with respect to other locations." This can be expressed in terms of distance or travel times from other locations, the cost of such travel, etc. Thus ... technology changes "relative location"—places that were once weeks apart in time are now only hours apart—and other mechanisms, such as alliances, can do likewise (Starr 2003, p. 5).

—**Agnew and Duncan, 1989**

The Himalayas, which run in the southeast curve along the northern front of India and separate it from the Tibetan Plateau, include several parallel ranges of the lofty mountains, with deep valleys between them. They cover a region about 2400 kilometers long and 250 to 300 kilometers in breadth. The Hindu Kush Mountains which runs from the Pamirs in the southwesterly directions, may be regarded as the natural boundary of India in the northwest, though considerable portions of the hilly regions to the South and East are now included in Afghanistan and

Pakistan. Further South, the Safed Koh, Suleiman and Khirthar Mountains (now in Pakistan) are generally regarded as the Western boundary of India, separating her from the table land of Iran. But large stretches of land to the West of the line in modern Afghanistan and Baluchistan (Pakistan) like those to the south of the Hindu Kush, were for long both culturally and politically parts of India.

There are several passes across the Hindu Kush, along almost all the chief rivers in this region, viz. Swat and Chitral running south; and the Kabul, Kurram, Tochi and the Gomal Rivers running east to the Indus. But by far the most important route is the one that crosses the Hindu Kush through one of its passes, runs along the Kabul valley, and then descends to Peshawar through the Khyber Pass, a winding and narrow defile of 32 km length. Another well-known route runs, beyond the fringe of the Afghan mountains from Heart to Kandhar, and then descends to the Indus Valley through the Bolan Pass or the Mula Pass further south. The third, well known route from the West followed the coastline and reached the Indus Valley through the narrow gap between the Khitar Range and the sea. But the inhospitable Makran Coast dissuaded invaders to follow this route. The two routes last mentioned were less important as gateways to India then the first. For just beyond the region where they debouched into the Indian Plains stretches the desert of Rajasthan (Rajputana), which bars access to the interior of India. The Khyber route on the other hand, leads directly across the plains of the Punjab to the interior through the narrow gap between the desert and the mountains. Hence, Khyber Pass has been most frequently used.

Actually the passes in the North-West are accessible, that from time immemorial have encouraged numerous invasions by Central and West Asian people. From Aryans, Greeks, the Persians, Huns, Turks to the Mongols all came down the passes located in the north-west.[15] Other passes in the North and North-East have allowed communication and movement between sparsely populated Tibetan Region and India.[16] **The importance of Himalayas is not that they kept invaders out but that they kept the Arctic Winds from entering and the monsoon from leaving the Indian Subcontinent. Thus providing the country the unique rain oriented climate.**

The Himalayan wall is no longer an impenetrable rampart in view of the modern developments of war and strategy including nuclear weapons; its geographical significance, however, remains intact. The high Himalayas impart climatic distinctiveness to the country typified by the monsoon character, an attribute not possessed by any single landmass of its size. In addition, this synonym of '**the abode of snow**' also serves as perennial source of water supply.

One decisive factor that has had a decisive impact on the sub-continent's history is the critical position of Afghanistan. Since the important overland routes between the subcontinent and The Central and Western Asia pass through Afghanistan, this mountainous tract witnessed the greatest interaction between India and the non-Indian Empires that rose in Central and Western Asia. Afghanistan lacked the physical features that could make a natural barrier, an ascendant empire based in Persia and Central Asia included Afghanistan in its fold. Afghanistan also lacked natural resources to sustain population and growth, hence, the empire which captured it, would invariably extend its borders into Northern India, stopping if at all at the Western Bank of Indus River. Conversely an ascendant India power could protect its Northern Border by capturing Afghanistan and extending the frontier to the Hindu Kush.

> Afghanistan's geography makes it central not only as a principal invasion route into India for terrorists in our day as for armies in days past, but also as a strategically vital rear base for Pakistan, India's primary adversary.

Island Territories and Maritime Area

The centuries following the rise of the Mongols set the stage for increasing importance of the sea.[17] India has a coastline of 7652 km with ten major and 180 minor ports. India has 1200 far flung island territories spread over Bay of Bengal and the Arabian Sea; a 220 million square km of ocean space as Exclusive Economic Zone.[18] The international maritime boundary extends up to Indonesia, Malaysia, Thailand, Myanmar, Sri Lanka and Pakistan. Ninety per cent of India's trade is by sea. **India meets five of the six critical elements as advocated by Admiral Mahan for a country to be a great sea power viz.** ***geographical position, physical conformation, and extent of territory,*** *population and national character, lastly the direction from the government.*[19]

> Patterns of movement and flows of people, culture, goods and information mean that it is now not so much physical boundaries—the geographical distances, the seas or mountain ranges—that define a community or nation's 'natural limits'. Increasingly we must think in terms of communications and transport networks and of the symbolic boundaries of language and culture—the 'spaces of transmission' defined by satellite footprints or radio signals—as providing the crucial and permeable boundaries of our age.
>
> **—Morley and Robins, 1995, p. 1.**

In view of the change in the International Law of the Sea, the Indian Parliament extended Constitutional Recognition to the new concept of the Exclusive Economic Zone in May 1976. As a result, **Article 297 of Chapter III, Part XII of the Constitution** reads as follows:

'All lands, minerals and other things of value underlying the ocean within the territorial waters, or the continental shelf, or the exclusive economic zone of India, shall vest in the Union and be held for the purposes of the Union.'[20]

India's exclusive economic is estimated at 2.02 to 2.2 million square km. The Territorial Waters, Continental Shelf, Exclusive Economic Zone and other Maritime Zones Act came into force in January 1977. By 2004, India would have an additional 1.5 million square km of exclusive Economic Zone, in view of legal provisions of extending the continental shelf.

Indian Ocean is the only ocean named after a country. The ice-free Ocean on which three Continents abut is the smallest and the warmest Ocean occupying 28 million square miles and cradles the peripheries of Africa and the Orient in the two separate geopolitical horse shoes in which one fourth of the world's population live and operate at different levels of political consciousness ranging from military dictatorship, monarchies, tribals, fundamentalism to democracies. Further due to historical disputes, internal insurgencies, narcotics, oil, arms sales, and strategic raw materials, the Ocean has become an **'object'** rather than **'subject'** with external powers actively bidding for clients states.[21]

It is bounded to the north by the Indian subcontinent; to the West and northwest by the east African coast and Arabian Peninsula, respectively; to the east by Thailand, the Malay Peninsula, Indonesia, and Australia; and to the south by the oceanic margin with the Southern Ocean at latitude 60°S, the northern limit of the area covered by the original Antarctic Treaty (1959). The Western extremity of the Indian Ocean is delineated from the Atlantic Ocean in two places—at the Suez Canal, and at the meridian running south from Cape Agulhas in South Africa. At its easternmost extremity, the Indian Ocean touches the Pacific Ocean at the 147°E

LOMBOK STRAIT

Lombok strait is not only a link between the Indonesian archipelagos, is also an important channel for Pacific and Indian Ocean sea shipping. Lombok Straits are safest natural waterways. Located in the Pacific and Indian Ocean maritime transportation hub for the global maritime corridor, an important strategic position, it is 80.5 km long from north to south. Width at the south is 65 km. In the north the mouth is 35 km wide. The north entry is shallower with depth at the most is of 1200 m, the deepest 1306 meters, no reef and no gravel bottom. Many vessels between the Persian Gulf and Southeast Asia, Japan, when unable to pass through Straits of Malacca, both by the way of this South Indian Ocean, or then by the Makassar Strait pass through Lombok Strait. There are 90,000 vessels passing from there every year. Due to its depth, 200,000 tons of ships have to pass through Lombok Strait. We can see the importance of Lombok strait in the economy.

meridian, running south from South East Cape on Tasmania to 60°S latitude. The northernmost extent of the Indian Ocean is the Iranian port of Bandar Imam Khomeini in the Persian Gulf. In addition, the Indian Ocean encompasses several regional seas and sea areas: the Andaman Sea, the Arabian Sea, the Bay of Bengal, the Great Australian Bight, the Gulf of Aden, the Gulf of Mannar, the Gulf of Oman, the Laccadive Sea, the Mozambique Channel, the Persian Gulf, and the Red Sea.

On land the Indian Ocean Region is bounded and variously influenced by 38 states: Australia, Bahrain, Bangladesh, Comoros, Djibouti, East Timor, Egypt, Eritrea, India, Indonesia, Iran, Iraq, Israel, Jordan, Kenya, Kuwait, Madagascar, Malaysia, Maldives, Mauritius, Mozambique, Myanmar, Oman, Pakistan, Qatar, Saudi Arabia, Seychelles, Singapore, Somalia, South Africa, Sri Lanka, Sudan, Tanzania, Thailand, United Arab Emirates, and Yemen. (France and the United Kingdom can also be counted among the Indian Ocean littoral states because of their island territories). Combined, these countries make up almost 40 per cent of the world's total coastline, dominated in order by Indonesia, Australia, India, Madagascar, Malaysia, Thailand, Somalia, South Africa, and Saudi Arabia.

India lies in the center of and dominates all the sea routes. The major focal points of contest in Indian Ocean are the entrances into the Ocean, this leads to three important waterways; first, Straits of Malacca and Singapore; second, Cape of Good Hope and third The Suez Canal.

Other routes of interest are a detour around Australia; however, these routes would add 3000 nautical miles in the sea journey.[22] The important other routes are: (a) Straits of Sunda, Lambok and Mokassar and other narrow Indonesian waters. Lambok Strait is the only strait that is deep enough to allow passage of the submerged nuclear submarines. All other straits are shallow for submerged submarines; (b) Around Australia—through Cape of York in North east, and Bass Strait in the South East.

The Straits of Malacca

The Strait lies between Malaya and Singapore in the East and Indonesia in the West. It is 400 nautical miles long and varies in width from 20 nautical miles at the Southern end, to 150 nautical miles in the northern end, the governing depth being only 25 feet. The strait is recognised as international strait by its major users Japan, United States, China and Russia. However, the three coastal states—Indonesia, Malaysia and Singapore are not International Waters or Straits, even while fully recognising their use for international navigation.[23]

The Cape of Good Hope

The Cape of Good Hope is located at the Southern tip of Africa. All the larger vessels, aircraft carriers, large oil tankers transit this waterway on way from Europe and Asia. The importance of the waterway was further highlighted when in 1967 Suez Canal was closed for eight years.

Strait of Hormuz

It is narrow Strait lying at the mouth of the Persian Gulf through which passes approximately 40 per cent of the world's energy requirements. For India it is extremely important, since approximately 70 per cent of the imported crude passes through it.

Climate of India

Location and physiographic factor have greatly influenced the climatic characteristics of the country. Although its considerable portion belongs to the sub-tropical zone, as a whole it shares characteristics of tropical monsoon climate, mainly because of the Himalayas, functioning as an effective meteorological barrier.

Five conditions—*latitude, the northern mountains, the elevation of Deccan Palteau, the neighbourhood of western desert and proximity to the Indian Ocean*—mainly determine the general features on the 'Climate of India'. The latitude produces tropical heat. Tampered on the southern Plateau by the general elevation of the land, intensified on the northern plains by the Himalayas, which refract the vertical summer solar sun rays, while in winter intercepting the cold atmospheric currents from the bleak central Asiatic Tablelands. The great desert intervening between the upper basin of the Ganga and the lower basin of the Indus helps to cause the hot blasts to blow over the North West provinces. The Indian Ocean surrounding the Peninsula on the two sides supplies a super abundance of moisture during the prevalence of the Southern Monsoons. None of the Ghats or the Southern Highlands is sufficiently elevated to arrest any large portion of the rain bearing clouds. Clouds at this time roll up continuously from the seething surface of the surrounding seas, sweeping over the Deccan Plateau, and penetrating far northwards through the head of the Bay of Bengal, thus precipitating all their remaining humidity on the southern slopes of the Himalayas. From these conditions it results that while great heat prevails everywhere, the provinces south of Satpura Range are, on the whole, cooler than the Indus and Ganga basins, and that an unusual quantity of moisture is pretty evenly distributed throughout the peninsula. At certain points the amount of this moisture surpasses the records taken on any other parts of earth's surface, varying on the Malabar Coast from

900mm to 1200mm, and in the Caldron—like Assam Valley exceeding 1500mm. The Indian Sub-Continent is warm, and on the whole productive. Hence, there has neither been temptation, nor necessity for inhabitants to venture on to the sea; they have remained at the early stage of land man to whom the sea is unfamiliar.[24]

Rhythm is the keynote of the monsoon climate.[25] The two seasons, the summer and the winter, roughly corresponding with the culmination of the Sun from the Southern to Northern hemisphere and vice-versa, and associated monsoon regimes are never mistaken and hence the climate can be discussed under two heads–the summer and winter monsoons. The imbalance in the regime, owe definitely to the differential heating and cooling as the temperature starts rising much before the vernal equinox, thus cutting short the winter season by about a month. Similarly, the related terrestrial radiation pushes its commencement further by about a month from the autumnal equinox reducing the duration to a little over four months. The summer season is bifurcated as a dry and wet or humid, roughly stretching from March to mid-June and mid-June and mid-October.

Lower temperatures, sometimes below freezing point, low humidity and scanty rainfall characterise winter season. In such vast region there is necessarily much diversity amidst this uniformity.

Influence of Geography on History

Like most countries of the world; history of India has been profoundly influenced by its geographical location and physical features.[26] In the first place, we must note the vast dimensions and the varied physical features of the country. In extent India is almost equal to Europe with the exclusion of Russia. It contains the highest mountain ranges, lofty plateaus, and plains only slightly higher than the sea level, sandy deserts, large rivers, fertile river valleys and forests of all types and descriptions. Every variety of climates from extreme cold to extreme heat is to be found in the country. All these factors tended to separate India from other countries and forming a compact territory, developed as distinctive political and cultural unit, as compared with the rest of the world. The Indian horizon was a large but limited one, and the common natural boundaries gradually led to a sense of common motherland. The vision of a fundamental unity always loomed large. It coloured the political ideals of the country. This ideal of political unity was rarely organised in actual practice. But, as apolitical theory it can be traced throughout the long course of Indian history. The cultural unity was, however, more manifest, being inspired by a common language, literature and religious and social ideals. In spite

> 'Geography and the chronology are the Sun and the Moon, the right eye and left eye of History.'

of seeming diversity there was a large measure of cultural unity and the goals of political union was never lost sight of. This unity in diversity is the keynote of the tangled history of India, and forms the background against which seemingly complex developments in the various aspects of Indian Civilisation must be viewed.

The natural barriers of hills and large rivers largely determined the different political (and partly cultural) units into which India was divided. These natural divisions favoured growth of a local and regional spirit and fostered separatist tendencies. The marked distinction between North India and Deccan Plateau led to the growth of regions, which maintained distinctive characteristics and generally played a separate role in politics throughout the long course of history.[27] The political history of India thus resolves itself into separate histories of the regions. But the points of contact between them, though infrequent, were not altogether absent.

The extensive valley of the Ganges has been divided into several local regions by the large rivers and the Indus Valley. Indus Valley though comparatively smaller, is broadly divided into two by the middle and lower courses of the river. Thus in Northern India the modern provinces of the Punjab, Sind, Uttar Pradesh, Bihar, Bengal as well as the tracts of Rajasthan, the plains of Northern Gujarat, plateaus of Malwa and Bundelkhand and the isolated hill tracts of Chota Nagpur have the roots of their separate entities as distinct units dug deep into the past. No doubt racial and linguistic factors played some part in creating these natural regions, but no one can ignore the very large influence of the geographical factors, including the strategic means of defence afforded by nature.

The Deccan Plateau was divided into several distinct regions by the two mighty rivers, the Godavari and the Krishna and their tributaries. Deccan is also separated from the coastal plains on the East and the West. The Odisha Hills and the estuaries of the two rivers named above divided the eastern coastal plains. The region south of the plateau was sharply split into an eastern and western zone by the Nilgiris and Cardamom Hills, and the Kaveri River again subdivided by the former, to a certain extent. All these regions generally speaking developed into separate distinct units and retained their individuality through the ages.

We find from time immemorial the influence of regional politics, with a surprising tenacity that has kept up the isolationist spirit even amidst political catastrophes and kaleidoscopic changes of rulers and dynasties, Empires rose and fell, the whole country passed through a series of foreign invasions but states under different names and ruling dynasties continued under their individual existence throughout the course of history.

The extensive coast line of India fostered trade and maritime activity and made the Indians hardy mariners. From an early period they navigated the seas, both in the East and the West. Herbold sea faring exploits carried them to distant and unknown parts of the world. **One of the greatest lessons of history has been that a nation that has confined to land has never won a war.** The commercial affluence and political prestige India historically enjoyed especially under the ancient South Indian Kingdoms stemmed from the naval power that was exercised. Again it is a fact that India-based British colonists could not have set up and strengthened an empire in the region without the unchallenged supremacy over the sea.[28] The over-sea and coastal movements of the people, for free trade in particular, have taken place even prior to the West European negotiations, the Indian people fanned out from the Persian Gulf region to the South East Asian realm.

The trade gave impetus to colonisation and Indian colonies were planted even in the most distant regions in the Far East. The maritime activities of India were, however, almost solely devoted to peaceful pursuits. This is mainly due to the vast expense of the sea on both sides of the peninsula. The direct voyage between the Indian Coasts and the opposite shore, either of Africa on the West or Indo-China and East Indies (Indonesia) in the east, was long and risky. The dubious chance of success afforded by the sea could scarcely tempt them to devote their energy and resources to building a powerful navy in order to establish an overseas empire.[29]

It is, a singular fact, that in numerous recorded instances of the foreign invasions from the West, the invaders have always (almost) defeated the Indians. This can hardly be regarded as a pure accident. Nor can it explained away by a lack of unity among the defenders, for the invaders did not always possess a numerical superiority over the opponents. Although culturally united since early times, political turmoil's could sweep the country from time to time with occasional sparks of organised Empires.

The true explanation seems to lie in India's ignorance of the outside world. The rise of political powers or new political combinations, the evaluation of military tactics, and the invention of new military weapons or fresh equipment, even in Central and Western Asia, not to speak of remoter countries, hardly ever interested India, though, as events proved, she fell a constant victim to one or other of them. The details of the defenders (Indian) campaigns leave no doubt that they were either both unaware of the impending danger or were outmatched by the new military formations or weapons to which they were complete strangers and consequently not sufficiently prepared.[30]

The reason for such ignorance is not merely to be sought in a spirit of isolation fostered by almost insurmountable barriers. It is also partly due to the fact that, for reasons stated above, Indian rulers had no occasion or temptation to carry on campaigns outside India. They lived and fought in their little world and cared little for what was happening in the outside world. How similar is the situation prevalent in India today. The political parties are fighting amongst themselves at the cost of national interest. Most of the political parties are individual satraps.

Unfortunately, the physical barriers, which shut off the vision of Indian rulers from the outside world, were not strong or powerful enough to keep out all foreign invaders from Indian soil. When some of them did cross the barriers into India, they brought with them new ideas and forces of the progressive world with which India could not cope. But so strongly did the geographical factors operate that as soon as these foreign invaders settled in India, they imbibed the similar spirit so congenial to her soil, and themselves fell victim to it. So it has been in the past, and so it is destined to be in the future. So long as the political vision of India confines itself within her natural boundaries of hills and seas, and does not look beyond to the outside world.

Centrality of India

Pandit Nehru, the first Prime Minister of India, had said in 1949 that India's position was strategic and that no power could ignore us. He said:

> "Look at the map. If you have to consider any question affecting Middle East. India inevitably comes into the picture. If you have to consider any question concerning South East Asia, you cannot do so without India, so also with the Far East. While the Middle East may not be directly connected with South East Asia, both are connected with India. Even if you think in terms of regional organisations in India, you have to keep in touch with other regions."[31]

For obvious reasons India figures prominently because geographically it is central to the region and accounts for three–quarters of the region's population, GNP etc.[32]

India is the gateway of both Middle East and South East Asia. Nehru had also stated, "India becomes a kind of meeting ground for various trends and forces and a meeting ground between what may roughly be called the east and the West". From time immemorial India has been a desirable destination for all kinds of people ranging from revelers to looters, from warriors to adventurers. Even the Aryans are to have come from outside. No wonder the theme caught eye of the Nobel Laureate Bengali poet Mr Rabindranath Tagore, who underlined the unbounded hospitality of India in his celebrated poem, ***'Bharat-tirtha'*** *(meaning Pilgrimage India).* The translation of the stanza would read:

> *No one knows to whose clarion call*
> *People responded and cam*

In gushing streams
And got merged into an Ocean?
Hither came the Aryans, the Barbarians,
The Dravidians, the Chinese, the Sakas,
The Huns, the Pathans, the Mughals,
To merge into one body and soul,
Today, doors to the West are open,
New ideas are flowing
Incessant giving's and receiving
Meeting and mixing are on
They will not return
From this supreme Ocean of Humanity,
That's India.

India lies amongst politically assertive and dynamic states. All the historical pretenders to global power originated in the vicinity of India or aimed to reach India. The world's most populous aspirant to power, as also, the entire potential—economic and political challengers—lie in her vicinity. After United States, the next three largest military spenders and two economies are here, as are four of the seven overt nuclear powers, and all but two covert ones. The region accounts for approximately 45 per cent of the world's population, 35 per cent of the world's GDP, and seventy five per cent of the world's energy resources.

The region is world's axial super sub-continent. A power that dominates the vicinity and India would exercise decisive influence of worlds two of the three most economically productive regions, Europe and East Asia. A glance at the map also suggests that the dominant power would almost automatically control the Middle East and Africa. With the area in and around India serving as the decisive chess board, it no longer suffices to fashion different policies for North America, Europe and other for Asia. What happens with the distribution of power in the vicinity of India viz. Asian Land Mass will be decisive not only for India but for the world as a whole.

One of the most striking things about the larger Asian strategic landscape is the arc of failing or troubled states around India. This harsh geographical reality is India's most-glaring weaknesses—one that weighs it down regionally. Its neighbourhood is so chronically troubled that India confronts what can be called a tyranny of geography.[33] As a result, it faces serious external threats from virtually all directions. It is locked in an arc of failing or authoritarian states that seek, in different ways, to undermine its secular, multiethnic, pluralistic character. To India's west lies "an arc of crises stretching from Egypt to Pakistan"—to use the title of one of the workshops.

There is continuing reluctance in the international policy discourse, however, to face up to a central reality: the political border between Afghanistan and Pakistan (or "Afpak" in Washington) has now ceased to exist in practice. The so-called Durand Line, in any event, was an artificial, British-colonial invention that left the large Pashtun community divided into two.[34] Today, that line exists only in maps. On the ground, it has little political, ethnic, and economic relevance, even as the Afpak region has become a magnet for the world's jihadists. A de facto Pashtunistan, long sought by Pashtuns, now lurks just below the horizon, on the ruins of an ongoing Islamist militancy.

ENDNOTES

1. Diehl, Paul F. (1991) "Geography and War: A Review and Assessment of the Empirical Literature," *International Interactions* 17: pp. 11-27.
   Diehl, Paul F., (1999) *A Road Map to War,* (Nashville: Vanderbilt University Press).
2. Ibid.
3. Zipf, G.K. (1949) *Human Behaviour and Principle of Least Effort',* (Cambridge, M.A.: Addison-Wesley).
4. Dikshit, R.D. (2006) *Political Geography: The Spatiality of Politics,* 9th Edition, (New Delhi: Tata McGraw-Hill Publishing Company Ltd).
5. Muni, S.D., and Muni, Anuradha, *'Regional Co-operation in South Asia',* (Delhi: National Publishing House, 1984), p. 162.
6. Cohen, Saul Bernard, *'Geography and Politics in The Divided World',* (London: Methun, 1964), p. 62. The Geo-strategic region is the expression of the interrelationship of a large part of the world in terms of location, movement, and trade orientation, cultural and ideological bonds. The geographical region is a subdivision of geo-strategic region. It is derived directly from geographic regions; this unit can provide a framework from common, political and economic actions. Contiguity of location and complementary resources are particularly distinguishing marks of the geo-political region. Geo-political regions are the basis for the emergence of multiple power nodes within geo-strategic regions. Also see, Chandershekar Rao, PVR, *'Regional Co-Operation in South Asia',* The Round Table, No. 293, January 1985, pp. 53-65.
7. Let us begin by drawing upon approaches to the idea of "place" by geographers (for example, Agnew and Duncan 1989):
   The first approach, space, is the one with which .... students of conflict are most familiar, emphasizing the location of things in relationship to other things, and how things are distributed. This idea of spatial contingency is picked up in Kirby and Ward's (1987:3) definition of "spatiality" as "a contingent factor within the operation of any social formation," in which society's "components are themselves dependent upon their spatial setting" (see also O'Loughlin and Anselin 1992:12).... This view of spatiality or location matches the two basic ways to think about location, as presented by Abler, Adams, and Gould in their classic text, Spatial Organisation (1971:59), "absolute location" and "relative location." According to Abler et al., "absolute location is position in relation to a conventional grid system designed solely for locative purposes." In this view, location is provided by such things as latitude and longitude or a street address. The concept becomes much more rich and trickier in the second way to think about location: "Relative location is position with respect to other locations." This can be expressed in terms of distance or travel times from other locations, the cost of such travel, etc. Thus .... technology changes "relative location", places that were once weeks apart in time are now only hours apart, and other mechanisms, such as alliances, can do likewise (Starr 2003:5, emphasis added).

8. The use of term sub-continent for India is a misnomer and the legacy of the British rule; this term has never been used for China or for Russia.
9. *Boundaries*, by definition, constitute lines of separation or contact. This may occur in real or virtual space, horizontally between territories, or vertically between groups and/or individuals. The point of contact or separation usually creates an 'us' and an 'Other' identity, and this takes place at a variety of socio-spatial scales. We identify four major themes within boundary studies: 1) the suggested 'disappearance' of boundaries; 2) the role of boundaries in the construction of socio-spatial identities; 3) boundary narratives and discourse; and 4) the different spatial scales of boundary construction. While this list is by no means exhaustive, we would argue that these are the key topics to be discussed within the context of the challenges facing the uncertain future of the nation-state and, by association, state boundaries. Changing impact of boundaries, however defined, on the creation of these multi-faceted identities:
    1. Recent/contemporary discussions of territoriality: the 'disappearance' of borders Patterns of movement and flows of people, culture, goods and information mean that it is now not so much physical boundaries ± the geographical distances, the seas or mountain ranges ± that define a community or nation's 'natural limits'. Increasingly we must think in terms of communications and transport networks and of the symbolic boundaries of language and culture ± the 'spaces of transmission' defined by satellite footprints or radio signals ± as providing the crucial, and permeable boundaries of our age (Morley and Robins, 1995:)
    2. *Constructing socio-spatial identities.* While a country could avoid Cold War alignment, it cannot lack an identity. The question: 'Which side are you on?' has been replaced by the much more fundamental one, 'Who are you?' Every state has to have an answer. That answer, its cultural identity, defines the state's place in world politics, its friends and its enemies (Huntington, 1996: 125).
    3. Territorial narratives: boundaries of exclusion and inclusion
    4. *Boundaries and spatial scale.*
10. Fairgrieve, James (1927), *Geography and World Power* (London: University of London Press Ltd.)
11. Hydro-hegemony is hegemony at the river basin level. The most stable situation in terms of riparian relations is when riparians share control of the resource, whereby the hegemon has negotiated a water-sharing agreement that is perceived positively by all riparians. This can be taken as the *positive* form of hydro-hegemony. At the other end of the spectrum is *negative/dominative* form of hydro-hegemony when the stronger competitor may seek to attain and consolidate maximum control of water resources through unilateral action. For hydro-hegemony, see Mark Zeitoun and Jeroen Warner (2006), "Hydro-Hegemony: A Framework for Analysis of Tran-boundary Water Conflicts", *Water Policy*, Vol. 8, No. 5, pp.435-60.
12. Geopolitics is an important and long established area of geographical inquiry, which regards spatial relationship to be a central importance in the constitution of international politics. Its contemporary usage should not, however, be confused with implicit governmental environmental determinism in much of political geography of the Ratzel-Mackinder era, or with German *geopolitik* of the inter-war period. As practiced currently, geo politics is a subfield focused on the search for rational explanation of the global geopolitical order from a geographical (spatial) perspective. Graham Smith (1994) has singled out three main approaches to its study:
    1. Traditional geopolitics with its roots in Mackinfer's Heartland thesis, and the related conceptual refinements on this basic theory to be discussed under "Global Strategic Views."
    2. *The power relations* perspective focused on the hierarchical character of States within the

global order by examining the polity's ability to influence or change the behaviour of other states in a desired direction. It's main source of inspiration being the *realist* school of international relations.

3. *The Political-economy approach* based on the assumption that geopolitics cannot be understood fully without considering the dynamics of global economy.

13. According to ancient literature, there were five divisions of India: one, **Uttarpathar or Udichya** (North and North West India); two, **Madhyadesh** (Indo-Gangetic Plains); three, **aparanta** or **Pratichya** (Western India); four, **Prachya** or **Purvadesh (Eastern Indai)** and five, **Dakshin pathar** (The Deccan).

14. 'The region is defined in terms of the entire content of the human occupancy of the area, is an association of the interrelated natural and societal features chosen from still more complex totality because they believed relevant to Geographic study.' Whittlessey terms this the *'compage'*. 'Compage' differs, in size or ranks, from the small locality to regions. From, 'The Regional Concept and Regional Method', by Derwent S. Whittlessey, P.E. James and C.F. Jones (1954), *'American Geography – Inventory and Prospect',* (Syracuse University), pp. 19-70.

Geographers recognise two forms of regions. One, is a single feature region: the other is a multi-featured or composite region. The multi-featured region is what geographers call the geographical region. The geographical region is the organisation of space, based on both qualitative and quantitative criteria, and expressing associations of various elements. Geographers consider the region to be merely a device separating real features. It is a community of physical; biotic and societal features that depict, or are functionally associated with man's occupancy of an area.

15. Vohra, Ranbir, *'The Making of India: A Historical Survey',* (New York 10504: ME Sharpe. Inc., 1977), p. 18.

16. It is important to note that the important recorded battle in the North were in Sikkim (Nathang Area) and in Jelep La, during the Younghusband Expedition to Tibet in the late 19th Century. These battles were fought in the thick of winters and hence the myth of Himalayas being a barrier or a wall in the north is not true.

17. The Sung's of China, occupied a leading position in China. The idea of training and supporting large land army was discussed at Sung's Court. **Instead of aggressive cult of the army and total militarization of the society, the Sung's promoted a measured, serene, and well calculated pride in the naval power and oversea commerce.** In 1132, responding to Chin invasion from the North, Sung responded by expanding navy and high sea's fleet for coastal defence, that was separate from river squadrons. [See George Modelski and William R Tompson, *'Leading Sectors and World Power's: The Co-evaluation of Global Economics and Politics',* (Columbia: University of South Carolina Press, 1996), pp. 168-69)].

The contest between Britain and France in the 1700's is compared with the contest of whale and an elephant. The basic pattern of Anglo-French Warfare can be traced to asymmetric evolution of military capabilities with Britain favoring Sea Power and France favoring the Land Power. Britain defeated the French because it controlled the sea, and hence could muster the resources.

The discussion can be further taken to contest between Soviet Union a Land Power and the United States a Maritime Power. Soviet challenge to United States military supremacy relied on persistent increase in the number of Intercontinental Ballistic Missiles, representing the land based component of triad. The United States combined share of Submarine Launched Ballistic Missiles and air launched bombs (from sea based launchers) was 72 per cent in 1962 and 70 per cent in 1988, with few fluctuations in between. To aggregate these indicators for 1970-90, the United Sates had three fourths of the sea and air launched nuclear delivery vehicles in the strategic forces balance with the Soviet Union. In contrast Soviet Union had an average 60 per cent cumulative share of the land.

The asymmetric distribution of military capabilities among incumbent and challengers has been an enduring feature at the global level since the Mongol's launched their bid for the Universal Empire. **The dominant forces all ruled the sea.** The main components of the victors military power, with some variations and few provisions transcended regional continental boundaries, were globally distribute, and were much more globally mobile by ruling the sea.

18. The concept of Exclusive Economic Zone (EEZ), along with varying rights and responsibilities of littoral and island states, is provided legal sanction by the Conference on United Nations on the Law of the Sea (UNCLOS III). After much debate and discussion, it was finally agreed to a new international Law of The Sea Convention in 1982. Some twelve years later, on November 16, 1994, the Law of the Sea entered into force, a year after sixty five (65) states ratified the convention. In the interim period it was considered as a part of customary international law. By late 1997, as many as 122 states had ratified the United Nations Law of the Sea Convention.

Mark Broughton, 'Electronics in the EEZ', *'EEZ Technology',* (1997), p. 123. The author states that The Law of the Sea provides vastly extended areas of sea to littoral and island states, comprising territorial sea of 12 nautical miles (NM), a contiguous zone of 24 nautical miles and an Exclusive Economic Zone of 200 NM, along with continental shelf of 200 to 350Nm where applicable. In this respect, it has been estimated a 500 kilometers of coastline of a state would provide an Exclusive Economic Zone of 1, 85,000 square kilometers.

Littoral states possess varying degrees of rights and responsibilities over these areas of sea. With respect to EEZ, they possess sovereign rights over all natural resources as well as certain economic activities in the area, along with the exercise of the jurisdiction over maritime research and environmental protection.

19. The four spatio-political aspects of sea power in world politics were basic to the strategic thinking of Mahan:
    1. There is a continuous and unbroken system of oceans and seas on the earth's surface leading to a unified system of oceanic communication.
    2. There is a vast trans-continental and almost completely landlocked State—the Russian Empire—extending without break from the ice-bound Arctic in the north to the rugged desert-mountain belt in inner Asia in the South, and from Eastern Europe to the extreme eastern margin of the Asian mainland.
    3. Around the trans-continental Russian Empire are the maritime States of Europe and countries of the South and East Asia, bordering on the Indian and the Pacific Oceans.
    4. There are three insular States disconnected from the Eurasian mainland—Great Britain, Japan and the United States.

To Mahan, the sea was a great highway; *"a wide common, over which men may pass in all directions, but on which some well-known paths show that controlling reasons have led them to choose certain lines of travel rather than others."* In a trade dominated modern world, therefore, suitable oceanic location offered a distinct politico advantage, and a land locked location was in that regard, definite advantage.

20. Roy-Chaudhry, Rahul (1993) 'The Indian Coast Guard in the 1990's', *Indian Defence Review* (New Delhi: Lancers, October 1993), p. 64.
21. The central location of India at the head of the Indian Ocean is considered of great significance because of the following reasons:
    1. The trans Indian Ocean routes which connect the countries of Europe in the West and the countries of East Asia provide a strategic central location to India.
    2. The Deccan Peninsula protrudes into the Indian Ocean; help India establish a close

contact with West Asia, Africa and Europe from the Western coast and with Southeast and East Asia from the eastern coast.

3. India has a long coastline on the Indian Ocean which becomes favourable trading ports and commerce hubs for other countries.
4. The coastal regions of India are famous for agriculture, trade & industrial centres, tourist centres, fishing and salt making. They provide important hinterlands for the ports.
5. Opening of Suez Canal in 1869 reduced the distance between India and Europe by 7000 kms.

The central location of India at the head of the Indian Ocean is considered of great significance because of the following reasons:

6. The trans Indian Ocean routes which connect the countries of Europe in the West and the countries of East Asia provide a strategic central location to India.
7. The Deccan Peninsula protrudes into the Indian Ocean, help India establish a close contact with West Asia, Africa and Europe from the Western coast and with Southeast and East Asia from the eastern coast.
8. India has a long coastline on the Indian Ocean which becomes favourable trading ports and commerce hubs for other countries.
9. The coastal regions of India are famous for agriculture, trade & industrial centres, tourist centres, fishing and salt making. They provide important hinterlands for the ports.
10. Opening of Suez Canal in 1869 reduced the distance between India and Europe by 7000 kms.

22. Abbinski, Henry, *'Australia and The Indian Ocean'*, International Conference on Indian Ocean Studies, held in August 1977 at Perth: R.G. Boyd, 'The Strategic Significance of the Malacca Straits: Report of the Department of National Defense Canada', reproduced in *'Strategic Digest'*, September 1977, (New Delhi: IDSA).
23. *'The Strait Times', 'The Djakarta Times'*, both of November 17, 1971.
24. Fairgrieve, James (1927), *Geography and World Power* (London: University of London Press Ltd.), p. 248.
25. See David S. Landes in his book, *'The Wealth and Poverty of Nations: Why some Are So Rich and Some so Poor'*, (New York: W.W. Norton, 1998).

Weather as Destiny.

If one approach to the historical study of economic growth can be said to be the most influential, it is that which takes technology as the fundamental force for growth. This was the focus of Abbot Payson Usher, as it has been for generations of historians of western technology. Their agenda has been to the consequences technological changes, but also its causes. Technical progress, in this view, accelerated in the West following the Renaissance and Reformation, which cultivated a culture of rationality and fostered systematic curiosity. It responded to the expression of trade in Smith's Century, increased economic mobility facilitated the flow of information and expanding commerce held out the line for greater profits. It encouraged and was encouraged by the limited state, which provided inducements for industry but allowed markets to operate with limited influence, by foreign marauders and the taxman. Recently, this tradition, emphasizing the singularity of western technological achievements, has fallen out of favour in the academy. In the now fashionable multi-culturalist view, Europe's knowledge and know-how did not surpass those of the civilisations until the beginning of the nineteenth century. Gunpowder, paper and printing, and the first long distance explorers all came from the East, after all. Europe was just luckier, or at best more systematic in exploiting the discoveries and resources of the region.

Landes launches an all-out counter-attack against cultural relativity in economic history. He insists that West is special, its achievement unique, and that to argue otherwise is bad history.

Its distinctiveness derives from two factors: geography and culture. Europe's Industrial Revolution was, at the deepest level, a product of the Gulf Stream. The continent's mild summers permit intense physical activity, unlike the tropics, whose heat and humidity force even the most energetic to seek shelter from the midday sun, and where the incentive to find others to do hard work labor accounts for the concentrations of wealth and ultimately explains the rise of slave society, a form of economic and social organisations incompatible with economic growth. As the author puts it with characteristics bluntness, "Where society is divided between privileged few land owners and a large mass of poor, dependent, perhaps un-free labourers – in effect, between a school of laziness (or self-indulgence) over against a sloughs of despond – what is the incentive to change and improve?" Europe's cold winters suppressed pathogens and rendered parasitism the exception, increasing the capacity of its native for work. The continent enjoyed just the right amount of rainfall, between the extremes of desert, where crops dried of thirst and topsoil eroded away, and the torrents of the tropics, where the jungle and rain forest crowded out settled agriculture.

All else followed from this favourable climate. The agriculture revolution followed in the seventeenth and eighteenth centuries, raising living standards, generating an investable surplus, and freeing labour for employment in industry. A state with capacity to fend off invaders followed, since the control of the river valleys that fed food supplies was vital to survival. The favourable climate sustained growth.

Lnades, saw technological change and capital accumulation as a powerful engines of economic growth sweeping aside all in their paths. Landes on the long-run viability of capitalism and offered a rather mechanistic rendition of the economic growth process, posting that less developed economy sees in the more advanced economy an image of the future.

26 **GEOGRAPHY AND NATIONAL POWER**

Geography,

Location, Napoleon said, *"Foreign Policy of a country is determined by its geography"*. Thus geography provides stable elements of national power in any state.

Neighbours. The immediate neighbours also determine the power and status of the nation.

Size, Shape, Climate, Fertility.

Population—Large number, Age composition, Occupation, Literacy

Resources—Natural, Food, Mineral, Technology.

Organisation, Leadership, National Character, Morale, Ideology and Diplomacy.

27. The popular view that India lacked political unity ignores the vastness of its area and natural barriers that tend to separate its different regions. When we deplore political disunity in India we really view it on the footing of comparatively small kingdoms like Egypt, Iran or a state in mediaeval or modern Europe.
28. Singh, Colonel Narendar, "India's Maritime Strategy', *Free Press,* Vol. XV, No. 142, November 26, 1997.
29. Only one Indian power, the Chola's, attempted such bold enterprise after having acquired possession of almost of the length of the eastern seaboard.
30. It may be noted as a typical example that the Indians opponents of Babur at the First Battle of Panipat were ignorant of the firearms which latter used for such deadly effect.

    The charge of compact and well-disciplined cavalry force, held in reserve, has often proved decisive against the mass of the elephants and infantry of the Indians. Yet, Indians have never learnt the value of cavalry or the strategic importance of reserve force.
31. Constituent Assembly Debates, Vol. 2, Part II, 8 March 1949.
32. Bercher, Micheal (1963) *'The New States of Asia',* (London: Oxford), p. 95.

    Micheal Bercher has pointed out six characteristics in order to delineate any regional system. These are:

(a) Its scope is limited with primary stress on a geographical region;
(b) There are at least three actors;
(c) Taken together, they are objectively recognized by the other as constituting a distinctive community, region or segment in global system;
(d) The units of power relatively inferior to units in dominant system using a sliding scale of power in both: and
(e) Change in the determinant system is greater in the subordinate system than the reverse.

33. Weiss, Stanley A. (2008) "India, the Incredible and the Vulnerable", *International Herald Tribune*, April 23, 2008.
34. Set up in 1893 as the border between British-led India and Afghanistan, the Durand Line had been despised and rejected by Afghanistan for long as a colonial imposition.

5

INDIA AND THE GREAT POWERS

Modi understood ***power is the currency of international/world politics***. Great powers— the main actors—pay careful attention to how much economic and military power they have, relative to each other. It is important not only to have substantial amount of power, but also to make sure that no other state sharply shifts the balance of power in its favour. Traditionally, great powers have played a dominant role in shaping international society. That role can be either responsible or predatory; Classical History was confined to three distinct areas —China, India and the Mesopotamia, with little awareness of events in the rest of the world viz. Greece, etc. In the Middle Ages, the policy of the European Powers was conducted in isolation from that of Asian Empires. With modern technologies, and in the face of the contemporary intellectual ferment, there is no longer any isolated area; any diplomatic or military move involves worldwide consequences. History indicates that a prominent power cannot long maintain its global leadership without the support and the cooperation of other nations in the pursuit of mutual interests.

> Since the dawn of civilisation, India has been blessed with a global vision, inspired by the age-old wisdom of the familiar dictum *Vasudhaiva Kutumbakam* ("The world is a family").

Apart from the always-vocal press and New Delhi's lively think-tanks, India and its leaders show little interest in military or strategic issues. Strategic defence reviews like those that take place in America, Britain and France, informed by serving officers and civil servants but led by politicians, are unknown in India. The armed forces regard the Ministry of Defence as woefully ignorant on military matters; with few of the skills needed to provide support in areas such as logistics and procurement (they also resent its control over senior promotions). Civil servants pass through the ministry rather than making careers there. The Ministry of External Affairs, which should be crucial to informing the country's strategic vision, is puny. Singapore, with a population of five million, has a foreign service about the same size as India's. China's is eight times larger. Hence, there is a deficiency with regard to security around India.

"India's grand strategy divides the world into three concentric circles. In the first, which encompasses the immediate neighbourhood, India has sought primacy and a veto over actions of outside powers in immediate neighbourhood. In the second, concentric circle encompasses the so-called extended neighbourhood stretching across Asia and the India Ocean littoral, India has sought to balance the influence of other powers and prevent them from undercutting her interests. In the third, which includes the entire global stage, India has tried to take its place as one of the great powers, a key player in international peace and security."[1]

At the eve of Indian Independence in 1947, World War II had just ended, and the new bi-polar world with all the play of Cold War just setting in. World was divided into two military blocs; on one side led by United States were the Western Powers (the United Kingdom, Germany, etc.), and other camp led by the Union of Soviet Socialist Republic (USSR) and its Warsaw Pact allies—also known as the Communist Bloc Countries. United States was, at the time, the champion of democratic way of life and was pursuing the policy of 'containment' of the Communism, by entering series of Military Agreements and establishment of blocs like North Atlantic Treaty Organisation, Central Treaty Organisation (original name Middle East Treaty Organisations), South East Asia Treaty Organisation (SEATO), Australia, New Zealand and United States (ANZUS).

Hence, one of the dominant realities of the 65 years of Indian independence has been the competition between the great powers of the day for global hegemony. The two World Wars were hegemonic conflicts with the combatants vying for political and military dominance. But in the post-1945 epoch of struggle for hegemony was expressed as a Cold War between the two rivals, whose power capabilities completely outweighed those of any other state, or even coalition of states. Super Power rivalry imposed its own logic on global politics, as Waltz[2] observed:

> 'In a bi-polar world, there are no peripheries. With only two powers capable of acting on a world scale, anything that happens anywhere is potentially of concern to both of them. Bi-polarity extends the geographic scope of both super powers concerned. It also brackets the range of factors included in the competition between them'.

In fact, Waltz suggested that super power rivalry transformed the globe into a single strategic arena. In the process, time and space have collapsed. Super Power rivalry has, therefore, been one of the most significant factors in the globalisation of politics of the post-Cold War period.

An examination of the history of the Indian engagement of Great Powers since Indian independence shows that there were three major occasions when the relationship might have developed along more positive lines. These were, first, in the period immediately after Independence; the second was in the aftermath of the Indo-China War of 1962; and the last was after the end of the Cold War and the dissolution of the Union of Soviet Socialist Republic (USSR).

THE FIRST PHASE: POST-INDEPENDENCE

India's Policy: 1947-54

The first phase commenced immediately on India achieving its independence. On the eve of Independence, India did try and offer everything that United States wanted. Nehru's first visit to a superpower was to the United States—as far back as in 1949. It was, in fact, the Pakistani Prime Minister who was scheduled to visit the USSR in 1949; the visit did not take place though. Nehru visited the USSR only in 1955, by which time American policies in South Asia were firmly locked down. And during his visit to the United States, Nehru did not lecture or hector any of his interlocutors but, instead, assured them that India would stand with the democracies in the event of war. This was more clearly spelt out by his trusted foreign policy aide, Sir GS Bajpai, who assured his American counterparts that he was speaking with the full authority of his Prime Minister. His remarks, made to Acting US Secretary of State Lovett in April 1948, deserve to be quoted in detail:

> "Sir Girja ... pointed out that two fundamental considerations prevented Indian adherence to the Soviet bloc. First, through its association with the British, unhappy as it had been in some aspects, India had acquired the ideals of democracy and individual liberty, which were held by the US and other nations of the West. Second, India can expect no effective assistance from the USSR in its primary objective of strengthening herself economically and militarily. In fact, the US is the only country which is in a position to aid India. ...Sir Girja stated that his remarks were being made with the full knowledge and authorisation of Prime Minister Nehru..."

However, America was by then moving towards containment of USSR. It is the policy of ***containment***[3] followed by United States that affected their stance in South Asia... An inter-agency study had come to the conclusion that America had only limited interest and stake in South Asia, and such interest as there was, lay in Pakistan. The assessment of the Joint Chiefs of Staff in their Memorandum of 24 March, 1949, reads as follows:

'It is widely understood that the United States is important to India. It is well less understood how important India is to the long-term interests of the United States. This importance derives from demographic considerations; from the growing importance of supporting and encouraging democracy, pluralism, secularism and preventing the spread of religious and ideological extremism, from considerations of regional security and global power balance: from the need to control international drug traffic and terrorism; from economic and trade considerations; and from issues related to the regional and global control and reduction of nuclear weapons'.

M. Granger Morgan, K. Subrahmanyam, K. Sunderji and Robert M. White, *The Washington Quarterly*

> "From the military point of view, the countries of South Asia, except Pakistan, have— under present and prospective conditions— little value to the United States. The Karachi-Lahore area in Pakistan may, under certain conditions, become of strategic importance. In spite of tremendous logistical difficulties, this area might be required as a base for air operations against central USSR, and as a staging area for forces engaged in the defence or recapture of Middle East oil areas."

The policy of ***containment*** followed by the United States also regulated their stance on the Kashmir question. The United States' stance on Kashmir is important because it was, by far, the most important issue facing India and Pakistan at this time; it was also the issue that dominated the conversation of both countries with the United States. Pakistan's foreign policy revolved round Kashmir. To a great extent, India's relations with other countries, especially the great powers, were also affected by the stand they took on the Kashmir dispute.[4] In 1948, shortly after India took the dispute to the United Nations for settlement under Chapter VI of the Charter, a discussion took place between American and British officials on the nature of the dispute. The American record of the conversation runs in part as follows:

> "The British representative, at first, attempted to minimise such an analogy by asserting that Kashmir was 'territory in dispute'. The US representatives agreed that Kashmir was a state about which a dispute had arisen between India and Pakistan, but stated that they found it difficult to deny the legal validity of Kashmir's accession to India. In the end, the British representatives agreed with the US point of view—that we had to proceed on the assumption for the time being at any rate India had legal jurisdiction over Kashmir."

By August 1949, Nehru was sufficiently tired of American badgering on the subject of Kashmir to admonish Ambassador Loy Henderson that *"he was tired of receiving moralistic advice from the US"*. Since this is a charge, the American leaders were later to level at Indian leaders; it is an indication of who went first. It is also true that the Indian leaders did not take the time to explain frankly and forcefully how pivotal this matter was to our overall foreign policy posture. In fact, all through the Indo-American relationship, this is a major failing perhaps on both sides, certainly on the Indian side, that they did not talk with sufficient candour.

However, by February 1950, that is, after the inter-agency discussion had focused on Pakistan as the country that presented some interest to them, this American position had changed; and the State Department was arguing against this very position. In an internal note, it was argued:

> "In the opinion of the Office of the Legal Adviser, execution of an Instrument of Accession by the Maharajah in October 1947 could not finally accomplish the accession of Kashmir to either Dominion in view of circumstances prevailing at that time..."

United States also supported Pakistan, because it perceived that Pakistan could lead a Muslim bloc to counter 'Hindu Imperialism', and to provide balance of power in Asia. India's policies were read to indicate 'national traits which in time, if not controlled, could make India Japan's successor in Asiatic imperialism'.

Worse was to come after the change of administration in United States in 1953. Whereas prior to this time, American military supplies were proceeding more or less even-handedly as between India and Pakistan, all this changed by 1954; America had undertaken to provide military assistance to Pakistan. The record shows that all sides declared that the assistance was meant for the fight against Communist aggression; in reality, Pakistan was arming against India. It was the United States leaning towards Pakistan that enabled the entry of the USSR into South Asian politics. For the first time in 1952, the Soviet delegate to the United Nations spoke about the Western designs over Kashmir. The Soviet Union expressed its support to the Constituent Assembly on the Kashmir issue, and criticised United Nations interference in the 'Affairs of Kashmir'. As a veto wielding permanent member of the United Nations Security Council, US and USSR contest effectively put an end to any realistic chances of a United Nations-brokered settlement of the issue.

Looking at the sequence of events described above, it is hard to escape the conclusion that this revision of the American position on the legality of the accession was a result of the conclusion drawn earlier that Pakistan was more important for America than India.

The USSR's entrance into the nuclear club in 1949 soon had a direct impact on its policy; it emboldened Stalin to support Kim Il-Sung's plan for a North Korean invasion of the South. As Evgueni Bajanov put it, when Stalin approved Kim's proposal, he "was now more confident of the Communist bloc's strength".[5]

India took keen interest in Korean War during 1947 to 1954. Pakistanis had also offered to the Americans that they would supply troops to the Korean War, but pleaded that until a Kashmir settlement was found, they were unable to spare any troops for the purpose. To the British, who were then setting up the Middle East Defence Organisation, the Pakistanis again offered to send troops—if they would help settle Kashmir, and address the Indian threat.

There were differences between United States and India about the policy and perception regarding issue pertaining to peninsular, regional and global issues. United States and India conducted themselves according to their respective perceptions. However, without exception, India voted for all the resolutions on Korea, including its first committee from September 1947 to December 1948. India supported the claim that the Korean issue could be discussed in the United Nations. Indian ambassador to the United Nations, Mr KPS Menon, played a key role as the chairman of United Nations Temporary Commission on Korea (UNTOCK). The commission was formed in 1948 to look at the political situation and possibility of general elections on the whole of the Korean peninsula. India supported Korea in her efforts to achieve full-fledged independence, and emphasised the importance of realising peaceful unification to the two Koreas—to the dislike of both, the United Sates and USSR.

Another issue of contention between United States and India was Japan. India played a limited role in the Allied Occupation of Japan from 1945 to 1952. Once India became independent, it expressed support for Japanese interests; its delegation at the Far Eastern Commission was sympathetic to Japanese concerns about rebuilding their nation, and to encouraging Japanese industry and finance. Justice Radha Binod Pal was the lone dissenting voice on the war crimes tribunal set-up to try Japanese war criminals, including Prime Minister Hideki Tojo. In 1949, the Indian delegation stopped pressing the question in the Commission regarding its share of reparations from Japan and proposed halting the reparations altogether— noting that the burden of making such payments told heavily on the living standards of the Japanese people.[6] India's interest in Japan's rapid economic recovery also found expression in other international forums. Further, India welcomed the relaxation of controls on Japan because of the flow of Japanese technical expertise to the rest of Asia.

As India emerged from the British rule, Prime Minister Jawarlahal Nehru quickly became the natural spokesman of the Third World (what we now call developing countries). His long association with decolonisation, his wide-ranging education and interests, and his skills as a politician and diplomat had brought him respect not only in the emerging Third World, but also far beyond. He was associated with an independence movement—the Indian National Congress—that continued to emphasise **non-violence, democracy** and **equality**, even after reaching formal independence of the country. Indeed, armed conflict played a much smaller role in India's independence struggle than civil disobedience and moral appeals.

> In short, it was American policies in South Asia that brought India and the USSR together. One thing which stood out very clearly that Great Powers intervened only to fulfill their national interests and not the states in dispute or contest.

This was the period in which three forces—Pakistan, the United Kingdom—United States and India—with Nehru's policies, built the expectation that India could be managed in a subsidiary type of state system. United States had made common cause with Pakistan. Collectively, United States and United Kingdom formed the framework that shaped the policy interactions amongst the external player's vis-à-vis India. This system had geographical limits (the India-Pakistan-Kashmir land theatre). It had the policy boundaries that centered on no general war policy of India towards Pakistan and UK-US policy via the United Nations to secure Indo-Pakistan ceasefire if war broke out. *The operative norm of the United States—the Great Power—was to maintain a situation of manageable instability in the region, and preventing any uncontrolled military escalation.* The Great Powers policy parameters avoided any meaningful measures that facilitated conflict resolution, other than put pressure on India to give concessions to Pakistan on the Kashmir issue. **The Great Powers during this period institutionalised conflict in the Indian sub-continent because well-defined policy boundaries existed and suited their interests.**

Two important conclusions may be drawn on Great Powers' influence on security issues at this stage:

(a) The first is the great importance and sensitivity of the Kashmir issue for India. The Indo-US relationship has been a difficult one because of differences in strategic outlook and interests as well as Indo-Pakistani dispute over Kashmir.[7] It appears that American policymakers did not grasp this reality.

(b) The second is that the USSR entered this issue much after the American policymakers had set course for a pro-Pakistan stance. In later years, i.e., in the late 1950s, senior Soviet officials were to tell their Pakistani counterparts that they took the stance on Kashmir and, by extension, on South Asia—only after Pakistan joined the anti-Soviet pacts, and started receiving United States military aid.

In short, it was American policies in South Asia that brought India and the USSR together. One thing which stood out very clearly was that Great Powers intervened only to fulfill their national interests—not the states in dispute or contest.

India's Policy: 1954-62

Defence Minister Fernandes famously asserted, "*China is potential threat number one ... China is and is likely to remain the primary security challenge to India in the medium and long-term ... the potential threat from China is greater than that from Pakistan and any person who is concerned about India's security must agree with that.*"[1]

[1]'Beijing No. 1 Threat Says India Official', *South China Morning Post* (4 May 1998); 'India's New Defense Chief Sees Chinese Military Threat', *New York Times* (5 May 1998).

It was in 1954 that China—the future Great Power—entered the scene in Indian Foreign Policy. The outlook of the People's Republic of China (PRC) on international relations was radically different than that of India. In the Chinese world order, China was, by all measures, the Middle Kingdom—at the center of the world, between heaven and earth, with the Mandate of Heaven bestowed upon the emperor and a superior military. China was surrounded by the inferior peoples of inner Asia (including those in Southeast Asia) who paid tribute, and the uncivilised barbarians beyond. Much like Chinese society, the Chinese world order was hierarchical, anti-egalitarian and closed to that part of the world that did not accept the concept of Sino-Centrism and the assumption of Chinese superiority. The system itself was manifested in a rather complex tribute system which, in essence, provided the framework for all the international relations in Asia. This system continued without challenge in Asia for centuries, until it was confronted by Europeans. With the arrival of Europeans, the tributary system gave way to the Guangzhou (Canton) trade—a short-lived compromise between the two world systems. The actual transition of China from the tribute system to a treaty system began with the Opium Wars, and ended in the first decade of the 20th century with the fall of the Ch'ing Dynasty.

The Chinese Communist Party (CCP) had won a brutal civil war that lasted on and off from 1927 to 1949. The party's supreme leader, Chairman Mao Zedong, summarised himself at the CCP's claim to power as early as 1938: "**Political power grows out of the barrel of a gun.**"[8] From the late 1940s to the early 1960s, Mao came to claim that the role of leading the Third World would naturally fall to China. In 1946, he argued that the world was divided into two hostile camps—the United States and the Soviet Union—"separated by a vast zone which includes many capitalist, colonial and semi-colonial countries in Europe, Asia and Africa."[9] But by the fall of 1962, he explicitly called for China to lead the Third World against Soviet and American hegemony.[10] Culture and ideology both supported this far-reaching claim. During the last millennium of imperial rule, Chinese monarchs had always asserted the centrality of the Middle Kingdom to the world. In 1962, Mao took up this idea when he called for Chinese leadership of the

Third World. ***Yet, in the late 1940s and the 1950s, Mao's China commanded only a fraction of the international respect enjoyed by Nehru's India.***

The pre-1949 experiences were cast in triangular terms, for example, in the interactions between Manchu China, Tibet and British India—and at times, between China, Tibet and Russia. Beijing's leaders also understood the importance of strategic triangles from their internal civil war that brought them over. They dealt with the US-Kuomintang-communist triangle during the civil war in the 1940s and the KMT-Japan-Chinese communist triangle in the 1930s. Communist China's ideology and diplomacy recognises that it cannot pursue its interests unaided. Mao said: "China's strength alone will not be sufficient, and we shall also have to rely on the support of the international forces (Great Powers), otherwise we shall not be able to win; this adds to China's tasks in international propaganda and diplomacy."[11]

IMPORTANCE OF TIBET FOR INDIA

Sir Charles Bell's Book "Tibet Past and Present" written in 1924 which still sums up admirably the essence of British Indian policy in this country, how apt it is even today. It runs as follows:

> "We want Tibet as a buffer to India on the north. Now there are buffers and buffers; and some of them are of very little use. But Tibet is ideal in this respect. With the large desolate area of the Northern plains controlled by the Lhasa Government, central and southern Tibet government by the same authority, and the Himalayan border States guided by, or in close alliance with, the Indian Government, Tibet forms a barrier equal, or superior, to anything that the world can show elsewhere."

Zhou Enlai pointed out the character of Chinese diplomacy. He made three points:[12]

(a) Does diplomacy refer to relations between countries or between peoples? Should we approach states or people? We must unite with the people of all countries—not only fraternal countries but also former colonial, semi-colonial countries and capitalist countries. *But the function of diplomacy is to deal with relations between states.*

(b) There are two kinds of friendly countries: (i) those that will be friendly more or less constantly; and (ii) those that are friendly just for the time being. Even these differ from each other. Some are our friends for a short time, while others remain so for a relatively long period.

(c) We should be flexible in our diplomatic work—relying on the progressives, uniting with the middle-of-the-road forces and splitting the diehards. In this way, we will open up new prospects for diplomatic work. It is wrong to think that the world is simply divided into two conflicting camps, and that there is nothing we can do to improve it.

Apart from radically different positions in international affairs, the two countries (China and India) faced a difficult territorial issue—Tibet. Tibet, situated on a high plateau between China proper and India, had long political ties to the former and cultural ties to the latter... In late 1949, the newly established Communist government had announced its plans to "liberate" Tibet; although it assured India that it had no plans to use force. But after a short military campaign in October 1950 which occurred in the shadow of the Korean War, Tibetan armed resistance collapsed. In order to gain the appearance of legitimacy, Beijing did not occupy Tibet at once, but offered "negotiations". Under Chinese pressure and clumsy in its own diplomacy, a Tibetan delegation signed the so-called 17-Point Agreement on May 23, 1951—which established Chinese sovereignty over Tibet.

> China's long-term geopolitical goals make seasoned diplomats twitch. Bill Emmott confirms that there is a very serious concern in the United States and Europe about the long-term aims of China. "The Chinese strongly believe that they have a Manifest Destiny to be the superpower of the world," Emmott said, adding that other nations see this belief as a danger signal. Even more worrisome is Emmott s assessment that the Chinese government would be willing to go to any extent to achieve this destiny, as they have done in invading Tibet, taking their uncompromising stand on reclaiming Hong Kong, and saber-rattling over their designs on Taiwan.[1]
>
> [1]Emmott, Bill (2008), *Rivals: How the Power Struggle Between China, India, and Japan Will Shape Our Next Decade* (Barnes and Nobel).

On April 29, 1954, Beijing and Delhi signed the "Agreement between India and China on Trade and Intercourse between Tibet Region of China and India".[13] It sanctified Chinese control of Tibet, the withdrawal of Indian troops from it, and the handing over of Indian postal and governmental infrastructure there.[14] The two sides, however, failed to agree on the precise demarcation of the Tibetan-Indian border. In the wake of the agreement on Tibet, during a visit by Chinese Premier Zhou to Delhi in late June 1954, the two sides also signed the joint statement on the five principles of peaceful coexistence (*Panch Sheel*), which included respect for territorial integrity and sovereignty, non-aggression, non-interference in internal affairs, equality and mutual benefit, and peaceful coexistence.[15] For the Chinese side, the agreement on Tibet marked a major step towards establishing firm control in Tibet.

In the absence of Chinese documentation, it is difficult to judge how Beijing valued the two agreements it had concluded with Delhi in 1954. Certainly, the

Indian renunciation of its claims in Tibet and *Panch Sheel* must have increased the Chinese feeling of having exclusive powers there, and of increased security, respectively. Yet, Beijing looked at the agreements probably also in instrumental terms. While India renounced its rights to Tibet, in particular, and committed itself to non-interference in the People's Republic of China, in general, the Chinese Communist Party continued to support the Communist Party of India for years.[16] Even Mao realised the obvious contradiction between the five principles of peaceful co-existence and clandestine Chinese support for communist parties in countries outside of the socialist camp. At the 1957 Moscow Meeting, the Chairman seemingly solved this dilemma by arguing that "support for the communist party's not holding power" with the aim of furthering the "inevitable course" of world revolution was not governed by principles of peaceful co-existence.[17]

According to the 17 Point Sino-Tibetan Agreement, China has given assurance to respect the autonomy of Tibet by various commitments. But the 1951 to 1959 era witnessed the gradual systematic breaking of major assurance contained in the Sino-Tibetan agreement, which ultimately resulted in open clashes between the Tibetans and the Chinese.[18]

Indian politicians and observers in 1954, in retrospect, chided Nehru for the agreement with China that curtailed Indian claims and rights in Tibet.[19] Yet, the Indian Prime Minister himself had thought at length about the complexities of the Tibetan issue and the possibility of Chinese foul play—which his writings from mid-June of 1954 testify. Obviously, he had come to some distressing conclusions, not only about Chinese intentions, but also about Indian impotence. While he asserted that "the Tibetans have our sympathy," he also called for "a realistic understanding of the situation and of our policy." He dismissed a strong Indian stand on the Tibet issue, since a "policy of encouraging the Tibetans to oppose Chinese vis-à-vis lordship over Tibet would be raising false hopes in the Tibetans which we cannot fulfil[l]". In fact, he was highly critical of the political institutions there, which he called "backward and feudal":

> Changes are bound to come there to the disadvantage of the small ruling class and the big monasteries. ...I can very well understand these feudal chiefs being annoyed with the new [Chinese] order. We can hardly stand up as defenders of feudalism.

Nehru's hands-off policy toward Tibet did not turn out to be a viable approach toward the subsequent developments north of the Himalayas. He quickly found himself in the quicksand of Sino-Tibetan relations. The deteriorating situation in Tibet naturally had a negative impact on Sino-Indian relations. In a circular of June to high-raking government officials, Nehru wrote that he was not concerned about the ideological disagreements among "Marxists" but about the way in which the Soviet Union and China are acting towards other countries:

> "[It] ...can only be interpreted as interference in the affairs of Yugoslavia. This is particularly strange for China to do. ... For the Chinese People's Government to interfere this way and in language of violence seems to me to be wholly without justification. ...Where do the Five Principles or the Panch Shila (Panch Sheel) come into the picture? In these principles, it is said specifically that there will be no internal interference, even ideological. What the Chinese Communist Party is doing with regard to Yugoslavia is clearly ideological interference and, in fact, something more than that. Therefore, the Five Principles have gone by the board. If the Soviet Union and China can do this with regard to Yugoslavia, there is no particular reason to imagine that they cannot or will not do so in the case of India."[20]

The ideological radicalisation in China, which Nehru hinted at in this circular, had already started the year before. Mao set out to plan and eventually to launch radical economic policies—the Great Leap Forward—which constituted a direct challenge to Soviet leadership in the communist world. This included both, a stress on Chinese national greatness—the creation of a siege mentality against alleged foreign aggression—and the militarisation of society and economy. In this context, it was no wonder that Chinese foreign policy radicalised, not only in general but also towards the ideologically more liberal Yugoslavia.[21]

What did this mean for India and her relationship to the PRC? At the time, the two were discussing unresolved border issues in the Himalayas. Nehru thus concluded his observations in the June circular:

> It seems to me that whatever the internal reasons might be in China, the attitude of the Chinese Government has stiffened somewhat even with regard to India. I am thinking of the long discussions about our frontier with Tibet. ... All this signifies that we have to be particularly careful in the future in what we say and do with regard to China specially.[22]

Indeed, in the spring, the PRC had published maps in which it claimed territories which India considered its own. The problem consisted in the lack of an agreed line of demarcation at the eastern sector between Burma and Bhutan, and at the Western sector between Nepal and Pakistan. In the East, the so-called McMahon line—named after a British colonial official Henry McMahon—from 1914 followed (roughly) the Himalayan crest line, but often crossed back and forth on both sides. Yet, neither China nor India had ever recognised it as a legal border. The territory between the McMahon line and the Himalayan foothills to the south was administered by India through the North East Frontier Agency (NEFA). The agency's temporary character suggests that India itself was not totally certain about its own claim to that territory. In the West, both sides claimed a triangular territory—Aksai Chin—which China controlled, and through which it had built a strategic road from Xinjiang to Tibet in the 1950s. Despite his knowledge about the disputed territorial situation, Nehru had dropped the issue of border demarcation in both sectors during his negotiations on *Panch Sheel* with Zhou in 1954.[23]

In December 1955, Khrushchev visited Srinagar and declared that Kashmir was an integral part of India and, in a pointed rebuttal of the Pakistani demand for self-determination, added that the people had already exercised their right of self-determination.

In March 1956, Khrushchev sent his aide, Anastas Mikoyan, to New Delhi. Having stopped in Pakistan enroute, Mikoyan in New Delhi warned Nehru that the Pakistani government intended to use the pacts in its dispute with India about Kashmir. Mikoyan assured Nehru of Soviet support. Nehru described his country's relations with Pakistan as "somewhat peculiar", and then volunteered a detailed account of his recent confidential talks about the pacts with the American and British leaders. He repeated his mantra that "the proper policy was to cultivate friendly relations with all countries," before joining Mikoyan in confidently—and correctly—predicting that both pacts would soon collapse anyway.[24]

The revolt in Eastern Tibet did not abate. By early 1957, the Chinese People's Liberation Army (PLA) controlled only the cities while the insurgents dominated the mountains. The unrest was a sign that China's minority policy towards Tibet had failed. In a misperception of political realities, Beijing even urged the Dalai Lama to use his authority to end the revolt. As Lhasa lacked any influence over the insurgents, the situation quickly spun out of control. Between mid-1958 and March 1959, neither Beijing nor Lhasa had much influence over vast parts of Tibet. Given the sudden prospect of an all-Tibetan uprising against Beijing's rule, the Guomindang and agents of the US Central Intelligence Agency perceived an opportunity to destabilise the PRC, and started to support the East Tibetan insurgents with logistics and weapons from bases in northern India.[25]

In a letter to Zhou in December 1958, Nehru referred to the new Chinese maps, pointing out that the two had discussed the border as late as 1956, and had agreed to respect the McMahon Line in the Eastern sector for the time being—although they both considered it a legacy of British imperialism. In a harsh reply on January 23, 1959, Zhou rejected Nehru's portrayal of the border situation, and denied that there was any implicit border agreement at all.[26]

Even before his flight to India, the Dalai Lama wrote a letter on March 26 to Nehru, explaining the crisis in his country that had occurred since March 10 and announcing his departure from his country to India.[27] First personal contacts between his officials and India representatives occurred on April 3 in India itself.[28] On April 5, Nehru received the Dalai Lama's letter and replied within 24 hours welcoming him.[29] A week later, Nehru decided to provide the Dalai Lama and his entourage of "120" with "suitable accommodation," but excluded armed

Tibetans from "seeking asylum".[30] On the 14th, India allowed the Dalai Lama to make a short and pre-approved statement without giving details on the situation in Tibet and his flight to India.[31] By late April, the Indian government had decided to keep the Dalai Lama's presence in India and its own relationship with him on a low level.[32] Obviously, India was willing to provide asylum but prevent Tibetan exiles from using Indian territory for political activities that might damage Sino-Indian relations.

In the second half of April, Mao, however, gave up his self-professed "restraint" toward Nehru's alleged anti-Chinese attitude,[33] and ordered the publication of propaganda on the Prime Minister's supposed role in the Tibetan uprising and his alleged cooperation with the British imperialists.[34] In his ideologically distorted world of contradictions, Mao still emphasised his desire for a "struggle for unity" with India, and saw the polemics he was launching as an "effort to safeguard Sino-Indian friendship."[35] The idea was to prove Nehru's alleged mistakes in India's relationship with the PRC, and magnanimously offering him forgiveness if he accepted Chinese positions with regard to the latest events in Tibet. Ultimately, Mao required from Nehru self-humiliation in the eyes of world public opinion, particularly in the Afro-Asian world. And so, he tried to paint Nehru as a traitor of the just aspirations of the Indian people, and placed him on par with those counter-revolutionaries who had led the Hungarian uprising against Soviet rule in 1956.[36] In this context, he accused India of resuming British expansionist policies towards Tibet.[37]

As India was a British-style deliberative democracy, the Chinese embassy in Delhi followed the public parliamentary debates in which Nehru had to (sometimes) deal with hostile and heated questions.[38] The very fact that the Dalai Lama, with his entourage, lived in Indian exile offered the Chinese embassy in Delhi a sufficient opportunity to link Nehru's government with the "Tibetan counter-revolutionaries".[39]

But on April 25, 1959, at a time when Mao determined to exert greater political pressure on Nehru, he also decided to subject the Sino-Indian borders to a stricter regime in order to prevent "the rebellious elements ... [from] coming and going". Thereafter, the border problems became acute, particularly because Nehru had decided—10 days before—which factors would guide India's policy towards Tibet. They included (in the following sequence):

(a) Maintenance of national security;
(b) Maintenance of friendly relations with China, and
(c) Deep sympathy for the Tibetan people.

Consequently, when the first Chinese border patrols appeared in the Himalayas, Nehru responded by implementing a military forward policy to assert

India's sovereignty.[40] Once both Beijing and New Delhi had sent their troops to the contentious Himalayan border, the open territorial questions returned with a vengeance. But Chinese troops stopped their advance roughly at the Himalayan crest line, which the Peoples Republic of China had observed since the early 1950s as the *de facto* border.[41]

The military conflict at the Sino-Indian border was an extension of the Tibet Question. With both sides sending troops to the non-demarcated border, the chances for violent clashes increased. When Indian troops arrived at the villages of Khinzemane and Longju in the eastern sector, the McMahon Line—or what they believed it to be—did not follow any natural and geographical features. New Delhi's agents decided to correct the situation on the spot by pushing the line of control a little bit towards Beijing's sentry posts. The Chinese troops replied with fire on August 7 at Khinzemane, and on August 25 at Longju. The second volley of shots started the Sino-Indian border conflict.[42]

The collapse of Sino-Indian friendship was a major blow to Sino-Soviet relations. The outbreak of the border conflict caught the Soviets during their painstaking preparations for Khrushchev's seminal visit to the United States. The Soviet leader recalled in his memoirs that Mao "started the [border] war out of some sick fantasy", with the mistaken idea that he could "dictate to the Soviet Union a foreign policy which contradicted the correct Marxist-Leninist position we held at the time".[43] These *a posteriori* quotes captured well the contemporaneous Soviet view that the start of the Sino-Indian border conflict was not an accidental event, but that the Chinese side deliberately tried to sabotage the Soviet policy of peaceful co-existence towards both, India and the United States.[44]

Despite being accused by China of collusion with the other great powers, Nehru sought support from both, the United States and the Soviet Union. During a visit to India in December, US President Dwight D. Eisenhower and Nehru discussed how to improve relations between India and Pakistan in the face of the Sino-Indian problems.[45] For the Chinese side, the visit was a welcome opportunity to mock the "peaceful attitude" of the imperialist Eisenhower's administration towards the world.[46]

America's containment policy, as implemented in South Asia, was to help India and Pakistan defend against external attack, to obtain bases and facilities from which the United States might strike the Soviet Union with its own forces, and to help both states meet the threat from internal (often communist-led) insurrection and subversion. Early American studies characterised India as the "pivotal" state of the region, and saw Pakistan as a likely place to base American long-range bombers as well as a potential ally in the tense Persian Gulf region.[47]

America also pursued Cold War objectives in South Asia on the domestic front. As the internal vulnerabilities of Pakistan and India became more evident (especially in light of the Comintern's 1949 call for revolutionary uprisings throughout the world), Washington mounted a variety of developmental, intelligence and information programs. The Indian communists were seen to be under the influence of the Soviet Union, and America provided huge amounts of surplus food, economic aid, and technical and agricultural missions in an effort to help India and Pakistan counter communist influence. Many of these programs assumed a correlation between poverty and susceptibility to communism: by encouraging economic growth (and redistributive policies, such as land reform) the communists could be beaten at their own game and democracy would have a chance, even in the poorest regions of India and Pakistan. Substantial information/propaganda campaigns were also developed, balancing the much larger Soviet operations. Although this ideological Cold War peaked in the 1950s and 1960s, Washington was still vigorously countering Soviet disinformation programs in the mid-1980s.

While Pakistan had become a useful ally in 1954, India was the main prize, and several American administrations believed that the most significant contest in Asia was that between communist China and Democratic India. Echoing Leninist logic (that the vulnerability of the metropolitan country lay in its colonies), India was seen by some as a key battleground in the Cold War.[48] The extreme form of this argument was expounded by Walt W. Rostow who justified the American intervention in Vietnam because if Communist aggression succeeded then India, the most important of all of the dominos, would ultimately fall to communism.[49] (It came as something of a surprise to Indian diplomats to learn from Rostow that their country was the reason why had intervened in Southeast Asia). John Foster Dulles once referred to Indian "neutrality" in the Cold War as immoral. Yet, he and other American officials eventually came to see Nehru's non-alignment as less and less problematic. Indians were very difficult to get along with. Not unlike Dulles, they were moralistic and preachy, but Delhi's influence in the non-aligned movement was an important fact of life and American critics concluded that as long as India was not an enemy, it need not be an ally. By the time of the "second" Cold War, 1980-89, Washington did not try to punish India for its close relationship with the Soviet Union, but sought an opening to New Delhi in the hope of luring it away from the Soviets and protecting Pakistan's southern flank. By this time, India was no longer a strategic prize to be courted and cultivated; it was seen as a state that had, at best, nuisance value, not in the same economic or strategic league as the other two major Asian powers, China and Japan.

While Indians had practical and conceptual difficulties with America's approach during the Cold War. The most persistent and important objection to

American policy stemmed from the military aspects of American alliance policy. This was objectionable on every ground. It seemed to establish a strategic and moral equivalence between India and Pakistan (at least in American eyes) that was not justified by the objective military, economic, and strategic capabilities of the two states, or India's stature as a free state with a liberal outlook. Indians resented this equivalence just as many Americans resented the way that non-aligned India seemed to equate the United States and the Soviet Union.

Further, by supporting Pakistan, New Delhi argued that America had forced India into an unnecessary and costly arms race.[50] The American arms program, agreed to in 1954, turned Pakistan into a lesser but still a significant military power. It enabled Pakistan to field an armored division equipped with first-line Patton M-48 tanks, to acquire a number of modern F-85 jet aircraft, and a small navy. The Pakistan military also received extensive training and technical support, including NATO briefings on nuclear war. These acquisitions, essentially completed by the end of 1959, made it unlikely that India could militarily dominate Pakistan.

Indians had other problems with the US-Pakistan relationship. American assistance gave Pakistan the means and the inspiration to challenge New Delhi. Air Marshal KD Chadha, a former Indian Air Force Chief expressed the Indian view of the relationship when he wrote that Pakistan's affiliation with the United States aroused "ambitions and delusions of grandeur" in Pakistan's power elite. Military officers exposed to American training and doctrines, "began to see themselves as invincible superior beings. They held the Indian Military Forces .... in derisive contempt. Arrogant, flamboyant and impregnated with American doctrinal proclivities, they were more than convinced that militarily India was a push-over." When coupled with the predominant view (in Pakistan) that one Pakistani soldier was the match for eight, or ten Indians, the Americans had made it even less likely that Pakistan would come to a settlement of Kashmir, and more likely that they might pursue a military solution to the dispute, or use force to pressure India into dangerous concessions.

Further, India attributed the distortion of Pakistan's politics to the American connection after the Army took power in Ayub Khan's 1958 coup. Delhi was concerned that the American-encouraged militarisation of Pakistan might spread to India itself. This was an additional reason to restrict the ties between Indian officers and their Pakistani counterparts, and between the Indian and the United States military establishments. Lastly, the Pakistan-US relationship came to be seen in Delhi as not directed against communism, but against India. Formally, the only American commitment to Pakistan was to consult, should the latter be faced with "communist" aggression.

Irrespective of what had been happening at the border, the shift in Chinese policy did not occur until Mao reasserted his authority at a secretive party conference at Beidaihe in August 1962. By endorsing Mao's view that "class struggle is fiercely under way in the international arena," the conference gave him a green light to demonstrate that his revolutionary strategy in foreign policy was superior to Soviet strategy. The expanding Indian probes offered him the opportunity to use India as a testing ground. On 6 October he decided to respond to another, widely expected Indian probe by resorting to military force, even while conceding to his intimates that "a war between China and India is truly a most unfortunate event".

In the fall of 1962 at the Sixth All-Country Foreign Affairs Conference, Mao stipulated a PRC foreign policy premised upon the dissemination of 'Mao Zedong Thought' overseas and support for national liberation movements across the Afro-Asian-Latin American world.[51]

THE SECOND PHASE: POST INDO-CHINA WAR 1962

India's Policy: 1962-65

The next phase opened after the Indian defeat at the hands of the Chinese in 1962. Enough has been written about how it affected Nehru and his foreign policy, so there is no need to go over that ground one more time. What has not received adequate attention is the brief period November 1962 to about the end of 1965. The war started on 20 October and continued until 21 November 1962. During this period each of the great powers had sufficient time to define their positions–even their changing positions. In the initial period, the USSR was cautiously neutral, even tilting towards the Chinese. The Americans, under President Kennedy, were much more forthcoming. In the early weeks, though, both these countries were caught up in the Cuban Missile Crisis, and yet Kennedy was strongly supportive. The Americans offered all help to the Indian Army and went much further in terms of offering air defence cover, manned by American forces.

However, once the actual battle stopped, the Americans all but made further military assistance conditional on India's reaching a settlement with Pakistan. It is a measure of the Indian desire for American aid that the Indian leaders undertook some of the toughest negotiations on the subject of Kashmir. In response to very active shuttle diplomacy by Governor Harriman and Secretary Sandys, India offered significant territorial concessions to Pakistan, despite Pakistan's signing a border agreement with China in March 1963, when the talks with India were at a very sensitive stage. However, the Pakistanis were unwilling to settle for anything less than the entire Valley, all the way south to the Chenab, and the talks ended without result. By this time, American positions were beginning to assert themselves, and it did not help that they offered to both sides what were called the "elements" of a settlement, which, in essence, backed the Pakistani territorial demands.

The Soviets, by now were over the Cuban troubles, however, were entering into a long struggle with the Chinese, stepped in again and offered India the fighter aircraft it had asked for—with no conditions attached. Nevertheless, India did not make any long-term commitment to either side. It is too President Kennedy's credit that Americans came up with Military Aid Programme assistance for India, and the two countries signed an Air Defence Agreement—the first and only such understanding between India and America during the Cold War. This was not easy, since the Pakistanis and their supporters in the Administration, were all for holding aid to India hostage to a Kashmir settlement.

India became one big factor in bringing Pakistan and the People's Republic of China together in 1962.[52] Pakistan fitted neatly within Beijing's larger foreign policy trajectory at the time. The relationship thus implicated and alleviated China's India problem while also transcending this single issue. It is therefore, critical to consider the consolidation and meaning of Sino-Pakistani ties within the wider scope of Chinese foreign relations in the early 1960s.[53]

Mention here should be made of President Kennedy for his role in strengthening Indo-US ties. Alone among the Presidents during the Cold War period, he saw the virtue of a strategic accommodation with India, and over-ruled all opposition in order to build one. It is idle to speculate on what might have been, but it is certain that, had he lived, there is a good chance that Indo-US relations would have been qualitatively different.

Anyhow, Kennedy did not live long enough to fulfill the promise of the new relationship. And once he was gone, things began to move to their by-then traditional pattern. An observer would not have to wait long for the hint of change. As early as 30 November 1963, President Johnson was recorded as telling his aides that he was unhappy at the way President Ayub Khan was being treated, and wanted that changed.

Change was not that easy to bring about, since President Ayub, and more particularly, his Foreign Minister Bhutto, were moving ever closer to China–at that time a source of growing difficulties for America especially in Vietnam. As for India, it was facing problems with American arms supplies, and was increasingly finding the Soviets a more responsive supplier. Soviet Union was not only; not insisting on any political conditions, but it was also willing to supply front-line aircraft, and to transfer production facilities too.

China conducted a nuclear test in October 1964, and its entry into the nuclear club triggered a divisive nuclear debate in India; it showed polarities between the pro-bomb lobby, the nuclear disarmers and the fence sitters who oscillated between nuclear security versus economic development or between 'guns versus butter'. Nehru died in 1964.

The immediate challenge faced by Nehru's successor, Lal Bahadur Shastri, did not come from China but from Pakistan, with which India went to war in 1965. China however, "added straw to the fire" by demanding that India destroy its fortifications on the border and withdraw its troops from there. There significant change was in India's military behaviour. In 1965, Mr Lal Bahadur Shastri, Prime Minister of India ordered the Indian Army to cross the Pakistani international border to relieve Pakistan's Military pressure in Kashmir. This broke the Nehru-Mountbatten taboo against no general war with Pakistan, as it challenged the Pakistani-Western idea that Kashmir was a legitimate target for Pakistan and its allies because it was 'disputed territory'.[54]

The Indo-Pakistan War of 1965 was another milestone in the evolving strategic equations. America was neutral between the two countries, even though they recognised internally that Pakistan had started the war. Peoples Republic China was eager to shed its hostile image after the Sino-Indian Border War of 1962. However, the 1965 Indo-Pakistani war offered an opportunity to stand behind Pakistan a Third World ally in the face of aggression from an India backed by both superpowers It was the Pakistanis that initiated hostilities in April 1965, after they provoked armed conflict in the Rann of Kutch, President Ayub Khan was convinced that an indigenous Kashmiri uprising would follow, though none came. Shortly after the invasion, the Peoples Republic China offered rhetorical support. A May 1965 statement appearing through the *Xinhua* newswire condemned India's "great power chauvinism", which "disrupt[ed] Afro-Asian solidarity" by pitting Asians against Asians.[55]

> Diplomatic historians may mark the 1962 war as the beginning of India's slow ascent to great power status and a force to be reckoned with in 21st century Asian power politics. Yet, to this day, India's foreign policy is—more than most other emerging titans—constrained by a quest for internal security and a deep introspection-making it a reluctant power and conducting a more or less "introverted foreign policy".

The Chinese made two important diplomatic interventions during the war, the first on 8 September, the second, a more serious ultimatum, on 18 September. On each occasion, the Indian Government sought the help of the American and Soviet governments to advise the Chinese to stay out of the conflict. After the second warning of 18 September, which was an ultimatum to India to dismantle some alleged structures on the Sikkim border in 72 hours, India had sought consultations and contingency planning with America in the event of China making good on its threat. The Americans refused to enter into such consultations, but assured the Indians that they had conveyed their concerns at the Warsaw talks that were then going on between the American and Chinese Ambassadors. The Soviets did not enter into any consultations either, but received an Indian diplomatic and defence delegation, and assured the Indian side that they had presented a strong demarche in Beijing. By this time, the Soviet-Chinese differences were out in the open, and it was clear that the Soviets were ready to confront the Chinese over this issue. The Indian Prime Minister was later to convey his thanks to the Soviets for having prevented the Chinese from taking any action in support of Pakistan during the war.

Shastri's military initiative against Pakistan caused alarm in Pakistan because the action broke the Nehru taboo against the general war against Pakistan; and it replaced in doubt the widespread belief that Hindus were talkers and not movers in the strategic sphere. However, the experiments of the initiative were short lived because the result of the initiative was the time honoured method of great powers' sponsored Indo-Pakistan ceasefire through the United Nation; and the Indian Government reverted to the old pattern of responding to aggression at a time of the enemy's choice. **A philosophy of defence of India, and not deterrence, remained the dominant Indian norm.**

To prevent another "hotbed of war" from arising, Soviet Premier Aleksei Kosygin undertook mediation and succeeded in brokering the Treaty of Tashkent to restore the status quo under international supervision. The treaty, though motivated by the narrow goal of preempting Western mediation, stands out as the most constructive accomplishment in the history of Soviet-Indian relations. Having restored the status quo under international supervision, the pact brought the two neighbors closest ever to a settlement of their sterile Kashmir dispute, but not close enough.

Diplomatic historians may mark the 1962 war as the beginning of India's slow ascent to great power status and a force to be reckoned with in 21st century Asian power politics. Yet, to this day, India's foreign policy is–more than most other emerging titans–constrained by a quest for internal security and a deep introspection-making it a reluctant power and conducting a more or less "introverted foreign policy".

India's Policy: 1965-71

War occurred in 1965 because Pakistan was militarised by Ayub Khan's regime, Indian rearmament, and the missed opportunity by Pakistan to attack India in 1962.

The years of 1965-75 were the best decade in USSR history. Socially and politically it was time unparalleled stability. From the military point of view, these years marked key breakthrough-parity with Western adversaries and, for all practical purposes and for the first time in USSR's history security from attack from abroad. It was also a period of growing USSR awareness of its international position and seeming potential for ever greater influence. The alliance with India looked strong and stable.

For the United States, the late 1960s and early 1970s were a time of trial and doubt, both internationally and domestically. Internationally, American economic and political dominance was already past its peak. Most importantly, the United States was committed to an increasing costly war in Vietnam. On the domestic front it was plagued by the civil violence and unrest and the divisiveness and other negative consequences of the Vietnam War.[56]

At Tashkent, Premier Kosygin had pressured a reluctant—and ailing—Prime Minister Shastri of India into accepting the reestablishment of the 1949 cease-fire-line in Kashmir as part of the agreement, thus obligating the Indian Army to withdraw from several strategic positions in that state, which had been seized at considerable cost of life during the 1965 War.

> Mrs. Indira Gandhi privately criticised the Soviet Union but expressed understanding. "Why should they listen?" she conceded to an interviewer. **"No power listens when it is a matter of national interest."**

The 1966 Tashkent Agreement between India and Pakistan had substantial impact upon United States policy toward both India and Pakistan, primarily characterised by an effort by the United States to assume a lower profile in the region. The primacy of United States commitment to Vietnam in the 1965-75 decade did not permit major commitments elsewhere in Asia except where "vital' American interests were seen as involved. United States was piqued at the failure of both India and Pakistan to endorse its support of the integrity of non-communist regimes in Indo China, and the United States Government was not inclined to respond sympathetically to overtures for great economic and military assistance from either.[57]

Shastri died at Tashkant. He was succeeded by Indira Gandhi. Indira Gandhi entertained no illusions about the Soviet Union or any other country, convinced that they all "were guided only by their own interests and had no obligations to other countries which did not conform to those interests." She wanted to calibrate Soviet arms sales to India and Pakistan in order to prevent the Soviet Union from "taking over management of the subcontinent."

Gandhi privately criticised the Soviet action but expressed understanding. "Why should they listen?" she conceded to an interviewer. "No power listens when it is a matter of national interest."

By the time the 1970's started, two other major issues divided India and the

United States: the Non-Proliferation Treaty and China. These issues have been aired and discussed over the years, and there is little to add to what is already well-known.

The struggle for independence in the erstwhile East Pakistan (now Bangladesh) gathered momentum in 1971, the possibility of a war between New Delhi and Islamabad loomed large in Asia. Pakistani President Yahya Khan said, "If India made any attempt to seize any part of East Pakistan, he would declare war and Pakistan would not be alone." Pakistan, with the tacit support of the United States, was trying for the UN involvement in East Pakistan, which was regarded by India as "an unnecessary interference in the internal affairs" of another country. China gave unqualified support to her "all-weather" friend Pakistan against India so that New Delhi would not dare to interfere in the domestic affairs of Pakistan. During the July 1971 meeting between Henry Kissinger and Chou-En-lai, the Chinese prime minister had clearly indicated to the then US Secretary of State that in case of the Indo-Pakistan war over East Bengal, Beijing would launch military intervention against India on behalf of Islamabad. India was desperate to avert Chinese intervention.

While Kissinger's visit to Beijing was a morale booster for Pakistan, it had an enormously demoralising effect on India as it felt diplomatically humbled and strategically isolated. India could see a US-China-Pakistan axis emerging against its vital national as well as geopolitical interests. This was perhaps the most perilous moment for India's independence in the history of the country. In keeping with the spirit of the US-China discussions held in Beijing, Washington took serious steps in July-August of 1971 that strengthened India's fears and enhanced Pakistan's intransigence.

Indira finding herself isolated and under constant inflow of refugees from East Pakistan, followed the old principle of survival find partners. Soviet Union fitted well in her calculations and hence she entered inn to a treaty with Soviet Union.

Indo-Soviet Treaty of Friendship and Cooperation was the closest thing to a mutual defence pact between India and the Soviet Union. The treaty of 1971 was like a pact of mutual cooperation meant to thwart any threats to Indian security during the Bangladesh war, and India, in turn, assured support to Soviet interests by tilting slightly towards the USSR camp in the Cold War rivalry. The treaty more than served its purpose when the USSR prevented American Navy's 7th fleet from coming to Pakistan's help in the 1971 war. It will be apt to point out that the treaty of 1971 reflected strong relationship between India and Soviet Union in the prevailing chaos emanating from the cold war politics.

The most important aim, from the USSR's point of view, to sign this treaty was its ambition to become dominant global power and to contain Chinese influence in the region. The Indo Soviet treaty reflects one of the most important aspects of global objectives. According to Bharat Wariavwalla, a known commentator, "the Soviet decision to enter into treaty with India is an aspect of Soviet globalism. An integral part of this globalism is no doubt the Soviet effort to construct an Asia-wide anti-Chinese condition. The simple and compelling desire to acquire all the attributes of a global power, which means global presence and global influence, are perhaps just as important in the minds of the present Soviet leadership as their need to contain China."[58]

The reputation of United States as a "guarantor" of Pakistani security had also been seriously damaged by what Pakistanis interpreted as Washington's "pro India" policy in 1965 War. By 1971 United States lacked much clout in Rawalpindi, particularly on issues that, in West Pakistan's eyes, struck at the very basis of their national existence.[59]

In the annals of diplomacy, the Indo-Soviet Treaty on Peace, Friendship and Cooperation, signed in August 1971, is a unique document that not only epitomised the special relationship between India and the then USSR, but also acted as a guarantor of regional peace. The treaty may have been replaced by its modern version, but its legacy continues to underpin the burgeoning strategic partnership between India and Russia.

India's Policy: 1972-1991

War occurred in 1971 because of the militarisation of India's civilian elite, and a strategic and diplomatic window of opportunity to attack Pakistan created by civil disorder. Indian official and military circles were rankled due Soviet Pressure at Tashkent and it was one of the factors in India's decision in 1972 to reject the Soviet offer to mediate after the 1971 war. India preferred to settle these matters directly with Pakistan on bilateral basis–accomplished in the 1972 Shimla Agreement, which defined a new "line of control" for the old cease fire line in Kashmir and allowed India to retain several key posts captured during the 1971 war that had been restored to Pakistan in Tashkent Agreement.

After Bangladeshi Independence, China actually withdrew political support for the Pakistani position of self-determination for Kashmir and endorsed the Simla Agreement, signed in July 1972 by Indian Prime Minister Indira Gandhi and Pakistani President Zulfikar Ali Bhutto, binding the two countries 'to settle their differences by peaceful means through bilateral negotiations'. It also cemented the Line of Control as something close to a permanent border. The agreement has been the basis of all subsequent bilateral talks between India and Pakistan, and equally important of all Chinese official pronouncements on the conflict.

Until 1971 nonalignment had a dual effect on United States policies in South Asia. On the one hand, Washington considered Indian economic and political stability necessary to prevent that important regional player from succumbing to communism and Soviet influence; hence the United States gave economic assistance and support to India during its 1962 war with China. On the other hand, India's nonalignment had led the United States in 1954 to ally itself with Pakistan, which appeared to support Western security interests. The United States-Pakistan alliance was renewed in 1959, with accompanying assurances from President Dwight D. Eisenhower to Nehru that the arms supplied to Pakistan would not be used in any aggressive war. When Pakistan and India went to war in 1965, the United States government refused to support India and suspended military transfers to both countries.

In 1971 the intertwining of the United States-Soviet, Chinese-Soviet, and Indian-Pakistani conflicts dragged India-United States relations to the nadir. That year, while Washington initiated a new relationship with Beijing, New Delhi signed a friendship treaty with Moscow to counteract United States and Chinese influence in South Asia. As the situation in East Pakistan deteriorated, India was unable to convince the United States to cease arms deliveries to Pakistan and persuade Pakistan's leaders to reach a political settlement with East Pakistan's elected representatives. Indira Gandhi's November 1971 visit to Washington failed to alter President Richard M. Nixon's pro-Pakistan stance. When war formally began after Pakistani strikes on Indian airfields in early December 1971, the United States and China voted for a cease-fire in the UN Security Council, but the Soviet Union's veto prevented any resolution from coming into effect. Washington's subsequent deployment of a naval task force to the Bay of Bengal left many in India convinced that the United States was a major security threat.

The next providential statement by a top Chinese leader was Deng Xiaoping's in 1988 when he met with the young visiting Indian Prime Minister Rajiv Gandhi, the first top-level visit since the 1962 border war. Deng told Gandhi: "If there should be an Asian Age in the next Century, then it could only be realised after both India and China become developed economies". It took another 15 years before relations between the two countries really started improving and only after India had embarked on 'playing the US card'.

THE THIRD PHASE: POST-BREAK-UP OF THE SOVIET UNION

India's Policy: 1992-2004

The period was full of turbulence. The end of the Cold War transformed the political landscape of Europe; it did little to ameliorate India's security concern.[60] In Asia, the secondary Cold War struggles of the past have emerged on to center stage. The struggle between United States and China intensified. Struggle is also between Japan and United States. This pertains to the economic spheres but here there were undercurrent concerning future destiny of Japan in World Affairs. A third arena of struggle concerns United States and regional powers—Iran and North Korea. Iraq had been occupied. Although the cases differ, a common theme runs through them. United States Government's interests lay in disarming regional military powers, reducing their military and diplomatic independence and their ability to pursue their interests, reducing, if not eliminating, centers of power that could challenge United States authority in regional and international affairs.

JAPAN'S VIRTUAL NUCLEAR CAPABILITY

Japan's long standing plutonium programme, its new geo-political position, and several statements by political figures espousing nuclear weapons have combined to make this idea plausible. As one journalist stated:

> Japan remains the only non-nuclear weapon country that is operating uranium enrichment and reprocessing plants, technically capable of production [of] fissile materials for nuclear weapons. The magnitude of these projects exceeds those of other nations that have either abandoned or postponed similar program.... Japans capability to acquire nuclear weapons is entangled with Tokyo's enigmatic diplomacy. On the one hand, it complies with its obligation to the International Atomic Energy Agency, making financial contributions, being open to inspections, and crusading for a nuclear free world as the world's sole victim of nuclear weapon attacks. On the other hand, the number of remarks made by political figures alluding to Japans ambitions for developing nuclear weapons has increased in recent years.... For the development of a nuclear weapons program, both political will and the technology represented by the plutonium program are necessary. Of the two, Tokyo's political will holds the key to preventing nuclear proliferation in Japan, but the nuclear umbrella provided by the United States will have the strongest influence on Tokyo's decision making.

During this period Japan was undergoing a fundamental period of change to its strategic environment. There were unprecedented flurry of *vision* books by political leaders in Japan, each with its own distinctive catch phrase. Mr Morihiro Hosokawa, Prime Minister, from August 1993 to April 1994, for one, saw Japan as embarking on the *'third opening up'*, the first having begun with Commodore Perry's visit to Japan in 1853 and the second with Japanese surrender in 1945.[61] He stated that the current global conditions are forcing Japan to play greater international role and engage more with the outside world. In the view of Ichiro Ozawa, officially the then number two and in fact the most powerful man in the *Shinshinto* [New Frontier Party (NFP)], Japan will soon be a *'normal country'*.[62] By this, Mr Ichiro Ozawa meant that Japan will be able to send its armed forces overseas under the auspices of the United Nations just like any other country. Japan will be free of constraints of the out dated 1947 Japanese Constitution. Taking quite a different view, Masayoshi Takemura, Head of the *Shinto Sakigake* (The Harbinger Party) and later the Finance Minister, saw Japan as a *'shinning country'*, making a significant contribution to resolving the worlds environmental problems.[63] The late Mr Michio Watanbe, former Deputy Prime Minister and a powerful and prominent figure in the Liberal Democratic Party who died in September 1995, envisioned Japan as a country *'whose opinion will be listened to carefully in the global community'*.[64]

Mr Hashimoto in September 1995 repeatedly referred to Japan as **'a nation that can stand on its own feet'**.[65] Mr Hashimoto on being sworn in as the Prime Minister of Japan in his first policy address to the National Diet in 1996 set out four priorities:

(a) Rebuilding a resilient Japanese economy;
(b) Building a society for the elderly in which people can be glad to have lived so long;
(c) Effecting administrative and fiscal reforms; and, in the international arena; and
(d) Developing a proactive foreign policy for the furthering of peace and prosperity.

Aside from minor differences, all these visions conveyed the same message: *'Japan should shed its old image of a lowly merchant state and play a more positive and larger role in world affairs,*[66] *as is appropriate for a nation of its economic stature. This would also involve opening its markets to foreign products and companies'.* The national polity of Japan was moving in the direction to reform its political and economic system drastically. The important policy tasks facing Japan then was less to do with individual and corporate wealth and more to do with international security issues and with domestic economic reforms needed to deal with the enormous economic transformation going on in Asia.

The question of defence and security had come to be discussed somewhat more openly than in the days of Liberal Democratic Party's (LDP) one party rule. Japan was facing more uncertainty than during the Cold War with regard to Korean peninsula,[67] Russia and China.[68] On the international front the Russian military threat, which had been the tie that bound Japan with the United States Armed Forces together, has almost disappeared, at least for the time being? But there was a new concern in the region: **China.** China had increased its military budget in real terms by 40 percent during the period.[69] There are talks of rivalry between Japan and China.

As a result of the review of Japan's defence posture after the Cold War, the National Defence Programme Outline in an after FY 1996 was adopted in 1995 by the then coalition cabinet led by the Socialist Prime Minister, Mr Murayama It's notable features are:

(a) Japan will continue to rely for its security on the combination of its self-defence capability and the deterrent provided under the Japan-United States Security Treaty.
(b) Though the possibility of a global armed conflict has become remote, unpredictability and uncertainty persist in the areas surrounding Japan: reorganisation of the Self-Defence Forces to make them more rational, efficient and compact, as well as their qualitative improvements will be affected. This entails a reduction in the number of the Ground Self-Defence Forces personnel from 1,80,000 to 1,60,000 (1,45,000 Regular and 15,000 ready reserve), of Maritime Self-Defence Forces destroyers from 60 to 50, and of Air Self-Defence Forces aircraft from 350 to 300.
(c) It is spelled out that the roles of the Self-Defence Forces include those of responding to large scale disasters, responding to situations arising in the areas surrounding Japan that might have an important influence on Japan's national peace and security (e.g. the Korean Peninsula) and participating in international peace cooperation activities (United Nations Peace Keeping Operations).
(d) Japan holds the largest quantity of fissile material (approximately 500 metric tonnes). Fissile material with rocketry provides the virtual capability. This capability cannot be overlooked by any strategic analyst.[70]

Given its adverse security environment in the early 1990s, India's pursuit of nuclear weapons as a deterrent against Chinese and Pakistani adventurism would have appeared not only wise but necessary, particularly when considered in conjunction with the relatively low costs of a nuclear programme, a multilateral order that threatened to recognise China's nuclear status in perpetuity while denying India entry, and an enabling domestic political environment. India carried out nuclear explosions in 1998, at the same time Pakistan carried out nuclear explosions.

This crumbled the strategic scheme of the US and, therefore, caused a wild response from Washington. As such, the Indian blasts suddenly punctured the burgeoning economic and security ties between India and the US. President Bill Clinton found the nuclear tests by India an affront to the US efforts to prevent nuclear proliferation. He stated that he was "deeply disturbed by the nuclear tests" and added that this action by India not only threatened the stability of the region, but also directly challenged the firm international consensus to stop the proliferation of weapons of mass destruction."[71]

But what has piqued Japan most is India declaring herself a nuclear weapon state. **Japan had signed the extension of Nuclear Non-Proliferation Treaty and the Comprehensive Test Ban Treaty only on the condition that no new nuclear weapon state would be added to the known five.** Japan had threatened to withdraw if any new nuclear weapon states are added. It is here that the clash occurs between the Japanese government and public opinion at home.[72]

With almost uncanny predictability Japan's reaction to India's nuclear test have been violently critical. Japan joined China and the United States in an anti-India rhetoric. Japan became one of the biggest critics of India. Japan was critical of India while supporting China and had suspended aid in 1962. Japan had also supported Pakistan both in 1965 and in 1971.[73]

United States imposed economic sanctions and export blockade of variety of equipment and components in the name of sensitive industrial uses, India could withstand US sanctions without much hardship. While the US government initially calculated that the Indian economy could lose several billion dollars of financial assistance and foreign investments due to sanctions, the Government of India kept issuing statements to the effect that India could sustain American pressures and sanctions. As a noted economist, Jagdish Bhagwati, observes, "the economic impact of US sanctions almost never work," sanctions did not hurt India beyond a point.[74]

India's Policy: 2005-14

Incomparable Henry Kissinger said: "The world faces four major problems—terrorism, the proliferation of weapons of mass destruction, the movement of the center of gravity from the Atlantic region to Asia and the impact of a globalised economy on the world order. The US and India have compatible, indeed overlapping, vital national interests in all four areas."

United States status as world's premier power was unassailable during the period. No state is likely to match the United States in the four key dimensions of power—military, economic, technological and cultural—that confer global political clout. President Clinton was correct when he said, "America has become world's '*indispensable nation*'."

The end of the cold war has created a belief in the United States that with Russia reduced the countries are vulnerable to United States pressure and blandishments. The model is the nuclear disarmament of South Africa. Just as United States pressure led to destruction of the South Africa's nuclear weapons the United States aims to achieve same with Iran and North Korea. Here the strategic concept had and still has timeless value; the goal was and today is to maintain United States hegemony in the strategic and economic spheres in order to make world safe for United States interests. And to enhance United States freedom of action to pursue its strategic objectives

As the international system in 21st Century evolves, the emergence of fledgling states with high propensities to employ force posed a serious challenge. More striking was the increasing frequency of overt use of force to settle disputes.[75] In short the era was a period in which individual states, either in isolation or as a member of interstate rivalry posed grave security problems to the international community and in particular to India.

> *"We must see foreign nations as they really are, not as we would like them to be. Let us not stake our future foolishly on one end card, let us not choose allies which others–better trained geo-politically–have considered doomed half a century earlier. By prudent, courageous analysis of our world political situation we shall always be able to preserve our sacred soil from shameful defeat. The admonitions 'see what is' and 'keep away from whatever our national honour can tolerate', are the pilot's lights of out voyage. They are modest enough and even hardly sufficient to help our ship of state against the open sea,"* said General Karl Haushofer in 1942, aptly applicable to India today.

Belief persisted and persists in many parts of the world, and in Pakistan, in the military solution as the ultimate option for state leaders and their internal and external opponent. This has resulted according to John Chipman[76] in:

> 'War has become politics by other means; government is the management of conflict; opposition has meant insurgency; and guerilla activities have become a life style'.

Strategic autonomy was the theme of Prime Minister Manmohan Singh's Government. It was criticised by many as not giving any directions. It was intended to make India remain equidistant from both US and China. However, critics of the policy saw this as a 'perverse policy' merely limiting India's cooperation with other countries citing China's sensitivities.[77]

> During the March 2010 visit of the Russian Prime Minister Vladimir Putin to New Delhi, the Indian Prime Minister Manmohan Singh described Russia in fulsome terms:
>
> 'Relations with Russia are a key pillar of our foreign policy, and we regard Russia as a trusted and reliable strategic partner. Ours is a relationship that not only stands independent of any other, but whose significance has grown over time. Our partnership covers areas such as defence, civil nuclear energy, space, science and technology, hydrocarbons and trade and investment.'

India has a long-standing ties with Africa that have been characterised by the presence of a large diaspora, especially in eastern and South Africa, solidarity with African states' anti-colonial struggles, non-alignment, South-South cooperation, which includes commercial linkages. Politically, however, India did not seek nor emulate the kind of high level engagement that has characterised China-Africa relations since the late 1990's. Throughout the period Indian Governments relations with Africa were largely conducted at the bilateral level. However, in 2008 India, Africa forum was launched. It was a more structured initiative with Africa.

The drivers that compelled these were clearly the hard material needs and impact of the financial crisis, which illustrated the importance of diversifying trade relations, and no doubt concern over China's growing presence in Africa.[78]

The second India-Africa Summit, under the theme 'Enhancing partnership: Shared Vision', was held in Addis Ababa in 2011. India offered further credit of $5 billion in credit lines and $7 million for the establishment of new institutions and training programs in consultation with African Union. Prime Minister Manmohan Singh announced establishment of India-Africa Food processing Centre, India-Africa Integrated Textiles Cluster, India-Africa Center for Medium range Weather Forecasting, India-Africa University for Life and earth sciences, India-Africa Institute of Agriculture and Rural Development. India's support for a $300 million deal to construct an Ethiopia-Djibouti railway line was also announced.[79]

Modi Doctrine in Relations to Great Powers

When Modi assumed office the world appeared as:

(a) There was only one superpower—US. It was embroiled in conflicts of its own making in Afghanistan and the Middle East;
(b) There were force power centre's at least economically France-Germany in Europe; Russia; China-Japan in the East and the US;
(c) The international system[80] was principally a self-help system;
(d) Africa was the future for the growth and progress of India. China had made many in roads in Africa; India had to make up for the lost time; and
(e) Anarchy defined by the absence of a central authority with coercive power, rather than order was the striking feature. Nation states were remained the main actors within the system. International regimes were being forced into place, alliances expanded, global norms were frequently invoked, and a multi polar world may eventually emerge. However, a genuine collective security arrangement[81] that enjoys widespread legitimacy[82] is unlikely to take shape in the foreseeable future. Barring a dramatic change, nation states will have to continue to defend primarily on their internal resources to remain stable and secure in the international system.

Given this perception, it was not be surprising that the Third World security analyst have considered arms control alien and not a high priority. Chandram Jeshurun perhaps best summarised this view describing attitudes towards arms control in South East Asia[83] where:

'Governments are inclined to embark on.... Measures that in no way touch upon issues relating to arms transfers, arms control and arms production in the current state of intra-regional and international strategic uncertainty'.

Article 2(7) of the United Nations Charter explicitly states that nothing contained in the charter shall authorise the United Nations to intervene in the matters, which are essentially within the domestic jurisdiction of any state. It, however, makes an exception in the case of the application of enforcement measures under Chapter VII of the Charter (Action with respect to Threat to the Peace, Breaches of Peace, and Acts of Aggression).

> Thomas L Friedman, three-time Pulitzer-winning columnist for the New York Times, is the ordained voice of US neo-liberalism. In his February 17 column, Friedman wrote: "The new world system is also bipolar, but instead of being divided between East and West (as in the Cold War) it is divided between the World of Order and the World of Disorder. The World of Order is built on four pillars: the United States, European Union-Russia, India and China, along with all the smaller powers around them. The World of Disorder comprises failed states (such as Liberia), rogue states (Iraq and North Korea), messy states—states that are too big to fail but too messy to work (Pakistan, Colombia, Indonesia, many Arab and African states)—and finally the terrorist and mafia networks that feed off the World of Disorder."

What Modi saw was the beginning of adjustments in Asia of what will be a protracted process of adjustments amongst great powers. There are two new powers emerging in the region—China and Japan—with no clearly articulated roles but greatly suspicious of each other, and a third country—India, that has an unrealised potential as a great power. Russia has, at least temporarily, lost its power base in almost every dimension, although it could re-emerge in the longer term as a disruptive power in the Asia-Pacific Region. Hence, today United States is the one actor that truly possesses all the attributes of superpower,[84] but there is questioning in the region whether it will hold the balance of power. Any new strategic balance in Asia is likely to rest upon relationships amongst the five powers, United States, Russia, China, India and Japan.

Modi also realised that in last two decades attempts to create a structure of international relations led by the United States, based on unilateral solutions to key problems was in the process. The United States elimination and change of government in Afghanistan and Iraq, isolation of Iran and North Korea, and the decision to attack Yugoslavia and dismember it, all pointed to one direction viz. **imposition of unilateral solution.** The formation of a **multipolar world** will be a lengthy process.

Although United States is militarily the only superpower,[85] as far as the economics[86] are concerned, we are living in a multipolar world. Three new centers of power have emerged–North America, dominated by the United States; Europe dominated by Germany and France, and Asia and the Pacific Region dominated by China and Japan. India is an emerging economic power. These centers are in competition with one another for the world market, raw materials and political influence. In spite of their competition *inter se* in the economic field, these powers have common security and strategic objectives. They have vested interest in maintaining the *status quo* in view of the rise of new powers, particularly in the Third World. Instead of two Power Blocks contending for hegemony as in the era of the Cold War, we have today a new alliance striving to establish its hegemony. This alliance consists of both East and West; and Japan against the rest of the world, particularly the Third World. Germany and Japan still depend for their security on the United States. China too has become a member, of the new economic alliance. Aware of the limits imposed upon it by economic factors, the United States now prefers to work through the new alliance then all by itself.[87]

> While Delhi and D.C. officially denied it, analysts said the union ultimately had Beijing in its sights. A Pentagon-commissioned report titled *The Indo-US Military Relationship: Expectations and Perceptions,* by a Virginia-based think tank, the Information Assurance Technology Analysis Center, had been released in 2002. It drew on interviews with America's top military brass to conclude, "As the US military engages India .... we cannot separate our thinking on India from our thinking on China. We want a friend in 2020 that will be capable of assisting the US military to deal with a Chinese threat. We cannot deny that India will create a countervailing force to China."

As far as India was concerned there was a possibility of a clash of interests if there is a future divergence between India's interest and powers in the region and the super powers. However, as of date or in the near future, say next 20 years, there is no major threat from the United States; on the other hand United States may solicit India's support if differences with China arise. A clash of interests between Russia and India appears unlikely, as their spheres of interest do not clash. On the other hand, there are chances of Russia soliciting India's support if it has serious policy differences with either China or the United States.

This also applies to other players in Asia. China and the United States have adjusted their military activities to new realities. The recent studies show renewed interests in military development in ASEAN, Japan and Australia. The United States favours international regimes that reduce the military capabilities of its enemies or potential enemies; it does not promote or encourage international regimes that affect its freedom of action and its interests. Selective disarmament and selective development of friendly regimes to constrain enemies is the essence of the United States approach to multilateral and bilateral diplomacy. This is also true of China and other Asian states.

The Asia-Pacific region has emerged as an extraordinary super region, bringing together powers of unprecedented military and economic capabilities. Never before in history has the world seen an arena inhabited by the kind of power represented by the United States, China, Japan and Russia at the centre, and by a host of major powers at the edges. The secondary powers include Australia, Association of South East Asian Nations, India, South Korea and Taiwan. Besides this correlation of forces, post-1945 Europe looks puny. The Asia-Pacific is extraordinary in terms of its structure which, with China at its core, features a stupendous and dangerous '**security dilemma**'. China abuts virtually every Asian region and is bounded by approximately twenty neighbours. It is in the politics of every region in the great Asian landmass; even in those regions it does not about it is a player. In addition, it has yet to settle boundary with several of its neighbours.[88]

The availability of **knowledge, nationalism** and **individualism**, has already brought **empowerment** of the individual, small groups, nation states. This has also resulted in number of non-governmental actors, multinational corporations, crime and drug cartels, religious fundamentalist groups capable of creating disorder and destruction. Approximately 38,000 Multi-National Corporations having a budget larger than the Gross National Products/Annual Budgets of some of the nations, speaks of awesome capabilities of non-governmental groups.[89]

The period of uncertainty in the international geopolitical scene will endure well into 21st Century. The resurgence of racial, religious and regional issues was on the rise to fuel conflicts between belligerent groups.

It was at this time Modi took reins of the Government in India. Modi based India's Foreign policy on '**nuanced, pragmatic realism**'. **Idealism is all very well, they say, but it cannot trump national interests in dealing with others states**. There were four Centres of Power—US, the sole superpower, resurgent Russia, China-Japan in the East and France-Germany in Europe. Modi found the Middle East burning and US taking unilateral actions to limit the capabilities of Iran and North Korea.

Hence, the India intensified its economic and diplomatic relations with United States and sought more military and political support. Vis-à-vis China, the India established robust economic relations, but at same time adopt military postures that minimise the risks of destabilising reactions in response. Finally, since material power and capability will define long-term Indian relations with China, Modi recognised the technological and economic challenges before her. He took a leaf from United States policy, 'Innovative technology and economic strength have been the traditional American assets and sources of its power;' hence, Modi went in for Make in India and Innovation.

Modi's solutions will also be influenced by the vagaries of domestic politics. The leadership changes in China has ushered a new generation into power that, appears, to be more internationalist and less nationalist in their strategic behavior.

Since independence, India has pursued non-alignment or poly-alignment, and has spurned the use of force as a tool of foreign policy. Non-alignment had become US bashing in India. Modi carried no hang-up of the past. He moved away hence, despite India's advocacy of a non-polar world, Modi and Indian policymakers nonetheless recognise the benefits of American sponsorship.

A pragmatic view is taken on the lasting US status as the sole super-power: US pre-eminence in the global strategic architecture is unlikely to diminish in the foreseeable future. Meaningful broad-based engagement with the United States spanning political, economic and technological interests and commonalties, will impact beneficially on our external security concerns with a resultant albeit less visible impact on our internal security environment.

Both nations agree that it serves neither US nor Indian interests for a powerful, authoritarian China to dominate the Asian landmass or for radical Islamic forces to wage wars that threaten the security of both states. Thus, as the United States perceives strategic advantage from assisting India's rise to great power status, and India is receiving tangible military and economic benefits from this relationship, for the foreseeable future, India's continued ascendance will be supported by the global hegemon.

- India's traditional strategy of non-alignment has shifted towards "poly-alignment".
- As a new regional power, India is increasing its naval, air force and missile capabilities.
- During this period of rapid development, domestic stability is a key challenge for India.

The US supports Indian expansion, with the aim of balancing Chinese influence in Asia. The United States faces a complex, dual challenge from Asia's two rising powers. It would be simplistic, therefore, to address China's rise by partnering with India, which fails to appreciate that China and India may have their own national self-interests that could clash with those of the United States. Besides, the interaction between China and India against the backdrop of a declining United States is another complicating factor. China-India is displaying several elements of convergence, but also binary features that characterise a zero-sum game. This milieu might persuade the United States to pursue a nuanced containment-cooperation policy towards China, but also play the arbiter between

India and China. Sino-Indian relations could also resolve into a complex mix with tensions and instabilities co-existing alongside collaboration and cooperation

United States has developed a growing stake in India's success. It has developed an interest, too, in a confident and reforming India—one that contributes to global growth, promotes market-based economic policies, helps maintain the global commons, and works to assure a mutually favourable balance of power in Asia, especially against the backdrop of a more powerful and assertive China.

The United States is trying to change India's reluctant stance and is attempting to forge closer ties with New Delhi. During his visit in June 2012, US Secretary of Defense, Leon Panetta, called India a "lynchpin" in the United States' strategic pivot to Asia. Behind all of this is the United States' desire to check the growth of Chinese power in the region. Mr Robert D. Blackwill,[90] former US Envoy to India, pointed out in a speech in New Delhi in 2009: "President George W. Bush based his transformation of US-India Relations on the core strategic principle of democratic India as a key factor in balancing the rise of Chinese power." Also he noted that: "[W]ithout this China factor at the fore in Washington, in my view the Bush Administration would not have negotiated the Civil Nuclear Agreement and the Congress would not have approved it."

Modi, for his part, clearly seeks a United States that helps to facilitate his economic goals—faster growth, technology acquisition and co-production, and expanded FDI in infrastructure and manufacturing. Previous governments, including but not limited to Modi's, have also sought American support for India's rise as a major power and recognition of its growing economic and strategic weight in Asia and around the world.

In fact, the emphasis on the Pacific is not new. As early as November 2001, US-India joint statements emphasised "common goals in Asia." A landmark 2002 speech by then-Ambassador to India Robert Blackwill positioned Asian geopolitics squarely at the center of his argument for strengthened partnership. Blackwill put this point directly: "Peace within Asia—a peace that helps perpetuate Asian prosperity—remains an objective that a transformed US-India relationship will help advance."

But in the decade of the 2000s, the principal lever to enable this cooperation was high technology—something tangible, touchable, and concrete. The two sides could set clear benchmarks: technology would be transferred or not; civil nuclear trade would be permitted or not; adaptations to the US Atomic Energy Act would be made or not; India would separate civilian and military nuclear facilities or not; and so on. And the manifestations of cooperation were many, including a defence technology security dialogue, missile defence cooperation, and Asia-focused military exercises.

By 2004, with the " Next Step on Strategic Partnership,"[91] initiative, the core of the expanded US-India strategic relationship had settled around three areas—civil nuclear activities, civilian space cooperation, and high technology trade—all of which focused on technology acquisition and collaboration. These came to dominate bilateral interaction for the rest of the Bush Administration.

Some of that momentum has continued into the current decade, especially in defence technology. The new US Secretary of Defense, Ashton Carter, has long placed an emphasis on co-development and co-production with India. And the two capitals agreed in 2012 to a potentially robust Defense Technology and Trade Initiative through which the United States would transfer various weapons and technologies and move toward co-production.

But the joint vision statement on Asia issued during Obama's visit marked a challenging change as well. It turned from a predominant emphasis on the *tangible* lever of high technology as the manifestation of cooperation to the less tangible, less touchable, less concrete lever of diplomatic coordination.

STRATEGIC PARTNERSHIP

What makes a partnership "strategic"? First, a strategic partnership must be ***comprehensive***, in order ***to allow linkages and tradeoffs between various policies***. Second, it must be built upon ***reciprocity***, short of which it cannot be deemed a partnership at all. Third, a strategic partnership has a ***strong empathic dimension***, which means that ***both partners share a common understanding of their mutual values and objectives***. Fourth, a strategic partnership must be ***oriented towards the long-term***, which is to say that it is not put into question by casual disputes. Finally, a strategic partnership ***must go beyond bilateral issues*** to tackle (with the potential to solve) regional and global challenges, **because that is its true raison d'être.**

Based on those standards, how strategic are the EU's "strategic partnerships"? Among the current ten strategic partnerships (with Brazil, Canada, China, India, Japan, Mexico, Russia, South Africa, South Korea and the United States) probably only the US-relationship qualifies as a true strategic partnership. The others are, among other things, not comprehensive (e.g. India and Japan), not oriented towards global issues (e.g. South Africa) or not based on reciprocity and empathy (e.g. Russia and China).[1]

In the new global environment, the EU cannot afford to have only one true strategic partner, even if that is the American superpower. In today's world, the EU needs to develop true strategic partnerships with tomorrow's great powers, because it takes time to build sustainable trust among partners in order to collectively address global threats and challenges. At the end of the day, what truly matters is not how much power you have or what kind of power you are, as the United States is now experiencing the hard way in Iraq and Afghanistan, but how you make use of that power. Strategic partnerships are precisely a blueprint for a smart use of the European Union's (and therefore Europe's) power.

The concept of strategic partnership emerged from the post-Cold War era.[2] Countries, particularly in Eurasia and in Asia, reacted to the demise of the bipolar order by developing new "hedging" strategies to deal in a flexible manner with the "lonely superpower" and with other regional powers at the same time, without committing to new forms of alliance in troubled and uncertain times. For a former superpower like Russia and for emerging powers like China and India, the international environment was simply too uncertain and evolving too rapidly to opt for a definitive bandwagoning or balancing posture at the global (vis-à-vis the US) and regional (vis-à-vis other regional powers) levels.[3]

[1]Renard, Thomas (2011), *The Treachery of Strategies: A Call for True EU Strategic Partnerships,* (Gent: Academia Press), p. 6.

[2]Kay, Sean (2000), "What is a strategic partnership?" *Problems of Post-Communism*, n°47, pp. 15-24.

[3]Nadkarni, Vidya (2010), *Strategic partnerships in Asia: Balancing without alliances* (Abingdon: Routledge).

Although Modi cosseted with US he did not leave Russia, China and Japan behind. India's partnership with Japan has witnessed the most dynamic growth. Several historic decisions have been taken, the most telling being the decision by Japan, the only country to have suffered a nuclear attack, to sign a civilian nuclear deal with India. Japan's commitment to invest $35 billion in India, a joint deal on constructing a high-speed railway, and cooperation on the Delhi-Mumbai Industrial Corridor, as well as joint participation in the Malabar Exercises and defence cooperation, provide evidence of the flourishing bilateral strategic, economic and technological partnership. The Agreement concerning other transfer of Defence Equipment and Technology Cooperation signed during the latest visit of Prime Minister Shinzo Abe on December 12, 2015 unveiled a new chapter in India-Japan defence cooperation by making available defence equipment and technology needed to carry out joint research, development and/or production projects.[92] Japan has been identified as a privileged partner in the *Make in India* campaign by Defence Minister Parrikar.[93]

Look East Policy (LEP), initiated by Prime Minister Narasimha Rao in 1992. Prime Minister Narendra Modi, renamed and advocated **Act East Policy** (AEP), which was launched at the East Asia Summit in Myanmar in November 2014. India Modi accorded a new focus to promoting connectivity through Myanmar and Thailand with other ASEAN states. Modi's allocation of $1 billion for promoting connectivity at the India-ASEAN Summit in Kuala Lumpur last November has brought the primacy of "connectivity, culture, and commerce" to the fore. India has recognised that success of AEP will be determined by its contribution to security and economic development of North-East India.

India's AEP has also impacted relations with the United States. During US President Barack Obama's visit to India as chief guest at India's Republic Day celebrations in January 2015, Modi stated, "For too long India and the US have looked at each other across Europe and Atlantic. When I look towards the East, I see the Western shores of United States." By aligning India's Act East Policy with the US pivot to Asia through the Joint Strategic Vision, India seeks to expand its geo-strategic space to contend with China's growing assertiveness and foster balanced relationship.

Modi just changed the game with China, he was candid and forthcoming. Panchsheel was out. The Five Principles of Peaceful Coexistence—are remembered by many in India as being honoured by China in the breach than in the observance in the late 1950s and early 1960s. No mention in joint statement and seems to have been replaced by this:

> The leaders agreed that the process of the two countries pursuing their respective national developmental goals and security interests must unfold in a mutually supportive manner with both sides showing mutual respect and sensitivity to each other's concerns, interests and aspirations. This constructive model of relationship between the two largest developing countries, the biggest emerging economies and two major poles in the global architecture provides a new basis for pursuing state-to-state relations to strengthen the international system.

Modi talked about the relationship being "complex," as well as about issues that "trouble smooth development of our relations" and held back the relationship. He urged China to think strategically (and long-term) and "reconsider its approach" on various issues. First and foremost: its approach toward the border, but also visas and trans-border rivers, as well as the region (read China's relations with Pakistan among others). The Indian position is that China continues to illegally occupy 38,000 km^2 of Indian Territory in Kashmir, besides the 5180 km^2 ceded by Pakistan to China. On its part, Beijing lays claim to 90,000 km^2 of territory in Arunachal Pradesh.[94]

China's approach on economic questions was also put on the table, with Modi stating that, in the long-term, the partnership was not sustainable if Indian industry didn't get better access to the Chinese market. China's approach on economic questions was also put on the table, with Modi stating that, in the long-term, the partnership was not sustainable if Indian industry didn't get better access to the Chinese market.

Modi also made clear that India wants China's support for a greater role in international institutions. He specifically highlighted that China's support for a permanent seat for India at the UN Security Council (UNSC) and Indian membership of export control regimes would be helpful to the relationship (interestingly, he explained India's desire for UNSC permanent membership as stemming from the same logic as the establishment of the Asian Infrastructure Investment Bank–part of Asia "seeking a bigger voice in global affairs."

Modi did not endorse China's One Belt, One Road initiatives. Modi noted that both China and India were "trying to strengthen regional connectivity and seeking 'to connect a fragmented Asia.'" But he distinguished between two types of projects: "There are projects we will pursue individually. There are few such as the Bangladesh-China-India-Myanmar Corridor that we are doing jointly."

Modi's geopolitical attention lies beyond the often mentioned race between India and China for African markets and resources. India sees Africa as a natural partner in the laborious process of reforming the United Nations Security Council. In India, as in parts of Africa, there is a strong feeling (not entirely unjustified) that the current constellation of permanent members of the Security Council—France, Britain, China, Russia and the United States—is outdated. Modi's foreign policy strategy has aimed to increase assistance to developing countries and vie for linkages with the African continent for increased trade, access to agricultural land, and cooperation on maritime security, in part to buffer China's influence in the region.

Modi has clearly pursued his "Neighbourhood First" and "Act East policies", which has prioritised improving relations with India's neighbours. India has also reached out to its maritime neighbours in the Indian Ocean Rim with proposals of enhancing economic and security co-operation. What underpins this strategy is also the desire to command strategic supremacy over the area.

While China is both a strategic partner and a global competitor, it has been Modi's policy to engage with China and court investment deals. He has done the same with Japan and Israel. He has also reached out to the Gulf Co-operation countries from which India derives energy security, trade, and employment for Indians who send home their remittances.

ENDNOTES

1. Raja Mohan, C. (2006), 'India and the Balance of Power', *Foreign Affairs,* July-August, pp.17-32.
2. Waltz, K.N. (1979), *'Theory of International Politics',* (New York: Addison-Wesley), p. 171.
3. George F. Kennan, a career Foreign Service Officer, formulated the policy of "containment," the basic United States strategy for fighting the cold war (1947–1989) with the Soviet Union. "The main element of any United States policy toward the Soviet Union," Kennan wrote, "must be that of a long-term, patient but firm and vigilant containment of Russian expansive tendencies." To that end, he called for countering "Soviet pressure against the free institutions of the Western world" through the "adroit and vigilant application of counter-force at a series of constantly shifting geographical and political points, corresponding to the shifts and maneouvers of Soviet policy." Such a policy, Kennan predicted, would "promote tendencies

which must eventually find their outlet in either the break-up or the gradual mellowing of Soviet power." See Chapter 2.

4. Lyon, Peter (1968), "The Foreign Policy of India" in F.S. Northedge (ed.), *The Foreign Policies of the Powers* (London, 1968), pp. 260-261.
5. US Atomic Energy Commission, "An Interim Report of British Work on Joe," 22 September 1949, Top Secret; Source: Harry S. Truman Library, President's Secret ary's Files, box 199, NSC-Atomic

   Holloway, David (1994), *Stalin and the Bomb: The Soviet Union and Atomic Energy, 1939-1956* (New Haven: Yale University Press), pp. 266-267.
6 See Narasimha Murthy, P.A. (1986), *India and Japan: Dimensions of Their Relations* (New Delhi: ABC Publishing House).
7. On the fitful improvement in Indo-US relations, see. Datta-Ray, Sunanda K (2002), *Waiting for America: India and the United States in the New Millennium* (New Delhi: HarperCollins).
8. Mao Zedong, "Problems of War and Strategy," November 6, 1938, *Selected Works of Mao Tse-tung*, vol. 2 (1967) (Beijing: Foreign Languages Press), pp. 219-235.
9. Mao Zedong, "Talk with the American Correspondent Anna Louise Strong," August 1946, *Selected Works of Mao Tse-tung*, vol. 4, (1967) (Beijing: Foreign Languages Press), pp. 97-101.
10. "Communication of the Main Points of the 6th All-Country Foreign Affairs Conference," no date, *Jiangsu Sheng Dang'anguan* [*Jiangsu Provincial Archives*], 3124, Zhang, pp. 145, 2-13. As quoted in Luthi, Lorenz, *Sino –Indian Relation 1954-1962* (Montreal: McGill U.).
11. Kapur, Ashok (2011), *India and the South Asian Strategic Triangle* (Abingdon, Oxon, OX14 4RN), p. 2.
12. Ibid., p. 2.
13. New China News Agency, "Agreement between India and China on Trade and Intercourse Between Tibet Region of China and India," April 29, 1954, Harold C. Hinton (ed.) (1980) *The People's Republic of China, 1949-1979: A Documentary Survey*, vol. 1, *1949-1957* (Wilmington: Scholarly Resources), pp. 165-166.
14. "Red China and India Sign a Pact on Tibet Vowing Nonaggression," *New York Times* [hereafter: *NYT*], April 30, 1954, pp. 1, 4.
15. "Text of Statement by Chou and Nehru," *NYT*, June 29, 1954, p. 4.
16. For one of the very few treatments of the subject, see: Sumanta Banerjee, (1995) "Mao and the Indian CommunistMovement," *China Report* 31 (1) 1995, pp. 37-66. It is interesting to note that Zhou in November 1959 claimed a Chinese right to influence the Indian masses in the Sino-Indian border conflict, see: "Talk with Zhou Enlai," November 11, 1959, Arkhiv Vneshnei Politiki Rossiiskoi Federatsii [Foreign Policy Archive of the Russian Federation; hereafter AVPRF], fond 0100, opis 52, delo 7, papka 442, ll. 145.
17. Wu Lengxi (1999), *Shinian lunzhan, 1956-1966: ZhongSu guanxi huiyulu, 1956–1966* [*Ten Years of Debate, 1956-1966: Recollections of Sino-Soviet Relations*] (Beijing: Zhongyang wenxian), p. 152.
18. Sali, M.L. (1998), *India-China Border Dispute: A Case Study of the Eastern Sector* (New Delhi: A.P.H. Publishing Corporation).
19. Brown, Judith (1999), *Nehru* (New York: Longman), p. 268.
20. "Prime Minister's Secretariat," June 15, 1958, NMML, Subimal Dutt Papers, Subject Files, File #32, p. 48.
21. Lüthi, Lorenz (2008), *The Sino-Soviet Split: Cold War in the Communist World* (Princeton: Princeton University Press), pp, 82-84.
22. "Prime Minister's Secretariat," June 15, 1958, NMML, Subimal Dutt Papers, Subject Files, File #32, p. 48.

23. Maxwell, Neville (1970), *India's China War* (London: Cape), p. 107. Swamy, Subramanian (2001), *India's China Perspective* (New Delhi: Konark), pp. 41-45, 54-67, 85. Liu Xuecheng (1994), *The Sino-Indian Border Dispute* (New York: Lanham), pp. 19, 26, 47-78, 87. Sinha, Mira (1979), "China: the Making and Unmaking of Nehru's Foreign Policy," *China Report* 15/2, p. 60.
24. Notes on Mikoyan-Nehru Conversations, 26–28 March 1956, in SDC, Subject File 19, 1956, NMML. Extracts of the conversations are reproduced in *Selected Works of Jawaharlal Nehru,* Vol. 32, pp. 397–401.
25. Shakya, Tsering W. (1999), *The Dragon in the Land of Snows: A History of Modern Tibet Since 1947* (London: Pimlico), pp. 162-184. Karan, P.P. (1973), "The Changing Geography of Tibet," *Asian Profile: Asia's International Journal Devoted Excl. to Asian Affairs* 1.1. p. 40. Craig, Mary (1992), *Tears of Blood: A Cry of Tibet,* (Harper Collins), pp. 54-55. Grunfeld, A. Tom (2015), *The Making of Modern Tibet,* (Routledge) pp. 107-111, 151-158. Norbu, Dawa, (2001), China's Tibet Policy (Richmond: Curzon,), pp. 215-227, 263-282.
26. Raghavan, Srinath (2010), *War and Peace in Modern India: A Strategic History of Nehru Years,* (London: Palgrave Macmillan), p.246. See also: Zhou Enlai, "Letter to Nehru," January 23, 1959, Hinton, Harold C. (ed.) (1980) The People's Republic of China 1949-79, A Documentary Survey volume 2, (Delaware: Scholarly Resource Inc.) pp. 807-808.
27. "Pt Jawaharlal Nehru, Prime Minister of India," March 26, 1959, *NMML,* Subimal Dutt Papers, Subject Files, File #6, p. 9.
28. "Summary of Discussion with Senior Tibetan Officers at Lumla on the 3rd April, 1959," no date, *NMML,* Subimal Dutt Papers, Subject Files, File #6, pp. 10-12. See also: "Resume of Discussion with His Holiness, the Dalai Lama on the Morning of the 6th April, 1959," no date, *NMML,* Subimal Dutt Papers, Subject Files, File #6, pp. 21-23.
29. "[Message received for His Holiness the Dalai Lama from the Prime Minster of India]," no date, *NMML,* Subimal Dutt Papers, Subject Files, File #6, p. 24.
30. "[Note]," April 12, 1959, NMML, Subimal Dutt Papers, Subject Files, File #6, 32-33.
31. "My dear Menon," April 14, 1959, *NMML,* Subimal Dutt Papers, Subject Files, File #6, p. 34.
32. "Message to be conveyed by Shri P.N. Menon on behalf of the Prime Minister to the Dalai Lama," April 29, 1959, NMML, Subimal Dutt Papers, Subject Files, File #6, pp. 41-42.
33. *Wu* Lengxi, ***Shinian*** lunzhan, zhongsu guanxi huiyilu, 1956–1966 (Ten-year polemical war, a memoir of Sino-Soviet relations), Vol. 1, (Beijing: Zhongyang) pp.198-202. Wu, Lengxi (1994) *Yi Mao zhuxi,* (Recalling Chairman Mao), (Beijing: Xinhua) pp. 123-124.
34. Ibid., 196.
35. Wu, Lengxi (1994) *Yi Mao zhuxi,* (Recalling Chairman Mao), (Beijing: Xinhua), pp. 125-126.
36. "Reception of the Vice-Foreign Minister of the People's Republic of China Zhang Wentian," May 4, 1959, *AVPRF,* fond 0100, opis 52, delo 5, papka 442, ll. 10-14. "Speech to the Soviet and other delegations from 11 countries and to the diplomatic envoys stationed in China," May 6, 1969, Mao Zedong, *JYMW,* vol. 8, 247-249.
37. Zhonggong zhongyang wenxian yanjiushi bian, *Zhou Enlai nianpu, 1949-1976* [*A Chronicle of Zhou Enlai's Life: 1949–1976*; hereafter: *ZELNP2*], vol. 2, *1957-1965* (Beijing: Zhongyang wenxian chubanshe, 1997), 224-225. Mao Zedong, "On the Tibet question and the Taiwan Question," *JYMG,* vol. 8, 65. See also: "Vice-Premier Chen Yi receives the Soviet ambassador in China Yudin," May 8, 1959, *WJBDAG,* 105-00659-01, 42-43.
38. "Nehru discussed yesterday in the people's assembly the Tibet question," May 9, 1959, *WJBDAG,* 105-00654-01, pp. 1-3.

39. Menon, K.P.S. (1963), *The Flying Troika: Extracts from a Diary* (London: Oxford University Press), pp. 235, 236.
40. Liu, Xuecheng (1994), *Sino-Indian Border Dispute and Sino-Indian Relations*, (Lanham, MD:University press of America), pp. 25-26.
41. Ibid., p. 26
42. Liu, Xuecheng (1994), *Sino-Indian Border Dispute and Sino-Indian Relations*, (Lanham, MD: University press of America), p. 26. Zafar Imam (1975), *Ideology and Reality in Soviet Policy in Asia: Indo-Soviet Relations, 1947-1960* (Delhi: Klyani), 181. Swamy, Subramanian (2001), *India's China Perspective* (New Delhi: Konark), 67. *Wu* Lengxi, ***Shinian*** lunzhan, zhongsu guanxi huiyilu, 1956–1966 (Ten-year polemical war, a memoir of Sino-Soviet relations), Vol. 1, (Beijing: Zhongyang), pp. 208-210.
43. Khrushchev, Nikita S (1974), *Khrushchev Remembers: The Last Testament* (Boston: Little, Brown), pp. 263, 307, 311.
44. Prozumenshikov, M.Y., "The Sino-Indian Conflict, the Cuban Missile Crisis, and the Sino-Soviet Split, October 1962: New Evidence from the Russian Archives," *CWIHP Bulletin* 8-9 (Winter 1996/97), p. 251. O. Arne Westad, "The Sino-Soviet Alliance and the United States," in: O. Arne Westad (ed.), *Brothers in Arms: The Rise and Fall of the Sino-Soviet Alliance, 1945-1963* (Washington, D.C.: Woodrow Wilson Center, 1998), 177.
45. "Record of a talk between President Eisenhower and Prime Minister on December 10, 1959," December 23, 1959, *NMML*, Subimal Dutt Papers, Subject Files, File #41, 132-134. "Memorandum of a Conversation, New Delhi, December 10, 1959, 11:30 a.m.," *Foreign Relations of the United States*, 1958-1960, XV, 521-524.
46. "Eisenhower visits India," December 31, 1959, WJBDAG, 105-00946-02, 3-6.
47. McMahon, Robert (1994), *Cold War on the Periphery: The United States, India, and Pakistan* (New York: Columbia University Press).
48. The view was developed fully by Chester Bowles, who twice served as US ambassador to New Delhi. For an authoritative account of Bowles' views, and his impact on American policy, see Schaffer, Howard B. (1993), *Chester Bowles: New Dealer in the Cold War* (Cambridge: Harvard University Press).
49. Rostow, W.W. (1972), *The Diffusion of Power: An Essay in Recent History* (New York: Macmillan).
50. Desai, Morarji (1974), *The Story of My Life*, Vol. II (New Delhi: S. Chand), pp. 171-72.
51. Lüthi, Lorenz M. (2011), "Chinese Foreign Policy, 1960-1979," in Tsuyoshi Hasegawa (ed.), *The Cold War in East Asia, 1945-1991* (Washington, D.C.: Woodrow Wilson Center Press), p.154.
52. See Goswami, B.N. (1971), *Pakistan and China: A Study of Their Relations* (New York: Allied Publishers); Syed, Anwar Hussain (1974), *China & Pakistan: Diplomacy of an Entente Cordiale* (Amherst: The University of Massachusetts Press,); Bhola, PL. (1986), *Pakistan-China Relations* (Jaipur: R.B.S.A. Publishers). Most studies of the Sino-Pakistani relationship offer scant attention to the nuances of China's larger foreign policy goals vis-à-vis Pakistan. A large number of these works summon the notion of a 'special relationship,' which asserts that the two states share a mutual understanding rooted in their common enmity toward India.
53. Tang, Christopher (2012), 'Beyond India:The Utility of Sino-Pakistan Relations in Chinese Foreign Policy, 1962-65', *Cold War International History Project*, No. 64 (Washington D.C.: Woodrow Wilson International Center for Scholars).
54. Kapur, Ashok (2006), *Indian from Regional to World Power* (New York: Routledge).
55. "Hsinhua statement on Indo-Pakistan border conflict, 4 May 1965," in Arif, K., (ed.). (1984). Documents on China-Pakistan Relations. (Lahore: Vanguard Books.), p. 64.
56. Bailer, Seweryn (1986), *The Soviet Paradox: External Expansion, Internal Decline* (London:

I.B. Tauris & Co Ltd.), pp. 309-310.

57. For discussion of the is crisis, see Ziring, Lawrence (1971), *The Ayub Khan Era: Politics' in Pakistan1958-1969* (Syracuse: Syracuse University press), Chapter 5.
58. Gaikwad, Sanjay, (1990), *Dynamics of Indo-Soviet Relations: The Era of Indira Gandhi* (New Delhi: Deep & Deep Publications)
59. DOS, *Sitrep*, 25 Aug 1971. In these discussions on 19 Aug 1971, Yahya indicated that A.K. Bohri would represent Mujib and also said that he had given consideration to Ambassador Farland's suggestion that a civilian governor be appointed though Tikka Khan had done a good military job, he had nevertheless acquired a reputation not conducive to return to normalcy. Yahya had thus decided to appoint Dr A.M. Malik, a Bengali with a career of public service, to replace him. Malik would have the authority to appoint a cabinet, all of whom Yahya indicated hehoped would be Bengali (letter from American Embassy, Islamabad, to Secretary of State, 20 August 1971), made available under Freedom of Information Act.
60. Singh, Jaswant (1998), 'Against Nuclear Apartheid', *Foreign Affairs*, September/October 1998, Vol. 77, No. 5, pp. 41-52.
61. Hosokawa, Morihiro (1993), *New Japan Party: Responsible Reform* (Tokyo: Tokyo Keizai Shinposha).
62. Ichiro Ozawa (1994), *Blueprint for A New Japan: The Rethinking of A Nation* (Tokyo: Kodansha International).
63. Masayoshi, Takemura (1994), *A Small but Shinning Country: Japan* (Tokyo: Tokyo Keizai Shinposha, 1994 (in Japanese).
64. Michio Watanbe (1994), *New Conservative Revolution* [Tokyo: Nesco Bungei Shunjusha, (In Japanese)].
65. Hashimoto, Ryutaro (1994), *Vision of Japan: A Realistic Direction for the 21st Century* (Tokyo: KK Best Sellers).
66 **Proactive Foreign Policy**

The national strategy Japan pursued after the San Francisco peace treaty of 1951 is usuallyreferred to as the **Yashido Doctrine**, taking its name after former Prime Minister Shigeru Yoshido, who was in office when the treaty was signed. The main thrust of the doctrine was that Japan should leave the task of national defence and security to the United States and concentrate on rebuilding its war ravaged economy. This strategy it was claimed, was good not only for Japan but also for the rest of the world. The Yoshida Doctrine in fact worked more effectively under the leadership of Ikeda—Prime Minister from 1960-64. Thus Japan succeeded in keeping its Self Defence Forces at an absolute minimum. Article 9 of the Constitution, which explicitly renounced war as *'as a means of settling international disputes'* and embodied the Japanese peoples support for the pacifist cause, was used to resist the pressure for major rearmament.

This lasted for forty years till Mr Yashuhiro Nakasone, became the Prime Minister in 1982. He had a keen understanding of his country's potential role. He stressed two things:

First, Japan should confront the Soviet Military threat by strengthening its defence capabilities in proportion to its economic power, in cooperation with the United States;

Second, Japan should introduce political and economic reforms.

In the area of international security, Nakasone pointed out, Japan played a unique role in the free world by countering Soviet threat. In what may have been effort to provoke discussion at home. Hitherto, Japanese Prime Ministers had shied away from the questions of Japans defence capabilities and responsibilities in international security measures for fear of inviting protests from powerful pacifist faction. As the arms race between United State and Soviet Union escalated and the United States pressed Japan to build u[p its defence capabilities; the

Prime Ministers of Japan chose the words carefully to characterise the security ties with the United States, referring to Japan as *'a member of Western Bloc' [Ohiro 1978-80];* and *'a United States ally' [Suzuki 1980-82],* so as to guide the thinking of their constituents on the subject [United States was able to change the course of the world on two occasions. In 1990-91]. In the Cold War era [See Advisory Group on Defence, "The Modality of the Security and Defence Capability of Japan: The Outlook for the 21st Century', (Tokyo, August 1994). During the Cold War, the frame work of Japans defence system was set out in the National Defence Planning Outline formulated in 1976, under which specific numbers of items such as tanks and warplanes were procured every five years. When Prime Minister Hosokawa succeeded Miyazawa in February 1994 he assembled a nine members council of experts and business men to assess policy needs and purpose changes in the outline. In August 1994, after five months deliberations the council submitted 29 pages report to Japans new Prime Minister Tomaichi Murayama. **'The Modality Report'**, recognised the changes. The report recommended that military dangers have changed both in form and nature but the thinking that Japan should maintain the minimum necessary level of basic defence capabilities as an independent state remains basically valid], Japan's identity as *'a member of the Western Camp'* served as one of its guiding principles in its security and foreign policies. The end of the Cold War has made it necessary for Japan to adjust its bearing in the world. This accords with the desire of its people to make their own decisions and to act to influence others. It is against this background the Prime Minister Hashimoto set out as one of his four priorities, *'developing a proactive foreign policy for the furthering of peace and prosperity'.* This means not just passively continuing to take the international political and economic situation as a given, but to think of it as something you can alter for the better. Secondly, it means advancing beyond the traditional concept of international contribution, which at times was derided, *'cheque-book diplomacy'.* Thirdly, it means taking initiative, or follow active diplomacy. Fourthly, you take initiatives for a purpose. This, in turn, means that you need to postulate ideals for which you can act in concert with others, that is to say universally acceptable ideals.

67. Although Japans relationship with the Republic of Korea is at times beset with problems arising from past history, care should be taken to ensure that these problems do not eclipse the overriding importance of the two countries working together. The two countries could work on the basis of shared values such as freedom, democracy and market economy, to achieve peace and stability in the region. The day before Prime Minister Hashimoto met President Clinton, he expressed Japan's support for the joint Republic of Korea-United States proposal to convene four party meeting (Republic of Korea, Democratic Peoples Republic of Korea (North Korea), United States and China). In the hope that this would lead to the relaxation of tension and the building of confidence on the Korean Peninsula. Japan's approach to the normalization of its relations with North Korea has two aspects. One is tonormalize the anomalous state of affairs that has existed between Japan and North Korea since the end of the Second World War, which would entail such questions as disposition of properties and claims. The other aspects are to contribute to peace and stability on the Korean Peninsula, which involves the problem of North Korean nuclear development and the promotion of the North-South dialogue. The normalization of talks were started in January 1991, but have been suspended since November 1992 when the North Korean delegation walked out.

68. 1994 Japanese Defense White Paper is more pessimistic than the 1993 paper. North Korea's Nuclear and Ballistic Missile Programme is described as a *'serious destabilizing factor'* and the need for Self Defense Forces to maintain a scientific and technological edge in the region is emphasised.

69. United State Department of Defense, 'United States Security Strategy for the East Asia and Pacific Region', (Washington D.C.: Government Printing Office, February 1995), p. 14.

70. See Singh, Narendar (1998), 'India Should Ignore Japanese Rhetoric', *Garha Chronicle,* Vol. V, No. 139 (Indore City Edition, June 15, 1998.
71. Cable News Network (CNN), Internet Web Site, June 18 1998.
72. See Singh, Narendar (1998), 'India Should Ignore Japanese Rhetoric', *Garha Chronicle,* vol. V, No. 139 (Indore, City Edition, June 145, 1998).
73. See, Singh, Narendar, "India Should Ignore Japanese Rhetoric", *The Garha Chronicle,* Vol. V, No. 139 (Indore: City Edition, June 15, 1998).
74. See Jha, Nalini Kant (1998), "Understanding Conflict and Cooperation between Two Democracies of the World," *Third Concept* (New Delhi), vol. 2, no. 14, April 1988, pp.51-52. Also his, (1988)"Indo-US Pakistan Triangle: Illusion and Reality", *Link* (New Delhi), vol. 30, no.23, January 10, 1988, pp.26-28.
75. The number of states that have used force has increased. According to one account, the year of 1994, witnessed 34 wars, almost 20 percent of the 186 wars initiated since the end of the World War II. See Gautzel, K. J., 'Die Kriegsherde der Welt", *Dur Binger im Staat,* vol. 45, No. 1, pp. 8-14, as quoted in Schireider Gerald and Patricia A. Weitsman, (ed.), (1997) *'Enforcing Cooperation: Risky States and Inter-Governmental Management of Conflict',* (London: Macmillan Press Ltd.), p. 4.
76. Chipman, John., (1991) 'Third World Politics and Security in the 1990's: The World Forgetting. By the World Forgot'. *The Washington Quarterly,* No 14 (Winter 1991) p. 164.
77. Tatna Tm (2014) 'How Narendra Modi could usher in India's greatest foreign policy era yet', *DNA,* 15 July 2014.
78. Rajrishi S, 'Banks and investment treaties: key for economic diplomacy with Africa', Policy Perspective, 8, 9 January 2015, p. 2, http://www.gatewayhouse.in/wp-content/ uploads/2015/01/Policy-Perspective_Economic-diplomacy-with-Africa.pdf, accessed 28 July 2015.
79. Second Africa–India Forum Summit 2011 Addis Ababa Declaration, http://summits. au.int/en/sites/default/files/Addis%20Declar-1_0.pdf, accessed 2 July 2015.

    Chaturvedi S. (2012) 'India and development cooperation: Expressing Southern solidarity', in Chaturvedi S, Fues T & E Sidiropoulos (eds), *Development Cooperation and Emerging Powers: New Partners or Old Patterns? (*London: Zed Books), pp. 182–183.
80. The international political systems are comprised of agents and structure. What is more, agency and structure are interrelated. This basic tenet of social theory is shared by the three most widely acclaimed modern social theorists—Durkheim, Weber and Marx. Durkheim recognises that social facts '*consists of manners of acting, thinking and feeling external to the individual, which are invested with coercive power by virtue of which they exercise control over him*'. But concomitantly, social facts '*are the beliefs, tendencies and practices of the group taken collectively*'. [Durkheim, Emile, *The Rules of Sociological Method,* translated and edited by W.D. Halls and Steven Lukes (New York: The Free Press, 1982), p. 52, 54.]
81. Prior to the League of Nations covenant, the settlement of disputes by force was legitimate, subject to limitation. In the era of nationalist legitimization settlement according to the distribution of nationals or by plebiscite was legitimate. There was no equivalent to this during the cold war.
82. International Court of Justice, Hague, in their Advisory opinion handed down on 8 July 1996 on the request of the United Nations General Assembly stated:

    'A threat or use of force by means of nuclear weapons is contrary to Article 2, paragraph 4 of the United Nations Charter and that fails to meet all the requirement of Article 51 is unlawful'.

83 Jeshurun, Chandram (1993), "South East Asia", in Jayanth Dhanapala (ed.) *Regional Approaches to Disarmament Security and Stability',* (Aldershot, U.K. Dartmouth for the Institute for

Disarmament Research.), p. 51.

84. Although United States is militarily the only superpower, as far as the economics are concerned, we are living in a multipolar world. Three new centres of power have emerged—North America, dominated by the United States; Europe dominated by Germany, and Asia and the Pacific Region dominated by Japan. These Centres are in competition with one and another for the world market, raw materials and political influence.

In spite of their competition *inter se* in the economic field, these powers have a common security and strategic objectives: they have vested interest in maintaining the *status quo* in view of the rise of new powers, particularly in the Third World. Instead of two rival Power Blocks contending for hegemony as in the era of the Cold War, we have today a new alliance striving to establish its hegemony. This alliance consists of both East and West and Japan against the rest of the world, particularly the Third World.

Germany and Japan still depend for their security on the United States.

85. Some analysts across the political spectrum agree that there have been few if any efforts at balancing Americas' resurgent hegemony. As Mastanduno, M. and Kapstein, Ethan B. (1999), *Unipolar Politics* (Columbia University Press), p. 5 write, "What is most striking, is the reluctance of other major powers to engage in an individual or collective strategy of balancing against the preponderant power of the United States in an effort to create an alternative international order." Kagan (2008, 38–39) reaches a similar conclusion:

"Sino-Russian hostility to American predominance has not yet produced a concerted and cooperative effort at balancing .... China and Russia cannot balance the United States without at least some help from Europe, Japan, India, and at least some of the other advanced democratic nations. But those powerful players are not joining the effort .... If anything, the most notable balancing over the past decade has been aimed not at American superpower but at the two large powers China and Russia."

Walt (2002, 127) echoes this same point:

"From the perspective of structural balance-of power theory, this situation is surely an anomaly. Power in the international system is about as unbalanced as it has ever been, yet balancing tendencies – while they do exist – are remarkably mild. It is possible to find them, but one has to squint pretty hard to do it. The propensity to balance is weak even though the United States has not been shy about using its power in recent years."

At most, there have been efforts at "soft balancing" against the United States (see below), but not concreted attempts to offset its overweening power.

86. Luttwak, Edward N. (1990), 'From Geo-politics to Geo-economics: Logic of Conflict, Grammar of Commerce', *The National Interest*, 20, Summer 1990; Also Luttwak, E.N. (1993), *'The Endangered American Dream',* (New York: Simon and Schuster). Luttwak claims, that instead of World Politics, the intersecting web of power relationships on the international scene, we would simply have **'World Business'** a myriad economic interactions spanning the globe. In some cases, the logic of commerce would result in fierce competition. In others the same logic would lead to alliances between economic entities in any location to capitalize ventures, vertically integrate, horizontally co-develop, co-produce or co-market goods and services. But competitively or cooperatively, the action on all sides would always unfold without regard to priorities. This would lead to logic conflict-displaced. This or something very much like this comes to mind when we speak of *'global Interdependence'.*

The geo-economic dimensions of the new world order involve the doctrine of transnational liberalism and neo-liberalism. The fundamental principle of this doctrine is economic liberty for the powerful, that is, that an economy must be free from the social and political *'impediments', 'fetter's'* and *'restrictions'* placed upon it by states trying to regulate in the name of public interest. 'These impediments'—which include national economic regulations, social programs and class compromises—are all considered barriers to the free flow of trade and capital and the freedom of the transnational corporations to exploit labour and environment in their best interest. Hence, the doctrine argues national economies should be deregulated.

87. United States built a formidable multinational force during Gulf War. It is one example of new alliance working.

88. Flak, Richard (1993), *'The Challenge of Globalisation and Emergence of Global Civil Society',* Rajiv Gandhi Institute of Contemporary Studies Paper No. 5, (New Delhi: Rajiv Gandhi Institute of Contemporary Studies, Rajiv Gandhi Foundation). Also see Bajpai, Kanti and Stephen P. Cohen, 'Cooperative Security and South Asian Insecurity', in Janne E. Nolan (ed.), *'Global Engagement: Cooperation and Security in the 21st Century',* [Washington D.C.: The Brookings Institute, 1994], p. 447. As per Bajpai and Cohen' One way of ameliorating security dilemma is through **'cooperative security arrangements'**. Cooperative security refers, minimally, to, **'a consensually arrived at commitment on the part of the military most significant states in the international system to regulate the size, the technical composition, investment patterns, and operational practices of their armed forces, such that surprise attack and extended offensive operations are implausible'**.

89. **Transnational Relations**

Describe the effects of the non-governmental groups, networks, associations or interactions which cut across national societies, creating linkages between individuals, groups, organisations and communities within different nation states.

Transnational Politics

Refers to all those relationships, associations, networks, interactions and organisations which cut across national societies and which intervene deliberately or unintentionally in domestic and international political processes. **'Greenpeace'**, is one such example.

TRANSNATIONAL POLITICS

Country A			**Country B**
Government			Government
	Public	Public	
	Religion	Religion	
	Science	Science	
	Professions	Professions	
	Revolutionaries	Revolutionaries	
	Labour	Labour	
	Arts, Sports, Culture	Arts, Sports, Culture	
	Ethnic	Ethnic	
	Sports	Sports	
	Education	Education	
	Business and Trade.	Business and Trade	

The above table depicts various non-governmental agencies and individual affecting the government decision and the choice of a particular course of action.

90. Speech delivered by Robert D. Blackwill, former US envoy to India, on "The Future of US-India Relations" in New Delhi on 5 May 2009.

91. *Statement by Prime Minister of India* Shri Atal Bihari Vajpayee on 13 January 2004:

"In November 2001, President Bush and I committed our countries to a strategic partnership. Since then, our two countries have strengthened bilateral cooperation significantly in several areas. Today we announce the next steps in implementing our shared vision.

India and the United States of America agree to expand cooperation in three specific areas:

civilian nuclear activities, civilian space programmes, and high technology trade. In addition, we agree to expand our dialogue on missile defence. Cooperation in these areas will deepen the ties of commerce and friendship between our two nations, and will increase stability in Asia and beyond.... The expanded cooperation launched today is an important milestone in transforming the relationship between India and the United States of America. That relationship is based increasingly on common values and common interests. We are working together to promote global peace and prosperity. We are partners in the war of terrorism and we are partners in controlling the proliferation of weapons of mass destruction and the means to deliver them.

The vision of the India-US strategic partnership that President Bush and I share is now becoming a reality".

92. List of documents exchanged during the visit of Prime Minister Shinzo Abe of Japan to India in New Delhi, December 12, 2015, Ministry of External Affairs, Government of India, December 12, 2015, at http://www.mea.gov.in/bilateral-documents.htm?dtl/26177/List_of_document..., accessed December June 17, 2017.
93. "Parrikar Meets Japanese Foreign Minister", *Press Information Bureau*, Ministry of Defence, Government of India, March 31, 2015, at http://pib.nic.in/newsite/PrintRelease.aspx?relid=117865, accessed Jun 17, 2016.
94. See Malik, J. Mohan (1989) 'Hands across the Himalayas', *Pacic Defence Reporter*, March, pp. 43–45; Mohan Malik, (1995) 'China–India Relations in the Post-Soviet Era: The Continuing Rivalry', *China Quarterly*, 142 (1995), pp. 317–355; Garver, John W., 'China and South Asia', pp. 68, 71.

6

INDIA AND REGIONAL SECURITY[1]

As Prime Minister-elect Narendra Modi had invited the heads of the governments of all South Asian states to attend his swearing-in on Monday, in a gesture, which diplomats and experts said was without precedent. Although foreign envoys stationed in New Delhi have attended past swearings-in, Ministry of External Affairs sources said, no world leader has been invited to attend what has traditionally been seen as a domestic event. The move startled regional diplomats-but also caused surprise in the corridors of power, which was not consulted on the decision. Mr Modi's surprise outreach, an advisor present at the meeting said, was intended to allay regional fears that his rise to power would herald a new hawkishness in Indian foreign policy. Modi sent a clear signal on Regionalism.

Regions[2] may be defined and distinguished according to an approximate combination of geographic, social, cultural, and political variables. Unambiguous distinctions, however, will always be elusive. As an analytical category in international relations, the "region" is fated to remain contingent and contentious. Geographical contiguity is clearly a prerequisite for regional identity, but drawing uncontested boundaries is usually an impossible task.[3] United Nations has classified the world into various regions and has lately classified South Asia (Afghanistan, Bangladesh, Bhutan, India, Islamic Republic of Iran, Pakistan, Maldives, Nepal and Sri Lanka) with Central Asia (Kazakhstan, Kyrgyzstan, Tajikistan, Turkmenistan, and Uzbekistan) to make it South Central Asia.[4] A very apt combination if one goes through the history. The two areas are interlinked from time immemorial.[5]

> **REGIONALISM**
>
> "*Good regionalism is good geopolitics; and bad regionalism is bad geopolitics.*"[1]
>
> [1]Henry Kissinger as quoted in Jay P. (1979), Regionalism as Geopolitics. *Foreign Affairs 58,* p. 485.

David Lake and Patrick Morgan define region minimally, as "a set of countries linked by geography and one or more common trends, such as level of development, culture, or political institutions."[6] Their definition has the advantages of simplicity, but it is potentially too broad to be really useful, and also possibly misleading. The nation-state is sometimes an inadequate building block for regional complexes.

South Asia has distinct geographic characteristics. Just from the map, it's easy to see that India is not only the biggest country therein, but it lies in the center of the subcontinent and on top of Indian Ocean. This means:

(a) All other states in the world see India as the main stake holder in regional security;
(b) Geographic centrality makes India the important hub for transporting goods and services. Because, India must give transit permission, or else, other bilateral trades and services communications face high transport costs.

India as center also suggests an asymmetry in regional relations reflected to a degree in physical indicators. For example, the land mass of India is 1.8 times of that of the sum of the rest of its regional partners. India's population is 2 times as large and its GDP is nearly six times as large. India's economy rate has maintained a steady rapid growth, and according to Forbes.[7] With respect to 'foreign trade', India's foreign trade volume accounted for more than 90 per cent of the trade of the whole of South Asia.

The Ministry of Defence defines India's strategic neighbourhood as that extending from the "Persian Gulf in the West to the Straits of Malacca in the East and from the Central Asian Republics in the north to near the equator in the South". The centrality of India in the South is a historical and geographical fact that its neighbours cannot deny. Most South Asian countries share a border with India, which is both porous and disputed. However, the overall asymmetry between India and its neighbours in South Asia is central to the persisting security dilemma in the South Asia. The threat perception of India's overt power by neighbouring countries has led them to use extra-regional powers or non-traditional means to keep India on the defensive. Pakistan's support to terrorists in Kashmir is part of this strategy.

> The Ministry of Defence, Government of India defines India's strategic neighbourhood as that extending from the "*Persian Gulf in the West to the Straits of Malacca in the East and from the Central Asian Republics in the north to near the equator in the South.*"

India's Strategic Neighbourhood

Is China part of the region? While China is not a part of South Asia it is a significant part of the regional security scenario. India's borders (a significant part of which are disputed) cover nearly 7,000 km of its 16,000 km of land frontiers. Here it should be remembered that over 94,000 km² of northeast India is claimed by China (not to mention another 60,000 km² in northwest India occupied by Pakistan). In fact, some aver that the region has been prey to "structural insecurity".

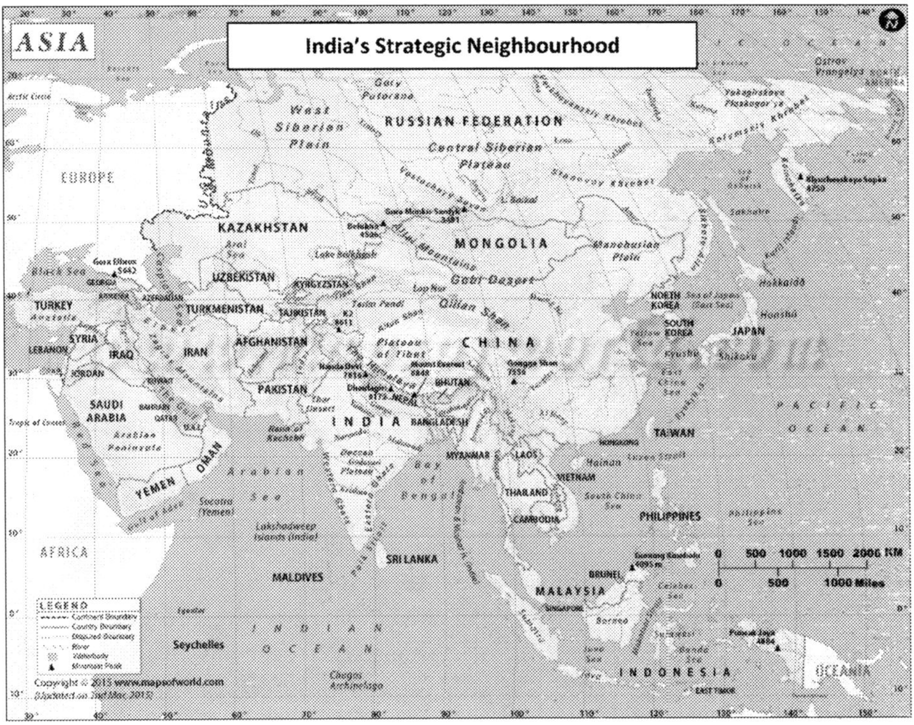

Regional conflict was a significant part of cold war competition, but it, too, usually was interpreted in a global perspective, as a projection of superpower rivalry into peripheral regions.[8] Architects of the US Cold War strategy like Henry Kissinger could opine publicly about the marginality of third world regions, and assert a great power orientation that perceived the essence of foreign policy as an elegant game of balance between power centers in Washington, London, Paris, Bonn, Moscow, and Beijing.[9] By the end of the Cold War, much of the rationale for foreign and security changed—the centrality of great power rivalry, the balance of power as the axis of interstate competition diminished, globalisation changed the concept of power where economic strength and various soft power options have accrued in importance, and there was a need for a competitive strategy to maintain and extend advantage. However, in 21st Century, the centrality of great powers rivalry is nearly but if not totally absent, the regions and sub-regions are today the primary forums for armed conflict and instability, with a variety of small wars and protracted stabilisation operations posing the greatest demands upon United Nations and United States the sole superpower.

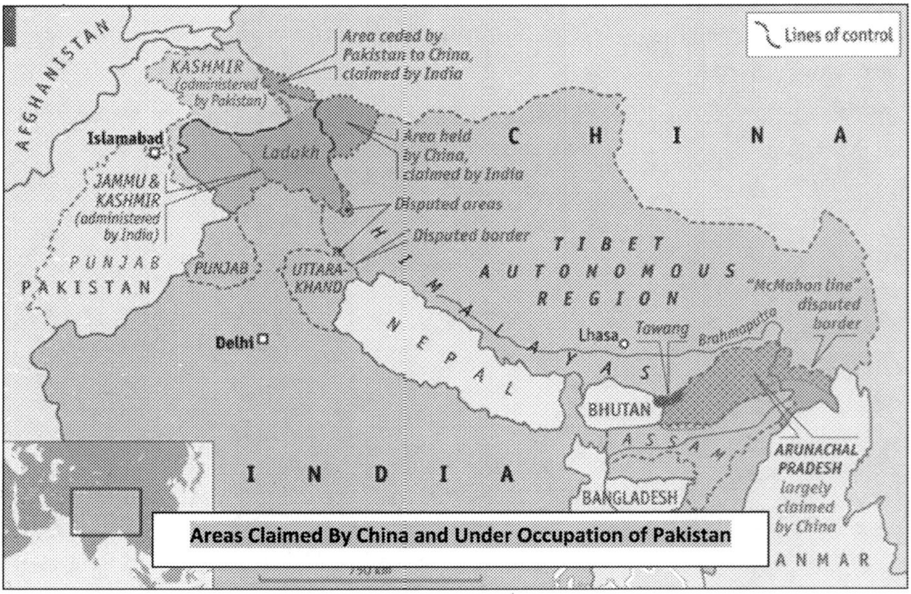

Areas Claimed By China and Under Occupation of Pakistan

Looking ahead, many nations have interests in this region, suggesting a renewal of the "Great Game" that once played out there and that in some ways continues unabated.[10] The growing threat posed by the twin risks of terrorism and instability linked with nuclear proliferation in Pakistan will command far greater attention in coming years. The threats posed by transnational terror groups—illustrated by the attacks on September 11, 2001 and the Mumbai attacks in 2008—will remain dominant concerns for the world. These groups remain both capable and deadly despite the death of al Qaeda's leader. In recent years, groups such as Lashkar-e-Taiba (LeT) and the Tehrik-i-Taliban Pakistan (TTP) have demonstrated increasing global reach, even though they were once thought to be focused solely on regional adversaries.[11]

> "The Indian elephant cannot transform itself into a mouse. If South Asia is to get itself out of the crippling binds of conflicts and cleavages, the six will have to accept the bigness of the seventh. And the seventh, that is India, will have to prove to the six that big can indeed be beautiful."
>
> **—Bhabani Sen Gupta**[1]
>
> [1]Gupta, Bhabani Sen (1984), "The Big Brother Syndrome", *India Today*, 30th April 1984, p.122

For India's policymakers, the challenge is to integrate regional perspectives, and sensitivities to national and regional dynamics, into a realistic and balanced approach to the pursuit of security; not to question the relevance of regional perspectives (which should be self-evident), but to better understand the ways in which they need to be joined to a comprehensive strategy for the pursuit of national interest.

Regional Perspectives of Security

One of the more influential recent attempts to delineate regions according to cultural criteria has been Samuel Huntington's clash of civilisations thesis. Huntington identifies nine world civilisational zones[12] based significantly, though not entirely, upon confessional affiliation.[13] The argument that geo-strategy will be dominated increasingly by civilisational conflict waged along the "fault lines" dividing these zones has been used widely to explain the apparent upsurge in ethnic conflict of the recent past. Huntington's argument, however, is neither entirely novel nor altogether convincing. Geopolitical analysis long has used the idea of the "shatterbelt", defined as a politically fragmented and ethnically divided zone that serves as a field of competition between continental and maritime powers.[14] Great civilisations cannot be bounded precisely spatially, and they are rarely either entirely homogenous or mutually exclusive. Huntington's attempt to designate geographically bounded civilisational zones, and to use these zones as the foundation for a theory of geo-strategy, rests on suspect premises.

> Defence Minister Shri A.K. Antony said political disturbances in West Asia and North Africa have forced fresh challenges for global security. "Security concerns of the future will increasingly be dictated by economic, geopolitical, environmental, social and demographic considerations. Terrorism, cyber-attacks and sea piracy are some of the major challenges facing the nation," said Antony. Antony was reported to have said that, "We are taking adequate steps to ensure any spill-over effect from any adverse development in Pakistan is successfully countered by our armed forces," he added, "Besides conventional threats, our armed forces have to reckon with non-conventional threats, cyber and information warfare. Though a conventional war is unlikely, there is need to maintain maximum level of operational preparedness to deal with such challenges."

Another thinker, Barry Buzan has developed the concept of the "regional security complex" in an effort "to offset the tendency of power theorists to underplay the importance of the regional level in international security affairs."[15] He makes the assertion that in security terms, 'region' means that a distinct and significant subsystem of security relations exists among a set of states whose fate is that they have been locked into geographical proximity with each other."[16] The existence of a "subsystem" of security relations presumes high levels of interdependence, multiple interactions, and shared sensitivities and vulnerabilities. Any attempt to identify such complexes empirically, however, poses obvious problems.[17]

Buzan and Weaver[18] have the regionalist perspective to post-Cold War security. They agree with Lake and Morgan[19] that in the post-Cold War world 'the regional level stands more clearly on its own as the locus of conflict and cooperation for states and as the level of analysis for scholars seeking to explore contemporary security affairs', and we believe this to be true even though we use an understanding of security more open that their rather traditional, military one.[20]

INDIRA DOCTRINE 1983

In 1983 Indira articulated a foreign policy, it stated that,

'India would not tolerate any intervention of outside powers in the internal affairs of other South Asian Countries. It also requited South Asian governments to desist from forging security relationships with countries deemed inimical to India's interests. Further it required South Asian governments to first request Indian economic and military assistance before turning to other countries, inform India prior to implementing any major security decisions and settle their internal disputes in a manner acceptable to India.'[1]

[1]Mazumdar Arijit (2015), *Indian Foreign Policy in Transition: Relations with South Asia,* (London and New York: Routledge), p. 29.

Regionalism

Regionalism[21] emphasises the uniqueness of a particular region, acknowledges the linkages between different regions, and centers on increasing the region's influence and political power, thus usually being regarded as the *middle* dimension (or bridge) of analysis between the domestic dimension and the global dimension.[22]

The Cold War (1945-1989) and decolonisation rolled back the imperial power, created dozens of new states, and allowed the regional security dynamics to start operating among these newly independent actors in most of Africa, the Middle East, South and South East Asia. The two superpowers United States and Soviet Union were both, for different ideological reasons opposed to the European and Japanese empires. The Soviet Union saw them as extension of capitalism and therefore as targets for socialist revolution. The United Sates saw them as an extension of European neo-mercantilism, and wanted them to be opened up to free trade and self-determination. The Cold War assisted the formation of several Regional Security Complexes in the Middle East, Africa and Asia.

First, can South Asia be called an independent region? Or, as Rafiq Dossani wonders, does South Asia exist?[23] Or, as Swaran Singh held, would it be more proper to call it Southern Asia?[24] If south Asia exists, what is the geographical scope of South Asia? How do we define the different powers? Then, in a geographically defined South Asia, does overarching security architecture exist? If partly yes, then what could be the key features of that security architecture? Could it help to address the current policy considerations or other security concerns of those players in that region? Or, if it is partly no, what will be the important catalysts and future scenarios for the evolution of security architecture? For example, in the Yearbook of the United Nations 2005, The Aden Colony, British Somaliland, and Singapore, though administered at various times under the Raj, have not been proposed as any part of South Asia. Furthermore, there exists a geographically defined South Asia region that clearly includes Afghanistan for both geo-political and geo-economical consideration. It defines South Asia in the domain of SAARC, namely India, Pakistan, Bangladesh, Nepal, Bhutan, Sri Lanka, the Maldives and Afghanistan. Although Myanmar has been historically and geo-politically part of the region, it is not included into South Asia by the United Nations classification. One of the unique features is that India shares boundaries with all the nations of South Asia while no two South Asia countries shares borders with each other excepting Afghanistan and Pakistan. The United States and Russia are defined as important external powers, and China is defined as an "important potential power of South Asia,"[25] mainly because it is an immediate nieghbour of South Asia.

What gives South Asia a Geopolitical Distinctiveness?

A major, almost defining, feature of South Asia is its diversity. Ethnically diverse, the region has over two thousand ethnic entities of varying size ranging between a few thousands and hundreds of millions. The region's linguistic diversity is both phenomenal and bewildering, although English does serve as a common language. In terms of religion, Hinduism and Islam dominate the landscape, with their inter-relations having moulded the area's history for over one thousand years, even though other religions—Buddhism, Jainism, Christianity and Sikhism—have flourished well.

South Asia's peculiar geography—a contiguous landmass ringed by the Himalayas in the north and surrounded by sea on three sides, with several rivers criss-crossing the region–favours mutual inter-dependence of SAARC member states. Other favourable factors are a common history, shared culture and languages, a similar mindset and collective memory of being children born from the same womb, influenced by an unbroken record of over five thousand years of human habitation and civilisational development.

What gives to South Asia geopolitical distinctiveness, apart from physical and cultural qualities, is its inward economic orientation. Though surrounded by water, the region has not been and is not a maritime one.[26]

India has long held a view that it has special place within the South Asian region. With respect to leadership, India has clearly established its preference for external powers to refrain from interfering within South Asia to extensively. Since 1987, it has made it clear that assistance in resolving intra-regional disputes should be directed toward India in lieu of outside powers.[27] This unique position as primary regional security manager was more fully institutionalised in Gujral Doctrine in the 1990s.[28] Aside from such claims to special management responsibilities though, India also views the intrusion of external powers as being an infringement upon its own position within the region. Gill quotes a senior Indian Foreign Ministry official who discusses India's role as a protector: 'India is the center of the region, so the region is India, and it is our job to protect it from outside'. Such a duty has' been an article of faith for many in the Indian strategic community.[29]

> If a South Asian country genuinely needs external help to deal with serious internal conflict situation or with an intolerable threat to a government legitimately established, it should ask for help from a number of neighbouring countries including India. The exclusion of India from such a contingency will be considered to be an anti-Indian move on the part of the Government concerned.[30]

In other words, New Delhi claimed a right to intervene in the internal affairs of the neighbouring countries if the internal conflict or disorder threatened to extend beyond national boundaries, or external military assistance with anti-India bias was received. Moreover, India has been blamed for pursuing the objective of creating asymmetrical power relations with South Asian states for playing dominant role in the region. Leo Rose argues that the primary purpose of India's regional policy is "to extract, in some form or another, recognition of India's hegemonistic status in the region from both of the major external powers, and from its neighbours in the region."[31]

SECURITY ARCHITECTURE

Security architecture is an overarching, coherent and comprehensive security structure for a geographically-defined area, which facilitates the resolution of that region's policy concerns and achieves its security objectives.

South Asian Security Architecture

Since, security architecture is an overarching, coherent and comprehensive security structure for a geographically-defined area, which facilitates the resolution of that region's policy concerns and achieves its security objectives; from the perspective of security architecture, South Asia is a relatively closed and unique strategic unit. It, in a whole, showed the features of asymmetry and fractures in security architecture from three different 'layers' or 'dimensions.'

(a) First, *in the dimension of power*, India enjoys absolute predominance in spite of different dependencies of other state powers on it;

(b) Second, *in the dimension of mechanism*, the design flaws on SAARC have shadowed double side impacts on both economy and society, which have resulted in the fragmentation of economic integration between the India-eastward camp and the Pakistan-westward camp, as well as the huge gap between official social communication or confidence building and unofficial people-to-people contacts.

(c) Third, *in the dimension of idea*, the bias of land first, sea later and military first, bread later have long and rooted origins, although now it might be the right time to redefine the gravity and priority between land power and sea power. This kind of asymmetric and fractured security architecture cannot adapt to new security situations and demands, nor satisfy the needs of South Asian people for a sustained peace and sustainable development.

GUJRAL DOCTRINE

In his famous Chatham House speech in London in September 1996, Gujral outlined his approach towards the neighbours and stated:

"The United Front Government's neighbourhood policy now stands on five basic principles: First, with the neighbours like Nepal, Bangladesh, Bhutan, Maldives and Sri Lanka, India does not ask for reciprocity but gives all that it can in good faith and trust. Secondly, no South Asian country will allow its territory to be used against the interest of another country of the region. Thirdly, none will interfere in the internal affairs of another. Fourthly, all South Asian countries must respect each other's territorial integrity and sovereignty. And finally, they will settle all their disputes through peaceful bilateral negotiations. These five principles, scrupulously observed, will, I am sure, recast South Asia's regional relationship, including the tormented relationship between India and Pakistan, in a friendly, cooperative mould."[1]

[1]Mr I K Gujral at the Royal Institute of International Affairs (Chatham House), London, 23 Sep 1996. The speech is reproduced in Gujral, I.K. (1998), *A Foreign Policy for India,* (New Delhi: Ministry of External Affairs), pp. 69-81.

One of the most striking things about the larger Asian strategic landscape is the arc of failing or troubled states around India. This harsh geographical reality is India's most-glaring weaknesses—one that weighs it down regionally. Its neighbourhood is so chronically troubled that India confronts what can be called a tyranny of geography.[32] As a result, it faces serious external threats from virtually all directions. It is locked in an arc of failing or authoritarian states that seek, in different ways, to undermine its secular, multiethnic, pluralistic character. To

India's west lies "an arc of crises stretching from Jordan to Pakistan"—to use the title of one of the workshops at the 2008 World Policy Conference at Evian, France.[33] A contiguous belt of political disorder stretches from Lebanon to Pakistan, with incalculable consequences for regional and international security. Rapid Talibanisation and spreading militancy threaten to devour next-door Pakistan, with a task force of the United States-based Atlantic Council warning in a report that, "We are running out of time to help Pakistan change its present course toward increasing economic and political instability, and even ultimate failure".[34]

The hasty retreat of the British Raj and the ensuring bitterness generated between the ruling elites of the two major South Asian states gravely disrupted the traditional complementarities and cohesion. Indeed, the legacy of state formation in South Asia bestows a unique complexity to the entire region. Thus, some of the contentious issues that inhibit cooperation in South Asia include those resulting from colonial legacies, issues of political and ideological character, issues of strategic conflict and military balance, issues that arise from the spill-over effect of internal conflicts and turmoil in a given country on its neighbours and issues that arise out of resource and developmental conflicts. The most pronounced security dilemma, however, stems from escalating arms race in South Asia, particularly between the two military powers—India and Pakistan. These disputes among countries further complicate the scenario and have created a lot of problems among the leaders for friendly talks. This situation deficits confidence building measures (CBMs).

Since independence South Asia has been a region of contest. Many authors have given various reasons, for India's inability to exercise influence in the region as it should have. First, all the nations of the region excepting Afghanistan were British Colonies. The partition of the South Asian subcontinent along religious lines (first into India and Pakistan, in 1947, then into India, Pakistan, and Bangladesh, in 1971) left India with a persistent conflict with Pakistan and an internal Hindu-Muslim divide. It also physically separated India from historically linked states such as Afghanistan, Iran, and the nations of Southeast Asia. The creation of an avowedly Islamic state in Pakistan caused especially profound problems for India's engagement with the Middle East. Such tensions intertwined with regional and global great-power rivalries to severely constrict India's room for maneuver in all three concentric circles.

The root cause of these manifold failures, in many minds, is the very artificiality of Pakistan itself: a cartographic puzzle piece sandwiched between India and Central Asia that splits apart what the British Empire ruled as one indivisible subcontinent. Pakistan claims to represent the Indian subcontinent's Muslims,[35] but more Muslims live in India and Bangladesh put together than in Pakistan. In the absence of any geographical reason for its existence, Pakistan, so the assumption goes, can fall back only on Islamic extremism as an organising principle of the state.

> "They can say what they want, but we have no doubt that the terrorists had come from Pakistan."
>
> **—Sriprakash Jaiswal, India's Minister of State for Home Affairs, shortly after the Mumbai bombings.**
>
> Buncombe, A. (2008): India lashes out at old enemy, in: The Independent, http://www.independent.co.uk/news/world/asia/india-lashes-out-at-old-enemy-1042720.html

Pakistan is, in many ways, the most dangerous nation in the world. Although designated a major non-NATO (*North Atlantic Treaty Organisation*) ally of the United States for security assistance purposes, (A tag which is lately under threat) Pakistan hosts myriad insurgent groups, radical Islamist political parties and a large military establishment well-armed with both nuclear and conventional weaponry. These disparate internal actors with highly divergent objectives illustrate the innate fissures and conflicts that characterise of this outwardly unitary state. As recent events have spectacularly revealed, Pakistan has, wittingly or unwittingly, also provided a hideout for the world's most wanted terrorist for years. Its populace has been cited as the most anti-American citizenry in the world. The government's authority throughout the country is uneven, and militant groups operating inside Pakistan directly threaten the stability of the regime and challenge its monopoly on the use of force. These groups are deeply connected with much of the country's radical Islamic religious leadership, as illustrated by the 2006 Red Mosque standoff and battle in Islamabad. State failure in Pakistan, triggered by extremism, popular uprising, or economic meltdown would have immensely dangerous repercussions for the United States and a host of regional actors.

Pakistan's willingness to continue baiting India is rooted in structural constraints that are ultimately personified by two simple realities. First, Pakistan remains the "anti-status quo"[36] state in South Asia. This phrase is not meant to convey any normative stance but is merely a description of Pakistan's circumstances: Islamabad today is not satisfied with the existing territorial order primarily because of its long-standing claims to the former princely kingdom of Jammu and Kashmir, significant portions of which are currently governed by India. Pakistan is not only weaker than India but probably growing weaker in absolute terms as well. This implies that Islamabad simply lacks the resources to secure its claims over Jammu and Kashmir by force. The military solution has in fact been tried on several occasions in the past and has in all instances been unsuccessful.

The second was Nehruvian policies. It may be due historic error or just coincidence due its problems at home. India adopted the 'socialist system', which caused a steady relative economic decline (similar as it happened in USSR and China) and a consequent loss of influence in the years after independence. The state-socialist model led India to shun commercial engagement with the outside world especially the West. As a result, India was disconnected from its natural markets and culturally akin areas in the extended nieghbourhood.

Thirdly, the Cold War, the onset of which quickly followed India's independence, pushed India into the arms of the Soviet Union in response to Washington's support for Pakistan and China—and thus put the country on the losing side of the great political contest of the second half of the twentieth century. Despite being the largest democracy in the world, India ended up siding with the opposite camp on most global issues. The United States had been pushing Pakistan as a frontline state in its contest with USSR, and Pakistan never would reconcile to living in peace with India.

There exists some possibility for adjusting or correcting those imbalances, fractures, and biases. This will mainly rely on India, and in the long run so do the people of South Asia, although in the short-term, some outside active or even assertive policies may in practice have certain positive results.

> **NEHRU DOCTRINE**
>
> India's foreign policy, according to Nehru, "is a policy inherent in the past thinking of India, inherent in the whole mental outlook of India, inherent in the conditioning of Indian mind during our struggle for freedom and inherent in the circumstances today. As a matter of fact, the traces of our foreign policy can be found even in our freedom movement. It was largely owing to Nehru's efforts that even since the mid-twenties the Congress party began to take interest in the international relations. He was the conscience of keeper the Indian National Congress with regard to the world-affairs in general. " In his Discovery of India, Nehru noted that: "the Congress gradually developed a foreign policy, which was based on the elimination of political and economic imperialism everywhere and on the co-operation of free nations. As early as 1920, a resolution on foreign policy was passed by the Congress in which our desire to co-operate with other nations, and especially to develop friendly relations with all our neighbouring countries was emphasised.

This region has seen democracy, socialism, martial law and monarchy.[37]

Militarisation of South Asia Post-Independence

Definitions say in simple words, "*Act of assembling (of arms, mightiness etc.) and putting into readiness for war.*" is Militarisation. Geyer[38] (1989, p 79) defines militarisation as "The contradictory and tense social process in which civil society organises itself for the production of violence".[39]

For India one of the remarkable features of the evolution since Independence has been gradual militarisation, interstate arms transfers, massive military development, and a violent culture at its periphery. Various levels of militarisation can be seen in the different countries, from outright military dictatorships such as in Myanmar, Pakistan has been saddled with direct military regimes, to military rule in certain areas of Thailand, to the arming of civilians in the Philippines.

Indian State has militarist responses on a number of issues. These include regions in India like the North East and Kashmir. Whenever the state feels a threat, either from internal or external sources a militarist response is considered the primary option. Thus whether it is the approach to tackling social justice movements or secessionist movements, from Naxalite to Khalistan, the state responds by the use of military methods. The effort is for conflict management through use of force. Not only is force used to resolve policy issues, but those wielding this force, army or police, also hold a certain status, power in society (e.g. Pakistan). What all these have in common is the notion that the use of force is necessary to the effective ruling of a population. Such a notion is in fact the premise of militarisation.

For more than 60 years now, the South Asian security structure has been marked by Indo-Pakistani rivalry, mistrust and violence. Since the independence of the Indian subcontinent and its partition into Hindu-dominated but nominally secular India and the newly created Muslim state of Pakistan in 1947, the relationship between both states was dominated by fear and enmity, leading to three full-scale wars[40] and a huge number of minor military skirmishes short of war. The disputed status of the Kashmir-region, "the root of all evil in Indo-Pakistani affairs"[41], fuelled the conflict repeatedly and tensions often escalated at the ceasefire line/Line of Control (LOC) between the Indian-administered part (Jammu and Kashmir) and Pakistan.[42] In the aftermath of the conducted nuclear tests of India and Pakistan in 1998, the tensions between them reached a new and much more threatening dimension and the arms race between both states increased. Strictly speaking, dangerous strategic competition is dominating the security paradigm of South Asia.[43]

> "There are few examples in the history of relations where two states have stagnated in a confrontationist mode, despite their civil societies having intense and wide-ranging commonalities. India and Pakistan, from their very inception as independent countries, have been stuck in an adversarial predicament owing to a number of reasons."[44]

In South Asia intra-state conflicts have amplified in the last few decades. Whether there are communal riots in India, sectarian and ethnic violence in Pakistan, rift with communist party in Nepal, rivalry and conflict between the main political parties in Bangladesh or the power struggle in Afghanistan, South Asia faces regional security threats because of internal crisis and conflicts of the states. Being one of the most ethnically, culturally and linguistically diverse regions, it has witnessed many inter-state and intrastate conflicts and war which have disturbed the overall security of the region.

There is continuing reluctance in the international policy discourse, however, to face up to a central reality: the political border between Afghanistan and Pakistan (or "Afpak" in Washingtonese) has now ceased to exist in practice. The so-called Durand Line, in any event, was an artificial, British-colonial invention that left the large Pashtun community divided into two.[45] Today, that line exists only in maps. On the ground, it has little political, ethnic, and economic relevance, even as the Afpak region has become a magnet for the world's jihadists. A de facto Pashtunistan, long sought by Pashtuns, now lurks just below the horizon, on the ruins of an ongoing Islamist militancy.

The disappearance of the Durand Line seems irreversible. While the writ of the Pakistani state no longer extends to nearly half of that country (much of Baluchistan, large parts of the North-West Frontier Province, and the whole of the Federally Administered Tribal Areas), even larger swaths of Afghanistan are outside the control of the government in Kabul. The Pakistani army has lost increasing ground to insurgents in the Western regions not because it is weaker than the armed extremists and insurgents but because an ethnic, tribal, and militant backlash has resulted in the state withering away in the Pashtun and Baluch lands. Forced to cede control, the jihadist-infiltrated military establishment and its infamous Inter-Services Intelligence (ISI) agency have chosen to support proxy militant groups, especially the Taliban. However, with its own unity unravelling, Pakistan is paying a heavy price for having fathered the Taliban. Indeed, an Islamist-ruled Pashtun state, even if a de facto one, would set in motion the unravelling of Pakistan and Afghanistan, two artificially created states that have searched endlessly for a national identity.

MILITARISM

Militarism is a belief system that endorses military values in civilian life; believes in the construction of a strong masculinity that is also a necessary component of state power; legitimizes the use of violence as a solution to conflict and dissent; and closely intersects with patriarchy and nationalism. Notions such as national honour, national pride and the ambition of being a great power form the basis of this militarised nationalism in India. Militarisation involves the increasing use of military power by states to further their national interests, with the option of using military threats and war as an extension of politics. It implies the growing dominance of militarist values in civilian institutions. Militarisation encompasses the process whereby military values, ideology and patterns of behaviour dominate social and political systems and influence gender relations, resulting in the militarisation of the

The international reluctance to come to terms with the disappearance of the Durand Line is because of the fundamental, far-reaching issues such acceptance would throw open. It is simpler to just keep up the pretence of wanting to stabilise Pakistan and Afghanistan within their existing political frontiers. Take US policy. As if determined to hide from this reality, the Obama administration is pursuing, at least outwardly, a military approach toward Afghanistan through a troop "surge" and a political strategy toward Pakistan pivoted on dispensing billions of dollars in additional aid—or what Pakistani Foreign Minister from (2008-11) Shah Mahmood Qureshi calls a "civilian surge". The Obama policy rejects the Bush administration's institution-building approach in Afghanistan as an attempt to create "some sort of Central Asian Valhalla". Yet, the new administration has unveiled $3.2 billion in annual civilian aid, a historic high, for an increasingly radicalized Pakistan to win hearts and minds there—a Valhalla even more distant. [United States has lavished Pakistan with nearly $8 billion in security assistance, $11 billion in economic assistance, and $13 billion in the lucrative program known as Coalition Support Funds (CSF)].

India has little choice but to brace up to the greater threats to its internal security that are likely to come from the Af-Pak belt. The international community had agreed to focus on institution building, demobilisation of existing militias, and reconstruction to help create a stable, moderate Afghanistan—goals that have prompted India to pour massive $1.4 billion aid into that country. But that investment now is at stake as the Obama administration abandons the goal of institution-building in Afghanistan and seeks to strike a political accord with the "moderate" Taliban (as if there can be moderates in an Islamist militia that enforces medieval practices). The whole security environment has led into massive militarisation of South Asia.

Incidence of War, Military Crisis and Terrorism

Year	Location	Parties Involved	Nature of Event
1947	Punjab and Bengal	Hindu, Muslims and Sikhs	Communal Violence
1947-48	Kashmir	Pakistanis, Kashmiris and Indians	Tribal invasion of Kashmir assisted by Pakistan Army
1962	Himalayan Frontiers	China and India	War
1965	Kutch (Gujarat)	Pakistan and India	War
1965	Kashmir and Punjab	Pakistan and India	War
1971	East Pakistan (Bangladesh)- the Indo-Pakistan Border on the West was Secondary	Pakistan, India and Bangladesh Guerilla	Indo-Pak War

Year	Location	Parties Involved	Nature of Event
1984	India (Punjab)	Sikhs, Indian Military Forces and Pakistan Army	Insurgency and Separatism
1984	Sri Lanka (Jaffna)	Sri Lankan Tamils, Indian Tamils, Sinhalese and Indian and Sri Lanka Government	Insurgency and Separatism
Mid-1980	Chittagong Hill Tracts	Chakma tribals, Bangladesh Military Forces and India	Insurgency and Separatism
1987	Indo-Pak Border	India and Pakistan	Military Crisis
1987	Sino-India Border	India and China	Military Crisis
1989-to date	Kashmir	Pakistan Army, Kashmiris and Indian Army	Insurgency and Separatism
—	North East India	Various Hill Tribes	Insurgencies
1999	Kashmir	Pakistan Army's incursion into India	Limited war
2001-02	India-Pakistan	Terrorist attack	Mobilisation of Forces
2003-	Kashmir, terrorist acts in other parts of the country	Terrorist attack	Insurgencies
1967-	Naxalite-Maosist Insurgency		Spread over a large area in Eastern and Central India

Nepal

Nepal, a land-locked country, has delineated its border both with China and India. Nepal has historical cultural and social relations with India. Indians and Nepalese share a common culture and terrain south of the Himalaya. Bound by languages and religions, marriage and mythology, the links of their civilisational contacts run through Lumbini to Bodh Gaya, Pashupatinath to Kashi Vishwanath, and Muktinath to Tirupati. At the people-to-people level, relations between India and Nepal are closer and more multifaceted than between India and any other country. Many partisans of Nepalese democracy also fought for India's freedom, for which they were jailed by the British, including Matrika Koirala, B.P. Koirala, and Man Mohan Adhikari, who became Prime Ministers of Nepal.

Indian strategists and policy makers consider Nepal as critical to India's security. The British Indian Empire saw Nepal as the buffer with China and after 1947 India continued with that policy. Any signs of close ties between Nepal and China are anathema to New Delhi.

While Nepal and India have close historical, religious and cultural ties, Nepal's strategic ties with India date to the Treaty of Sugauli of 1816 signed between the Nepalese monarch and the British East India Company. As per the treaty, large parts of the Nepalese kingdom (including parts of present day Uttaranchal, Himachal Pradesh and Sikkim) were annexed by the British empire, a British resident was stationed at Kathmandu, Nepal agreed to defer to the British with respect to its foreign policy and Gorkhas were recruited in large numbers by the British for military service. Nepal regained some of the lost territory when the monarch helped the British during the 1857 uprising. However, even today Nepal lays claim to certain parts of Indian Territory, like Kalapani, along the India-Nepal border.

Modern day India and Nepal signed a Treaty of Peace and Friendship in 1950 which in addition to respecting each other's sovereignty and territorial integrity granted rights to Nepalese and Indian citizens to reside and work (and even obtain citizenship) in India and Nepal respectively. Further, India granted Nepal the right to transit trade across its territory and to the use of Indian ports for importing and exporting commodities free of customs duties. Furthermore, Gorkhas still form a key part of the Indian army.

Over the decades New Delhi has consistently sought to influence Nepalese politics, sometimes directly, often indirectly. India was instrumental in helping the Nepalese monarch regain his traditional power and reduce the powers of the powerful hereditary Prime Ministers, the Ranas.

Many Indians believe independent India never had foreign combat troops deployed on its soil. Nepalese troops were the exception. Aside from those recruited to India's Gurkha Regiment, an outsized Nepalese Army brigade drawn from all its 18 regiments was loaned to India in 1948-49, when Indian troops were deployed in Kashmir and for the integration of Indian States. The commanding officer of this force, General Sharda Shamsher Jang Bahadur Rana, was the son of the then Prime Minister of Nepal, Maharaja Mohan Shamsher Jang Bahadur Rana. Yuvraj Karan Singh's marriage to Yasho Rajya Lakshmi, Sharda Shamsher's daughter, was arranged during the General's stay in India.

The external threat to Nepal is minimal at the moment. However, the political history of Nepal is a series of events of violence whether it is in the process of unification of modern Nepal or the process of regimes thereafter have led to militarisation of society. It is difficult to pinpoint exact dates and events to succinctly answer to the question as to when and how the violence of politics in Nepal began.[46] The past has been witness to dozens of violent political conflicts that occurred in different times and places in Nepal. However, the trend of violent politics was intensified after the Shah dynasty came into existence. Defeating Ghale Gurung, Drabya Shah became the king of the Gorkhas and his immediate descendant, Prithvi Narayan Shah, unified Nepal by annexing Baise state (twenty-two) and Chaubise (twenty-four) principalities through violence.[47]

In the inception of modern Nepal, there were violent disputes between the ruling families generally known as 'Vardars' (Thapa, Basnett and Pandy) for sharing power and resources. The 14 September 1846 Kot massacre was the first. Many leading nobles were killed or assassinated and some many were exiled. The events at Kot weakened power of Shah family and other Vardar—Thapas, Pandes and Basnets—the then ruling clans; and power came in the hands Jung-Bhadur Rana.[48]

Janga Bahadur Rana, imposed the hereditary, Prime Ministerial, autocratic, rule of 104 years[49]. Within the last six decades, Nepal has experienced many instances of internal political violence, among them; anti-Rana armed revolution (1940s), "exterminate the class enemy" campaign (1970s), and royal abolishment violence (1980s) are significant.

From historical readings it is revealed that Nepali Society has suffered either a violent armed struggle or people's movement at about each 10-year interval since the formation of Modern Nepal. In the 1970s; the communist party (Marxist-Leninist) started armed struggle in eastern Nepal (Jhapa district) against "feudals." They named it Barga Shatru Khatam Abhiyan (exterminate the class enemy campaign). It was inspired by Latin American revolutionary literature and the Naxlanbadhi Kisan Aandholan (known as Naxalbari Agricultural Movement) in India.[50]

In February 13, 1996, under the leadership of Baburam Bhattarai, the United People's Front (UPF) declared the beginning of what they called the 'people's war', an armed struggle dedicated to sweeping away the semi-feudal based social structure and establishing a new democratic people's republic. The escalation of people's war and the states corrosive response to it resulted in grave political violence. Both the nature and degree of (CPN) Maoist and state counter violence is unprecedented in the Nepal's history.[51] Dahal and Rai (2007)[52] succinctly write, "The escalation of the Maoist insurgency and the state's counterinsurgency in the aftermath of the Maoist 'people's war' has made political violence and terror an everyday reality of Nepali society to the degree and scale never experienced before".

Long practices of violent politics have socialized the common people to them. That violence is a normal element in politics has been taken for granted. The Maoist insurgency normalised violence at a societal level. That has made violence in politics more acceptable than before. The growing trend of using violence in the social sphere to achieve end goals, and the practice of "youth force formation" as militia of political parties have socialised the youth as a "fierce segment" of society. History shows that practices of routinenisation and ritualisation of violence creates tension and insecurity at a societal level.

Table 2: Main Militant Groups Formed by the Political Parties/Groups

Sl.No.	Youth Organization	Mother organization	Geographical Influence
1.	Young Communist League	UCPN (Maoist)	All over the country
2.	Youth Force	CPN (UML)	All over the country
3.	Madhesi Youth Force	Madhesi Janaadhikar Forum (MJF)	Eastern, Central and Mid-Western Terai regions
4.	Security Brigade (Rakshya Bahini)	Nepal Sadbhawana Party (Rajendra Mahato)	Central and Mid-Western regions
5.	Madhesi Commando	Nepal Sadbhawana Party	Central and Mid-Western regions
6.	Terai Madhes Sewa Surakshya Sangh	Terai Madhes Loktantrik Party	Mid-Western and Western regions
7.	All Nepal Democratic Youth Organisation	Rastriya Janamorcha Party	Mid-Western and Western regions
8.	OBC Regiment	Pichhada Varga Mahasangh	Central Terai Region
9.	Limbuwan Volunteers and Limbuwan Liberation Army	Sanghiya Loktantrik Rastriya Manch/Limbuwan Rajya Parishad	Eastern region
10.	Janasurakshya Bal	CPN-Maoists	Some districts
11.	Madhesi Raksha Bahini	Sadbhawana Party	Some of the Terai districts
12.	Khas Ksherti		

Source: Various Journals and Newspapers.

While India and Nepal share close ties, as seen from the high peaks of the Himalayas, however, the Nepalese leaders have always feared absorption by India, not just of a physical nature but also economic and cultural. The fear of physical absorption increased after India's role in the creation of Bangladesh in 1971 and Indian absorption of Sikkim in 1974.

In the economic arena Nepalese resent the large Indian business diaspora and friction over transit trade has never been amicably resolved. While India and Nepal share rivers, they have not been able to come up with a solution whereby India could fund hydro-electric projects in Nepal and benefit from the large energy production. Over the decades many Hindi-speaking ethnically Indian migrants settled in the deltaic Terai region of Nepal. Nepal has been reluctant to offer these madhesis citizenship which has only aggravated existing tensions with India.

The close relationship between India and Nepal has been aptly summed up by Mr Rakesh Sood, former Indian Ambassador to Nepal: "Not many are aware of the extensive economic linkages and cooperation between the two countries."

"Two-thirds of Nepal's foreign trade is with India which also accounts for half of Nepal's foreign direct investment. The Nepali currency is pegged to the Indian rupee. Over the years, India has built highways, optical fiber links, medical colleges, trauma centers, polytechnics, schools, health centres, bridges, etc. For flood protection and embankment construction in Nepal, India provides more than Rs 75 crore annually. To facilitate the movement of goods and people, India is providing Rs 270 crore to build four integrated check posts on the border, Rs 650 crore for extending two railway links out of the five proposed, and Rs 700 crore for the first phase of rebuilding old postal roads in the Terai region. In addition, there is a second EXIM Bank Line of Credit for $250 million available and another $125 million for the power transmission line upgrades. About Rs 1,300 crore is disbursed annually to the 1.25 lakh Indian Army pensioners in addition to other welfare schemes. The provision of iodised salt, conducting cataract and trachoma camps, gifting of ambulances and school buses in the remotest of Nepali villages are initiatives that have made a difference to life in rural Nepal." Still, an undercurrent of resentment against India has persisted."

WHAT IS IT ABOUT INDIA'S BEHAVIOUR THAT NEPALIS DISLIKE?

1. Big-brother attitude: Many Nepali citizens feel that India holds a "big-brother" attitude towards Nepal and interferes in its internal affairs. Time and again, India is accused of utilising diplomatic power for its vested-interests. A case in point is the recent "undeclared blockade" by India.
2. "Unfair" treaties: There exists a long list of treaties which are considered unfair by the Nepali side. This list includes 1950 Indo-Nepal Treaty of Peace and Friendship, Koshi and Mahakali water treaties, among others. Nepali people feel that they are not provided with their fair share of water and also they are angry about how Nepal's political leadership easily bows down to India's terms.
3. No respect for sovereignty: People think that Nepal finds it necessary to consult India on every important matter including its internal issues. Nepali people are angry about India's unwarranted objection over its new constitution which was endorsed by more than 90 per cent of people's representatives elected to the Constituent Assembly—the body mandated to draft the constitution.
4. Mistreatment at border entry points: Nepali migrant workers who work in India complain that officers of Indian border security force, Seema Suraksha Bal, mistreat them at border entry points. Indian Prime Minister Narendra Modi, during his Nepal visit last year, had promised to improve that situation but the problem still persists.
5. Encroachment of border areas: Complaints of encroachment of Nepali territory often create tension between these two countries. For instance, the Nepali side accuses India of encroaching key strategic areas like Kalapani and Lipulekh (also bordering China) which lie within the Nepali territory.

6. "Insensitive" Indian media: Indian media, especially TV news channels, are considered weapons to spread sensationalism and ultra-nationalism in Nepal. Many people feel that Indian media is insensitive towards its smaller neighbouring countries and does not respect their concerns, and disregards important facts. When Indian media was covering Nepal in the aftermath of the April 25 earthquake, the hashtag #GoHomeIndianMedia trended on microblogging site Twitter. A lot of criticism came from within India.
7. Relationship: Nepali people like many Indian things such as holy places, Bollywood movies and food that have become part of the daily life of Nepali people. But Nepali people do not take any criticism hinted towards the country lightly. In the year 2000, Indian actor Hrithik Roshan's alleged anti-Nepal statement provoked riot in some places of Nepal. However, Hrithik Roshan denied making such a statement.
8. Influence of China on Nepal: People feel that India keeps unnecessary concerns about "China's increasing proximity" with Nepal. A majority of Nepalis think that no other nation can be as close with Nepal as India is because of many similarities between the two countries. People are unhappy about India's inability to understand the difficult situation faced by Nepal even when it tries to maintain balance between the two big countries which surround it.

Source: http://kathmandupost.ekantipur.com/news/2015-10-02/8-things-nepalis-dislike-about-indian-interference.html

It is often argued by the Nepalese that Indo-Nepal relationship is highly "unequal" because of the unequal Treaty of Peace and Friendship which the two countries signed in 1950. However, the fact remains that it was Nepal that had wanted this treaty in order to maintain the special ties with independent India that it had with British India. Moreover, many a time over the last 65 years India has asked the Nepalese side what provisions of the treaty were unequal; but there has been no concrete response."

It may be noted here that according to Articles VI and VII of the treaty, citizens of both countries have equal rights in matters of residence, acquisition of property, employment and movement in each other's territory. As Ambassador Sood says, "The treaty provides for an open border between the two countries and allows Nepali nationals to work in India without a work permit, to apply for government jobs and the civil services (except for the IFS, IAS, and IPS), to open bank accounts and buy property. Incidentally, India had waived its rights under reciprocity as a sign of goodwill. The provisions of the 'secret' side letters to the Treaty, which required Nepal to consult India on its defence requirements, which Nepalese perceive as unfair and which are often used by politicians to whip up anti-India sentiment, are no longer secret or even observed."

As American Scholar late Leo Rose[53] writes in his book, *Nepal: A Profile of a Himalayan Kingdom*, the strategies available to countries in Nepal's geostrategic situation are limited in number: isolation from the surrounding world to the greatest extent possible, acceptance of subordinate position to the dominant power in the region or delicate exercise in the balancing off of surrounding powers in order to limit their capacity to interfere.

"Small countries situated in highly strategic areas between two larger and more powerful neighbours must, by necessity, formulate strategies and policies that reduce their vulnerabilities and exploit opportunities," said Rose.

Recently, Nepal's leadership has failed to formulate the policies to reduce the vulnerabilities. As Nepal's relations with its southern neighbour India are at the lowest level with eroding trust, its relations with northern neighbour are also not the warmest yet.

The UPA brought the Maoists to the centrestage in 2006, after assessing that they were the emerging force that India should be working with. But the action against the civil war guilty, as demanded by India now, targets the very Maoists to a large extent. This indicates that India's next policy in Nepal would be to move against the alliance of the two communist parties currently in power in Kathmandu.

Modi has to revisit the open border system. Time for a hard decision to close the border has come. Let Nepal, like any other landlocked country, be allowed few trade and transit points by India as permissible under international law. And let Indians and Nepalese visit each other with VISA only. Let nothing special remain between India and Nepal. Let the two interact as "normally" as possible.

Bhutan

The Kingdom of Bhutan is increasingly important strategically to both New Delhi and Beijing. The reason for this interest is not untapped mineral riches or a large consumer class, but Bhutan's geographical location. As the Kingdom has only in recent years begun to open itself up to the outside world, it finds itself caught up in a discreet but high stakes diplomatic battle being waged between India and China. The main issue is territory is the Chinese claim on Bhutanese territory, China has laid claim to three areas:

(a) The Jakarlung and Pasamlung Valleys on the Bhutan-Chinese North central Border are of interest to China due their proximity to Tibet, as well as what China perceives as its "historic claims:

(b) The Doklam Plateau in eastern Bhutan, China covets most is Doklam Plateau. The claim on Doklam Plateau is of grave concern to India, strategic importance has been aptly described by Centre of Land Warfare Studies (CLAWS):

"The Doklam Plateau lies immediately east of Indian defences in Sikkim.

The Chines occupation of Doklam would turn the flank of Indian defences completely. This piece of dominating ground not only has a commanding view of the Chumbi Valley but also overlooks the Siliguri Corridor further to the east".

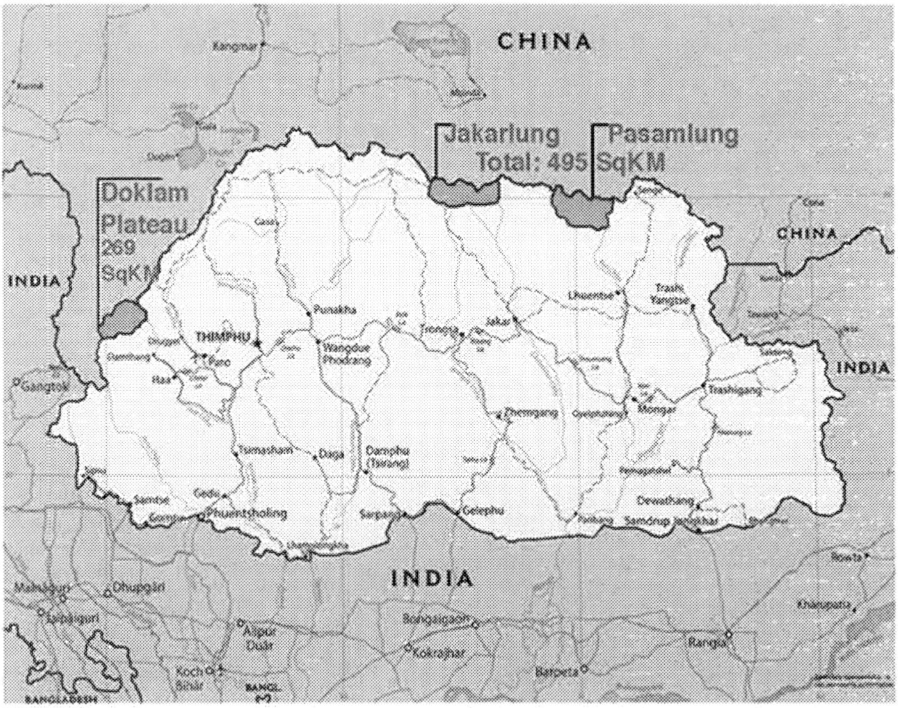

Disputed areas between Bhutan and China

After the British had left the subcontinent, the relationship between India and Bhutan saw a continuity of this pattern. The Bhutanese agent in India continued to function as before while political representative from India based in Sikkim contributed in looking after Bhutan.

In April 1948, a Bhutanese delegation arrived in India and urged the Ministry of External Affairs to revise the treaty signed between the British India and Bhutan in 1865 after the Duar War. India reciprocated and reiterated its respect for Bhutan's independence provided the latter also maintained the same rapport it had with the Britishers. India also agreed to return the Dewangiri Hill strips in return for a revision of the essential provisions of the 1910 treaty. Bhutan also agreed to forgo its subsidy (as per the 1910 treaty) which it had received from India if it had returned 800 square miles of territory that the British had taken through the 1865 treaty.

In 1949, The Treaty of Friendship between India and Bhutan was signed.

Article 2 states that *"On its part the Government of Bhutan agrees to be guided by the advice of the Government of India in regard to external relations."* India was Bhutan's primary force in foreign affairs until 2007, when the treaty was altered during Bhutan's transition from an absolute monarchy to a parliamentary government, and the clause that provided India's guidance on external affairs was not retained. Judging by recent visits of Indian officials to Thimpu, however, it would appear that India still expects to play a significant role in shaping Bhutan's decision-making process in sensitive areas of its foreign affairs.

Bhutan proved to be India's trusted friend in 2003 when it launched Operation All Clear and Operation Flush out against Indian insurgents taking shelter in its territory. Co-incidentally, a BJP-led government was in power in India at that time.

In addition to its lengthy diplomatic relationship, India is far and away Bhutan's most important economic and trading partner, accounting for nearly 60 per cent of Bhutan's exports, and 75 per cent of its imports, as well as being a vital donor of economic aid to the country. It is widely suspected that during election in Bhutan that the Indian government used this leverage by cutting subsidized gasoline and kerosene to the country in response to what it saw as then Bhutan's Prime Minister Jigme Thinley's warming of relations with China, resulting in his government's eventual defeat at the polls.[54]

China steps up its soft power diplomacy; as its rich increasingly travel to Bhutan as tourists and as the massive investments in Tibet make that area a possible access points for the nascent Bhutanese traders. Mr Le Yucheng, the Ambassador of the People's Republic of China to India, made his first trip to Bhutan. Another area of convergence is the Chinese government's much heralded crackdown on corruption.

Seeking to repair relations, India's new Prime Minister Narendra Modi chose Bhutan as his first visit abroad, and came bearing gifts in the form of a fifty per cent increase in aid and loans from the previous year, while Nepal and Bangladesh, two recipients of Indian aid, saw their funding decrease slightly. Modi's visit also raised the prospects of moving forward on Bhutan's 10,000MW initiative, in which the Indian government is to fund three hydroelectric projects that upon completion are expected to produce up to $1.7 billion worth of electricity. This is expected to significantly boost the country's GDP. The energy sector also represents a very significant share of government revenues. While Indian policy towards Bhutan appears to consist primarily of economic carrots (and perhaps a subtle stick when necessary), China's approach historically has been one that bears many similarities to its current strategy in the East and South China Seas.

Sri Lanka and Maldives

The relationship between India and Sri Lanka is more than 2,500 years old and both sides have built upon a legacy of intellectual, cultural, religious and linguistic interaction. In recent years, the relationship has been marked by close contacts at the highest political level, growing trade and investment, cooperation in the fields of development, education, culture and defence, as well as a broad understanding on major issues of international interest.

The specific geo-strategic location of Sri Lanka in the Indian Ocean and ethnic affinity of the Indian Tamils with the Sri Lankan Tamils have been the most important factor in their relationship. India is the closest neighbour of Sri Lanka, separated from it at its narrowest point by 22 miles of sea called the Palk Strait. The implication of such a close proximity is that developments in each country have affected the other. Sri Lanka's strategic location caused concern to Indian security particularly because of the possibility of the involvement of external powers in the ethnic conflict. The presence of external powers there can possibly pose a serious threat to the security and unity and integrity of India as well as to regional stability.

India-Sri Lanka relations in the post-1990 period have undergone a contextual change together with changes in India's foreign policy perceptions. After the end of the Cold War and the emergence of the US as the sole superpower, India's foreign policy perceptions too have changed. In keeping with the changing global economic and trade scenario, India's strategic priorities in the Indian Ocean region have also undergone a change during the last two decades. India's national security perceptions have now been enlarged to include economic security, free trade and commerce, energy security, and social security of the population in addition to territorial integrity.

India-Sri Lanka relations are now affected by the regional power dynamics, with external powers seeking to increase their own influence and counter those of others. India is the most important foreign supporter of Sri Lanka, and remains its largest trading partner.

China's interest in Sri Lanka is much more due to the island's geographic location. As vanguard of the peninsular part of South Asia, Sri Lanka dominates the Indian Ocean shipping lanes are vital to China's global trade. Secondly, Sri Lanka's close proximity to India makes it part of any activity – strategic or commerce – relating to India and offers immense trade and military potential when China deals with India.

China is currently one of Sri Lanka's major military suppliers, but also has a potential for economic investments and infrastructure projects. The Sri Lanka Government under President Mahinda Rajapakse exploited the geopolitical struggle unfolding in the Indian Ocean between China and India, with the United States having its own agenda for retaining its influence. While Pakistan is playing for stakes in Sri Lanka with Chinese knowledge to queer the pitch for India, the Russians too are keeping a hawk eye on any activity in the Indian Ocean. Pakistan's engagements in Sri Lanka are also strategically sensitive to India. Strategically, it is in India's interest to keep its rivals out of its sphere of influence.

The Sri Lankan government's decision to review, and in effect suspend, the $US1.4 billion, Chinese-backed Colombo Port City (CPC) project has strained relations between Beijing and Colombo. The project, which was sealed with the Rajapakse government, is part of Xi's ambitious plan for a Maritime Silk Route, involving substantial investment in Asia and Africa aimed at boosting trade and tourism. Beijing is pushing the scheme as a means of extending its influence in the Indo-Pacific region and securing shipping routes on which it relies for importing energy and raw materials from Africa and the Middle East.

A major stumbling block in India-Sri Lanka relations is the ethnic reconciliation issue. In Sri Lanka, the government did win the war as they defeated the LTTE in 2009 however; winning the peace remains a much greater challenge. India was not directly involved, however its influence was decisive India played a crucial role in the military defeat of the LTTE, but never claimed credit for it.[55] Many of the underlying conflicts which had driven the LTTE's violent struggle for Tamil self-determination remain unresolved. The brutality of the war, the centralized and Sinhalese-dominated political system, and the Sri Lankan government's lack of interest in political reforms or power sharing and minority rights suggest that the 2009 victory has failed not only to address many of the problems underlying the conflict, but also aggravated some of them. While the LTTE are virtually eradicated in Sri Lanka, the support for Tamil separatism remains high among the large Tamil Diaspora, which was a key contributor of funds for the LTTE during the war.[56]

It has long been assumed that if any country could encourage Sri Lanka to seek a sustainable political settlement/peace to its ethnic conflicts it would be India. No lasting settlement is possible to ethnic issue without Indian acceptance. With India's rise as a global economic power and its growing ambition to play an influential role internationally, many analysts and Western diplomats continue to hope that India can help influence Sri Lanka's post-war policies. To date, India, like other governments that support a sustainable peace in Sri Lanka, has struggled to contain administration's strong Sinhala nationalist and authoritarian policies.

At the core of India's foreign policy is a reiteration of the Indian Government's commitment to protect Sri Lanka's unity, sovereignty and territorial integrity. India's pragmatic policy of non-intervention in the internal affairs of Sri Lanka and Sri Lanka's commitment towards India's security concerns created a credible atmosphere and consequently brought a new era in the relations between the two countries. India's new policy has contributed to removing the cultivated fear complex of Sri Lanka. The leadership and the people in Sri Lanka have changed their mindset and thinking about India; for the first time, India is considered as an asset rather than a threat to Sri Lanka's security.

India's clear, sincere and abiding commitment to the unity, sovereignty and territorial integrity of Sri Lanka and its support for a peaceful, negotiated settlement of the Sri Lankan ethnic conflict put hatred behind and sowed the seeds for eliminating all irritants in the political relations between the two countries. Keeping in view New Delhi's changing foreign policy perceptions and India's earlier experience of the Indo-Sri Lanka Agreement of July 29, 1987 and subsequent mission of the IPKF from 1987 to 1990, India has resisted the option of mediation or intervention in the ethnic conflict of Sri Lanka. The events that unfolded between 1987 and 1990 imparted a new dimension to bilateral ties and these were the most troubled and by and large conflictual years in India-Sri Lanka relationship.

India has already been engaging with Sri Lanka and Maldives in a trilateral format.[57] Both Sri Lanka and Maldives are crucial for India—not just because these island nations constitute India's backyard. From the point of view defence and geography, Sri Lanka and Maldives need to be clubbed. Therefore, one will have to wait and watch for the fledgling trilateral partnership of India, Sri Lanka and Maldives.

Till recently, both Sri Lanka and Maldives were difficult countries for India to manoeuvre as the two island nations have found it increasingly difficult to ignore China. Moreover, China has been pursuing cheque book diplomacy and enticing Sri Lanka and Maldives with multi-billion dollar investments.

India, which is already engaging rather pro-actively with Sri Lanka and Maldives in a trilateral format, will have to convince both of them that being their immediate neighbour can be far more useful than any other foreign power, including China.

Myanmar

Geo-strategically, Myanmar's importance for India arises from these factors:

1. Myanmar is the second-largest of India's neighbours and the largest on our eastern flank.
2. Myanmar provides the eastern littoral of the Bay of Bengal. An unfriendly Myanmar hosting foreign naval presence would be a grave threat to India's security.
3. Myanmar has a big border with China in the north, contiguous with the

Sino-Indian disputed border. Military analysts can gauge the various strategic complications that arise from such a configuration in case Myanmar is under unfriendly influence.

4. Myanmar bridges South Asia and India with South-East Asia. It also acts as a buffer between India's North-Eastern States and the Southern provinces of China.

Geopolitically, with a friendly Myanmar, India could add more substance to her 'Look East' policies of building up relationships with South-East Asia, as Myanmar shares common borders with Laos and Thailand. With no contentious issues looming over India-Myanmar relations, a viable strategic partnership is more easily achievable. This can counter-act the negative image being propagated that India is unfriendly with her neighbours.

Geo-economically, Myanmar is rich in natural resources and has appreciable production of crude oil, and natural gas. It has sizeable deposits of copper, lead, tin, tungsten, steel and gold.

Together with Thailand and Laos, Myanmar is also part of the notorious 'Golden Triangle' region of the narcotics trade, and is a source of drug trafficking and HIV AIDS in Manipur, Mizoram and Nagaland. To counter these non-traditional security threats, better management of the Indo-Myanmar border is required. India needs to ensure that its pace of engagement does not slacken, and would do well to learn from countries such as Thailand and Japan. New Delhi also needs to be careful that the any number of issues does not impede its inroads into Myanmar.

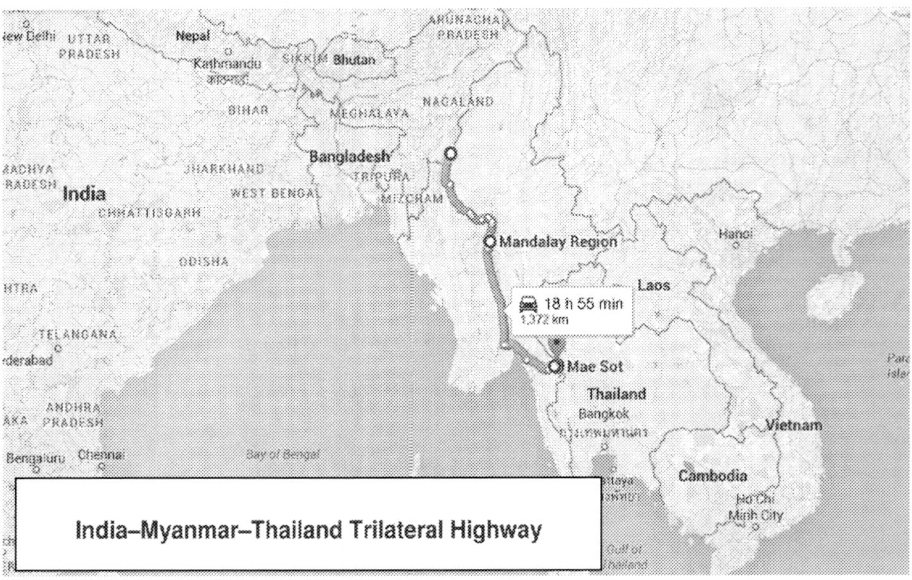

India–Myanmar–Thailand Trilateral Highway

First, the tense situation in Assam has obliterated other priorities of the North East, and it is possible that the distress in Assam may obliterate other important priorities in the region, especially upgrading infrastructure at border posts in both Arunachal and Manipur. The border infrastructure is abysmal at both Moreh (Manipur) and Champhai (Mizoram). While trade between India and Myanmar has witnessed an increase over the last five years, and is estimated at US$1.3 billion, only a negligible percentage of this—less than one per cent—is through Moreh. Poor infrastructural development on the Indian side is also responsible for the delay of the Imphal-Mandalay bus. In stark contrast to India, China has been quick to connect its Yunnan province with Myanmar and converted the former, which was not particularly developed, into an economic hub. In fact, the destination of the Myanmar-China pipeline is close to Kunming town in Yunnan.

Second, domestic political problems and other foreign policy priorities should not be allowed to overshadow important policy decisions pertaining to Myanmar.

This is the time when New Delhi needs to keep an eye on all these developments in Myanmar and continue to increase its clout in different ways.

First, New Delhi should find common cause with Thailand, since it shares cordial relations and common interests. Other countries are also jointly exploring opportunities in Myanmar. For example, a Philippines company SL Agritech corp has signed a deal with both Thailand and Myanmar for developing and selling rice in Asia. Indian companies could also look at such opportunities. To begin with, Indian and Thai companies could partner in the Dawei Port project, which Thailand is very interested in, especially since it will connect Chennai with the Dawei Sea Port in Myanmar and Laem Chambang Port in Thailand. Some discussions have already taken place and it remains to be seen what happens.

Second, there should be more emphasis on people-to-people contact and students from Myanmar should be encouraged to study at Indian universities. India should learn its lessons from SAARC, where it has been extremely slow at taking the right initiatives vis-à-vis other countries in South Asia. While New Delhi has already committed itself to setting up an IIT and a high class agricultural institute, it should set up scholarships for students from Myanmar. For both purposes, the Mekong Ganga Basin is an excellent platform, as Thailand and Myanmar both are members of the organization. The decisions taken at the recent ministerial level meeting held at New Delhi for accelerating the pace of work on the Indo-Myanmar-Thailand trilateral and extending it up to Cambodia as well as the proposal for India-Myanmar-Lao PDR-Vietnam-Cambodia, and for enhancing people-to-people contact is a welcome step.

Third, India itself should from time to time do a serious appraisal of important projects, such as the Kaladan multi-modal project which is imperative for connecting India's mainland to its North-East, so that there is no further delay in implementation.

Modi visited the eastern neighbour to attend a couple of multilateral meetings including the East Asia Summit.[58] He met President Thein Sein for the first time on 11 November 2014 and they identified three 'C's to strengthen their bilateral relations; those are connectivity, cultural links and people to people contacts.[59] Among which connectivity is all set to get a big boost with projects like upcoming Imphal-Mandalaya Bus service, *India-Myanmar-Thailand trilateral highway, Kaladan Multi-modal Transit Transport Project* and the two sides also focused on the need of direct air links.[60] The two sides also discussed the possibility of Indian investment in Myanmars's special economic zones and ways to enhance bilateral trade which stands at US$2 billion, well below the potential.

Fourth, perhaps it is time that India allowed states greater leeway in the economic realm, as China has, while not letting the guard down on the security front. To that extent, exchange of delegations between states of Arunachal Pradesh, Manipur, and other border states with Myanmar are necessary for strengthening India's presence and increasing linkages between the North-East. A recent visit by a business delegation from Arunachal Pradesh, headed by the state's agriculture minister, visited Mandalay and met politicians and businessmen. Apart from exploring business opportunities, possibilities for greater people-to-people contact were also discussed.

Fifth, the efforts of chambers of commerce are important. A proposal by the Indian Chamber of Commerce, which has helped India push bilateral trade with Bangladesh, to push for greater trade between the North East and Myanmar is indeed welcome and a its idea of setting up a trade promotion office at Guwahati would give a thrust to this.

Finally, increasing the pace of improving infrastructure and the quality of the Integrated Check Post at Moreh will not disappoint.

It would indeed be a pity if India cannot make a success of its forays into Myanmar, since it has inherent advantages. Cultural linkages between the two countries date back to centuries, with Buddhism of course being one of the strongest links. Also, Myanmar is in the process of making a transition from a military rule to open democracy, and there is no better example for Myanmar in the region than India. India can understand the ethos of Myanmar better than the West, and therefore can play a key role in helping it set up democratic institutions. While India's Prime Minister has sought to infuse dynamism into the bilateral relationship, there have been occasions when India has seemed to be patronizing. New Delhi should also avoid sound byte diplomacy.

While India should seek to build its presence in Myanmar, it should not lose sight of the fact that there will be synergies with China in the context of the Bangladesh, China, India, and Myanmar Corridor (BCIM). The corridor, an important component of China's One Belt, One Road vision passes through the four countries. For long, India has been wary of the project, but now it is working on some of the **important stretches** of the project, realising the benefits of being part of the project.

Afghanistan

During the Great Game of the 19th Century, the British designed a multi-layered frontier between the Russian empire and their own sphere of influence, British India.[61] This British policy has been root cause of many problems in contemporary Afghanistan. Afghan borders are contested as they cut across ethnic and tribal lines—a destiny which Afghanistan shares with many postcolonial states. Afghanistan, landlocked and poor in agricultural land,[62] also has an inherent economic problem.[63] Weak government and internal conflicts are a consequence thereof. Today even the limited goals for Afghanistan, namely, a crackdown on Islamist and the ousting of the Taliban regime, seem distant.[64] Afghanistan lies at the crossroads of the Middle Eastern, Central Asian, and South Asian security environments. It was crafted not as a nation-state but as a buffer zone intended to separate the then dominant regional powers Britain, Russia, and Persia. Today, Afghanistan is more of a connector between the surrounding security environments than an insulator. It draws together various security-related issues (for example, narcoterrorism with an Islamist background) and spills them over to all bordering regions. Furthermore, today's regional powers in the broader nieghbourhood around Afghanistan—Iran, Pakistan, India, Russia, Uzbekistan, China, and Japan—are all involved in the country's affairs.

> *Afghanistan has been a prize that Pakistan and India have fought over directly and indirectly for decades.*[1]
>
> [1]Kaplan, D. (2008), 'Behind the Indian Embassy Bombing', *The Atlantic,* July 2008.http://www.theatlantic.com/magazine/archive/2008/08/behind-the-indian-

India's relations with Afghanistan have steadily improved since the fall of the Taliban. As for Afghanistan, it is already a misfit in the SAARC context. Any talk of forging transportation and infrastructural connectivity among all eight SAARC nations would be meaningless if Pakistan is not on board. Afghanistan is dependent on Pakistan like no other SAARC country is. India will have to find another geographical route to rope Afghanistan in its gambit.

India views Afghanistan as a gateway to the Central Asian region, where India hopes to expand its influence Central Asia is crucial for India not only because of its oil and gas reserves especially to secure energy. India's other interest is to make sure Islamist extremism remains under control in its neighbourhood. India's struggle against Islamist extremism is closely intertwined with the rise of extremism in Pakistan and Afghanistan.

The India-Afghanistan Strategic Partnership signed on October 04, 2011 was the first agreement that Afghanistan has formally entered into with any country to reconstruct Afghanistan, help guarantee its security and is linked with the drawdown of US forces from Afghanistan. Afghanistan views the strong ties with India as a means to assuage the sense of insecurity and capable of assisting the war-torn nation to stabilize the helpless nation on account of the debilitating power struggle anticipated in the power vacuum following the withdrawal in 2014 of the US and NATO forces. Pakistan is concern about the agreement and is quite suspicious of encirclement by India.

India has pursued a ***soft power*** strategy towards Afghanistan sticking to civilian rather than military matters. In consonance with the priorities laid down by Afghanistan's government, Indian assistance has focused on building human capital and physical infrastructure, India is building roads, providing medical facilities and helping with educational programs in an effort to develop and enhance long term local Afghan capabilities. India has undertaken construction of important Zaranj-Delaram Road, which enables Afghanistan to have access to sea via Iran and provides a shorter route for Indian goods to reach Afghanistan.

All of Afghanistan's nieghbours also have distinct ethnic and economic interests in the future of Afghanistan as allied military forces draw down, raising the specter of a proxy civil war if the tenuous ethnic and political comity breaks down. The United States, China, India, Russia, Turkey, Iran and other nieghbouring states will continue to compete for influence in the region—peacefully or otherwise.

Bangladesh

Since inception of Bangladesh in 1971, it has experienced some serious internal crisis, primarily due to political reasons. Besides political instability that crops up from time and again in the country, Bangladesh also faces challenges from extreme Islamist groups which have been time and again disrupting the peace.

The extreme rivalry between two main political parties, Bangladesh Nationalist Party (BNP) and the Bangladesh Awami League (AL) have contributed more on disrupting the political process than strengthening it. The struggle for power has pushed both the parties towards violence.[65] Bangladesh is also experiencing ethnic conflict in its tribal areas that led to violence and displacement of great number of people. The Chittagong Hill Tracts (CHT) is a diverse region, comprising of thirteen (13) different ethnic groups and they differ in religion, customs and tradition from the rest of Bangladesh. Through military intervention by the

Bangladesh Army, the government tried to control the area. Bangladesh Government also tried to change the demographic composition of the area, which led to the creation of the militant wing of Parbattaya Chattagram Jana Sanghati Samity (PCJSS). The civil war ended through a peace accord. However, thousands of families are still displaced.

"For India, the ethnic expansion of Bangladesh beyond its political borders not only sets up enduring trans-border links but it also makes New Delhi's already-complex task of border management more onerous. As brought out by Indian census figures, Indian districts bordering Bangladesh have become Bangladeshi-majority areas. It is perhaps the first time in modern history that a country has expanded its ethnic frontiers without expanding its political borders. In contrast, Han China's demographic onslaught on Inner Mongolia, Xinjiang and Tibet was a consequence of the expansion of its political frontiers."[66]

ASSASSINATIONS IN SOUTH ASIA

Afghanistan: Emir Habibullah Khan (1919), King Mohammed Nader Shah (1933), President Mohammed Daoud Khan (1978), President Nur Mohammad Taraki, (1979), Prime Minister Hafizullah Amin (1979), President Mohammed Najibullah (1996) Vice-President Abdul Qadir (2002)...

Bangladesh: President Mujibur Rahman (1975), Politicians Fazlul Haq Mani (1975), Abdur Rab Serniabat, (1975), Tajuddin Ahmed (1975) and Syed Nazrul Islam (1975), Prime Minister Mohammad Mansoor Ali (1975), Coup Organiser Khaled Mosharraf (1975), and President Ziaur Rahman (1981).

Bhutan: Prime Minister Jugme Palden Dorje (1964).

India: Mahatma Gandhi (1948), Prime Minister Indira Gandhi (1984), Prime Minister Rajiv Gandhi (1991), Kashmiri Muslim leader Abdul Ghani Lone (2002)...

Pakistan: Prime Minister Liaquat Ali Khan, (1951), Governer Hayat Sherpao (1975), Women leader Meena Keshwar Kamal (1987), President Muhammad Zia-ul-Haq (1988), former Prime Minister Benazir Bhutto with her hundreds of followers (2007)...

Sri Lanka: Socialist PM Solomon Bandaranaike (1959), Vice Chancellor of the University of Colombo Stanley Wijesundara (1989), President Ranasinghe Premadasa (1993), General Parami Kulatunga (2006)...

Identity-based Political Violence

"Identity" politics has become the cause of political violence in South Asian Region. Ethno-nationalism is a feeling of collective identity which sometimes is sufficiently strong and exclusive to lead to genocide, as in Sudan, Rwanda or elsewhere. Ethno-nationalist violence may be the most intense and frequent in modern days. The growing trend of ethno-nationalism over the world has sidelined the ideology and the boundaries of territory. The ethno-communal based political violence between: Sikh-Hindu and Muslim-Hindu in Kashmir; Sinhala and Tamil in Sri Lanka; Catholic and recent political violence between Pahade and Madeshe inter-ethnics in Nepal are visible examples of identity based political violence.

> 'For many people in Bangladesh, life is just unbearable, because they have to choose right side, and if they don't choose the right side they're persecuted.[1]
>
> [1]John W. Lewit, *Immigration Law Firm.*

Another cause of the security problem lies in the condition of uncertainty about the others adversaries intentions—a 'dilemma of interpretation'[67]—as a result of anarchy in international politics. As Kenneth Waltz[68] described almost half a century ago, the system of international politics is marked by an anarchical character due to the absence of a political authority above sovereign states which could enforce law, resolve disputes and, especially, offer transparency.[69] John Herz identified that this social constellation of groups of people (states) lacking a coherent organisational unity at higher level is creating a 'security dilemma' among them.[70] Under anarchy, the decision-makers in one state cannot get fully into the minds of their counterparts for understanding their intentions—"intentions are impossible to divine with 100 per cent certainty"[71]—which creates an existential condition of 'unresolvable uncertainty'.[72] In context to hostile relations and a violent history—a 'shadow of the past'—like between India and Pakistan, such uncertainty may result into fear and worst-case planning, what Butterfield named the 'irreducible dilemma' fueled by 'Hobbesian fear'. Thus, the condition of anarchy in the international system in combination with the shadow of the past in Indo-Pakistani relations paves the ground for a full-scale security dilemma between both states.

Illegal Immigration

Illegal immigration is one of the most serious threats confronting India. India's geostrategic location, its relatively sound economic position vis-à-vis its neighbours, and its liberal democratic credentials have long made it a magnet for people in other parts of the region who are fleeing persecution in their countries of origin or looking for a better life. Refugees/Illegal immigrants from Tibet, Afghanistan, Sri Lanka, Myanmar, Pakistan and Bangladesh have found shelter in India. Illegal immigration into the country occurs through its huge porous borders. While refugees coming from other areas-including Tibet, Sri Lanka, Afghanistan and Myanmar—have been dealt with in a somewhat systematic, although ad hoc, manner, the influx from Bangladesh has been largely unattended.

According to the Ministry of Overseas Indian Affairs, Government of India more than 20 million people are illegal immigrants' in India. Bangladesh in particular, poses a problem for India, with large numbers of immigrants and difficulties in regulating flows. Though the seriousness of the problem is well recognised, it is nevertheless difficult to tackle because it is entangled in domestic political issues. According to estimates there are approximately 15 million Bangladeshi's citizens living in India. Bangladesh of course refuses to accept the immigrant's as Bangladeshi citizens. Illegal Bangladeshi immigration is a significant cause for ethnic conflict in North-Eastern India, where it has shifted the balance of ethnic communities, setting off inter-ethnic violence. Bangladeshis have been moving out of their country due to economic, political and social reasons. There is a crisis of '***lebensraum***' (living space) in Bangladesh due alarming population growth. The population is 1252.08 per km^2 in 2016, one of the highest in the world. The gravity and scope of threats was highlighted by Lt Gen S K Sinha, former Governor of Assam in his report. *Inter alia*, he points out:

> 'This silent and invidious demographic invasion of Assam may result in the loss of the geo-strategically vital districts of Lower Assam. The influx of these illegal migrants is turning these districts into a Muslim majority region. It will then only be a matter of time when a demand for their merger with Bangladesh may be made. The rapid growth of international Islamic fundamentalism may provide the driving force for this demand. In this context, it is pertinent that Bangladesh has long discarded secularism and has chosen to become an Islamic State. Loss of Lower Assam will sever the entire land mass of the North East, from the rest of India and the rich natural resources of that region will be lost to the Nation.'[73]

There are tens of thousands of Sri Lankan Tamils who fled the fighting in that troubled island and settled in India. It is known that approximately 2,78,480Tamil refugees are living in India. In addition there are thousands of Nepalese citizens in India who fled the country during the period of Maoist insurgency in Nepal.

Illegal immigration has also become a source of trans-national criminal enterprise. Crime syndicates dominate the trade in South Asia, and the number people trafficked from the region runs into millions. Women are trafficked from Nepal and Bangladesh. These are then sold to Arab countries. The sex trade has caused another problem that is of HIV/AIDS. Dubai remains a popular destination/ transfer point for sex trade workers organised by criminal syndicates.

Muslims in Myanmar, most of whom are Sunni, constitute about 4 per cent of the country's entire population, with the largest concentration in the north of Rakhine State (also known as Arakan), especially around Maungdaw, Buthidaung, Rathedaung, Akyab and Kyauktaw. Muslims in Rakhine State refer to themselves as 'Rohingya': their language (Rohingya) is derived from the Bengali language and is similar to the Chittagonian dialect spoken in nearby Chittagong, in Bangladesh. There is some dispute as to whether the Rohingya are indigenous to the region or are more 'recent', being in the main the descendants of those who arrived in Rakhine State during the British colonial administration. Since 1982 and their loss of citizenship, Rohingya have been persecuted and oppressed to an astounding level. They have been particularly targeted by the Myanmar's army (the tatmadaw) such as torture, cruel, inhuman and degrading treatment and punishment, extra-judicial killing and summary execution, arbitrary arrest and detention, rape, destruction of homes, forced labour, forced relocation and eviction, confiscation of land and property, etc. Large number have now come and settled down around Jammu after Bangladesh stopped their entry into Bangladesh.

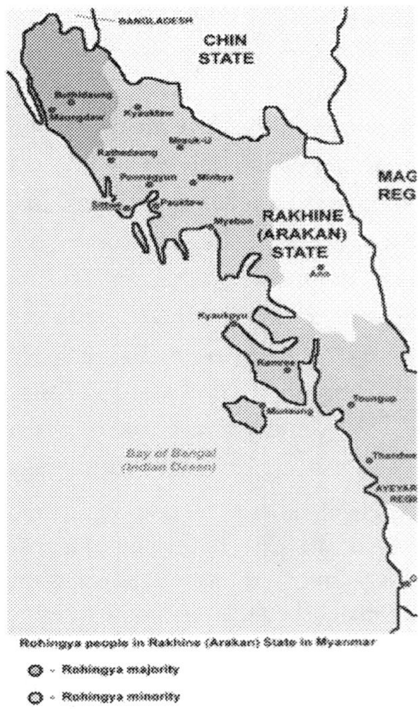

Money Laundering (Hawala Transactions)

Terrorists, Anti National Element's, Criminals need money to fund their activities. This means that they need their funds laundered successfully throughout the world. The raison d'etre for organised crime is the production of ill-gotten funds. For both The Financial Action Task Force, an inter-governmental body that develops and promotes national and international policies to combat money laundering, financing of terrorism, and proliferation of terrorism, has placed three countries—Iran, Pakistan and Sri Lanka—on its blacklist of nations that fail to meet international standards with regard to the task force's recommendations.[74] India alone lost over USD 125 billion in illicit outflows between 2000 and 2008, and total estimated capital flight accounted for approximately 16.6 per cent of India's gross domestic product (GDP) in 2008 India alone lost over USD 125 billion in illicit outflows between 2000 and 2008, and total estimated capital flight accounted for approximately 16.6 per cent of India's gross domestic product (GDP) in 2008. India alone lost over USD 125 billion in illicit outflows between 2000 and 2008, and total estimated capital flight accounted for approximately 16.6 per cent of India's gross domestic product (GDP) in 2008.[75]

'***Hawala***' has offered the worldwide Muslim community an efficient means of monetary transfer for over 1,000 years. With origins in Islamic scripture, the system dates back to the Middle Ages, and was originally designed to enable Muslim traders to circumvent restrictions on lending in the Roman Empire. In recent times, hawala transactions have constituted an alternative remittance system, enabling expatriates from Muslim countries to deliver funds to family members. However, given strict regulations on the worldwide banking system in the aftermath of 9/11, transnational terrorist groups such as LeT have found that this web of trust and honour suits their needs very well. Criminals, terrorist financiers, money launderers, and drug traffickers have all been able to accrue substantial benefits. Unregulated and evasive on the Islamic street, the web of ***hawala*** continues to stymie the efforts of counterterrorism agencies.

Another widely used practice is the creation of ***benami***, or false nominee, accounts. These accounts enable the transfer of money by way of an intermediary to the intended receiver. Nominal account holders often assist criminal or terrorist organisations, and shield their financial dealings by merging them with legitimate or unrelated business transactions. In a system with no oversight, the identities of many account holders may be entirely fictional.

The twin revolutions in communications and technology have further compounded this problem. With nerve centers in Pakistan, India, the Gulf States, and the city of Dubai in particular, hawala now offers individuals the opportunity to reach street corners across the globe.

Even though zeroing in on illicit hawala transactions is not impossible, they remain a boon to money launderers and terrorists. In the case of money laundering, the hawala system is conducive to each major stage of the process: (i) *placement*, at which point funds exit normal financial channels; (ii) *layering*, which refers to the complex monetary movements that aim to confuse authorities; and (iii) *integration*, at which point funds reenter the financial system in the form of a legitimate investment. Because they leave no paper trail, hawala transfers are particularly useful in the layering phase: The system's legitimate ties with trade-intensive businesses like those of jewellery, import and export sectors, and travel and foreign exchange services, all provide a good cover for the critical interface between legal and illegal channels. Hawala provides an effective path for integration for the same reason.

The implications for terrorist financing are similarly striking. For transnational terrorist groups like the LeT, JeM, etc., *hawala* represents a significant asset in a highly diversified funding system. The five main funding sources for such groups are (1) donations from charities, (2) individual contributions—whether they are coerced or spontaneous, (3) state sponsorship, (4) profits from legitimate businesses, and (5) profits from criminal enterprises. The hawala system has bolstered these fundraising efforts by providing a secure channel for transfers between legitimate companies and criminal enterprises.

Drug Trafficking

UN Secretary-General Mr Ban Ki-Moon, while addressing Security Council meeting on grave nature of narcotic drug stated, "In recent years, drug trafficking has emerged as a leading threat to international peace and security. This sobering reality underscores three fundamental points:

(a) First, drug trafficking is evolving into an ever graver threat that is affecting all regions of the world. It will require sustained political will and significant resources to counter this challenge.
(b) Second, the trans-national nature of the threat means that no country can face it alone. This fight requires a comprehensive international approach based on a strong sense of shared responsibility. States must share intelligence, carry out joint operations, build capacity, and provide mutual legal assistance. So far, cooperation between Governments is lagging behind cooperation between organised crime networks.
(c) Third, we need a more balanced approach to drug control. Such an approach should focus on reducing demand for drugs and the harm done by them; on promoting alternative development and the rule of law at the source of the supply; and on disrupting trafficking routes."

The South Asia region is a primary source of heroin for the international drug trade, primarily for the West Asian, European, and Eurasian markets. India is caught between the three largest heroin and opium producers in the world such as the countries like Afghanistan, Pakistan (Golden Crescent) and Myanmar (Golden Triangle), resulting in conflicts on her borders adjoining major drug production /transporting areas. Afghanistan is the world's largest producer of illicit opium. Pakistan is a major transit country for Afghan-produced opiates and is also a source of illicit opium poppy. Around the world, approximately 16.5 million people use opiates annually, generating yearly revenue of USD 68 billion.[76] Afghanistan alone produces almost 90 per cent of the world's illicit opium, with most of the cultivation concentrated in provinces in the south, including Helmand, Kandahar, and Zabul, which remain among the most insecure in the country.[77] Although ordinary farmers actually produce much of this opium supply, they earned only 0.6 per cent, or USD 440 million, of the total worth of the global opiate market in 2010. Indeed, it is international criminal networks that generate record profits from the trade.[78]

In India, substantial amounts of opium are diverted to the black market from legal production for pharmaceutical industries. International terrorists and drug traffickers have been able to operate with impunity in Afghanistan.

One of the critical problems arising of two major narco-producing and trading regions—the Golden Crescent and the Golden Triangle—is the cementing of diabolic relationship between insurgent groups, arms dealers and narco-terrorists. Such relationship is quite common with the groups operating in the region.[79]

Economic incentives facilitates interaction between narcotics and insurgent groups by explaining the 'specific dynamics' of the drug trade which 'enables insurgents to increase their capabilities and challenges they pose to states' and also affecting the 'motivational structures of insurgent groups.'[80] In India, Bengal, Bihar and Malwa Region have been traditional poppy growing regions.[81] The Maoist involvement in illicit poppy production and trade lends credence to the theory of strong linkages between armed conflicts and drug production. The Maoist influence and activities has been on the increase since 2010. "The drug lords of this area earn at least 200 crore a year from poppy cultivation. ... The Maoist are trying to control the drug lords for funding as it can bring huge amount of money," remarked an investigating officer, which further arguments concern at what could possibly escalate into a major law and order crisis in the entire region.[82]

Link West

In the context of international relations in the Persian Gulf, it becomes important to analyse the fundamental security dilemmas that countries of the region face as a whole. First, the Gulf monarchies and emirates continue to contract with outside powers, such as the USA, to provide for defence and safeguard energy security in the region.[83] Second, each of these countries has to confront the challenges posed by non-state actors against their rule.[84] And third, each state faces the dilemma of balancing allies, adversaries, and ethnic communities regardless of the commonalities between them.[85] GCC countries, therefore, continue to reflect vast differences in ideology and have to leverage diplomatic action as the only solution for maintaining peace in the region.[86]

The 1973 increase in the oil price and the beginning of large scale development activities in the Gulf, there was an upsurge of white-collar workers and labourers from India. The initial years of the 1970s required huge human resource investments by the GCC countries in development activities in industry, agriculture, communications, transport, and infrastructure. Instability in the region provided the driving force for peaceful developing countries like India to send in their unskilled labour, registering an almost 200 per cent growth in the years between 1970 and 1975—and in the following years, the Indian expatriate community in the region grew to some 39.1 per cent.[87]

The Saudis and the Gulf are deeply troubled by what they perceive as America's abandonment of its traditional partners either in the name of democratisation, as in Egypt, and the embrace of their adversary, Iran, in the name of political realism. Discarding the traditional caution, the Gulf have chosen to take charge of their own destiny and are spending much treasure to limit Iran's influence, from Lebanon to Yemen and from Basra to Damascus.

To make matters worse, the steep fall in oil revenues has begun to squeeze the Gulf Countries economy. For the first time in decades, Saudi Arabia is compelled to look at changing its national business model and diversification of its strategic partnerships. As it looks for new friends and partners, India has begun to figure prominently in their calculus.

For the last four decades and more, India was interested only in oil, diaspora and remittances from its growing number of expatriate workers. In its determination to keep out of the conflicts in the Middle East, Delhi had apparently lost all capacity to empathise with the region's real concerns. Delhi had branded key countries like Saudi Arabia and Turkey as pro-Pakistan, and did little to explore India's own bilateral opportunities with them.

INDIAN DIASPORA

The term "Indian diaspora" refers to all persons of Indian descent living outside India, as long as they preserve some major Indian ethnocultural characteristics. Only nationals of Pakistan and Bangladesh are excluded from this term since those countries were part of the larger British India before 1947 and thus constitute a special case.

A common distinction with regard to ethnic Indians outside India, often referred to as overseas Indians, is made between non-resident Indians (NRIs), who hold Indian citizenship, and persons of Indian origin (PIOs), who do not.

India already has two main working security understandings in the region, namely with Saudi Arabia and Qatar. While details of India's strategic understanding with Riyadh remain largely unknown, New Delhi signed an expansive defence agreement with Doha in 2008, thought to be a "one of a kind," not signed with any other country since. Under the agreement, New Delhi has committed to protect Qatar's assets and interests from external threats.

China is becoming a major player in global politics and in the regional politics of West Asia, and its influence in the Gulf region is on the rise. China is bolstering its ties with major Gulf countries and Beijing has been active in establishing a soft power presence in the region through trade links and cultural ties.

Qatar Petroleum and the China National Offshore Oil Company concluded a range of deals that included a 25-year Exploration and Production-Sharing Agreement which will make Qatar the largest supplier of liquefied natural gas to China.[88] Both Saudi Arabia's Aramco and the Kuwait Petroleum Corporation have entered into agreements with the China Petroleum and Chemicals Group to participate in joint ventures for integrated refinery and petro-chemical conversion processes of crude oil supplied by the two Gulf countries to the Fujian and Guangdong provinces in China.[89] Gulf countries are major consumers of Chinese light manufactured goods, marketing infrastructure, machinery and equipment, vehicles, foodstuffs, and engineering and labour services.

Looking forward, some basic ideas are worth keeping in mind. First, India's interests in the Gulf Region and Middle East are strategic and enduring. For more than a half century, Indian interests have centered on energy security and foreign remittances; securing the stable, uninterrupted flow of oil at reasonable prices.

Second, Chinese interests in the Middle East are significant and growing. China is acutely aware of its need to import oil to support its growing economy, and much of that oil will come from the Middle East for many decades to come. That plain fact is the consequence of two realities: first, the Middle East has the largest proven reserves of oil in the world, and second, China is far closer to the Middle East than other potential sources of oil. While many Chinese scholars perceive a strategic imperative in conservation and pursuit of alternative energy, their nation's immediate needs suggest a deepening of economic ties to the region. Additionally, the increasingly sophisticated behavior of China's state-owned energy conglomerates demonstrates that they are no longer simply seeking equity oil to meet China's needs. This further suggests that even if China's demand for oil were reduced, or China sources oil from other sources like Central Asia the future prosperity of large Chinese companies is now inexorably linked to that of the global oil market as a whole and Middle Eastern oil in particular.

Third, the Middle East's interests in the India and China are evolving. As recently as a few decades ago, the Middle East looked almost exclusively westward for both its markets and its security. Westerners helped develop the region's oil production, Westerners purchased much of that oil, and Westerners helped create the state of Israel in their midst. The Soviet Union had relatively less influence. For all of its efforts in the region, the Soviet Union never transcended principally military relationships with regional governments, and in the event, those relationships were mostly with relatively poorer countries such as Egypt and Syria, or very poor ones such as south Yemen. The idea of developing deep ties with

China seemed far-fetched not only for the region's governments, but even for the armed movements that opposed them. India has recently stepped being a very large importer of oil. Indian economy is the fastest growing and is now a larger market for oil from the region. There is deep suspicion of United States whether it will come to assistance of the Gulf Countries.

Finally, Energy is undoubtedly the primary driver of the Gulf-India relationship today, and will remain so in coming decades. To fuel its growth, India needs to devise an energy security strategy that acknowledges the centrality of Gulf oil, Arab and Iranian. India already buys almost 80 per cent of its imported oil from the Middle East and, combined, the Arab Gulf states are already India's largest foreign oil supplier. Although economic and energy ties, as well as expatriate remittances, remain critical, India–Gulf relations are currently diversifying into security and defence cooperation. New counterterrorism and counter-extremism cooperation pledges targeting Pakistan are expected to bring dividends in India's ties with the UAE, Saudi Arabia and Qatar. India has been active to wean away Middle east from Pakistan.

A New Great Game[90]

Important geopolitical events were taking place in Central Asia after break up of USSR. Central Asia is the Jewel in the Crown that was now up for Grabs. Indian cannot remain isolated; it has stake in Central Asia. Once part of Soviet Union the CIS States are rich in vast natural resources with large Oil/Gas reserves in areas near the Caspian Sea & Nuclear Material like Uranium. From a Geo-political point of view, Central Asia has always been important. From the middle to the end of the 19th century, while the region was part of the Russian Empire, the oil-bearing areas of Baku were producing half of the world's oil supplies. In World War II, during his campaign against Russia, Hitler tried to capture Baku and the Caucasian oil fields as part of his strategy for world domination. After the war, the Soviets retained these areas as reserves, choosing to exploit oil deposits on Russian soil, in Tatarstan and Siberia. Following the collapse of communism the ex-Soviet republics of Central Asia, especially Turkmenistan and Kazakhstan, have been trying to exploit their natural resources, since they consider oil to be the prime means of securing their economic and political independence.

Uzbekistan, Tajikistan and Kyrgyzstan—the other three post-Soviet countries in Central Asia—are not yet seen as major energy players. That could change though, with new investments being considered. Tajikistan and Kyrgyzstan, with no substantial raw materials deposits—though it is believed oil and gas resources in Tajikistan's Bokhtar field are significant—rely on hydro power. They account for more than 70 per cent of Central Asia's total capacity. Energy today is a key factor in domestic and external policies of all states. Crucial role of energy in international politics and security policies is explained by Alexandross Petersen and Katinka Barysch as, "Energy has come to symbolize the geopolitics of the 21st Century, reflecting countries' diminishing reliance on military and political power. Today, energy is an instrument of geopolitical competition, like nuclear weapons and large armies were during the Cold War."[91]

The Central Asian Republics have been mostly in the sphere of influence of Russia having close geographical & strategic positioning being energy rich former soviet states. Russia has long standing political, historical & cultural ties with Central Asian States. Moscow too has upped its game to consolidate its position in its backyard with Floating a Eurasian Economic & Customs Union with countries like Kazakhstan being part of it.

China's presence and influence in Central Asia—Kazakhstan, Kyrgyzstan, Tajikistan, Turkmenistan, and Uzbekistan—have been increasing. The Westward strategy articulated by Chinese President Xi Jinping in his "New Silk Road economic belt" highlights Central Asia's importance for Chinese economy and development. Central Asia is resource rich, and, because of its proximity to China offers a great opportunity for cheap, reliable energy imports. China has been investing billions of dollars in the energy sector. China's strategic aims in central is to secure an alternate energy route preparing for eventual standoff in Indian Ocean & South China Sea in future which has the potential to choke off China's Crucial energy supplies from Gulf Region via the Andaman Sea.

China upgraded relations with Kyrgyzstan to a strategic level. Kazakhstan is the leading oil producer in the region, with output of roughly 1.6 million barrels per day (bbl/day), of which approximately 90 per cent is exported. The Baku-Tbilisi-Ceyhan network that came online in 2006 is not the only Kazakh attempt to break Russia's monopoly. Astana is already one of the most significant oil suppliers to China. The first pipeline connecting the Caspian shore with China's Xinjiang province is one of the longest links in the world at nearly 2300 km. China in fact controls around 20 per cent of Kazakhstan's oil production and is its key trade partner.

China and India both face looming resource scarcities in fuel, water and other materials that will force them to look outward and increasingly toward other more resource-rich South and Central Asian states.[92]

U.S. policy toward Central Asia comprising five countries of the region the region—Kazakhstan, Kyrgyzstan, Tajikistan, Turkmenistan, and Uzbekistan—that gained their independence in 1991, which lasted from the dissolution of the Soviet Union until the terrorist attacks on September 11, 2001, focused on three priorities: securing the legacy of Soviet weapons of mass destruction; helping the Central Asian countries attain and defend their newly won sovereignty, independence, and territorial integrity against a potential resurgence of Russian neo-imperialism; and breaking up Russia's monopoly over pipelines and transit routes for Central Asian oil and gas as a means of ensuring the region's independence from Russia. The United States explicitly rejected the geopolitical approach to Central Asia, and instead embarked upon a long-term effort to support the creation of democratic governance, free-market economies, and regional economic integration. Despite at times lofty rhetoric, U.S. policymakers generally viewed the region as a relatively low priority, and American engagement to achieve greater stability, security, and prosperity as well as better governance remained limited.

Russia and China formed the Shanghai Cooperation Organisation (SCO). SCO is a Eurasian political, economic, and military organisation which was founded in 2001 in Shanghai by the leaders of China, Kazakhstan, Kyrgyzstan, Russia, Tajikistan, and Uzbekistan primarily to counter US and have access to energy. India has formerly become member of SCO.

India entered into the Great Game by the International North-South Transport Corridor (INSTC) is said to connect South and Central Asia to North Europe via Russia. Iran is a partner nation in INSTC along with Russia, India, Azerbaijan, Armenia, Kazakhstan, Kyrgyzstan, Tajikistan, Turkey, Ukraine, Belarus, Oman, Syria and Bulgaria. INSTC is key transit link for the most cost-effective transportation corridor for European-Indian Ocean trade and will determine its growing influence on the world at large.

Modi on assuming power realized the importance of Central Asia to secure energy for the nation. As astute student of realpolitik he immediately embarked upon securing energy needs. Modi was well aware that Pakistan will never allow free flow of trade nor the TAPI gas pipeline will see the light of the day. Pakistan will always put hurdles in the construction. An important cog in this wheel is The Chabahar Port. The port of Chabahar is located in the south of Sistan and Baluchistan Province on the Makran coast (overwhelming majority [of the city's inhabitants are ethnic Baluch) located 300 km east from the Strait of Hormuz and is the only Iranian port with direct access to the Indian Ocean as well as the Oman Sea and Persian Gulf. It is also officially designated as a Free Trade and Industrial Zone by Iran's government. In April 2013, the Iranian Ambassador to Afghanistan had said, "Afghanistan will be connected to the Central Asian 14 states by bringing the Chabahar route to operation". Iran has already constructed the route from Chabahar to Milak on the Iran-Afghanistan border. From Milak, this route is connected to the Zaranj Delaram route that India built for Afghanistan for about $100 million which connects with the main Kandahar–Herat highway from where goods can be transported to other parts of Afghanistan. A number of other initiatives have also been announced or are in the process of completion. These include the Chabahar-Faranj-Bam railway, the rail link between Hajigak and Chabahar and the Chabahar-Zahedan-Mashhad rail link, which will be further, extended to Herat and Mazar-e-Sharif and be finally connected to Termez in Uzbekistan.

Chabahar vs. Gwadar: India vs. China

Both these ports and the strategic politics around them prove that India and the Pakistan-China axis are now expanding the base of the competition, instead of limiting everything to bi-party conflicts. Both sides know that war and battles are meaningless and suicidal. The real victory today resides in checkmating the enemy through a power struggle which is more aimed at economic benefits.[93] On Fen 18, 2013 Pakistan government transferred operational control of its strategically located deep sea port Gwadar, Balochistan Province to China. As per the Gwadar port website, it has 3 berths at present with a plan to add 3 more (a multipurpose, a grain, and an oil berth). Its projected draught is 12.5 metres with which it claims it will be able to handle 50,000 DWT (Dead Weight Tonnes, which denotes carrying capacity) vessels.

Chabahar has 10 berths already, and is expanding to include a deep water berth which would be able to handle VLCCs (Very Large Crude Carriers) of 22 m draught or more. Gwadar only connects to Xinxiang Province, but Chabhar connects everyone to everyone.

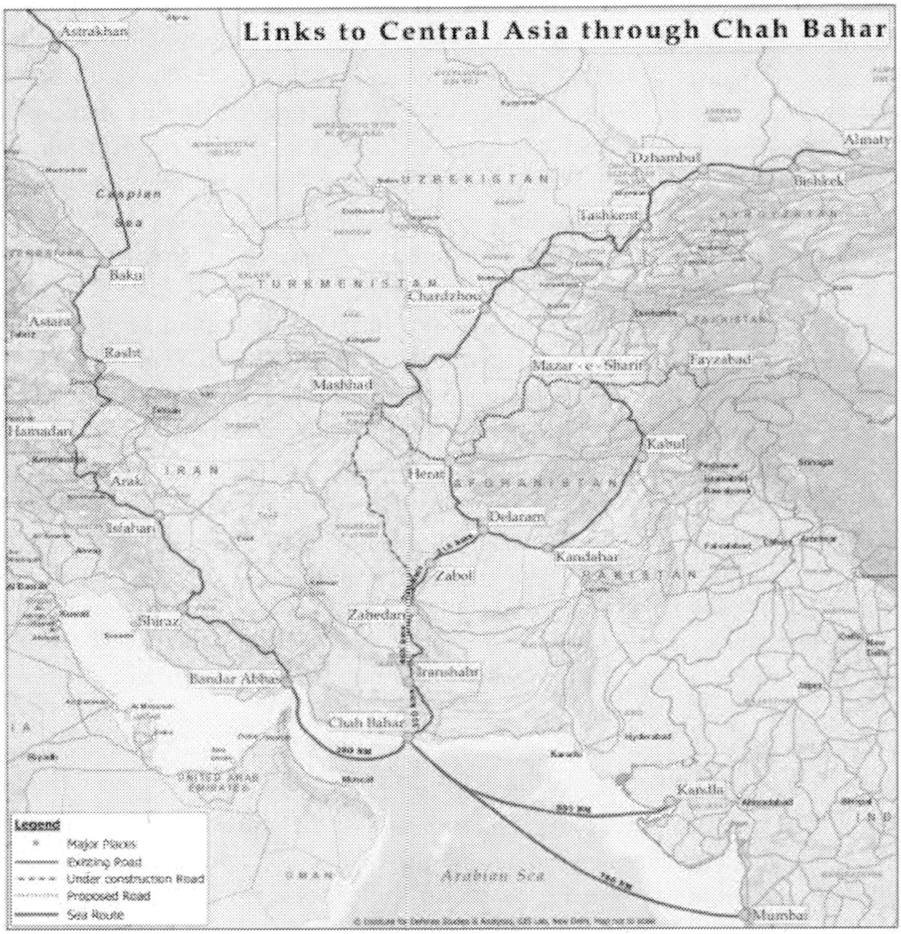

All of Afghanistan's nieghbours also have distinct ethnic and economic interests in the future of Afghanistan as allied military forces draw down, raising the spectre of a proxy civil war if the tenuous ethnic and political comity breaks down.[94] The United States, China, India, Russia, Turkey, Iran and other nieghbouring states will continue to compete for influence in the region—peacefully or otherwise.

OCEAN ZONES: RIGHTS AND RESPONSIBILITIES UNDER THE UN CONVENTION ON THE LAW OF THE SEA

The ocean is classified into eight zones:

Territorial Sea: The coastal seas extending as far as 12 miles from shore, in which the coastal state has sovereign authority, subject to the recognition of the right of innocent passage for ships on their way from one location to another.

Contiguous Zone: An area extending 12 miles beyond the territorial sea, in which the coastal state may enforce its fiscal, customs, immigration, sanitary, and security laws.

Exclusive Economic Zone (EEZ): The seas beyond the territorial sea extending to 200 nautical miles, in which the coastal state has the sovereign right to manage, exploit, and protect mineral and living resources, subject to providing access to unused portions of what the coastal state determines to be the maximum allowable catch of the living resources. Other states are guaranteed high seas navigation rights and the right to lay and maintain cables and pipelines.

Continental Shelf: Both the seabed of the EEZ and the areas of the seabed beyond the EEZ that meet geological requirements specified in UNCLOS. The coastal state manages there sources of the continental shelf (and shares revenues derived from exploitation of mineral resources of the shelf beyond the EEZ) with the international community.

High Seas: The waters beyond the EEZ in which vessels and activities are under the authority of the flag state, and subject to only a limited number of international prohibitions, such as measures outlawing piracy and the slave trade.

The Area: The portion of the ocean floor beyond the limits of national jurisdiction. Mineral resources of the Area are managed by the International Seabed Authority, as established by UNCLOS.

International Straits: Straits that are used in international navigation regardless of whether they are sufficiently narrow to otherwise be considered territorial seas subject to innocent passage. International straits are subject to the regime of Transit Passage, in which ships and aircraft may pass through or over international straits in their "normal mode" without the restrictions imposed on innocent passage.

Archipelagic Waters: Those waters within boundary lines drawn to encompass the islands of archipelagic states. Passage through archipelagic waters is subject to conditions similar to Transit Passage in designated sea lanes and innocent passage in other areas of the waters.

Indian Ocean

"*The Indian Ocean area will be the true nexus of world powers and conflict in the coming years. It is here that the fight for democracy, energy independence and religious freedom will be lost or won.*"—Robert D. Kaplan

Long acknowledged as 'globalisation's cradle', the IOR has latterly grown considerably in its strategic importance. This has been for two main reasons. Firstly, the IOR has emerged in the post-Cold War period as the epicenter of the West's ongoing struggle against violent transnational jihadist extremism.[95] This struggle has in turn played out against the backdrop of endemic state fragility in many regional polities. [96] The resulting conjunction of political extremism and local governance failures has resulted in the IOR becoming the principal post-Cold War theatre of engagement,

Secondly, India and China's accelerating economic transformation in the last two decades has spurred a profound growth in IOR maritime commerce, the ocean constituting an indispensible 'super-highway' conveying the natural resources of Africa, the Middle East and Australia to the region's voracious rapidly industrializing demographic giants.[97] (Green and Shearer 2012: 177).

This area is important for India's supreme national security interest of survival". For China, it is vital transit route for energy imports sourced from West Asia and Africa. This makes China highly vulnerable in case of a Sino-Indian military conflict.

Indian Ocean is a hub of energy; India is seeking to enhance its involvement in the region, seeking to increase its influence from the Plateau of Iran to the Gulf of Thailand. India is soon to become the world's fourth-largest energy consumer, after the United States, China, and Japan—is dependent on oil for roughly 33 per cent of its energy needs, 65 per cent of which it imports, and 90 per cent of its oil imports could soon come from the Persian Gulf. Another reason behind developing naval power is India's "Hormuz dilemma," its dependence on imports passing through the strait, close to the shores of Pakistan's Makran coast, where the Chinese are helping the Pakistanis develop deep-water ports.

Though Beijing deflects claims of hegemonic aspirations, it identifies security in the IOR as a primary concern for Chinese "core interests." In 2015, a white paper charting China's military strategy[98] indicated a shift of People's Liberation Army Navy to focus on both offshore water defence and open seas' protection. Chinese behavior suggests that Beijing seeks to establish a persistent regional maritime presence. It now boasts a semi-permanent naval presence through its counter-piracy activities in the Indian Ocean and has more aggressively asserted itself in the Pacific with extensive patrols and land reclamation projects in disputed waters.

The Chinese government has already adopted a "string of pearls" strategy for the Indian Ocean, which consists of setting up a series of ports in friendly countries along the ocean's northern seaboard like, Gwadar, Pakistan, a port in Pasni, Pakistan, 75 miles east of Gwadar, which is to be joined to the Gwadar facility by a new highway; a fueling station on the southern coast of Sri Lanka; and a container facility with extensive naval and commercial access in Chittagong, Bangladesh. The Chinese government is also envisioning a canal across the Isthmus of Kra, in Thailand, to link the Indian Ocean to China's Pacific coast—a project on the scale of the Panama Canal and one that could further tip Asia's balance of power in China's favour by giving China's burgeoning navy and commercial maritime fleet easy access to a vast oceanic continuum stretching all the way from East Africa to Japan and the Korean Peninsula. Besides this strategy, China is cultivating its relations with the countries of the region through aid, trade and defence agreements. One important factor pushing China to built alternative routes is the fact that Indian navy, soon to be the third largest in the world after those of the United States and China, will function as an antidote to Chinese military expansion.

Maritime terrorism also poses a potentially serious danger to the region. Although there has been little in the way of seaborne terrorist attacks in the IOR over the past decade, extremist groups affiliated with al-Qaeda (particularly al-Qaeda in the Arabian Peninsula) have expressed a continuing interest in closing down strategic maritime chokepoints, such as the Bab al-Mandeb that separates Yemen from Djibouti. While the ability of al-Qaeda affiliated groups to successfully execute attacks on commercial vessels in the area remains the source of much speculation, there exists little doubt about these groups' intentions.

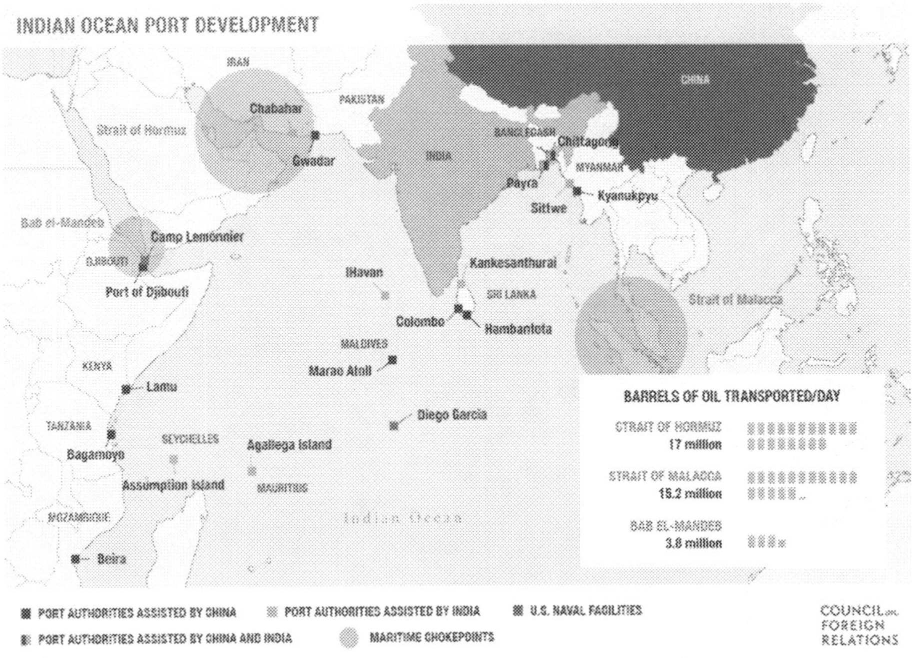

Herbert-Burns considers the ongoing shift of the Cold War-centric geopolitical gravity from the Atlantic and Pacific Oceans to the Indian Ocean, as more world naval powers turn their attention and resources to the IOR. This shift has been driven by the astonishing economic growth of China, the steady rise of India's trade and productivity, increasing exports of raw materials from developing countries, and rising exports of crude oil from the Middle East to Asia. When this economic and trade shift is fused with the reality of the numerous, serious ongoing security challenges in the IOR, it comes as no surprise that major naval powers and regional navies have placed the Indian Ocean as a priority area in current and future operations and strategic planning.

In terms of new vessel construction in recent years, activity has been concentrated primarily in South Korean, Chinese, and Japanese shipyards. Ongoing concerns about the shipping industry's greenhouse gas emissions have combined to drive innovative ship design that prioritizes economy of scale, energy efficiency, and environmental sustainability. However, some of these new larger ships will be unable to use any port in the Americas, or pass through the Panama Canal. Instead, these vessels have been designed specifically to service trade routes connecting Europe with Asia via the Indian Ocean using the Suez Canal and Singapore Straits as key transit points. The industry trend of commissioning new ships customised to travel through waters of the IOR is based largely on the projected growth of exported Chinese manufactured goods over the coming years.

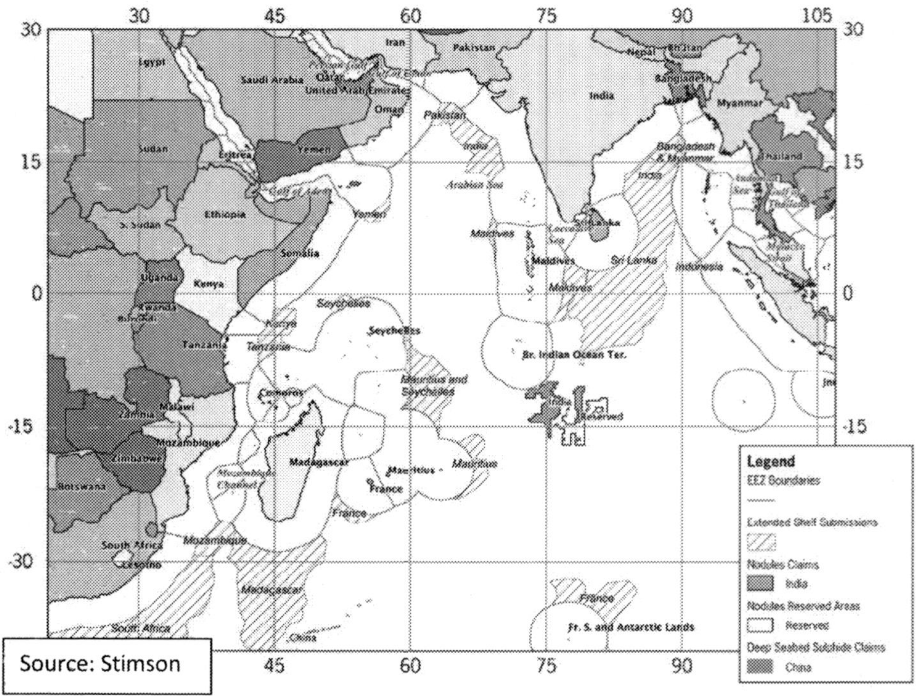

Source: Stimson

All parties to UNCLOS are also members of the International Seabed Authority (ISA), the agency that manages the mineral resources of the seabed beyond the limits of national jurisdiction. There are three known classes of hard minerals on the world's deep seabed:

1. Polymetallic nodules of manganese and iron oxides enriched in nickel, copper, cobalt, and rare earth elements are found on the abyssal plains;
2. Cobalt crusts consisting of iron and manganese oxides enriched in cobalt and rare earth elements, and found on the slopes of seamounts; and
3. Polymetallic sulfides of copper and zinc, sometimes enriched with gold, that are found near spreading centers and subduction zones.

Over the past decade, rising demand (particularly in China) for seabed minerals with industrial applications drove metal prices upward, resulting in increased commercial interest in seabed mineral deposits. India and China have each sponsored national applicants for ISA recognition of exclusive rights to explore mineral sites in the Indian Ocean. India's claim is for a deposit of polymetallic nodules, while China's claim is for a deposit of polymetallic sulfides.

Modi, the first by any Indian Prime Minister in nearly three decades. In an address to the Australian Parliament, Modi outlined his view of Australia "as a major partner in every area of our national priority," noting that "Australia will no longer be at the periphery, but at the centre of India's vision."[99] Prime Minister Modi also used the visit to reach out to Australia's significant Indian-Australian community, addressing a 16,000-strong crowd of Indian community groups in Sydney.

In such a vein, as "natural allies," Secretary of State Colin Powell publicly stated "India has the potential to keep the peace in the vast Indian Ocean and its periphery. We need to work harder and more consistently to assist India in this endeavor."[100]

Rupert Herbert-Burns assesses the variety of sources of insecurity that afflict the region, ranging from insurgent conflict, terrorism, and political instability to illicit trafficking and piracy. These security threats exist within one of the world's most important strategic and commercial spaces, with the Persian Gulf serving as the world market's most significant source of crude oil and the northern Indian Ocean rim constituting a critical sector of the globe's east-west-east trading belt. Taken together, the myriad security threats facing the region may exceed the international and regional community's capacity to effectively manage such challenges. Indeed, without policy coherence, creative thinking, longevity of participation, and significant resources, there is a likelihood that the various security threats facing the region will further increase in coming years, contributing to the area's geopolitical fragility.

Piracy and armed robbery at sea—particularly off the Somali coast—remain top maritime security concerns in the IOR. Despite the efforts of a multinational coalition to patrol the waters off east Africa, the area impacted by Somali piracy remains enormous at approximately 2.5 million square miles, with pirates' use of mother ships enabling Piracy Attack Groups (PAGs) to stage vessel hijackings at great distances from the coast.

Modi's Grand Strategy for Indian Ocean region has been rightly summed up by American naval analysts Eric Margolis. Eric Margolis rightly discern that "driving India's naval strategy is the concept that the vast Indian Ocean is its mare nostrum...that the entire triangle of the Indian Ocean is their nation's rightful and exclusive sphere of interest."[101] Mahan would have understood this a century ago. In 1945/49 Panikkar and Vaidya talked of India's oceanic destiny needing around 50 years to come into play. This time period has now elapsed, and Vaidya's hopes in 1949 of an "India well on the path to becoming a mighty seapower which she is destined by nature and which alone can ensure national greatness" are perhaps now starting to be realised.

Modi laid out five-fold framework for India's engagement with Indian Ocean Littoral:

(a) India will do whatever is necessary to secure India's mainland and island territories and defend its maritime interests. India will, "will work to ensure a safe, secure and stable Indian Ocean Region that delivers us all to the shores of prosperity."[102]

(b) Focuses on deepening security cooperation with regional partners. India has long had close security partnerships. India launched a coastal surveillance radar project. The radar initiative is part of an ambitious project to build a maritime domain awareness network across the Indian Ocean. It calls for the establishment of eight surveillance radars which will be linked with over 50 sites on the Indian coast and connected to an integrated analysis center near Delhi.

(c) Relates to building multilateral cooperative maritime security in the Indian Ocean. Modi said India will help strengthen regional mechanisms in combatting terrorism and piracy and responding to natural disasters. PM Modi expressed the hope that Mauritius, Seychelles and other countries will join the trilateral security initiative it already has with Maldives and Sri Lanka. India's access to strategic facilities in Seychelles and Mauritius marks a major departure from its traditional opposition to foreign military bases. Although calling these arrangements "bases" might be premature, they point to future possibilities for an expanded Indian strategic footprint in the littoral.[103]

(d) Sustainable economic development, Modi announced a joint working group to expand cooperation on the "blue economy" that will increase littoral states' understanding of ecology, resources, and allow them to harness the ocean in a sustainable manner.

(e) Modi has discarded India's longstanding reluctance to cooperate with other major powers in the Indian Ocean. While insisting that Indian Ocean states hold the primary responsibility for peace, stability and prosperity in those waters, Modi indirectly referenced the role that the United States plays in the region through dialogue, exercises, economic partnerships, and capacity building efforts. This was evinced during the recent visit of US President Barack Obama, when Modi and Obama announced the renewal of their defence framework agreement and signed a broad framework for expanding cooperation in the Indian Ocean and Asia Pacific.

Terrorism

South Asia is the quintessential "bad nieghbourhood." Overpopulated, poor and poorly governed, it has messy borders and a messier history of conflict, as well as an incendiary mix of strong ethnic identities and diverse religious communities, many of which are concentrated within exclusionary ghettoes. Islamist extremism has flourished in this intemperate soil, and it is here that the world's first *global* Islamist terrorist movement was bred and nurtured, and from where it was exported-first into the immediate neighbourhood, and then across the continents, until it finally struck the heart of "fortress America" on September 11, 2001.

The truth is that the terrorist threats confronting us today were sown decades ago-not just in the anti-Soviet *jihad* in Afghanistan of the 1980s, but in the radical Islamic ideologies that were revived in the early decades of the 20th Century. The history of these movements, and the ideologies that provoked them, is much too long to consider here. But it is useful to recall that, in undivided India in the mid-1920s, Maulana Sayyid Abu A'la Maududi, the founder and head of the Jamaat-e-Islami in India (and, following Partition, in Pakistan), began to articulate an ideology of political Islam that gave primacy to *jihad* over and above all the other duties imposed by Islam. The four pillars of Islam (prayer, fasting, alms giving and pilgrimage), Maududi said, were "acts of worship... ordained to prepare us for a greater purpose and to train us for a greater duty": *jihad*.[104] Islam was, in this conception, in irreducible conflict with all nationalisms, as well as with every form of governance-whether authoritarian or democratic-other than *sharia* (Islamic law).[105]

There is, moreover, more than sufficient evidence of Pakistan's continued support for a wide range of *jihadi* groups in its covert war against India. Most prominently, no action whatsoever has been taken against the fifteen constituents of the United *Jihad* Council (UJC), which is responsible for a major proportion of terrorist crime in Jammu and Kashmir. The UJC continues to operate openly from Muzaffarabad in Pakistan-occupied Kashmir, and receives visible support from the state and intelligence structures there. With regard to other terrorist organizations, peripheral tactical readjustments have indeed been made; where most were previously operating openly out of various locations in Pakistan, the majority has now ostensibly shifted their camps and headquarters to Pakistani-occupied territory to exploit the apparent ambiguity of its "disputed" status. Nine of these Pakistani groups are currently on the US list of terrorist organizations. Harkat-ul-Mujahideen (HuM), Jaish-e-Mohammed (JeM), Lashkar-e-Toiba (LeT) and Lashkar-e-Jhangvi (LeJ) are listed as Foreign Terrorist Organizations. The al Badr Mujahideen, Harkat-ul-Jehad-e-Islami (HuJI), Hizb-ul-Mujahideen (HM), Jamiat-ul-Mujahideen and Sipah-e-Sahaba Pakistan (SSP) are identified as Other Selected Terrorist Organizations. Five of these-the HuM, HuJI and JeM (collectively known as the Harkat Triad), the JeM and LeJ-are members of Osama bin Laden's International Islamic Front.

Modi Doctrine in the Region

The ongoing power shifts in the world are primarily linked to Asia's phenomenal economic rise. How far and rapidly Asia has come up can be gauged by reading the 1968 book *Asian Drama: An Inquiry into the Poverty of Nations*, by Swedish economist and Nobel laureate Gunnar Myrdal, who bemoaned the manner impoverishment, population pressures, and resource constraints were weighing down Asia.[106] With the economic rise, the strategic landscape in Asia also is changing rapidly. *"The security dilemma is a two-level strategic predicament in relations between states and other actors [...]. The first and basic level consists of a dilemma of interpretation about the motives [...], the second and derivative level consists of a dilemma of response about the most rational way of responding."*[107]

Modi has taken the issues headlong:

(a) 'Neighbourhood First' policy

(b) **Act East Policy**. From the very beginning the Modi led government made it ample clear that India would focus more and more on improving relations with ASEAN and other East Asian countries as per India's Look East Policy which was formulated during PM Narasimha Rao's government in 1992 for better economic engagement with its eastern neighbours but successive government later successfully turned it into a tool for forging strategic partnership and security cooperation with countries in that region in general and Vietnam and Japan in particular. In her recent visit to Hanoi, Vietnam Sushma Swaraj has stressed on the need for an **Act East Policy**[108] that she said should replace India's over two decade-old **Look East Policy** emphasising a more proactive role for India in this region.

(c) **India's Link West Policy.** During the first term of the UPA, Prime Minister Manmohan Singh talked of a "Look West" policy and cited the importance of the Middle East in India's energy security. During UPA's second term of the UPA, the idea of a "Look West" policy surfaced again. Nothing much came out though. India has strategic interest to secure it is energy needs as also to wean away the nations from Pakistan. Middle East is facing a vacuum and China has stepped in big way to fill the vacuum. For India and these countries a peaceful and conflict-free environment is a sine qua non for their development process. Socio-political turmoil in the Gulf region including the stirrings of the Arab Spring and the consequent tough response by the regimes, the Shia-Sunni divide and its shadow on the ethnic conflicts in Syria, Yemen or in Iraq itself, the rapid rise of the highly radical group Islamic State of Iraq and Levant (ISIL) and the extreme violence perpetrated by them are all developments of deep concern not only for the region but for the world at large. Meanwhile, in the backdrop is the longstanding Arab-Israeli dispute which persists with no sign of abatement. Relations of the major power in the Gulf, namely, Saudi Arabia with Iran, Iraq or Syria also constitutes an important factor of the equations in the region. India has pushed for economic association.

(d) **India's 'Connect Central Asia' Policy.** India's "critical and strategic" diplomatic outreach to these five countries—all former republics of the erstwhile Soviet Union. A significant reason for India's move to engage more closely with the Central Asian region is geostrategic. The need to boost India's energy security in the backdrop of abundance of natural resources like hydrocarbons and uranium in the region and the growing threat of extremist outfits like the ISIS too has prompted India to seek deeper engagement with the five "Stans". China's growing inroads into these countries has India concerned, propelling it to seek deeper engagement with the "Stans". China, in fact, has been increasing its presence in the Central Asian nations by constructing expansive pipelines as well as road and railway networks across the region, with an eye firmly on the rich mineral resources of these countries. Besides, China's "One Belt, One Road" initiative that envisages connectivity via rail, road and sea too has New Delhi worried with the "belt" taking within its swathe Central Asia too. Modi pushed for "North South Transport Corridor". The proposed "corridor" aims to reduce the cargo transportation time and transactions cost among India, Central Asia and Russia. And also bypass of Gwadar Port in Pakistan. The North South Corridor reduces the distance to sea port for the countries of the region for export trade

(e) **Indian Ocean Outreach.** Unlike the rhetoric of the past, the Modi government truly perceives the Indian Ocean as India's "immediate and extended neighbourhood", vital for its security and for which India must assume a degree of responsibility in shaping its future. Modi's four-pronged vision for the region was unveiled during his visit to Mauritius last month. This focuses on defending India's maritime territory and interests; deepening economic and security cooperation with maritime neighbours and island states; promoting collective action for peace and security; and seeking a more integrated and cooperative future for sustainable development. This policy appears to be driven by three factors:

(i) Counter China's expanding influence in the Indian Ocean. This was most vividly seen by the presence of Chinese submarines off Sri Lanka last year. China has also proposed a 'maritime silk road' plan, intended to revive a trade route running from China through Southeast Asia and the Indian Ocean to Europe. A key contract for the expansion of Male international airport in the Maldives was granted to a Chinese company after the controversial cancellation of its Indian contract three years ago. To counter China's 'maritime silk road' plan, the Modi government has recently launched 'Project Mausam', a transnational initiative to revive India's ancient maritime routes and cultural linkages with countries in the region. And, the new Sri Lankan government has suspended the contract given to a Chinese company on the Colombo Port City project, reportedly at India's behest.

(ii) Build expand India's and security links with island states to ensure its role as a 'net security provider' in the Indian Ocean. Modi's visit to the Seychelles, Mauritius and Sri Lanka demonstrated this. This included the gifting of a second Dornier maritime aircraft and the launching of a coastal surveillance radar project in Seychelles, and the provision of an offshore patrol vessel to Mauritius. Alongside, India agreed, for the first time, to develop Assumption Island in Mauritius and the Agalega Island in the Seychelles, both of which could be used for surveillance purposes. India also agreed to the politically significant development of the oil tank farm near Trincomalee in Eastern Sri Lanka.

(iii) To maintain maritime dominance over the Indian Ocean. India is currently bolstering its naval profile with the acquisition of aircraft carriers and nuclear-armed ballistic missile submarines. The government recently unveiled an $8 billion naval building plan. The first of six French-designed diesel-electric Scorpene submarines has just begun sea trials in an attempt to stabilise the navy's dwindling submarine numbers. Plans are being made to accelerate the construction of India's second indigenously-built aircraft carrier after the first one is expected to enter service in four years

(f) Modi government has rhetorically expressed "zero tolerance" towards terrorism, and last month India's Home Minister publicly criticised Pakistan for supporting terrorism in India.

ENDNOTES

1. Kapur, Ashok (2011), *India and the South Asian Strategic Triangle,* (Abingdon, Oxon, OX14 4RN).
2. Buzan, Barry and Weaver Ole (2003), *Regions and Power: The Structure of International Security* (Cambridge: Cambridge University Press).
3. Russett, Bruce (1967), *International Regions and International Systems,* (Chicago, IL: Rand McNally).
4. The regions Southern Asia and Central Asia are combined into South-Central Asia. esa.un.org/ .../country-classification.pdf
5. Kelly, Robert E. (2007), "Security Theory in the 'New Regionalism.'" *International Studies Review* 9), p. 197–229.
6. Lake, David A., and Morgan, Patrick M. (1997) "The New Regionalism in Security Affairs," in David A. Lake and Patrick M. Morgan (eds.), *Regional Orders: Building Security in a New World,* (University Park, PA: The Pennsylvania State University Press), p. 11.
7. Forbes, Nov 30, 2015 *India Now Fastest Growing Large Economy at &.4% Third Quarter GDP growth,* http://www.forbes.com/sites/timworstall/2015/11/30/india-now-fastest-growth
8. Solingen, Etel (1998), *Regional Orders at Century's Dawn: Global and Domestic Influences on Grand Strategy* (Princeton, NJ: Princeton University Press).
9. Kissinger, Henry (1994), *Diplomacy* (New York: Simon & Schuster), pp. 703-732.
10. The "Great Game" traditionally refers to the 19th Century competition between England and Russia over the Central Asian corridor for access to India and East Asia. For more, see Peter Hopkirk, (1994) *The Great Game: The Struggle for Empire in Central Asia* (New York: Kodansha America).
11. Tankel, Stephen "Lashkar-e-Taiba: From 9/11 to Mumbai," *The International Center for the Study of Radicalization and Political Violence* (April/May 2009), http://icsr.info/news/attachments/1240846916ICSRTankelReport.pdf.
12. Huntington divided the world into the major civilisations of his thesis as:
    (i) Western Civilisation comprising as United States and Canada, Western and Central Europe, Australia and Oceania;
    (ii) Latin American, includes Central America, South America (excluding Guyana, Suriname and French Guiana), Cuba, the Dominican Republic, and Mexico;
    (iii) The Orthodox world of the former Soviet Union, the former Yugoslavia (except Croatia and Slovenia), Bulgaria, Cyprus, Greece and Romania;
    (iv) The Eastern World is the mix of the Buddhist, Chinese, Hindu, and Japonica civilisations;
    (v) The Muslim World of the Greater Middle East (excluding Armenia, Cyprus, Ethiopia, Georgia, Israel, Malta and South Sudan), northern West Africa, Albania, Bangladesh, Brunei, Comoros, Indonesia, Malaysia, Pakistan, and Maldives;
    (vi) The Sub-Saharan Africa;
    (vii) Lone Countries, Ethiopia and Haiti;

(viii) Israel;

(ix) Cleft Countries—countries with a large group of people identifying with separate civilisations.

13. Huntington asserts that "religion is a central defining characteristic of civilisations," and cites Christopher Dawson's observation that "the great religions are the foundations on which the great civilisations rest." Samuel P. Huntington, *The Clash of Civilisations and the Remaking of World Order*, New York: Simon & Schuster, 1996, p. 47.
14. Kelly, Philip (1986), "Escalation of Regional Conflict: Testing the Shatterbelt Concept," *Political Geography Quarterly*, Vol. 5, No. 2, pp. 161-180.
15. Buzan, Barry (1991), *People, States & Fear: An Agenda for International Security Studies in the Post-Cold War Era*, 2nd edn., (New York: Harvester Wheatsheaf), p. 186.
16. *Ibid.*, p. 188, and the entire discussion on pp. 186-229.
17. For an example of regional analaysis inspired by Buzan's premises, see Svante E. Cornell, (2002), *Small Nations and Great Powers: A Study of Ethnopolitical Conflict in the Caucasus*, (Richmond: Curzon Caucasus World).
18. Buzan, Barry, and Ole Wæver (2003), *Regions and Powers: The Structure of International Security* (Cambridge, UK: Cambridge University Press).
19. Lake, David A., and Morgan, Patrick M. (1997), *Regional Orders: Building Security in New World Order* (Pennsylvania : Pennsylvania State University Press), pp. 6-7.
20. Nye, Joseph S., Jr. (1968), *International Regionalism: Readings* (Boston: Little, Brown).
21. See Louise Fawcett (1995/1997), "Regionalism in Historical Perspective," in Louis Fawcett and Andrew Hurrell, (eds.), *Regionalism in World Politics: Regional Organization and International Order* (Oxford University Press), p.10; Edward D.Mansfield and Helen V. Milner (1999), "The New Wave of Regionalism", *International Organization* Vol. 53, No.3, Summer; Andrew Wyatt-Walter (1995/1997), "Regionalism, Globalisation, and World Economic Order", in Fawcett and Hurrell (eds.), *Regionalism in World Politics: Regional Organization and International Order* (Oxford University Press), pp.92-97.
22. Lemke, Douglas (2002), *Regions of War and Peace* (Cambridge, UK: Cambridge University Press).
23. See Rafiq Dossani, Daniel Sneider and Vikram Sood (2009), *Does South Asia Exist?* (Washington D.C.: Brookings Institute).
24. See Swaran Singh (2003), *China—South Asian: issues, equations, policies*, (New Delhi: Lancer's Books). United Nations, Yearbook of the United Nations,, Office of Public Information, 1947, United Nations p.297.
25. United Nations, Yearbook of the United Nations, Office of Public Information, 1947, United Nations, p.297.
26. Pacione, Michael Ed (1988), *The Geography of the Third World: Progress and Prospects* (London: Routledge).
27. Hilali, A.Z. (2001), "India's Strategic Thinking and its national Security Policy," *Asian Survey*, 41, pp. 737-764.
28. Ayoob, Mohammed (2000/2001), "Nuclear India and Indian-American ... US Policy and Asian Security," *Survival* 42:4 (Winter 2000/2001), pp. 51-71.
29. Mohan, C. Raja (2004), *Crossing the Rubicon: The Shaping of India's Foreign Policy* (New York: Palgrave), p. 127.
30. Sen Gupta, Bhabani (1983), "Regional Security: The Indian Doctrine," *India Today*, August 31, 1983, p. 20.
31. Rose, Leo E. (1989) in Robinson, F. (ed.), *Cambridge Encyclopedia of India, Pakistan, Bangladesh and Sri Lanka* (Cambridge: California University Press), p. 236.

32. Weiss, Stanley A. (2008), "India, the Incredible and the Vulnerable", *International Herald Tribune*, April 23, 2008.
33. 2008 World Policy Conference at: http://www.worldpolicyconference.com/
34. Atlantic Council, (2009), *Needed: A Comprehensive U.S. Policy Toward Pakistan*, Report of Task Force co-chaired by former Senator Chuck Hagel of Nebraska and Senator John Kerry of Massachusetts (Washington, DC: The Atlantic Council, February 2009).
35. ***The Muslim Experience*** in South Asia begins with the concept of *al-Hind*, the Arabic word for India. Al-Hind invokes the vast tracts of the northern and north-western parts of the Indian subcontinent that came under mainly Turko-Islamic rule in the Middle Ages and were protected from the horse-borne Mongols by lack of sufficient pasture land. The process of Muslim conquest began in Sindh, the desert tract south and east of Iran and Afghanistan, adjacent to the Arabian Sea, easily accessible to the Middle East by land and maritime routes. The Umayyad Arabs conquered and Islamicised Sindh in the early 8th Century. Then came the Turkic Ghaznavids (based out of Ghazni, in eastern Afghanistan), who conquered parts of northern India in the 11th Century. The Ghaznavids were followed by the Delhi Sultanate, a military oligarchy between the early 13th and early 16th Centuries, which preceded the splendorous rule of the Persianised Mughal dynasty on the subcontinent. All these Muslim warriors governed immense inkblots of territory that were extensions of the Arab-Persian world that lay to the West, even as they interacted and traded with China to the north and east. It was a land without fixed borders that, according to University of Wisconsin historian Andre Wink, represented a rich confection of Arab, Persian, and Turkic culture, bustling with trade routes to Muslim Central Asia.

    To the extent that one area was the ganglion of this Muslim civilisation, it was today's Pakistan. Fertile Punjab, which straddles the Pakistan-India frontier, "linked the Mughal empire, through commercial, cultural and ethnic intercourse, with Persia and Central Asia," writes University of Chicago historian Muzaffar Alam. This area of Pakistan has been for centuries, the civilisational intermediary connecting the cool and sparsely populated tableland of Central Asia with the hot and teeming panel of cultivation in the Indian subcontinent. Pakistan's many mountain passes, especially those of Khyber and Bolan, join Kabul and Kandahar in Afghanistan with the wheat- and rice-baskets thousands of feet below. The descent from Afghanistan to the Indus River, which runs lengthwise through the middle of Pakistan, is exceedingly gradual, so for millennia, various cultures occupied both the high plateaus and the lowland riverine plains. This entire middle region—not quite the subcontinent, not quite Central Asia—was more than a frontier zone or a bold line on a map: It was a fluid cultural organism and the center of many civilisations in their own right.
36. Joeck, Neil (1985), "Pakistani Security and Nuclear Proliferation in South Asia," *Journal of Strategic Studies*, Vol. 8, No. 4, December 1985, p. 80.
37. Nepali, R.K. (2009), "Democracy in South Asia," *International Institute for Democracy and Electoral Assistance* (Stockholm, Sweden).
38. Geyer, M. (1989), "The Militarization of Europe, 1914–1945," in Gillis J. (ed.), *The Militarization of the Western World* (New Brunswick, NJ: Rutgers University Press), p. 79.
39. Ibid.
40. Namely: 1947-1948, 1965, and 1971. Some scholars argue that the Kargil crisis in 1999 has to be counted as a war. However, this is not my point of view.
41. Stephens 1964, p. 238.
42. "Their most intractable conflict is the one over Kashmir, the mostly Muslim state whose Hindu ruler chose to join his lands to India in 1947. Pakistan contested that arrangement and invaded the territory, touching off the first Indo-Pakistani war. By the end, Pakistan controlled

about one third of Kashmir. The status of the state has remained unresolved ever since", Ganguly, S. (2002), 'Back to Brinkmanship – How India and Pakistan arrived at a nuclear standoff,' in: CERI/CNRS Sciences-Po, p.2. http://www.cerisciencespo.com/archive/july02/artsg.pdf

43. Ganguly and Hagerty call the post-1998 era in Indo-Pakistani relations, marked by a nuclear arms race, a period of 'fearful symmetry', see Ganguly, S., and Hagerty, D.T., (2006), *Fearful Symmetry: India-Pakistan Crises in the Shadow of Nuclear Weapons,* (Washington: Washington University Press). But, I would argue that there do not exist a situation of strategic symmetry. The striking disparity in resources and power between Pakistan and India is identifiable and creates a much more dangerous situation due to the possibility of desperate pre-emptive strikes. For a distinguished analysis of this aspect, see Kapur (2005).
Kapur, P.S. (2005), "India and Pakistan's Unstable Peace: Why Nuclear South Asia Is Not Like Cold War Europe," in: *International Security*, volume 30, issue 2 (Fall 2005), pp. 127-152.
44 Dixit, J.N. (2002), *India-Pakistan in War and Peace* (London: Routledge).
45. Set up in 1893 as the border between British-led India and Afghanistan, the Durand Line had been despised and rejected by Afghanistan for long as a colonial imposition.
46. INSEC (1996) *Human Rights Year Book* (Kathmandu: Informal Sector Service Centre), pp. 133-147.
47. Karky, Jaya (1982), "A Study in Revenue Collection System in Nepal 1846-1923," *Contribution to Nepalses Studies,* Kathmandu: CNAS (9) pp. 55-64.
48. Bista, Dor Bhadur (2001), *Fatalism and Development: Nepal's Struggle for Modernization* (New Delhi:Orient Longman), 1001-116.
49. Pathak, Bishnu & Uprety, Devendra (2009), *Terai–Madhes Searching for Identity Based Security,* (Kathmandu: Conflict Study Center), p.5.
50. Pathak, Bishnu & Uprety, Devendra (2009), *Terai–Madhes Searching for Identity Based Security,* (Kathmandu: Conflict Study Center), pp. 1-17
51. Shah, Saubhagaya (2002), "From Evil State to Civil Society," in Dixit, K & Ramachandran, S. (eds.) *State of Nepal* (Lalitpur: Himal Books), pp.137-160.
52. Dahal, Dilli Ram and Janak Rai (2007), "Anthropology, Conflict and Development in Nepal," in Pyakural, Kailash *et al.* (eds.), *Nepal in Conflict* (Katmandu: SASON), p.59.
53. Rose, Leo E., (1989) in Robinson, F. (ed.), *Cambridge Encyclopedia of India, Pakistan, Bangladesh and Sri Lanka* (Cambridge: California University Press).
54. "How India is losing Bhutan, its last 'friend' in South Asia," *Firstpost World,* New Delhi, July 9, 2013, at http://www.firstpost.com/world/how-india-is-losing-bhutanits-last-friend-in-south-asia-942269.html (Accessed on December 16, 2015).
"Ties strained as India cuts fuel subsidy to Bhutan", http:// articles.timesofindia.indiatimes.com/2013-07-06/india/40407054_1_subsidy-cutfuel-subsidy-indian-oil-corporation (Accessed on December 16, 2015).
55. Manoharan, N. (2012), "Convert Military Victory into Political Opportunity of Reconciliation," *Indian Foreign Affairs Journal,* Vol. 7, No. 2, April–June 2012, 115-155.
56. International Crisis Group (2010), "The Sri Lankan diaspora after the LTTE," *Asia Report No. 186* (Colombo/Brussels, International Crisis Group).
57. India's naval and defence documents defined the maritime strategy of India and provided broad approach for cooperation. For instance, India's Maritime Strategy Document (2007) speaks of achieving "maritime security through non military aspects, such as economic, political, sociological and psychological. The document adopts an oceanic approach to strategy rather than focusing only on protecting India's coast line." This strategy is reflected in the trilateral

maritime agreement. India has been involved in and, to some extent, it is successful in maritime diplomacy with Sri Lanka and Maldives that consists of 'training of naval officers, regular exchanges, transfer of military equipment, manning of military installations, hydrological explorations, patrolling of borders and EEZs and humanitarian assistance'. Therefore, the identification of shared interests between these three countries led to cooperation.

58. "Time to demonstrate an 'Act East' Policy", *The Hindu*, 12 November 2014. Retrieved 12 November 2014.
59. "PM Modi meets Myanmar President U Thein Sein," *The Times of India,* 12 November 2014. Retrieved 12 November 2014.
60. "PM Narendra Modi pushes for regional connectivity, increased cultural contact in Myanmar", *The Indian Express,* 12 November 2014. Retrieved 12 November 2014.
61. Rubin, Barnett R. (2007), "Saving Afghanistan," *Foreign Affairs* 86(1), p 62f.
62. Khosla, I.P. (2007a), "India and Afghanistan," in Sinha, Atish/Mohta, Madhup (ed.), *Indian Foreign Policy: Challenges and Opportunities*, New Delhi: Academic Foundation, pp. 529-555.
63. Rubin, Barnett R. (2007), "Saving Afghanistan," *Foreign Affairs* 86(1), p 62; Baev, Pavel K. (2008), 'Sad Wisdom of Hindsight: Soviet intervention in Afghanistan (1979-1989)', in Bernard, Cheryl et al. (ed.), *Afghanistan: State and Society, Great Power, Politics and the Way Ahead* (Santa Monica: RAND), p 38.
64. Starr, S. Frederick (2008), "A Regional Approach to Afghanistan and Its Neighbors," in Tellis, Ashley J et al., (eds.), Challenges and Choices (Strategic Asia 2008-09), Seattle: National Bureau of Asian Research, p. 351.
    Rasmussen, Mikkel Vedby (2008), 'Afghanistan and the Boomerang Effect', in Bernard, Cheryl et al. (eds.), *Afghanistan: State and Society, Great Power, Politics and the Way Ahead,* (Santa Monica: RAND), p. 20).
    Bernard, Cheryl (2008), 'The Next Afghanistan', in Bernard, Cheryl et al. (eds.), *Afghanistan: State and Society, Great Power, Politics and the Way Ahead*, Santa Monica: RAND, p. 47.
65. Dahal, S.H., Gazdar, H., Koothaponclam, S.I., and Murth, P. (2003), *Internal Conflict and Regional Security in South Asia Approaches, Perspectives and Policies.*
66. Chellaney, Brahama (2007), *Asian Juggernaut: The Rise of China, India and* Japan (New Delhi: HarperCollins), p. 117.
67. Booth, K., and Wheeler, N. (2008), *The Security Dilemma – Fear, Cooperation and Trust in World Politics,* (New York: Palgrave Macmillan), p. 2.
68. Ibid., p. 2.
69. "With many sovereign states, with no system of law enforceable among them, with each state judging its grievances and ambitions according to the dictates of its own reason or desire— conflict, sometimes leading to war, is bound to occur. To achieve a favourable outcome from such a conflict, a state has to rely on its own devices, the relative efficiency of which must be its constant concern", Waltz 1959, p. 159.
70. Anarchy is a mayor feature of International Relations (IR) theory, although constructivists dispute the fundamental character. See for example Wendt (1992).
    Wendt, A. (1992), "Anarchy is what States make of it: The social construction of power politics," *International Organization*, volume 46, issue 2, pp. 391-425.
71. Herz, J.H. (1950), "Idealist internationalism and the security dilemma," in *World Politics*, Vol. 2, No. 2, pp. 157-180 (p.157).
72. Mearsheimer, J.J. (2001), *The Tragedy of Great Power Politics* (New York: W.W. Norton), p. 31.
73. See Group of Ministers Report on Reforming National Security System, Chapter II, Para 24 of the Report. D.O.No. GSAG.3/98, dated 08 November 1998, full text of the report is

available at http://www.satp.org/satporgtp/countries/india/states/assam/documents/papers/illegal_migration_in_assam.htm, accessed on 08 August 2015.

74. Reuters, "Pakistan, Indonesia, Ghana join money-laundering blacklist," Feb 16, 2012, http://news.yahoo.com/pakistan-indonesia-ghana-join-money-laundering-blacklist-173108562.html.

75. Curcio, Karly, "Corruption in India Stifles Economic Growth, Fosters Violence Against Whistleblowers," September 13, 2010, www.financialtaskforce.org/2010/09/13/corruption-in-india-stifles-economic-growthfosters-violence-against-whistleblowers/;
Global Financial Integrity, "The Drivers and Dynamics of Illicit Financial Flows from India: 1948-2008," November 2010, http://india.gfip.org/.

76. United Nations Office on Drugs and Crime, "The Global Afghan Opium Trade: A Threat Assessment, 2011," July, 2011: 7, www.unodc.org/documents/data-and-analysis/Studies/Global_Afghan_Opium _Trade_2011-web.pdf.

77. Bureau of International Narcotics and Law Enforcement Affairs, "2011 INCSR: Countries Reports—Afghanistan through Costa Rica," March 3, 2011, www.state.gov/j/inl/rls/nrcrpt/2011/vol1/156359.htm;
United Nations Office on Drugs and Crime, "Opium Production in Afghanistan shows increase, prices set to rise," October 11, 2011, http://unama.unmissions.org/Portals/UNAMA/Documents/October11_UNODC_Opium_Survey_Press_Release_ENG.pdf.

78. Ibid., p.16.

79. Bhalla, Abhishek (2016), "Pathankot attack: Drug Cartels –India officials' nexus under scanner," *Mail Today* (January 6, 2016), (New Delhi).

80. Cornell, E.S. (2005), "The Interaction of Narcotic and Conflict," *Journal of Peace Research,* 42(6), pp. 751-760.

81. Excise revenue, chiefly accruing from trade opium for foreign as well as domestic consumption had formed the mainstay of the British Empire.

82. "Maoist menance: Revolution feeds on drug money," *Times of India,* 15 Februrary 2011.

83. CSIS (Center for Strategic and International Studies) (2007), *The United States, India, and the Gulf: Convergence or Divergence in a Post-Iraq World* (Report of the Persian Gulf Initiative Workshop), (Washington, DC: CSIS).

84. CIRS (Center for International and Regional Studies) (2009) *International Relations of the Gulf* (Report of Working Group 1), (Doha: CIRS).

85. Chapman, D. and N. Khanna (2004), *The Persian Gulf, Global Oil Resources, and International Security* (Working Paper no 419), (Binghamton, NY: Department of Economics, Binghamton University).

86. Dadush, U. and L. Falcao (2009), 'Regional Arrangements in the Arabian Gulf,' in *Carnegie Endowment Policy Outlook* (Washington, DC: Carnegie Endowment for International Peace), pp.1–13.

87. Khadria, B. (2007), *India: Skilled Migration to Developed Countries, Labour Migration to the Gulf* (Report of the 'Red Internacional Migracion y Dessarollo' Conference Proceedings, Madrid, Spain), pp 5–37.

88. Ulrichsen, K.C. (2010), *The GCC States and the Shifting Balance of Global Power* (Occasional Paper no 6), (Doha: Center for International and Regional Studies).

89. Alterman, J.B. (2009), 'China's Soft Power in the Middle East', in McGiffert, C. et al (eds.). *Chinese Soft Power and its Implications for the United States* (Washington, DC: Center for Strategic and International Studies), pp.63–76.

90. The "Great Game" traditionally refers to the 19th Century competition between England and Russia over the Central Asian corridor for access to India and East Asia. For more, see Hopkirk,

Peter (1994), *The Great Game: The Struggle for Empire in Central Asia* (New York: Kodansha America).

91. Petersen, Alexandros and Barysch, Katinka, *Russia, China and the Geopolitics of Energy in Central Asia,* The Center for European Reform, p. 1 available at http://www.cer.org.uk/sites/defaults/files/publications/attachments/pdf/2011/rp_010-4118.pdf
92. Peter H. Gleick, "China and Water," *The World's Water 2008–2009* (Washington: Island Press, 2009); and Minqi Li, "Peak Oil, the Rise of China and India, and the Global Energy Crisis," *Journal of Contemporary Asia* 37 (November 2007), pp. 449-471.
93. Read more at: http://www.oneindia.com/feature/chabahar-versus-gwadar-geopolitics-of-ports-2106871.html
94. Rashid, Ahmed (2011), "The Way Out of Afghanistan," *The New York Review of Books* (11 January 2011).
95. Kaplan, R.D. (2009), "Center Stage for the Twenty-First Century: Power Plays in the Indian Ocean," *Foreign Affairs* 88(2), pp. 16-32.
96. Cordner, L. (2011), "Progressing Maritime Security Cooperation in the Indian Ocean Region," *Naval College War Review* 64(4), pp. 68-88.
97. Green, M.J. and A. Shearer (2012), "Defining US Indian Ocean Strategy," *The Washington Quarterly* 35(2), pp. 175-189.
98. The seas and oceans bear on the enduring peace, lasting stability and sustainable development of China. The traditional mentality that land outweighs sea must be abandoned, and great importance has to be attached to managing the seas and oceans and protecting maritime rights and interests. It is necessary for China to develop a modern maritime military force structure commensurate with its national security and development interests, safeguard its national sovereignty and maritime rights and interests, protect the security of strategic SLOCs and overseas interests, and participate in international maritime cooperation, so as to provide strategic support for building itself into a maritime power. www.mod.gov.on IV. Building and Development of China's Armed Forces accessed on June 18, 2016.
99. 2016 Narendra Modi, "Address to the Joint Session of Australian Parliament" (speech, Parliament of Australia, Canberra, 18 November 2014). http://www.narendramodi.in/prime-minister-narendra-modis-address-to-the-joint-session-of-the-australian-parliament-6909 accessed June 18.
100. Blank, S. (2005), *Natural Allies, Regional Security in Asia and Prospects for Indo-American Strategic Cooperation* (Carlisle: Strategic Studies Institute), p. 20; Powell, C. (2001), "U.S. Looks to its Allies for Stability in Asia and the Paciûc," *International Herald Tribune*, 27 January 2001.
101. Margolis, E. (2005), "India Rules the Waves," Proceedings. *U.S Naval Institute*, 131.3, March 2005, pp, 66–70.
102. Prime Minister Narendra Modi's Speech at the International Fleet Review 2016 at Vishakhapatnam, India.
103. Sakhuja, Vijay (2016), "Forecast 2016: Indian Ocean Politics and Security", IPCS, accessed on June 28, 2016.
104. Khurram Murad (ed.) (2002), *Fundamentals of Islam* (New Delhi: Markazi Maktaba Islami Publishers), p. 285.
105. Ibid., pp. 296-302.
106. Myrdal, Gunnar (1968), *Asian Drama: An Inquiry Into the Poverty of Nations* (New York: Pantheon).
107. Booth, K., and Wheeler, N. (2008), "The Security Dilemma—Fear, Cooperation and Trust in World Politics" (New York: Palgrave Macmillan), p. 4.

108. Narendra Modi, "Media Statements by Prime Minister of India and Prime Minister of Vietnam in New Delhi," media statement, 28 October 2014, http://www.mea.gov.in/incomingvisit detail.htm?24143/Media+Statements+by+Prime+Minister+of+ India+and+Prime+ Minister+of+Vietnam+in+New+Delhi+October+28+2014;
Narendra Modi, "Opening Statement by Prime Minister at the 12th India-ASEAN Summit," (speech, India-ASEAN Summit, Nay Pyi Taw, Myanmar, 12 November 2014), http:// www.mea.gov.in/incomingvisitdetail.htm?24143/Media+Statements+by+Prime+ Minister+of+India+and+Prime+ Minister+of+Vietnam+in+New+Delhi+October+28+2014

7

India and International Institutions

History indicates empires have relied upon broad range of tools, incentives, and policies to establish and maintain dominance, ranging from political persuasion and cultural influence, to coercion and force.[1] Most empires have sought domination rather than direct and full control within their territories and dependencies. **Although military power (hard power) has often been instrumental in empire building, but it is the soft power that has been essential in maintain that rule.**

> When a conqueror felt that he was in a position to invade the foreigner's country, he sent an ambassador with the message: '**Fight or submit.**' More than 5000 years ago India recognised that the person of the ambassador was inviolable. This was a great service that ancient Hinduism rendered to the cause of international law. It was the religious force that invested the person of the herald or ambassador with an inviolable sanctity in the ancient world. The Mahabharata rules that the king who killed an envoy would sink into hell with all his ministers.

No country could lead an isolated life. As societies evolve, expand and multiply their governing frame work of rules and institutions become correspondingly more complex and functionally more specific. The strength of societies is to a large extent determined by the quality of the institutions: the formal and informal rules of human interaction it has. These institutions—laws, customs, networks, organisations, etc—enable or constrain an open, democratic and equitable society. They also determine a society's ability to absorb shocks, and its sustainability. In contemporary societies, national governments can satisfy only a small and diminishing proportion of needs of human beings as social animals. Consequently, citizens look to more and more to additional actors and layers of governance. 'Civil society' refers to the social and political space where voluntary organisations/associations attempt to shape norms and policies to regulate public life in social, political, economic and environmental dimensions. These layers of institutions now extend from local to global level. In last hundred years International Institutions have become an increasingly common phenomenon of our life. The international institutions refer to concrete cooperative problem solving arrangements at the international or global level.

The rise of international organisations should be attributed to increasing interdependence among nation states[2] in the 21st Century. This phenomenon is the result of the dramatic progress in the technology since the industrial revolution, which led to developments in transportation and communication.[3]

The approach to international politics in the 21st Century rests on the belief that institutions are a key means of promoting world peace.[4] According to former Secretary of State Warren Christopher, "No single institution is expected to play a dominating role; instead, the aim is to create 'a framework of complementary, mutually reinforcing' institutions."[5] The proliferation of international organisations,[6] the growth in treaty arrangements (both bilateral and multilateral) among states[7] and the deepening of regional integration in South Asia as South Asian Association of Regional Cooperation; European Union and efforts in Central and South East Asia all represent formal expressions of the extent to which internal politics has become more institutionalised. The construction or formation of all international, regional and multi-lateral organisations is designed for privileges state autonomy over the collective organisational needs. However, as the community of states becomes more and more interconnected, certain obligations and duties must be performed to guarantee certainty and security in other states.

COOPTIVE POWER

According to Nye, cooptive power is 'the ability of a nation to structure a situation so that other nations develop preferences or define their interests in ways consistent with one's nation.'[9] Nye also argued co-optive power emerges from soft power and immaterial sources such as 'cultural and ideological attraction as well as the rules and institutions of international regimes.' As a result, the difference between hard and soft power relies on their relative materiality as soft power is mostly based on intangibles such as the power of example. Soft power is therefore the ability to modify other states' because of their perception of you.

[1]Nye Jr. Joseph S. (1990), "Soft Power", *Foreign Policy*, Vol. 80, pp.124–44.

States engage in highly complex exchanges and interconnected relations, not only in the most apparent domain of commercial transactions, but in almost all spheres of their daily activities. Nye argued countries that are likely to be more attractive in postmodern international relations are those that help to frame issues, whose culture and ideas are closer to prevailing international norms, and whose credibility abroad is reinforced by their values and policies;[8] or the **captive** power. It should also be understood that conduct at these international institutions are today providing security and power to states.

Alliance, treaties bilateral and multilateral, image cultivation, propaganda and activities that we would now label as public diplomacy are nearly as old as diplomacy itself. Even in ancient times, prestige-conscious princes and their representatives never completely ignored the potential and pitfalls of public opinion in foreign lands. References to the nation and its image go as far back as the Ramayana, Mahabharata, the Bible, and ancient Chinese, Indian, Greeks and Romans, were familiar with international relations in diplomatic activity aimed at foreign publics (modern international relations). Identity creation and image projection – nation-branding in today's parlance were all actively pursued since ancient times. From very ancient times states have attempted to increase their strength by getting in bilateral or multilateral agreements against a common adversary or protect themselves from a stronger foe.[10]

> *'Make friends, make friends, however strong or weak they be: Recall the captive elephants that mice set free.'*
> —**Panchtantra Stories**

Over two thousand years have passed since Mahabharata was fought and it is possible to identify certain key elements in the conduct of war. From the study certain major facets come to mind, the first is **technology**; the second is the complex question of **organisations**; the third; is **creation of allies to increase strength** [*'Make friends, make friends, however strong or weak they be: Recall the captive elephants that mice set free.'*—**The Panchtantra**] and deprive the adversaries of the same; fourth is the **leadership**; both political and military and lastly, the **public opinion** or support which is generally attained from 'dharm yudh' or just war.[11]

World War I and II brought the nations states to collectively come together and evolve a mechanism to prevent war in future. It is not that forming of groups or association is a new phenomenon, but increased speed of communication did open new vistas for collective action either to dissuade, or limit the ability of nation states to carry out independent actions. In the era of growing inter-state conflict between the two world wars, E.H. Carr wrote that 'power over opinion' was 'not less essential for political purposes than military and economic power, and has always been closely associated with them'.

In twentieth century Fascism and Communism—directly challenged and gave an impetus towards communication with foreign publics. Political leaders' battles for overseas 'hearts and minds' are therefore anything but a recent invention. **It is in creation of allies that international organisation, multilateralism and military diplomacy comes into play.**

The international institutions are closely bound up with power. These institutions are not just concerned with liberal purposes of solving common problems or promoting shared values; these are also sites of power and reflect and entrench power hierarchies and the interests of powerful states. Indeed sovereignty may be increasingly defined not by the power to insulate one's state from external influences but by the power to participate effectively in international institutions of all kinds.

International Organisations have a direct impact on the internal policy, states actions are rarely confined to national borders: acts performed by one country—even if directed at managing purely internal affairs—have consequences for the affairs of other states. For example, a health policy decision that decreases the availability of vaccinations to a certain population in Country A may result in the increase of the disease in Country A's neighbouring countries.

On the other side, focusing on the external dimensions, states need the execution of internal and external acts by other states to perform their functions, maintain safety and eventually even for their existence. This situation can again be exemplified with a health policy example. In fact, campaigns to eradicate certain diseases—like the recent campaign to eradicate polio—can be successful only if all countries implement common and coordinated policies directed at the eradication of the disease.

India spent many years since 1947 struggling to achieve the international status that it expected because of its civilisational greatness and geopolitical uniqueness. But a lack of material resources and military capability long prevented it from securing a place under the "diplomatic sun."[12] The Cold War global confrontation between East and West offered shelter through alliances, but threatened India's new found independence. **During those early years, India turned to soft power through multilateralism as a way of magnifying its influence in international affairs until it could exert influence more materially.**

In the early stages, India's policy was dedicated to the realisation of her objectives through the United Nations which, she thought, was to be used in the fullest measure. She also thought that the United Nations was to be guarded from the efforts of the Great Powers to abuse it and make a sterile instrument of power politics. It is ***Soft Power*** perhaps in terms of this dependence that one can better understand Indian impatience the transcendent ideological rivalry of the Great

Powers, which has constantly threatened to engulf the United Nations. This was realised by India in the early stages of the cold war and made Mrs Vijay Lakshmi Pandit to remark... "The conflict in ideology, that is plunging the world into gloom and tension, seems so sadly irrelevant to these great human problems that vitally affect a half, and perhaps more than half, of the human population".[13] India has been of the view that the great power harmony would make it more effective, but at the same time the view is being developed now that even a Great Power agreement cannot force decisions which are against the interests of the rest of mankind.

Nye (2004) developed the concept further in his book, *Soft Power: The Means to Success in World Politics*. Soft power in international politics arises from factors such as the dominant values, internal practices and policies, and the manner of conducting international relations of a State. Soft power is the ability to obtain what you want through attraction rather than coercion or payments.[1] It arises due to the attractiveness of a country's culture, political ideals, and policies, that is, through elements which are 'real but intangible'.[2]

[1]Joseph S. Nye Jr. (1990), *Bound to Lead: The Changing Nature of American Power*, New York: Basic Books, Inc., Publishers, p.188.
[2]Raja Mohan, C. (2003), "Indian Diaspora and 'Soft Power", *The Hindu*, 06 January.

There is a perceptional change in the manner international organisations are operating. Richard N. Haass argues that "twenty-first century international relations is turning out to be non-polarity: a world dominated not by one or two or even several states but rather by dozens of actors possessing and exercising various kinds of power", indicating a shift from the previous world order.[14] Fareed Zakaria argues that "the age of American uni-polarity—which began with the collapse of the Soviet Union—has ended".[15] United States and many countries in Europe have faltered in their economic stability which has eroded their international political power and domestic political cohesiveness. These nations are not as able to use their traditional power resources to achieve their purposes as in the past. Private actors and small states have become more powerful on many issues. At least five trends have contributed to this diffusion of power: economic interdependence, transnational actors, rise of nationalism in weak states, the spread of technology and changing political issues.[16]

The five trends[1] have contributed to this diffusion of power and made private actors and small states more powerful are:

1. Economic interdependence; 2. Transnational actors; 3. Rise of nationalism in weak states; 4. The spread of technology; and 5. Changing political issues.

[1]Joseph S. Nye Jr. (1990), 'Soft Power', *Foreign Policy*, No. 80, Fall 199.

India today has outgrown its Cold War role as a third world, non-aligned nation to exercise influence as an emerging power through global governance by oligarchy—be it as part of the Five Interested Parties in the World Trade Organisation (WTO); the Brazil, South Africa, Russia, India, and China (BRICS) group at the Copenhagen climate change negotiations of 2009; or the Group of 4 (G4) coalition of countries (Brazil, Germany, India, and Japan) demanding permanent membership in the UN Security Council. India is pushing hard for greater voice in the bedrock institutions of global governance, but finding its quest for a permanent seat in the UN Security Council (UNSC) frustrated despite some success in the international financial institution. India's global presence has been acknowledged in various multilateral and bilateral global arenas. India is seen as a rapidly rising global power by virtue of being the largest democracy and having younger demographics, and is one of the top five economies of the world today. As a member of the World Bank, International Monetary Fund (IMF) and Asian Development Bank (ADB), India has increased its stakes and influence following the global financial crisis of 2008. In new multilateral mechanisms like G-20, IBSA and BRICS, India's influence is increasingly being felt. Indian business enterprises (both public and private) have been making their presence felt around the world. Indian investment abroad in 2012 was higher than foreign investment in India.

Joseph Nye says that a country's foreign policy can increase its soft power if its foreign policy is perceived by other countries and people to be 'legitimate and having moral authority'.[17] Today, in almost every international forum, India has explicitly engaged with smaller groups of powerful nations to affect outcomes at the expense of the more broad-based universalist approach that it traditionally espoused (or claimed to). India does not extensively rely on the multilateral treaty-based system, preferring instead bilateral relationships or strategic partnership with major and regional powers in almost every field of international cooperation from trade to nuclear technology.

India's soft power, in any case, got a major boost with the way it achieved independence. The legacy of the Indian freedom movement and that of its leader, Gandhi, certainly built India's soft power from the very beginning as a country which had achieved independence with non-violent methods. This soft power was consolidated by the foreign policy agenda set by Nehru. India's foreign policy has been based on moral values from the time of Prime Minister Jawaharlal Nehru, who remains a tremendous influence on Indian foreign policy even today.

The rule-taker instinct is most apparent in India's unquestioning adherence to the dominant Western liberal economic and democratic model, albeit with Indian characteristics. India is unlikely to jettison parliamentary democracy or return to the state-dominated "license raj" economy, even if its practice of democracy remains imperfect and its efforts to dismantle the overbearing regulations that curtail economic growth are inept.

The Ministry of Defence *Annual Report 2011-12* says, "India has strengthened its participation in multilateral institutions and deepened its strategic partnerships with various countries so as to effectively contribute, as a responsible stakeholder, to regional and global peace and stability." India has entered into number of strategic alliances.

What are International Institutions?

There are no widely agreed upon definition of institutions in the international relations literature.[18] For example defining institutions as "recognised patterns of behaviour or practice around which expectations converge" allows the concept to cover almost every regularised pattern of activity between states, from war to tariff bindings negotiated under the General Agreement on Tariffs and Trade (GATT) thus rendering it meaningless.[19] McCormick defines international *organisation* as "a body that promotes voluntary cooperation and coordination between or among its members."[20] Shanks, Jacobson, and Kaplan defined intergovernmental organisations (IGOs) as: those associations established by governments or their representatives that are sufficiently institutionalised to require regular meetings, rules governing decision-making, a permanent staff, and a headquarters.[21] Russett, Oneal, and Davis defined International Organisations as: formal continuous institutions established by treaty or other agreement between governments, long-range in nature, multilateral, with a secretariat and more-or-less regular meetings, and an 'international legal personality' with legal standing.[22] Mearsheimer defines institutions as, "a set of rules that stipulates the ways in which states should cooperate and compete with each other.'[23]

> **INTERNATIONAL ORGANISATIONS**
>
> Organisations themselves are important units of analysis, precisely because they take on a life and character of their own. And those lives and characters, emerging from the process of organised action, should receive direct and critical observation. International relations will be enhanced if we pay greater attention to how modern international organisations emerge and what they do in action—in short, if we pay greater attention to organisational performance.
>
> Ness, G.D., and Brechin, S.R. (1988): "Bridging the Gap: International Organisations as Organisations," *International Organisation*, 42(2), p. 270.

The authors prescribe acceptable forms for state behaviour, and proscribe unacceptable kinds in behaviour. The rules are negotiated by the states; they entail the mutual acceptance of higher norms, which are "standards of behaviour defined in terms of rights and obligations."[24] The rules are typically formalised in international agreements, and are usually embodied in organisations with their own personal and budgets.[25] Although rules are usually incorporated into a formal international organisation, it is not the organisation per se that compels states to obey the rules. States must choose to obey the rules they created. International institutions, in short, call for "decentralised cooperation of individual sovereign states, without any effective mechanism of command."[26]

Two other terms use are the intergovernmental organisation and the supranational organisation, these are defined in succeeding paragraphs.

Intergovernmental Organisations

An intergovernmental organisation (IGO) is composed of nation-states and it promotes voluntary co-operation and coordination among its members.[27] Decisions and agreements reached in this type of organisation however are not enforceable, and the members remain independent. ***The crucial aspect of an IGO is that the members do not surrender any power (or sovereignty) to it.*** The United Nations is an intergovernmental organisation.

Supranational Organisations

A supranational organisation is different because member states do surrender power in specific areas to the higher organisation. Decisions taken by a supranational organisation must be obeyed by the member states. Often there are courts to determine when violations have occurred, although frequently enforcement mechanisms are not as effective as they are within nation states.

Supranationalism[28] has tended to erode certain norms, prerogatives, and images of national sovereignty, without however, fundamentally altering the position of the nation-state as still the single most important actor in the international system.

Need for International Organisations

The world of 1945 has evolved dramatically, fundamentally, and irrevocably. New rules and institutions of global governance will need to take into account several fundamental changes in world politics. These include:

1. ***A shift in power to the global "South":*** While the United States remains at the apex of the international system, the global distribution of power—political, economic, demographic, technological, and to some degree military—is shifting toward the developing world, driven by the rise of China, India, Brazil, and other nations and the relative decline of Europe. Core international institutions, from the UN Security Council to the

Group of Eight industrialised nations (G-8), have not yet adapted to accommodate these shifts, reducing both their perceived legitimacy and their practical effectiveness.

2. ***The rise of transnational threats***: The principal foreign policy challenges of the twenty-first century are likely to be transnational threats—from terrorism to pandemics to climate change. Such challenges will necessitate new forms of institutionalised cooperation and pose particular challenges to India, historically ambivalent toward multilateral institutions.
3. ***The specter of weak and failing states***: For the first time in modern history, the main threats to world security emanate less from states with too much power than from states with too little (e.g., Afghanistan). The goal of collective security has thus shifted from counter-balancing aggressive powers to assisting fragile and post-conflict countries in achieving effective sovereign statehood, including control over "ungoverned spaces."
4. ***The mounting influence of non-state actors***: A corollary to state weakness is the rise of non-state groups and individuals that are capable of operating across multiple sovereign jurisdictions. These include illicit organisations motivated by political grievance (e.g., al-Qaeda) or simple greed (e.g., crime syndicates). But non-state actors also include more benign forces, such as humanitarian NGOs and civil society actors, philanthropic institutions like the Reliance Foundation, Gates Foundation and "super-empowered" individuals like Bono, all clamoring for entrée into decision-making forums that have traditionally been the purview of states alone. How to integrate these new stakeholders into multilateral deliberations remains a major challenge for global governance.

> Successful institutions treat everyone equally and impersonally.
>
> Robert D. Kaplan, (2014) Elections Don't matter, Institutions Do, *Global Affairs* (Stratfor Global Intelligence), 15 Jan 2014.

5. ***Evolving norms of sovereignty and intervention***: There is growing recognition that each state owes certain fundamental obligations to its own citizens and to wider international society. These responsibilities include an obligation not to commit atrocities against one's own population; a prohibition against sponsoring or providing a safe haven to transnational terrorist groups; and a duty to prevent the proliferation of weapons of mass destruction. Yet the effort to make these new norms operational and enforceable remains a Herculean challenge.
6. ***The spread of regional and sub-regional organisations***: Although the UN Charter of 1945 explicitly endorsed regional organisations, such bodies truly began to flower only with the end of the Cold War, both as complements to universal-membership organisations and as substitutes

for them. The task for US policymakers is to assess the comparative advantages of different institutions and encourage a judicious division of labor (between, say, the UN and the African Union) that ensures effective burden sharing, rather than unwarranted "burden shifting."

7. ***The increasing prominence of transnational government networks***: In past decades, the process of multilateral cooperation and rule-making tended to be hierarchical and centralised, reflecting formal negotiations among high-level national delegations. In the 21st Century, multilateral cooperation frequently unfolds in a distributed and networked manner, through the collaboration of transnational networks of government officials from regulatory agencies, executives, legislatures, and courts.
8. ***A growing reliance on coalitions of the willing***: A recent trend in global governance has been to rely less on large, formal organisations (like the UN), which are vulnerable to paralysis and inaction, than on narrower collective action among like-minded countries, as in the Proliferation Security Initiative (PSI). An ongoing dilemma for US policymakers will be to exploit the flexibility of such coalitions without undercutting formal, large-membership organisations whose technical expertise, legitimacy, and resources the United States will need over the long haul.

Role of International Organisation

International institutions are associated with the vastly increased normative ambition of international society and with the attempt to institutionalise a wide range of values that regulate almost every aspect of inter-state relations and also profoundly affect how societies are organised domestically. The role that international organisations can play depends on the interests of their member States. States establish and develop international organisations to achieve objectives that they cannot achieve on their own. By the same token, States will not permit international organisations to do things that constitute, in the eyes of these States, interference in their internal affairs. The proliferation of international institutions is commonly associated with globalisation and with increased levels of transnational exchange and communication.

According to Archer,[29] international organisations fill three principal roles in the international community:

1. They strive to serve as an instrument for the attainment of aims common to the members.
2. They occasionally constitute the arenas or forums within which interrelationships among the members are pursued;
3. Less frequently. International organisations play the role of an independent actor in the global system.

Advantages of International Institutions

There is no great puzzle as to the advantages that often lead states to favour bilateral, multilateral agreements or acting through international institutions. The international institutions empower weaker states by constraining the freedom of the most powerful through established rules and procedures (the dispute settlement mechanisms of the WTO is a good example). International Institutes provide political space for important middle-level players to build new coalitions in order to try and affect emerging norms in ways that are congruent with their interests. It also helps to counter-balance or at least deflect the preferences and policies of the most powerful. The international institutions provide a stage or a forum to provide 'voice opportunities' to states make known their interests and to bid for political support in the broader marketplace of ideas. States also seek to use international institutions either to defend themselves against norms or rules or practices that adversely affect their interests or, even in optimistic moments, to change dominant international norms in ways that they would like to see.

The rush lately by all countries to join these institutions suggests that countries have found them to be more beneficial than the alternative of staying out, but it does not moot the question of whether they would be better off without any of these multilateral institutions in the first place. Four reasons are often theorised for the existence of these institutions: (1) constraining the great powers; (2) providing information and reducing transaction costs; (3) facilitating reciprocity; and (4) promoting reform in domestic politics.

Constraining the Great Powers

International institutions may exert a constraint on the underlying anarchy of the international system. They make the use of force and power by states to achieve their goals less likely; the rules, norms, and procedures established by these institutions replace to some extent the pursuit of national interest by power. Most importantly, as Inkberry claims, they help to harness the behaviour of the most powerful states.[30] By creating and complying with these institutions, the Great Powers, or hegemony, can reassure other states that they will not take advantage of them. The strongest bind themselves to a set of norms and rules that the other states voluntarily agree to accept.

Evidence for this effect is mixed. As the WTO points out, "trade is likely to expand and be more profitable under conditions of certainty and security as to the terms of market access and the rules of trade—pre-commitment around a set of rules also diminishes the role of power and size in determining outcomes."[31]

Providing Information and Reducing Transaction Costs

Some argue that a major reason for the popularity of institutions is the lowering of transaction costs and the provision of information to facilitate multilateral cooperation in an anarchic world. As Ethane writes, international institutions "facilitate agreements by raising the anticipated costs of violating others' property rights, by altering transaction costs through clustering of issues, and by providing reliable information to members. [They] are relatively efficient institutions, compared to the alternative of having a myriad of unrelated agreements, since their principles, rules, and institutions create linkages among issues that give actors incentives to reach mutually beneficial agreements."[32] For him, international institutions also reduce uncertainty by monitoring the member states' behaviour and allowing decentralised enforcement through reciprocity strategies.[33]

Others have noted the expertise role of the IFIs. "The World Bank is widely recognised to have exercised power over development policies far greater than its budget, as a percentage of North/South aid flows, would suggest because of the expertise it houses.... This expertise, coupled with its claim to "neutrality" and its "apolitical" technocratic decision-making style, has given the World Bank an authoritative voice with which it has successfully dictated the content, direction, and scope of global development over the past 50 years."[34] The claim is that the policy expertise given (or imposed via conditionality) has not been beneficial. For instance, Stiglitz, Bhagwati, and others have all criticised the IMF for pushing the developing countries into opening their capital markets.[35]

Facilitating Reciprocity

International institutions facilitate reciprocity strategies among countries in an anarchic environment. Cooperation in anarchy relies on reciprocity, but more cooperation can be sustained if it need not require simultaneous and perfectly balanced exchanges. "International regimes can be thought of in part as arrangements that facilitate non-simultaneous exchange."[36]

There is little evidence that this reciprocity has extended to the developing world. Many developing countries did not join the WTO until recently; most of the developing country members did not reciprocally liberalise their trade in the trade rounds.

> "In the period until the launch of the Uruguay Round and the formation of the WTO, only the industrial countries were meaningful participants in multilateral trade negotiations. They bargained amongst themselves to reduce trade barriers, while developing countries were largely out of this process and had few obligations to liberalise. The latter availed themselves of the benefits of industrial country liberalisation, courtesy of the Most Favored Nation (MFN) principle, but that defined pretty much the limits of their contribution to or

benefits from the General Agreement on Tariffs and Trade (GATT). Industrial countries were content with this arrangement, in part because it alleviated the pressure on them to liberalise sensitive sectors such as agriculture and clothing, but perhaps more importantly because the markets of developing countries were not at that stage sufficiently attractive."[37]

Facilitating Reform in Domestic Politics

Some scholars have speculated that joining an international institution and publicly agreeing to abide by its rules, norms, and practices has important domestic political consequences. It can help domestic leaders to alter policies at home that they otherwise would not be able to do. It can help them lock in "good" policies (that is, ones that enhance general welfare) and resist pressures by special interests to adopt "bad" policies (that is, ones that benefit special interests only). Or it can help domestic leaders to activate interest groups to counterbalance other groups' pressures and thus introduce different policies than otherwise. Once a nation joins an institution it becomes hard for their leaders to violate institutional practices since leaders who do so tarnish their international reputations and are less capable of making new agreements; their publics lose from this and are more likely to evict the leader, making noncompliance more costly than otherwise.[38]

> One of the most efficient pronouncements on India's foreign policy in general is given by Prime Minister Jawaharlal Nehru in his Columbia University address in the United States on October 17, 1949—a statement that seems as helpful today as when it was pronounced. In explaining India's Foreign Policy an attempt "to combine idealism with national interest," Nehru went on to add:
> "*The main objectives of that policy are: the pursuit of peace, not through alignment with any major power or group of powers, but through an independent approach to each controversial or disputed issue; the liberation of subject peoples; the maintenance of freedom, both national and individual; the elimination of racial discrimination; and the elimination of want. Disease and ignorance which affect the greater part of the world's population.*"

India and International Institutions

Most international institutions were not drafted for the specific needs of 'developing countries' or India. The Bretton Woods institutions are prime examples. The organisation of International Corporation and development (OECD) describes their initial tasks: "The International Bank of Reconstruction and Development [IBRD] was there to guarantee European borrowing in international (North American) markets; and the International Monetary Fund

(IMF) was there to smooth the flow of repayments.' The presence of delegation from the nations of what is now referred as South including Indian delegation (*pro forma* led by British officials as India was in transition to independence) insisted on resources financing development as well as European reconstruction.

India's concept of her membership of the international society is one in which the concept of State sovereignty is limited by the overriding considerations of internal solidarity and international co-operation. While, like every other state in the world, she is zealous of her independence and territorial integrity, she is also fully cognizant of the compelling need for the advancement of that society to some form of world order.

By choosing this variation on multilateralism, India is buying into a strategy developed largely by the United States, Russia, China, and several Western European powers to co-manage international economic and, to a lesser degree, security systems. However, India has so far been tentative about its willingness to assume much responsibility within these systems.

Two major developments are currently transforming the multilateral system. The first is the trend towards multi-polarity as expressed by the rising number of states that act as key players. There have been times when only a few or even one player dominated the geopolitical game. But today it seems that several states are becoming dominant players as global or regional actors. The (voting) behaviour of the BRICS countries (Brazil, Russia, India, China and South Africa) in the UN and their presence in the G20 illustrates this trend.

Indian diplomacy has undergone significant change and maturation in the last fifty years. India has moved from a Cold War relationship with the USSR to establishment as a nuclear power, a burgeoning relationship with the US and a shift in its regional relationships based on a new 'Act East', 'Link West', 'Neighbourhood First', policy.[39] There are also indications that Indian diplomacy is moving beyond its pre-occupation with border security, specifically at its North Eastern and North Western land borders with China and Pakistan respectively.[40] This is evidenced by developing relations with South-East Asia and its maturing diplomatic approach to its traditional enemies, Pakistan and China, and its newest friend, the US.

GLOBAL GOVERNANCE

Global governance refers to complex of formal and informal institutions, mechanisms, relationships, and processes between and among states, markets, citizens, and organisations—both intergovernmental and non-governmental through which collective interests are articulated, rights and obligations are established, and differences are mediated.[1]

[1]As quoted in Thakur, Ramesh and Van Langenhove, Luk (2006), 'Enhancing Global Governance Through Regional Integration', *Global Governance*, Vol. 12, No. 3 (July-September 2006), p. 233.

The emergence of truly global problems such as climate change, proliferation of weapons of mass destruction and many others have indeed led to an increasing paradox of governance. As Thakur and Van Langenhove put it in Global Governance[41] "[t]he policy authority for tackling global problems still belong to the states, while the sources of the problems and potential solutions are situated at transnational, regional or global level". As such the building blocks of multilateralism, the states, seem to be less and less capable of dealing with the challenges of globalisation. But because the multilateral world order is so dependent on the input of states, multilateralism itself is not functioning well.

India and the United Nations

The United Nations was developed after World War II to oversee global peace and security. Post-independence India was an enthusiastic supporter of the multilateral system, at that time comprised largely of the United Nations and its associated organisations. In September 1946, Jawaharlal Nehru professed "wholehearted co-operation and unreserved adherence, in both spirit and letter" to the UN Charter.[42] Parts of India's subsequently drafted constitution laid out directive principles of state policy on international affairs that adhered noticeably to principles of the UN Charter such as promoting peace and security, promoting international law, and settling international disputes through arbitration.[43]

India has used the General Assembly platform for voicing strongest opposition to imperialism, colonialism and apartheid. In 1954, India took a leading part in securing political sanctions against the racialist regime of South Africa. In 1965, it supported fully the UN sponsored economic boycott of Rhodesia. It gave full support to the Angolan liberation movement and to the cause of Independence of Namibia. India also played an active role in setting up of the United Nations Conference on Trade and Development (UNCTAD) and calling for the creation of a New International Economic Order (NIEO). India led a group of developing countries whose support proved valuable in getting 16 countries admitted in 1955. India forcefully pleaded for representation of Communist China in the United Nations.

India encountered a major setback at the UN on the issue of Kashmir in the winter of 1947. Faced with the choice of unilaterally repelling a Pakistani attack and consolidating India's hold on the erstwhile princely state, or referring the matter for arbitration to the UN, Nehru chose the latter option. Much to his disappointment, the Security Council failed to endorse India's claim to Kashmir; instead, insisting on a plebiscite of the state's population. India realised belatedly that "the Security Council was a strictly political body and that decisions were taken by its members on the basis of their perspective of their national interest and not on the merits of any particular case."[44]

The Kashmir episode permanently colored Indian thinking on the UN. Since then, India has been loath to allow any form of multilateral intervention in the South Asian region.[45] Pakistan's consistent efforts to internationalize the Kashmir issue at the UN doubtless contributed to India's growing preference for bilateralism over multilateralism.[46] The induction of Pakistan into United States Regional Alliances such as the CENTO and SEATO made India deeply critical of the United States alliance system. New Delhi's aversion to any UN inclination to override state sovereignty is evident even in its approach to peacekeeping—India's most celebrated contribution to the UN, through its generous provision of military and civilian staff—for which it emphasizes the need for consent of the parties involved.

Post-Cold War, the UN became considerably more active than it had been over the previous two decades, marked initially by the 1992 Rio Summit on Climate Change, at which India played an important role.22 In other UN conferences, including that leading to the indefinite extension of the NPT in 1995, and the adoption of the Comprehensive (Nuclear) Test Ban Treaty (CTBT) in 1996, New Delhi occasionally opted for a stance viewed by some as a would be "spoiler."[47]

When United Nations was founded there were 51 member states. Today it stands at 198. Alongside with growth in the number of states has occurred the rise of civil society actors who have mediated state-citizen relationships and given rise to the concept of **"We the peoples of the World"**. The international policy making space is congested as private and public non-state actors jostle alongside national governments in setting and implementing the governance agenda. United Nations continues to serve several critical functions. First, the United Nations upholds basic normative standards on the use of force. Second, it offers critical mechanisms to mediate international disputes. Third, it provides inclusive regulatory frameworks and regimes that ensure transparency, predictability, and stability, and offers mechanisms for redress when these regimes break down. Fourth, it serves as a legitimate vehicle for collective action to keep and restore the peace, including through preventive deployments, peace operations, and post conflict peace-building. In addition to these traditional roles, the United Nations has in recent years sought to adjust to a new suite of security threats, ranging from the threat of global pandemics to transnational terrorism to the proliferation of weapons of mass destruction.

India's role in the comity of nations is also important because there has been a general lack of appreciation of her role in the United Nations and the efforts she has made in the Organisation for conciliation and solution of the world's problems have created some sort of disappointment and disillusionment. Though, even now, India regards the United Nations as the agency for peaceful solution of problems and a medium of co-operation, it has to be noted that the role of the Great Powers and the cold war, which has clouded the issues that are presented in the United Nations, has cooled some of her early enthusiasm manifested in the beginning. The Indian focus is still global, thanks to presumed leadership of the Non-aligned movement.

The United Nations cannot displace the responsibility of local, state and national governments but can and should be the locus of multilateral diplomacy and collective action to solve problems shared in common by many countries.

The Prospects for UN Reform

India believes that the United Nations must undertake reforms that will make it truly representative while enhancing its credibility and effectiveness. In particular, the composition of the Security Council needs to change thereby reflecting contemporary realities. The United Nations must play an active role in ensuring inclusive growth within nations, and inclusive globalisation across nations. India also believes that the UN should play an active role in ensuring genuine global counter-terrorism cooperation, in particular, the conclusion of the continuing negotiations on a Comprehensive Convention on International Terrorism.

Despite these indispensable roles, the United Nations also suffers from five major shortcomings. First, ***it is largely a reactive organisation***, despite its attempts to develop a culture of prevention. Second, ***classic collective action challenges persist*** at the United Nations, including lowest-common-denominator negotiations, free-riding, and lack of sufficient funding. Third, the UN Security Council is ***increasingly anachronistic, failing to reflect shifts in global power*** or include even a single country from Africa or Latin America. Fourth, the United **Nations** ***remains racked by ideological divisions***; particularly between North and South, which frequently obstruct international cooperation. Finally, the United Nations as an institution remains in dire ***need of management reform.***

When trying to tackle transnational threats over the past decade, global leaders have often turned to alternative groups like the G-20 or regional organisations, rather than the United Nations. Many participants anticipated that this trend would persist, as the United Nations faces competition from ad hoc and regional arrangements. Therefore, to remain relevant, they said, the United Nations will need to reform.

India, of course, is a leading candidate if permanent seats are added to the UN Security Council, and many workshop participants spoke in favor of the United States declaring its support for India's candidacy. *Permanent membership of the UN Security Council has traditionally been considered a key criterion for being counted as a great power. China is permanent member of UN Security Council.*

A major uncertainty, however, was how India would behave if it did obtain a permanent seat. Some participants expressed concern that India would import its nonaligned rhetoric into the UNSC, and that it would resist using the UNSC's coercive tools to defend international norms. Others disagreed, suggesting that a UN Security Council seat would encourage India to become a guarantor of the global system. Referring to India's campaign for a permanent seat, former foreign secretary M.K. Rasgotra commented in 2007 that "things of that kind will come to India unasked as its economic and other strengths grow."[48]

International Economic Institutions

The roles of the three main institutions have changed over time; in addition, their membership has become nearly universal. All of these institutions were created by the victors in World War II and were intended to help them avoid another global depression. Part of the problem for these institutions lies in their legacy as these was designed to help the developed countries create a cooperative and stable world economy in a non-globalised world.[49]

The IMF was established to support the fixed exchange rate system created at the Bretton Woods Conference in 1944; its role was to aid countries that were experiencing difficulties in maintaining their fixed exchange rate by providing them with short term loans. It was a lender of last resort and a provider of funds in crisis, enabling countries to avoid competitive devaluations. Ensuring a stable international monetary system to promote trade and growth was its central mission. From an initial membership of 29 countries, it has become almost universal with 184 members.

With the collapse of the Bretton Woods fixed exchange rate system in the early 1970s, this role changed. The IMF dealt less with the developed countries and more with the developing ones. It provided long and short term loans at below-market interest rates for countries in all sorts of economic difficulty, making it less distinct from the World Bank. It began attaching increasing numbers of conditions to those loans ("conditionality"), negotiating with countries to make major changes in their domestic policies and institutions. Promoting economic growth as well as resolving specific crises became its mission, which meant that ever more countries became involved in these so-called structural adjustment programs. Indeed, as Vreeland notes, in 2000 alone the IMF had programs with sixty countries, or more than one-third of the developing world.[50] These changes made the IMF more similar to the World Bank.

Formed after World War II, the Bank concentrated mostly on reconstruction and later on development; in 1960, with the formation of the International Development Association (IDA), the Bank moved further toward economic development programs. Many countries over the years have received both IMF and World Bank loans, often simultaneously. The World Bank also gives interest free loans and grants (similar to foreign aid) to the poorest developing countries. This aid has been heavily used in Africa; indeed, in 2003, 51 per cent of it went to sub-Saharan Africa. This overlap of missions, proliferation of adjustment loans, and expansion of conditionality are central issues today.

In 2001, the then Goldman Sachs Group economist Jim O'Neill coined the term BRIC to describe the growing prominence of Brazil, Russia, India and China in the global economy. Not yet considered developed countries, the four were grouped together for being at the same stage of economic development. South Africa joined them later. BRICs Bank was born because the countries that represent this have long realised they need an alternative system to IMF/World Bank, one in which they have greater say. BRICS account for about 40 per cent of the world's population and a combined economy of about $16 trillion. Although they account for over one-fifth of the global economy, together they garner only 11 per cent of votes at IMF. On the other hand, developed countries such as the US, Japan, Germany, the UK and France hold 40 per cent of the voting power. In the BRICS bank, the founding members have equal voting rights. The articles of the bank do say that its creation is to complement "the existing efforts or multilateral and regional financial institutions."

Global Trade

The dominance of market, resources, economic goals have always been significant element's in international affairs, the interdependence of national economies has increased with accelerated and expanded flows of trade, investment and technology across political frontiers. *"Markets cannot play a dominant role in the way in which a political economy functions unless allowed to do so by whoever wields power and possesses authority."*[51] Rules governing international commerce, like those governing international politics, reflect the interests of the dominant players.

India was one of the 23 founding contracting parties to the General Agreement on Tariffs and Trade (GATT) that was concluded in October 1947. The country's leaders served as spokesmen for developing-countries, and raised their concerns in the discussions that led to the GATT, and India has often led groups of less developed countries in subsequent rounds of multilateral trade negotiations (MTN) under the auspices of GATT.

The WTO, which replaced GATT in 1995 mandated for trade in goods as well as services and issues affecting international trade. Hence, WTO has considerably greater influence on trade among nations. The WTO is a multilateral framework (an agreement among governments) for conduct of international trade in goods and services and also for protection of intellectual property rights, i.e., patents, copyrights, trademarks, etc. and for discussion of trade related issues.

The WTO has a set of multilateral agreements primarily on the rights and obligations (of governments) that prescribes for governments in formulation of rules, procedures and practices related to international trade.

The WTO disciplines are in three parts: (i) for the trade in goods, contained in the GATT and some specific agreements on goods; (ii) for the trade in services, contained in the General Agreement on Trade in Services (GATS); and (iii) for the protection of Intellectual Property Rights, contained in the Agreement on Trade Related Aspects of Intellectual Property Rights (Agreement on TRIPs). The principle objective of the WTO is to work for reduction of tariff on international trade. There is an agreement called the Dispute Settlement Understanding (DSU) for enforcement of the rights and obligations and for resolving disputes between governments in areas covered by agreements of WTO.

Over the past twenty years, India has become increasingly integrated into the global economy. In the early 1990s, the country first embarked on a process of economic reform and liberalisation. Since then, the share of trade in India's gross domestic product has risen from around 25 per cent to 50 per cent, and India's share of the global export market has doubled as well. India has also become more integrated into global financial and capital markets, and the capitalisation of the Indian stock market has increased tenfold as a result.

A more confident India also asserted itself in the multilateral trading regime, as it formed a loose coalition of developing countries seeking to prevent the launch of a new post-Uruguay trading round.[52] Largely a passive spectator in the GATT/WTO regime until the late 1990s, India had spoken up at the 1999 Seattle meeting of the WTO against the inclusion of labour and environmental standards on the WTO agenda.[53]

India has been pressing for greater economic cooperation within the subcontinent. India always had fairly open trading regimes on a bilateral basis with Nepal and Bhutan, and in 2000 it unveiled a similar arrangement with Sri Lanka. India has actively supported the negotiation of a free trade agreement (FTA) for the region, but enduring conflict between India and Pakistan and the wariness between India and smaller neighbours has prevented an accelerated movement toward regional integration.

Climate Change

Environmental matters received scant attention within the Indian government. India's position had long been to stick closely to the terms of the Kyoto Protocol to the UN Framework Convention on Climate Change, under which industrialised countries committed to specific targets for emission reductions while developing countries were not required to do so under the "common but differentiated" responsibilities approach that had characterised UN discussions and agreements on the issue since the Rio conference. India is wary of intrusive monitoring, reporting, and verification requirements that might infringe on its sovereignty and impede its ability to reach domestic development targets. India has remained adamant that the global climate change regime maintain a two-track approach that differentiates between the "common but differentiated responsibilities" of developed, OECD countries and those of developing countries like India.

Prime Minister Manmohan Singh appointed one of India's most talented and media genic younger politicians, Jairam Ramesh, to the environment portfolio. Ramesh at first yielded little. However, it soon transpired that within the government, Ramesh was arguing in favor of flexibility in line with the reported determination of Prime Minister Singh that, at the Copenhagen conference, India should be "part of the solution to the problem."[54]

Ramesh was quoted as arguing that "India must listen more and speak less in negotiations" because its stance is "disfavored by the developed countries, small island states and vulnerable countries. It takes away from India's aspirations for permanent membership of the Security Council."[55] India offered (voluntary) emissions goals that would be subject to international "consultation and analysis," but not scrutiny or formal review.[56] He was soon challenged by two of India's long-time negotiators. Specifically, they questioned an offer articulated by Ramesh that India could reduce its carbon intensity by 20 per cent to 25 per cent of 2005 levels by 2020,[57] because New Delhi had not yet elicited reciprocal concessions.[58]

The outcome of the Copenhagen talks, widely perceived as a fiasco and criticized by India's Prime Minister, actually served India's interests well in allowing it to be "part of the solution." A last-minute truncated accord offered by the BASIC (Brazil, South Africa, India and China) powers and the United States, acknowledged—however reluctantly and only by taking "note" of it—by the conference plenary, underscored that India was now an indispensable negotiating partner on key global challenges such as climate change.

Many at home in India perceived the results as positive rather than negative on the global climate conference and its limited outcome.[59] All in all, in contrast to its positions at the WTO in 2008, India demonstrated agility in the run-up to the Copenhagen conference and dexterity during the meeting, allowing it to emerge as one of the forgers of a compromise. Not surprisingly, it also adopted a flexible negotiating stance at the follow-up UN conference in Cancun in December 2010.[60]

"Climate change is a major global challenge. But it is not of our making. It is the result of global warming that came from prosperity and progress of an industrial age powered by fossil fuel," Modi said while inaugurating the India pavilion at the summit, toughening his country's stand in the face of recent US criticism of India.

"But we in India face consequences. We see the risk to our farmers. We are concerned about rising oceans that threaten our 7,500 km of coastline and 1,300 islands. We worry about the glaciers that feed our rivers and nurture our civilisation." He clearly outlined India's strategy, saying the developed world should provide easy access to cleaner technologies, climate finance and right to carbon space, technologies, climate finance and right to carbon space.

India played its role to get the accord cleared at Paris Summit. The Paris accord, as agreed upon by member countries, sets the architecture for carbon emission reduction after 2020. It safeguards the principle of common but differentiated responsibility that has remained a non-negotiable aspect of India's climate position. This principle squarely puts the major responsibility on developed nations to drastically cut their carbon emissions and provide the necessary finance, technology and capacity building for developing economies to mitigate and adapt to climate change.

Modi in his opening speech at the negotiations highlighted the need to operationalise the principle of equity and fair distribution of the remaining carbon space (i.e. the amount of carbon we can further emit before breaching average temperature threshold).

Key elements of the Paris accord:

- **Long-Term Goal:** The long-term objective of the agreement is to make sure global warming stays "well below" 2 degrees Celsius (3.6 degrees Fahrenheit) and to "pursue efforts" to limit the temperature rise to 1.5 degrees Celsius (2.7 degrees Fahrenheit). Temperatures have already increased by about 1 degree Celsius (1.8 degrees Fahrenheit) since pre-industrial times.
- **Emissions Targets:** In order to reach the long-term goal, countries agreed to set national targets for reducing greenhouse gas emissions every five years. More than 180 countries have already submitted targets for the first cycle beginning in 2020. Only developed countries are expected to slash their emissions in absolute terms; developing nations are "encouraged" to do so as their capabilities evolve over time.
- **Reviewing Targets:** The initial targets won't be enough to put the world on a path to meet the long-term temperature goal. So the agreement asks governments to review their targets in the next four years and see if they can "update" them. That doesn't require governments to deepen their cuts. But the hope is that it will be possible for them to do so if renewable energy sources become more affordable and effective.

- **Transparency:** There is no penalty for countries that miss their emissions targets. But the agreement has transparency rules to help encourage countries to actually do what they say they will do. That was one of the most difficult pieces to agree on, with China asking for softer requirements for developing countries. The agreement says all countries must report on their emissions and their efforts the reduce them. But it allows for some "flexibility" for developing countries that "need it."
- **Money:** The agreement says wealthy countries should continue to offer financial support to help poor countries reduce their emissions and adapt to climate change. It also encourages other countries to pitch in on a voluntary basis. That paves the way for emerging economies such as China to contribute, even though it doesn't require them to do so. Actual dollar amounts were kept out of the agreement itself, but wealthy nations had previously pledged to provide $100 billion annually in climate finance by 2020.
- **Loss and Damage:** In a victory for small island nations threatened by rising seas, the agreement includes a section recognizing "loss and damage" associated with climate-related disasters. The US long objected to addressing the issue in the agreement, worried that it would lead to claims of compensation for damage caused by extreme weather events. In the end, the issue was included, but a footnote specifically stated that loss and damage does not involve liability or compensation.

What set apart from India's previous efforts was the approach of the negotiating team, "There was a great deal of cohesion within the Indian Negotiating team, between the Minister and the officials, and between Paris and Delhi," said a member of the delegations support team. India emerged from Paris talks as a proactive and progressive player. Through initiatives like the International Solar Alliance, New Delhi demonstrated its willingness and ability to think out of the box in moving away from fossil fuel-based path to development. India made it clear that it was willing to look to ways in which the global effort to address the challenge of climate change could be pursued in partnership with countries without jeopardising its development push. *In a sense Mr Javadekar, Minister, was able to do all the things the Mr Jairam Ramesh had wanted to as India's Chief Negotiator,* " a veteran observer from the G-77 groups of nations said.[61]

In the end India was able to project itself. India was able to protect it development space by ensuring the idea of differential responsibilities of developed and developing countries was embedded in the elements such as Finance, transparency, efforts to reduce emissions, capacity building. New Delhi also secured a key demand for a financial provision to help meet the costs of intellectual property rights crucial in the transfer of technology.[62]

New Forums

The emergence of the G-20 at the leader level and India's inclusion represent a politically significant graduation for the country rather than an introduction to serious consultations on global financial issues. After all, India had long been involved in such consultations at the International Monetary Fund and at the Bank for International Settlements in Basel, cutting an impressive figure in many instances. India's "finance diplomacy" has been one of its strongest contributions to international relations writ large. The G-20's emergence at the leader level while Manmohan Singh was India's Prime Minister was a happy coincidence, as group insiders report that, given his extensive background in economic issues, he has consistently been one of the two or three voices most keenly anticipated and listened to around the table.

India's desire to be a "canny negotiator" that effectively walks the North-South line could shape the country's engagement with the multilateral system in years to come.[63] However, as Nitin Desai argues, this approach may work less well in an era in which India is increasingly seen internationally as advancing its own interests rather than seeking to champion (more than rhetorically) those of a highly differentiated developing world as a whole.

At Indian Ocean Rim-Association for Regional Cooperation (IOR-ARC), Indian Commerce Minister Anand Sharma called for an institutional mechanism to facilitate business interaction among members. Though the IOR-ARC has existed since 1995-96, it has so far failed to emerge as a common economic platform, and India's trade ties in the IOR region have progressed chiefly along bilateral lines. But with China's economic overtures increasingly frequent and backed by commercial heft, India finds that it can no longer take its geo-economic position in the region for granted. To counter China's commercial bilateralism, India seems to be trying to establish a multilateral mechanism for overseeing trade and investment that China may later have to join.[64]

India's tightrope walk is increasingly evident. It consistently voted with Washington against Iran's nuclear program at the IAEA while continuing to maintain friendly bilateral relations with Iran and defend its own nuclear program. It promotes the notion of Brazil, India, Russia, and China (BRIC) as a coalition of emerging economies championing developing nation causes, but is careful not to antagonise Washington by endorsing an alternative international currency to the dollar, something for which China and Russia have expressed support.[65] It has joined Brazil in criticising China's exchange rate policies, making clear that BRIC solidarity is selective.[66]

Strategic Partnerships

Strategic Partnerships, unlike the Cold War type of alliances, do not bind nations to support each other on all strategic issues in all situations. The partnerships are entered into in those areas of common interest where mutual help and collaboration can be of long-term benefit to both. Being bilateral in nature, they do not have the stigma of a multilateral alliance, which may be presumed to be a power bloc meant to countervail some big power or another power bloc. These partnerships are considered strategic in nature because of the importance of the issues involved and the long-term nature of cooperation that is visualised. India has entered into strategic partnerships with more than a dozen countries in the last 10 years. They pertain to core areas of national interest like supply of defence equipment and technology, military exercises, cooperation in the field of nuclear energy, trade and investments, diplomatic support on critical issues, cooperation in science and technology, education, agriculture, information and communication technology, banking, insurance, and various other sectors. Each partnership has a specific character focusing on certain issues. It is in the nature of things that some partnerships are more comprehensive than others, depending on the number of areas in which the two sides can fruitfully and actively engage to mutual benefit and the scope and depth of their relations.

For a country like India which has built its reputation on value based and rule based foreign and security policies, and has exhibited its economic potential by consistent growth in the last two decades, it is important to be exacting and serious in building an architecture of its bilateral relationships Since the end of the Cold War, India relationship with US, Japan, Russia, EU, South Africa, Brazil has been evolving and "reaching new heights". In this budding relationship, the most visible manifestation is cooperation in the sphere of defence. It is quite apparent from the increasing frequency and scope of bilateral military exercises, seminars, personnel exchanges, high level and unit visits, officer and unit exchanges, as well as the defence technology sales. India has also moved away from its traditional emphasis on the "power of the argument" towards the "argument of power".[67] The extent of support provided by a foreign country to India on issues that are critical to its national security is a measure of how useful a partner that country is.

Russia emerges as the most important strategic partner of India. It has given us strong political and diplomatic support and helped us enormously in building our defence capability. But the economic content of the partnership is extremely weak. Urgent and vigorous steps need to be taken to improve economic relations if this partnership is to be sustained and made durable

The United States is a strong competitor with Russia and is currently the second most important partner. The strategic partnership with the US usually acquires a higher profile because of its image as a global power. But the US has been very lackadaisical in providing political and diplomatic support to India on vital issues. Even its defence cooperation with India has been subjected to lots of 'ifs' and 'buts' driven by domestic political and economic considerations. The United States needs to take India more seriously if this strategic partnership is to be placed on a robust footing because it has tremendous potential for the benefit of both countries.

France occupies the third position in terms of the importance of strategic partners. Its political and diplomatic support to India has been valuable. There is greater potential for India–France defence cooperation than has been exploited so far. But India and France need to pay greater attention to strengthening their economic ties. France and India are both independent-minded nations and have a certain similarity of world-views. No opportunity should be missed to widen and deepen the strategic partnership with France.

Strategic partnerships with Germany and Japan seem to be taking off. The potential for economic cooperation with both these countries is already visible. This potential needs to be further exploited. Even if defence cooperation takes time to develop, efforts should be made to seek the support of both these countries on political and diplomatic issues of concern to India more strongly and consistently...

However, strategic partnership that needs special mention is with Japan. India and Japan established a 'Strategic and Global Partnership' in 2006. Ever since, their relations have continued to evolve and they are jointly exploring ways to strengthen their strategic ties. In this regard, an action plan covering security and counter-terrorism exchanges was unveiled in 2009. Japan's appreciation of India as a strategic partner stems out of the geopolitical concerns it faces with regard to China's rise and the North Korean threat. India has been an important axis of most Japanese initiatives in Asia such as the Quadrilateral Initiative in 2007. Moreover, Japan is also aware of the importance of the Indian Navy in ensuring the security of the Sea Lanes of Communication (SLOCs) in the Indian Ocean and across the Strait of Malacca, which ensures a regular supply of oil for Japan. For India, Japan's importance is primarily economic. Its strategic importance, however, is gradually unfolding.

Defence diplomacy has been used as an effective tool of foreign policy and forms one of India's main forms of engagement with many countries such as Russia, Singapore, UK, USA, France, Indonesia, Israel, Japan, Mauritius, Myanmar, Maldives, Nepal, Sri Lanka, Bangladesh, South Africa, Tajikistan, Oman and Bhutan. India's international military cooperation arrangements include formal defence arrangements which could be bilateral or multilateral. Military to military activities include high level visits, attending courses at military training institutions, defence and military expert exchanges, joint exercises, defence equipment and technology-transfers, military assistance programmes, sports and adventure activity and cooperation in UN peace keeping operations.[68] Obviously the levels of military cooperation with each and every country cannot be at the same level. However, these are determined by national interests and foreign policy goals and priorities.

Modi Doctrine

The Bhartiya Janta Party election manifesto speaks of regions and regional forums rather than countries. This is in sharp contrast to past, the manifesto clearly states, "We will create a web of allies to mutually further our interests. We will leverage all our resources and people to play a greater role on the international high table".

The BJP manifesto further says that "There is a need to integrate our soft power avenues into our external interchange, particularly, harnessing and focusing on the spiritual, cultural and philosophical dimensions of it. India has always played a major role in world affairs, offering a lot to the World. India has believed in what is said in Sanskrit, *vasudhaiva kutumbakam* (the world is one family). This has been its tradition since time immemorial. The magnetic power of India has always been in its ancient wisdom and heritage, elucidating principles like harmony and equity. This continues to be equally relevant to the world today in today's times of Soft power. We will adopt Proactive Diplomacy to spread the same. India was reckoned ... as ... also a vibrant trading society. Our ancestors used to trade with foreign nations through the routes of sea, centuries ago. This was based on the strength of our business acumen and integrity, our products and crafts. The symbols of our ancient civilisations stand as a testimony to our architectural and urban planning excellence. We will revive Brand India with the help of our strengths of 5-T's: Tradition, Talent, Tourism, Trade and Technology". This is typical of the Modi stamp on the manifesto. Similarly, Modi thinks that non-resident Indians (NRIs), people of Indian origin (PIOs) and professionals settled abroad are a vast reservoir to articulate the country's national interests and affairs globally; he will want to harness this resource – a known support base of his – to strengthen what he calls Brand India

UN Security Council: The US and USSR had emerged as the two superpowers and were battling a 'Cold War'. US had managed to get its allies UK and France into the UNSC but Communist Russia was the only country from the Warsaw Pact in the elite body. Now there was a proposal for a permanent Asian seat and there were two possible candidates: India and People's Republic of China (There was another in Formosa called the Republic of China which was then member of the Council, but since that was a government in exile with the only thing running in its favor being US recognition). The United States wanted to get

India into the UNSC because it did not want a communist country in UNSC. Nehru refused to take the seat. Modi set out aggressively to seek support for India on the high seat.

Paris Climate Talks: Leading up to the negotiations and through the conference, India's role was often made out to be as one that could either make or break the Paris negotiations. But under Prime Minister Narendra Modi, India has deftly managed its PR and signed onto a final agreement that is balanced in its immediate interests. India managed to:

1. Put back the important principle of equity and "common but differentiated responsibilities" in text, which India has been pushing for. The US and developed nations wanted to dilute this plank.
2. Though developed countries use fossil fuel—coal and gas—they wanted developing countries to cut emissions. It is still not clear if the developed nations will be forthcoming with funds and technology for clean energy or the modalities if they do.
3. The big challenge met was ensuring the agreement established the idea of climate justice—acknowledging that industrialised nations have been the major emitters since 1850.
4. India also wanted a mention of sustainable lifestyle and consumption, which is there in the text

Missile Technology Control Regime: The members of the Missile Technology Control Regime, an international anti-proliferation grouping, have agreed to admit India, diplomats said, in a win for Prime Minister Narendra Modi. Admission to the MTCR would open the way for India to buy high-end missile technology, also making more realistic its aspiration to buy surveillance drones such as the Predator. India becomes a significant Arms Exporter as India hopes to sell makes a Brahmos supersonic cruise missile, in a joint venture with Russia that both countries hope to sell to third countries.

Nuclear Suppliers Group: PM Narendra Modi is leaving no stone unturned to get members of the 48-nation bloc to support India's membership request. India has been pushing for membership of the bloc for last few years and had formally moved its application on May 12. The NSG had granted an exclusive waiver for India in 2008 to access civil nuclear technology after China reluctantly backed India's case based on the Indo-US nuclear deal. China nowever is blocking entry of India as fall member of NSG.

Strategic Partnerships: The 21st Century has witnessed a new pattern of international relationships in which nations enter into freewheeling partnerships with other nations based on complementarity of interests in specific but vital areas. These partnerships, unlike the Cold War type of alliances, do not bind nations to support each other on all strategic issues in all situations. The partnerships are entered into in those areas of common interest where mutual help and collaboration can be of long-term benefit to both. India has built its reputation on value based and rule based foreign and security policies, and has exhibited its economic potential by consistent growth in the last two decades, it is important to be exacting and serious in building architecture of its bilateral relationships. Today, Russia emerges as the most important strategic partner of India. It has given us strong political and diplomatic support and helped us enormously in building our defence capability. But the economic content of the partnership is extremely weak. Urgent and vigorous steps need to be taken to improve economic relations if this partnership is to be sustained and made durable. The United States is a strong competitor with Russia and is currently the second most important partner. The strategic partnership with the US usually acquires a higher profile because of its image as a global power. But the US has been very lackadaisical in providing political and diplomatic support to India on vital issues. Even its defence cooperation with India has been subjected to lots of 'ifs' and 'buts' driven by domestic political and economic considerations. US has recognised India as a major defence partner.

Prospects for effective multilateral cooperation in the twenty-first century will inevitably reflect the distinct national interests of the great powers—and their willingness to share the burdens of providing global public goods. But the identity and number of the world's leading states is changing, creating new challenges and opportunities for global governance. The world order that ultimately results from this transition period will reflect difficult negotiations on global rules and institutions between established powers—including the United States, European Union, and Japan—and emerging ones—including China, India, and Brazil.

This calls for, in the short-term a new international initiative to bring structural reform in the world's financial system with more effective regulation and stronger systems of multilateral consultations and surveillance as well as a collaborative and cooperative global effort for successfully overcoming climate change that leads to an outcome that is fair and equitable while recognising the principle that each citizen of the world has equal entitlement to the global atmospheric space.

While India seems willing to play its part in international summits and negotiations, New Delhi prioritises bilateral ties, regional forums, small caucus groups within wider institutions, and new forums of particular relevance to India's interests. The US relationship has already paid rich dividends in terms of nuclear technology, trade, agriculture, science and technology, military cooperation, and a host of other areas. Buoyed by these successes, New Delhi has established strategic partnerships (of varying depth) with a host of powers, including the EU, Russia, Japan, Israel, Brazil, South Africa, and China.

ENDNOTES

1. Simes, Dimitri K. (2003), America's Imperial Dilemma', *Foreign Affairs,* Vol 82, No. 6, November/December 2003.
2. The term 'interdependence' is described in the Encyclopedia of Public International Law as the fact that States are mutually dependent on each other in ensuring the subsistence and advancement of their nations. Zemanek, K. (1984) 'Interdependence', In Bernhardt, R (ed.) *Encyclopedia of Public International Law,* (New York: ELSEVIER) pp. 275-276.
3. Jacobson, H.K. (1979), *Networks of interdependence: International Organisations and Global Political System* (New York: Alfred A. Knopf), p.13.
4. The other prominent theme in Western policymaking circles is the importance of spreading democracy and capitalism across the globe. Prosperous democracies, so the argument goes do not fight each other. Thus, the aim is to increase the number of stable democracies in the international system.
5. Chritopher, Warren (1993), "The CSCE Vision: European Security Rooted in Shared values," Statement to the Plenary Session of Conference on Security and Cooperation in Europe, Rome, November 30, 1993, as quoted in Mearsheimer, John J. (1994/95) 'The False Promise of International Institutions', *International Security,* Winter 1994/95, Vol 19, No 3, pp. 5-49.
6. Shanks, Cherly, Jacobson, Harold K., and Kaplan, Jefery H. (1996), 'Inertia and Change in the Constellation of International Governmental Organisations, 1982-2992', *International Organisation,* 50(4), pp. 593-626.
7. Goldstein, Judith (1996) 'International law and Domestic Institutions: Reconciling North America "Unfair" trade laws', *International Organisation,* 50, pp. 531-564.
8. Nye, Joseph S. (1990) 'Soft Power', *Foreign Policy,* Vol. 80, autumn 1990; Joseph S. Nye and William A. Owens, 'America's Information Edge', *Foreign Affairs,* vol. 75, no. 2, March/April 1996; and, for a recent elaboration of this concept, see Joseph S. Nye (2004), *Soft Power: The Means to Success in World Politics* (New York: Public Affairs, 2004).
9. Singh, Col Narendar (2006), *Conduct of War* (New Delhi: Manas Publishers).
10. Ibid.
11. Jawaharlal Nehru quoted in Reddy, T. Ramakrishna, (1968) India's *Policy in the United Nations* (Cranbury, NJ: Associated University Presses), p. 30.
12. United Nations Official Records, 2nd Session of General Assembly 1947, 1.138.
13. Haass, Richard N. (2008), "The Age of Nonpolarity: What will follow US Dominance", *Foreign Affairs,* May–June 2008.
14. Zakaria, Fareed (2012), "The World has changed, Mr. Romney", *The Washington Post,* 1 February 2012, at http://www.washingtonpost.com/opinions/the-post-american-worlddemands-a-new-approach-from-the-us/2012/02/01/gIQAba5ziQ_story.html
15. Nye, Jr.Joseph S. (1990), 'Soft Power', *Foreign Policy,* No. 80, Fall 1990, pp 153–170, cited in Raghavan V.R. (2007), Working Paper, The Stanley Foundation's Conference: After the Unipolar Moment: Asia and Regional and Global Order, May 31, http://www.stanley foundation.org/publications/working_papers/RAGHAVAN_working_ paper_ May_ conference_ FINAL.doc, accessed 16 January 2013.
16. Paul, T.V., and Nayar, Baldev Raj (2003), *India in the World Order: Searching for Major Power Status* (Cambridge: Cambridge University Press), p.59.
17. See Keohane, Robert O. (1988), 'International Institutions: Two Approaches," *International Studies Quarterly,* Vol. 32, No. 4 (December), p. 384.
    Keohane, Robert O. (1989), *International Institutions and State Powers: Essays on International Relations Theory* (Boulder, Colo.: Westview Press), pp. 3-4;

Young, Oran R., (1989) *International Cooperation: Building Regimes for Natural Resources and Environment* (Ithaca, N.Y.: Cornell University Press), Chaps 1 and 8.

18. Young, Oran R. (1982), 'Regime Dynamics: The Rise and Fall of International Regimes', in Krasner, Stephen D. (ed.), *International Regimes,* Special Issue of *International Organisation,* Vol. 36, No. 2 (Spring 1982), p. 277.
19. McCormick, John (1999), *The European Union: Politics and Policies* (Boulder Colo.: Westview Press), p.10.
20. Shanks, C., Jacobson, H.K., and Kaplan, J.H. (1996), "Inertia and Change in the Constellation of International Governmental Organisations, 1981–92," *International Organisation, 50*(4), pp. 593–627.
21. Russett, B., Oneal, J.R., and Davis, D.R. (1998), "The Third Leg of the Kantian Tripod for Peace: International Organisations and Militarized Disputes, 1950–85," *International Organisation, 52*(2), pp. 441–67.
22. See, North, Douglas C., and Thomas, Robert P. (1970), "An Economic Theory of the Growth of the Western World," *The Economic History Review,* 2nd series, Vol. 23, No. 1 (April), p.5.
23. Krasner, Stephen D. (ed.), *International Regimes,* Special Issue of *International Organisation,* Vol. 36, No. 2 (Spring), p. 186. Non-realist institutions are often based on higher norms, while few, if any, realist institutions are based on norms. The dividing lines between norms and rules are not sharply defined in the institutionalist literature. See Koehane, Robert O. (1984), *After Hegemony: Cooperation and Discord in the World Political Economy* (Princeton, N.J.: Princeton University Press), pp. 57-58. One might argue that rules, not just norms, are concerned with rights and obligations. The key point, however, is that for many institutionalist, norms, which are core beliefs about standards of appropriate state behaviour, are the foundation on which more specific rules are constructed. This distinction between norms and rules applies in a rather straight forward way. Both collective security and critical theory challenge the realist belief that states behave in a self-interested way, and argue instead for developing norms that require states to act more altruistically. Liberal institutionalism, on the other hand, accepts the realist view that states act on the basis of self interest, and concentrates on devising rules that facilitate cooperation among states.
24. International organisational are public agencies established through the cooperative efforts of two or more states. These administrative structures have their own budget, personnel, and buildings. John Ruggie defines them as "palpable entities with headquarters and letterheads, voting procedures, and generous pension plans." See Ruggie, John G. (1992), "Multilateralism: The Anatomy of an Institution," *International Organisation,* Vol. 46, No. 3 (Summer), p.573. Once rules are incorporated into an international organisation, "they may seem almost coterminous," even though they are "distinguishable analytically." Keohane, Robert O. (1989), *International Institutions and State Powers: Essays on International Relations Theory* (Boulder, Colo.: Westview Press), p. 5.
25. Lipson, Charles (1994), "Is the Future of Collective Security Like the Past?", in Downs, George W., (ed.) *Collective Security Beyond the Cold War* (Ann Arbor: Univerity of Michigan Press), p. 114.
26. McCormick, John (1999), *The European Union: Politics and Policies* (Westview Press: Boulder Colorado), p.10.
27. The terms supranational organisation, Supranational Organisations (SNOs), and supranationalism to refer to all organisations, institutions and political and social processes involving more than a single state or at least two non-state actors from different nation-states. Supranational encompasses formal organisations, institutions, and political and legal agreements related to transnational interaction. These range from the cross-border movements of people, commodities, and information (and the agreements and political frameworks that legitimise

and regulate these) to more structured, ormalised inter-state activity organised and supervised by multilateral institutions and organisations, including IGOs. The broad definition of the term supranational is akin to the term transnational but differs from it in that supranational is not intended to focus primarily on the distinction between the state as an actor in international politics versus non-state actors acting alone or together with state-actors. The purpose will be rather to suggest and illustrate the continued decline and the crisis of the independence of the nation-state both as an apolitical actor and as a justifiable ideological stereotype and construct.

28. Archer, C. (1983), *International Organisations*, pp. 130-141. Also see Coplin, W.D. (1962), *The Functions of International Law*, p. 152.
29. Ikenberry, G. John (2001), *After Victory: Institutions, Strategic Restraint, and the Rebuilding of Order after Major Wars* (Princeton: Princeton University Press).
30. World Trade Organisation (2003), *World Trade Report 2003* (Geneva: World Trade Organisation).
31. Keohane, Robert O. (1984), *After Hegemony: Cooperation and Discord in the World Political Economy* (Princeton: Princeton University Press), p. 97.
32. These arguments tend to overlook the distributional effects of institutions, and to focus on the mutual gains from cooperation within the institution. See Martin, Lisa, and Beth Simmons (1998), 'Theories and empirical studies of international institutions', *International Organisation* 52 (4): pp. 729–57.
33. Barnett, Michael N., and Martha Finnemore (1999), 'The politics, power, and pathologies of international organisations,' *International Organisation* 53(4): pp. 699-732, pp 709–10.
34. Stiglitz, Joseph E. (2002), *Globalisation and its Discontents* (New York, NY: W.W. Norton), chap. 3; Bhagwati, Jagdish (2004), *In Defense of Globalisation* (New York: Oxford University Press), p. 204.
35. Keohane, Robert O. (1984), *After Hegemony* op. cit.
36. Mattoo, Aaditya, and Arvind Subramanian (2004), 'The WTO and the poorest countries: The stark reality,' *IMF Working Paper* 04/81, p.6.
37. McGillivray, Fiona, and Alastair Smith (2000), 'Trust and cooperation through agent specific punishments,' *International Organisation* 54 (4), pp. 809–24.
38. Kapur, Ashok (2006), 'India: From Regional to World Power', *India in the Modern World* (London Routledge).
39. Behuria, Ashok & Smruti Pattanaik & Arvind Gupta (2012), 'Does India Have a Neighbourhood Policy?', *Strategic Analysis*, Vol. 36, No. 2, March 2012, pp. 229-246.
40. Thakur, Ramesh and Van Langenhove, Luk (2006), 'Enhancing Global Governance Through Regional Integration', *Global Governance*, Vol. 12, No. 3 (July-September 2006), pp. 233-240.
41. *Indian Annual Register: July–December 1946* (Calcutta: N.N. Mitra, 1947), pp. 252–253, cited in the Indian Council of World Affairs, *India and the United Nations* (New York: Manhattan, 1957), p. 28.
42. Chamling, Dhiraj R. (1978), *India and the United Nations* (New Delhi: Associated Publishing House), p. 9.
43. Chinmaya R. Gharekhan (2007) "India and the United Nations," in Atish Sinha and Madhup Mohta (eds.), *Indian Foreign Policy: Challenges and Opportunities* (New Delhi: Academic Foundation), p. 200.
44. See C. Raja Mohan, "India and the New World Order," *Seminar* 529 (September 2003), www.india-seminar.com/2003/529/529%20c.%20raja%20mohan.htm
45. See Muchkund Dubey (2007), "Reform of the UN System and India," in Atish Sinha and Madhup Mohta, eds., *Indian Foreign Policy: Challenges and Opportunities* (New Delhi: Academic

Foundation), p. 186.

46. Mallik, Amitava (2004), *Technology and Security in the 21st Century: A Demand-Side Perspective,* SIPRI Research Report No. 20 (Oxford: Oxford University Press, 2004), p. 74.
47. Rasgotra, Maharajakrishna, "Foreign Policy Must Meet 21st Century Needs," Observer Research Foundation Analysis, 24 August 2007, www.orfonline.org/cms/sites/orfonline/modules/analysis/AnalysisDetail.html?cmaid=10325&mmacmaid=10326
48. Stiglitz, Joseph E. (2002), *Globalisation and its discontents* (New York, NY: W.W. Norton), p. 3.
49. Vreeland, James Raymond (2003), *The IMF and economic development* (New York: Cambridge University), p.1.
50. Strange, Susan (1988), *States and Markets: An Introduction to International Political Economy* (London: Printer Publishers), p. 23.
51. Blustein, Paul (2009), *Misadventures of the Most Favored Nations: Clashing Egos, Inflated Ambitions, and the Great Shambles of the World Trade System* (New York: Public Affairs), pp. 67, 96.
52. Sengupta, Dipankar, Chakraborty, Debashis and Banerjee, Pritam (2006), *Beyond the Transition Phase of WTO: An Indian Perspective on Emerging Issues* (New Delhi: Academic Foundation), p. 29.
53. See text of a conversation between Prime Minister Manmohan Singh and Council on Foreign Relations President Richard Haas, 22 November 2009, www.cfr.org/publication/20840/conversation_with_prime_minister_dr_manmohan_singh.html
54. Sethi, Nitin "Jairam for Major Shift at Climate Talks," *Times of India,* 19 October 2009, http://articles.timesofindia.indiatimes.com/2009-10-19/india/28079441_1_greenhouse-gas-emission-reduction-climate-negotiations-change-negotiations
55. Feigenbaum, Evan A. (2010), "India's Rise, America's Interest," *Foreign Affairs,* Vol. 89, No.2 (March/April): 90.
56. Some participants questioned whether India should so closely align itself with China on this issue (especially since Chinese emissions far exceed India's own), but most participants agreed that China and India have similar overall objectives for climate change governance.
57. Dhar, Aarti, "Jairam Irons Out Differences With Negotiators," *The Hindu,* 7 December 2009, www.thehindu.com/news/national/article61104.ece
58. For editorial responses from two prominent Indian newspapers, see "Silver Linings," *Indian Express,* 21 December 2010, www.indianexpress.com/news/silverlinings/ 556927; "Far from Inspiring," *The Hindu,* 21 December 2009, www.thehindu.com/opinion/editorial/article67768.ece.
59. See T. Jayaraman, "Taking Stock of Cancun," *The Hindu,* 13 December 2010, www.thehindu.com/opinion/lead/article948372.ece
60. Goswami, Urmi (2015), "How India weathered a storm in Paris during COP21 climate summit" *The Economic Times,* Dec 22, 2015, New Delhi. http://economictimes.indiatimes.com/news/politics-and-nation/how-india-weathered-a-storm-in-paris-during-cop21-climate-summit/articleshow/50275528.cms
61. Ibid.
62. Michel, Davis (2009) "Introduction," in David Michel and Amit Pandya, eds., *Indian Climate Policy: Choices and Challenges* (Washington, DC: Henry L. Stimson Center), p. 1.
63. Green, Michael J., Gill Bates (eds.) (2009), *Asia's New Multilateralism: Cooperation, Competition and The Seach for Community* (New York: Columbia University Press).
64. "India Reluctant to Join De-Dollarization Chorus at BRIC," *Economic Times,* 15 June 2009, http://articles.economictimes.indiatimes.com/2009-06-15/news/27648497_1_bric-summit-

treasury-bonds-sdrs India also does not hold as much in US Treasuries as China and Russia do, and this might add to its reluctance to join their chorus.

65. Geoff Dyer, "Brazil and India Add to Pressure on China," *Financial Times,* 21 April 2010, www.ft.com/intl/cms/s/0/1d692fd2-4d1c-11df-baf3-00144feab49a.html#axzz1NVKEEeFP
66. With the end of the Cold War and the collapse of Soviet Union, how India made fundamental foreign policy changes to cope with the new geo-strategic realities of the post-Cold War world see Mohan, C. Raja (2003), *Crossing the Rubicon: The Shaping of India's New Foreign Policy,* New Delhi: Viking; and also see "India's New Foreign Policy Strategy", Draft paper presented at a Seminar in Beijing by China Reform Forum and the Carnegie Endowment for International Peace, Beijing, May 26, 2006, available at http://carnegieendowment.org/files/Mohan.pdf; "Rising India's Great Power Burden", *Asia Report,* Issue No. 7, Washington DC: The Sigur Centre for Asian Studies, 2010.
67. Key Note Address by the Honourable Raksha Mantri, Shri A.K. Antony, at the National Seminar on "Defence Cooperation as a Tool for Enhancing National Interest" organised by the Centre for Land Warfare Studies (CLAWS), New Delhi, May 27, 2008, available at http://www.claws.in/index.php?action=master&task=66&u_id=5.

8

CULTURAL ASPECT OF SECURITY POLICY

The maxim "Know Thy Enemy" is often counted as the acne of strategic wisdom; it is unfortunate that the maxim is not highly respected by the political community in India. War has an **organisational**, structural and technological dimensions which make it a rigorous, practical, and precise enterprise, ***but war are also fought between calculating rivals in a domain of uncertainty, and by distinctive political communities in ways that reflect deeply rooted, culturally conditioned preferences.***

> Attempts to salvage the secularisation model have interpreted evidence of burgeoning religiosity in many contemporary political events to mean that we are witnessing merely a fundamentalist, anti-modernist backlash against science, industrialization, and liberal Western values ... Religious fervour is often dismissed as ethnic hostility ..., typically explained away as an isolated exception to unremitting trends of secularization and seldom recognised as part of a larger global phenomenon.[1]
>
> [1]Sahliyeh, E. (ed.) (1990), *Religious Resurgence and Politics in the Contemporary World* (New York: Albany State University of New York Press).

Samuel Huntington, in his book *The Clash of Civilisations and the Remaking of World Order*, argues that, since the end of the Cold War, **the significant divide that is found in societies no longer reflects ideological, political or economic systems, *but cultural differences.*** In other words, it is the confrontation of identities that matters in the post-Cold War world.[1] In his work History of Warfare, John Keegan suggests that throughout history war has been essentially a cultural phenomenon, an atavism derived from patterns of group identification and interaction rather than the purposeful activity implied in Clausewitz's famous dictum that "war is the continuation of politics by other means."[2] Keegan offers,

> "Had his [Clausewitz] mind been furnished with just one extra intellectual dimension—and it is already a very sophisticated mind indeed—he might have been able to perceive that war embraces much more politics: that is always an expression of culture; often a determinant cultural forms, in some societies the culture itself."

Today 'security' as a political value, at least in India, has no independent meaning and is related to individual or societal value systems. As a social science concept, "*security* is ambiguous and elastic in its meaning." There seems to be agreement between many foreign defence policy practitioners and theoreticians that perceptions of identity are of importance as a psychological frame of reference in defence and security policy. In both ancient and contemporary human societies, one can witness the cultural creations of warfare, religion, and social stratification interacting to help form and perpetuate the existence of each other. In addition, these cultural factors have lent themselves to help produce, regulate, and justify specific technologies.

Wolfers[3] pointed to two sides of the security concept: "Security in an *objective* sense, measures the absence of threats to acquired values, in a *subjective* sense, the absence of fear that such values will be attacked". From the perspective of social constructivist approaches in international relations [4] security' is conceived as an outcome of a process of social and political interaction where social values and norms, collective identities and cultural traditions are essential. From this perspective, security is always *intersubjective* or "security is what actors make of it."[5]

> Social structures have three elements: shared knowledge, material resources, and practices. First, social structures are defined, in part, by shared understandings, expectations, or knowledge. These constitute the actors in a situation and the nature of their relationships, whether cooperative or conflictual. A security dilemma, for example, is a social structure composed of intersubjective understandings in which states are so distrustful that they make worst-case assumptions about each other's intentions, and as a result define their interests in self-help terms. *A security community is a different social structure, one composed of shared knowledge in which states trust one another to resolve disputes without war. This dependence of social structure on ideas is the sense in which constructivism has an idealist (or 'idea-ist') view of structure.*
>
> Wendt, Alexander (1992), 'Anarchy is What States Make of It: The Social Construction of Power Politics', *International Organisation,* 46 (2): p. 73.

The *perception* of security dangers depends on the worldviews or traditions and on the mind-set of policymakers[6] that have often distorted the assessment of 'new challenges' and that "freeze international relations into crude images, portray its processes as mechanistic responses of power and characterise other nations as stereotypes".

As early societies began to group together and form conglomerations of people that eventually became towns and cities, they discovered a 'need' for warfare in order to protect and expand their territories, resources, and populations. In the words of Ehrlich, it is important to remember that "(c)onnecting 'genes for aggression'...to the actions of warring governments is a bit of a stretch, just as would be connecting genes for conciliations to the deployment of United Nations peacemakers."[7] Basically, Ehrlich wants us to realise that there are no "war" or "peace" genes, but that cultural micro- and macro-evolutionary conditions (that is, societal or environmental conditions) may drive a group of people to be either warring or peaceful.

These global changes have meant that an increasing number of people now lack the protective cocoon of relational ties that shielded community members and groups in the past.[8] In this wider sense, globalisation tends to break down

> "...the protective framework of the small community and of tradition replacing these with many larger, impersonal organisations. The individual feels bereft and alone in a world in which she or he lacks the psychological support and the sense of security provided by more traditional settings."[9]

Philosophies world over are 'society centered,' or 'this world centered' and directs man to find fulfillment here in this world through socio-political activities, whereas Indian Philosophy looks upon the world as *fleeting, transitory* and *'unreal'* and encourages human beings to seek spiritual realisation of the 'Absolute'.[10]

Indian philosophers in olden days never concerned themselves with theories of kingship and nature of Government, but were grappling with the problem of transmigration of souls and underplaying the importance of life in *this* world. Religious and no politics dominated Indian social life. In spite of periodic invasions and few eras of internal breakdown India never oriented her thoughts to military power, or the socio-politically oriented ideology of a unitary, humane government, and lacked a strong unifying credo.[11] The early Indians, lacking a concept of unitary political state, never desired a single name for this sub-continent. By the fourth century CE, the term "**Bharatvarsha**" (homeland of the mythical King Bharat) may have been used to refer to the sub-continent.[12] The word '**Hindustan**' which became current during the Mughal period technically applied only to the Northern Indo-Gangetic Plains area and excluded the area of the Deccan.

The only book worth mention is the Kautilya's **Arthashastra.**[13] It is believed that Kautilya the author of the tremendously influential manual on statecraft engineered the rise of the Mauryas. Kautilya rose to be the Chief Political Advisor of the first Maurya Emperor.[14] However, the teachings of Kautilya were soon lost. India under the Mughals also failed to evolve into a state as European countries did. The Mughals Emperor was a *Shah-en-shah* (Kings of Kings) rather than a

King of India. Another work of importance appeared just as India was about to achieve Independence by Anand Coomaraswamy. In his work *Spiritual Authority and Temporal power in The Indian Theory of Government*, Anand Coomaraswamy has drawn extensively from texts like the *Vajasneyi Samhita,* and the *Satpatha Brahmana* to arrive at an alternative understanding of kingships, its responsibilities and goals. According to Coomaraswamy, **'the only royal road to power is to become one's own master; the mastery of whatever else follows'**; this is the traditional secret of government.[15]

The abstract character of modern society, with its implicit anonymity and alienation, has made the lives of more individuals migratory, ever-changing, and mobile as they are uprooted from their original social milieu. The result, according to Berger, has been increasing attempts to "de-modernise" in order to seek "reversal of the modern trend that left the individual 'alienated' and beset with the threats of meaninglessness."[16]

Most wars today, it seems, are civil wars in which one religious group are contesting for supremacy over other. Religion, we tend to believe, purports to bring inner—and outer—peace. It seems contradictory, then, that religion should provide the source for so much conflict. It might be easy to blame "those Muslims" or "the Hindus" or "the Christians" for the religious intolerance that fuels modern religious warfare. However, the conflicts are far more complex than they may appear on the surface, and the solutions are far less readily apparent than we would like to believe. Let's also not forget that Christianity is rooted in Judaism, and that the Messiah foretold in the Old Testament was supposed to be a great king who would lead Israel to victory. Therefore, the same God who urges us to "love our neighbour" also tells us (in Deuteronomy) "when the Lord your God gives [your enemies] over to you, and you defeat them; then you must utterly destroy them; you shall make no covenant with them and show them no mercy."

> Terrorism could be defined as the deliberate creation and exploitation of fear for bringing about political change. The acts are often by non-governmental groups or individuals not officially serving governmental agencies.

Strong, even extreme, attachments to ethnic, religious, national, and clan identities have appeared to push individuals and groups to engage in what often seem to be inhumane and improbable acts toward those perceived to be the enemy.

Victor Hanson argues that the ancient Greek preference for physical confrontation and quick decision created a "Western Way of War," dominated by a search for decisive battle strategies of annihilation, a tradition that remains alive to this day.[17] Such conclusions could be extreme, but they are useful in underlining the fact that wars are conceived, plotted, and waged by socially conditioned human agents.

A definition of war—'warfare among the peoples'—in addition to that between the peoples, is a theme expressed by Rupert Smith, a retired British general in his book *The Utility of War.* "Warfare nowadays is non-linear, pervasive and paradoxical. The neat symmetry of me and my enemy is manifestly not something one finds in Baghdad or Faluja, Darfur or the Pakistan-Afghanistan border."[18]

Martin van Creveld, in his book *The Culture of War*, observes that wars are fought mainly to expand interests, but that they also attract men and women, as can be seen from decorated instruments of war, such as weapons and uniforms. In fact, it is the culture of war that motivates people to fight on, even at the cost of their lives.[19]

Definition of Culture

Culture can be defined as, "A culture is a shred system of beliefs, values, customs, behaviours and artifacts that the members of a society use to cope with one another and that are transmitted from generation to generation through learning."[20]

Culture, as defined by *Webster's Dictionary*, is: "the integrated pattern of human behaviour that includes thought, speech, actions, and artifacts, and depends upon man's capacity for learning and transmitting knowledge to succeeding generations; the customary beliefs, social norms, and material traits of a racial, religious, or social group."[21] According to Ralph Linton, anthropologists tend to define culture as "the sum total of the knowledge, attitudes, and habitual behavioural patterns shared and transmitted by the members of society."[22] Cultural geographers also study the imprints of culture to determine patterns of behaviour throughout the globe; they seek to understand how the cultural themes of geography interact with the interrelationships of the natural environments and human societies.[23] One noted geographer, Carl Sauer, oriented his focus around the concept of the "cultural landscape." He defines the cultural landscape as the "forms that are superimposed on the physical landscape by the activities of man." He emphasises that *forms* result from the operation of cultural processes (causal factors that shape cultural patterns) that unfold over a long period of time and involve the cumulative influences of successive occupants.[24]

> If, taking your stand on egotism, you think, "I will not fight", vain is the resolve of yours; nature will drive you to act.
> **—Bhagavad Gita, Chapter 18.**

Warfare and Religion

The likelihood that religious cleavages will lead to political violence may depend on many factors, including the size of religious minorities, their geographic distribution, the history of conflict, external support, capacity for mobilisation,

> The thesis of Kirby's excellent introduction is that the Cold War was one of history's great religious wars, 'a global conflict between the god-fearing and the godless'. (p. 1) It was a war in which 'Christianity was appropriated by Western propagandists and policy-makers for their anti-communist arsenal' (p. 2), nowhere more so than in the USA. But in addition, as this volume demonstrates, Christianity was not simply a tool of psychological warfare. Church leaders were not merely pawns in a political game; they were active participants. Their flocks were not only recipients of propaganda; for millions religious faith was central to their lives. This fact is most vividly demonstrated in the several chapters that deal with the Catholic Church and Pope Pius XII during the early years of the Cold War.

and whether religious groups are internally divided. Religious divisions appear to have less salience where people of one religious group identify with different ethnic groups, geographic locations, or class divisions.[25] In many conflict and post-conflict cases it has been observed that religious institutions and leaders are critically important, and religious values often motivate either violence or peace building.

With the development of warfare came the development of religion. A causative relationship is not necessarily implicated between warfare and religion, but it is clear that these cultural components greatly influenced, shaped, and sometimes legitimised the other. Indeed, it can be argued that at some points in time, war and religion are not two separate entities at all, but one unit with two halves, each promoting the other (the Crusades are an excellent example of a time when religion was fused with war, and each half was inextricable from the other).

Colin Chant explains that "(d)efence was a prime consideration in the foundation of Greek cities: the earliest usually centred on a Rocky Hill, or Acropolis."[26] This concern for defence was a priority for the Greeks, and was one of the main factors in planning layout. Greek cities were typically set back from the sea so that they would not suffer direct sea-borne attacks. [27] The Mycenaeans were adept in the skills of building stone defensive walls that not only surrounded the city and thus protected it from attack, but also were extended to surround and protect their water supply. Later, underground aqueducts, closed-pipe systems, and other techniques could help supply a walled city with the necessary water.[28] The same is in case of cities of India. These were built around places which were easy to defend. On the plains to the West of Yamuna more than 20 cities have been built one over the other for good reasons in Delhi; it laid at the most dominating area before the outsiders cross into the plains of India. It was on the plains around it that the wars were fought for over 5000 years.

Most Chinese elites are proud of their civilisation and historical pre-eminence but also shamed by the "century of national humiliation" (*bainian guochi*). Since the founding of the Peoples Republic China, the primary goals of Chinese leaders have been to build a prosperous and strong (*fuqiang*) China, and to regain what they perceive as their country's rightful place in the world. Throughout the Cold War, China's foreign policy was seriously constrained by its strategic relations with the United States and the Soviet Union. As Gilbert Rozman observes, "A great power's identity focuses on the country's past, present and the future in international relations; concentrating on its capacity to project power in comparison to other countries with their own ambitions."[29] Seen from this angle, the foreign policy and security strategy of other great powers are connected to China's identity formation, assisting or hindering its pursuit of a great power status.[30] *China is one of the nations that are hindering India's identity formation.*

Three world religions with their roots in the Middle East adopted, at some stages of their history, the idea of a 'Holy War', as well as that of a 'Just War'.

Judaism: Judaism is not a pacifist religion. The idea of Holy War occurs in the Hebrew Bible, but it was not about making others Jewish, but about survival. The idea of 'Just War' is clearly expressed both in the Old Testament (see Deuteronomy 20:10-15, 19-20) and in the later rabbinical tradition. So while revenge and unprovoked aggression are condemned, self defence is justified.

Christianity: Christianity, during its 2,000 year history, has taken up all three positions on war: Pacifism, Just War and Crusade or Holy War

Islam: 'Islam' means 'submission' or 'surrender' to the will of God (Allah). Muslims have three orders viz.

1. If you are a Muslim you are my brother.
2. If you are not a Muslim either you convert or pay tax for allowing you to follow your religion.
3. If your state is not a Muslim country you agree to pay tax for protection or you surrender.

China is increasingly assertive in articulating its conception of a future order based on Chinese civilisation and philosophy. For example, the idea of building a "harmonious world" (*hexie shijie*) has been widely advocated. In constructing and spreading China's cultural values, it is suggested, Chinese socialist theory should also be integrated with traditional Chinese culture.[31] Their perception of each other's national identity is to some degree shaped by a "discourse of danger."[32]

Religion has been a relevant factor in efforts to achieve objectives and win support in communities. Militant groups have enjoyed direct state support, sought political power by forming political parties, made deals of convenience with the state, and sought to become the state. The mujahideen, the Taliban, SSP, and JeM all depended on direct support from Pakistan at various times.[33]

For its part, Pakistan has used money and religion to keep the groups on its side. In only a few years, the Pakistani Taliban already has a long history of signing and breaking peace treaties with Islamabad when needed.[34]

National Identity

National identity is a form of collective identity, whereby the identity of a group of people is defined and shaped by its internal cohesion and external relationship with other groups of people. Anthony Smith believes that it is "perhaps the most fundamental and inclusive" collective identity which provides "a powerful means of defining and locating individual self in the world through the prism of the collective personality and its distinctive culture."[35]

National identity is closely linked to different conceptions about sovereignty and statehood. It has since the early 19th century promoted the idea that the source of individual identity and loyalty lies with 'a people'—the nation, which is seen as the source of sovereignty which the state, in turn, is founded on.

Membership of a political community is institutionalised spatially within territorial states.[36] The framing of foreign policy follows as a consequence of the political community being recognised as a sovereign state in the international system. Wallace[37] has called this the 'grand strategy' definition of foreign policy —"that foreign policy is about national identity itself: about the core elements of sovereignty it seeks to defend, the values it stands for and seeks to promote abroad."

According to Breuilly,[38] nationalism is a political doctrine built upon three assertions to legitimise state power.

1. There exists a nation with an explicit and peculiar character.
2. The interests and values of this nation take priority over all other interests and values.
3. The nation must be as independent as possible. This usually requires at least the attainment of political sovereignty.

In India the National Identity is questionable and Indian Passport holder can be a Bengali, Assamese, Tamilian and host of other sub caste and geographic identity but rarely an Indian'. The management of internal security, therefore, assumes great importance. If the internal security issues are tackled effectively, subversion by the external forces to that extent becomes more difficult. Unfortunately, the rise of contentious politics based on sectarian, ethnic, linguistic or other divisive criteria, is primarily responsible for the many communal and secessionist movements flourishing in India. The presence of hostile neighbours enables the internal conflicts to get external support, which includes money, arms and sanctuaries. The vested interests exploit these conditions to pursue their own agenda.

Indian Culture and Strategic Policies

Unlike most civilisations Indian civilisation did not grow along one river valley. There were six different cultural growths in India. The Indus Valley had the rivers flowing to the West and South. It had more of affiliations with the West, viz Afghanistan and Central Asia. In later stages some movement did take place along coastal route. It was separated from the Ganges Valley which flows to the east and had an insulated development. The three rivers of the South flowing to East, Mahanadi, Krishna and Cauvery all had rich civilisations along its banks but isolated from other.

> Guru Nanak (1469-1534), the first Sikh Guru wrote this hymn:
>
> *'No one is my enemy*
> *No one is a foreigner*
> *With all I am at peace*
> *God within us renders us*
> *Incapable of hate and prejudice.'*

The only thing that connects them by fine thread is Ganga. "The Ganga, especially, is the river of India, beloved of her people, round which are intertwined her memories, her hopes and fears, her songs of triumph, her victories and her defeats. She has been a symbol of India's age-long culture and civilisation, ever changing, ever flowing, and yet ever the same Ganga." Words of Jawaharlal Nehru, first Prime Minister of India,

How does Indian culture conceptualise "the enemy"? The enemy is an alien (organised) force whose aims or actions would deprive India of its sacred territory or subvert its society by undermining its civilised values. Three major world religions have their roots in India: Hinduism, Buddhism and Sikhism. Buddhism and Sikhism both grew from Hinduism. All three share the idea of non-violence (ahimsa).

"Whereas among other nations it is usual, in the contests of war, to ravage the soil and thus to reduce it to an uncultivated waste, among the Indians, on the contrary, by whom husbandmen are regarded as a class that is sacred and inviolable, the tillers of the soil, even when battle is raging in their neighbourhood, are undisturbed by any sense of danger, for the combatants on either side in waging the conflict make carnage of each other, but allow those engaged in husbandry to remain quite unmolested. Besides, they never ravage an enemy's land with fire, nor cut down its trees."[39]

While the strategic culture is historical in its conscious roots, proponents of Indian strategic culture have ample historical reference points for enemies over the last millennium.[40] Chinese empires as such did not figure prominently in this South Asian history. Rather, the subcontinent was invaded over land by successive waves of Muslim armies, typically from the northwest—through what we know today as Afghanistan. Muslim rulers overthrew numerous pre-existing Hindu monarchies in north and south India, and established their own hegemony by force, conversion and institutions of government.

> The term *'non-violence'* was actually coined in English (about 1920) by Mohandas Karamchand Gandhi (1869-1948) as a direct translation of 'ahimsa', 'avoiding harm to others'. The idea of non-violence was very important to Mahatma Gandhi's thinking and actions as a Hindu leader during India's approach to independence in 1947. He wrote:
>
> 'I object to violence because when it appears to do good, the good is only temporary; the evil it does is permanent.'

India was partitioned in the backdrop of large-scale communal riots, but the partition of the country on religious lines, without taking into consideration its multiple identities, instead of bringing the communal tensions down, in fact, worsened the situation. The two-nation theory created Pakistan, and it still survives on this theory. Pakistan finds it difficult to accept the reality that India continues to be a democratic, plural, multireligious society and that India today has more Muslim citizens than Pakistan. Jinnah declared: "Islam and Hinduism are not religions in the strict sense of the word, but in fact different and distinct social orders, and it is only a dream that the Hindus and Muslims can ever evolve a common nationality.... To yoke together two such nations under a single state ... must lead to a growing discontent and final destruction of any fabric that may be so built up for the government of such a state."

The Government of Pakistan has taken upon itself the responsibility of not only protecting its own citizens, but also the Indian Muslims. The power structure in theocratic Pakistan, dominated by the army, the feudal landlords, the bureaucracy and the religious leaders has been able to retain its hold over the levers of power by playing the anti-India and Islamic cards. Pakistan plays the Islamic card in its foreign policy also. It misses no opportunity to club India as an anti-Islamic country where Muslims are not safe. The continuing tensions between India and Pakistan have a direct bearing on the internal situation in India. They have further complicated the internal security situation.

Yet in the event, the fabric of India's secular state proved tougher than that of confessional Pakistan. Pakistan originally consisted of eastern and western sections, connected by a common religion but different in language and culture. The religious bond proved insufficient, and East Pakistan in 1971 seceded and became the independent state of Bangladesh. Secular India, however, has held together. There are now almost as many Muslims in India as there are in Pakistan. Muslims and Hindus in India may perhaps not have "evolved a common nationality," but they—and Sikhs also, so far—have managed to live together, within one state, for more than sixty years now, whereas the "common nationality" of the Muslims of Pakistan burst asunder after 24 years.

Cultural Impact on India's Security Policy

The viability of the secular and democratic system in India is a remarkable phenomenon, and one that has received less attention in the West than it deserves. Yet there have been continuing challenges, both internal and external, to India's secular democracy, and to the very existence of an Indian state.

In India especially, religion plays a vital and influential role in the society that was manifested itself as a potent force in the political development of the India state from pre-independence to post-independence.

There are core traits of Indian strategic culture that have persisted since independence despite shifts in India's strategic foreign and security policies during and after the Cold War, and notwithstanding the gathering momentum of the forces of globalisation. However, it is foreseeable that some of the core traits may be subject to modification in the coming decades due to generational changes in Indian leadership who are less steeped in tradition, the rise of new business entrepreneurs in high technology spheres who operate with a less parochial and more globally oriented paradigm, and the impetus of regional political leaders and upward mobility of lower strata of society who are less easily socialised in a standard strategic outlook.[41]

Before one arrives at security ends and means, the *content* of what is strategic and what is to be secured under the rubric of Indian "security objectives" must be recognised as based on metaphors of "Indian-ness" (or *Bharatvarsha* and *Hindutva*), an outlook that transcends the Republic of India—the divided nation and territory—that emerged after partition from British colonial rule in 1947.[42]

India's Defence and Security policy, most broadly defined, is central to people's sense of national identity, and to an understanding of their nation's purpose, role and values. A nation, and an administration, without a realistic and well-articulated defence and security policy; which explains the bewildering present and illuminates the uncertain future are rudderless.

India is characterised by more ethnic and religious groups than most other countries of the world. Aside from the much noted 2000-odd castes, there are eight "major" religions, 15-odd languages spoken in various dialects, and a substantial number of tribes and sects.[43] Religious identity has been constantly present in the antagonisms that have for centuries pitted neighbour against neighbour, with Muslims, Shias, Sunnis, and Hindus struggling for power in Western India.

The conventional clause in India's inchoate foreign policy that emphasised non-interference in internal affairs of neighbouring countries sounds absurd in this era of economic liberalization and globalisation where the challenges as well as opportunities are transnational.

Three ethnic or religious conflicts have stood out of late: two occurred in the states of Assam and Punjab; another, the more widely known Hindu-Muslim conflict continues to persist. The Assam problem is primarily ethnic; the Punjab problem was based on both religious and regional conflicts, while the Hindu-Muslim problem is predominantly religious.

Trans-Border Identities

Migration is as old as human civilisation. Population movements have always played a vital role in the structural transformation of societies and economies. However, unlike in the past when migration involved establishment of new habitations in fertile and virgin lands, migration today is characterised by movement of populations to other countries with people and cultures of their own. It therefore raises issues regarding loyalty, identity, development and security.

Being the most developed of all South Asian countries; India has been the most sought after destination by immigrants from neighbouring countries. Migrant Bangladeshis are concentrated in West Bengal and Assam. India and Nepal share a 1900 km border that runs along Uttar Pradesh, Bihar, West Bengal and Sikkim. Migration between Nepal and India has been easy due to an open, porous border and strong familial links. Geographical contiguity, socio-cultural affinity, the kinship factor and historical reasons have left the Indo-Bangladesh and Indo-Nepal borders vulnerable to migration.

Bangladeshi migrants to India consist of Muslim migrants and Hindu refugees, both categories having different sets of reasons to migrate. But the overriding consideration in both the cases is ethnic commonalties with Indian Bengalis. Although Bangladeshis have their national identity within the nation-state framework, they identify themselves as Bengalis and share a common ethno-cultural ethos and heritage with Bengalis across the border. However, the basis of a separate nation-state for many Bangladeshis is that they are Muslims and their culture, language and religion is different from that of the Bengali Hindus of West Bengal. The unfolding and enforcement of Bangladeshi nationalism, promoted by the Bangladeshi National Party, had its effects on Bangladeshi migrants to India, in the sense that they carried with them their new-found national identity. It has been difficult, particularly for Bangladeshi Muslims, therefore, to merge into the Indian mainstream.

However, problems arise when Nepalese in India try to assert their Nepali identity in exclusive terms vis-à-vis mainstream India. The Gorkha National

Liberation Front [GNLF] in Darjeeling illustrates this tendency, even though it claims to protect the interests and rights of Indian Gorkhas only.

Given the ethnic and cultural similarities between India on one hand and Bangladesh and Nepal on the other, the "ethnic-cultural space" of each intrudes into the "geographical-territorial space" of the others. It is natural that ethno-cultural contiguity and continuity give opportunities and scope to immigrants to India to relate to their respective country of "origin".

For the Indian state, the security implications of large-scale migration from both Bangladesh and Nepal are varied but inter-related, given the complex nature of migration and the multiple identities that migrants profess. They cover demographic changes, growth of radicalism, particularly Islamic fundamentalism, regionalism, and, more importantly, involvement and even encroachment of foreign powers on the country's "sovereign space". All these threats to territorial integrity, core values or socio-political practices of the Indian state interact, sometimes reinforcing each other.

In general, however, in depth knowledge of national and regional cultural dynamics has not been strong point for Indian strategy, which has tended to rest on sturdy pillars of relative invulnerability and the capacity to mobilise force. In the volatile and uncertain security environment of the years to come, however, the assumption of technological and material advantage may not be safe one, nor will these advantages always suffice to ensure superiority in every possible contingency. The main adversary for India, Peoples Republic of China represents long term rival with considerable assets and great self confidence, derived in part from a highly distinctive and ancient culture.[44] Russia lost some influence after end of Cold war and break up of Soviet Union, but eventually the inherent strengths that made Union of Soviet Socialist Republic so formidable will reassert them. India confronts a long term struggle to manage the dilemmas of the Muslim World and the associated dynamic of terrorism, that will demand of India sophisticated cultural awareness. Effective engagement in complex contingencies will demand from India and in depth knowledge of real and potential rivals. Strategy is not uniquely the product of culture, and culture itself is not lucid or

> Colin Gray, defines strategic culture as "the socially constructed and transmitted assumptions, habits of mind, traditions, and preferred methods of operation.... That are more or less specific to a particular geographically based security community." The foundation of strategic culture are the fundamentals of culture itself; shared experience, language, common governance, and values. The cultural orientation that derives from these commonalities, it can be argued, affects the ways in which politics conduct diplomacy, define and pursue interests, and wage war.

unambiguous construct. But all strategy unfolds in cultural context, and cannot be fully and properly understood outside it.

As a major power India will be called upon to intervene with force and wage war in a variety of contexts in years to come. A better understanding of the strategic cultures especially of potential adversaries will place another weapon in the arsenal and strengthen prospects for success. In Bernard Brodie's classic formulation, "good strategy presumes good anthropology and sociology. Some of the greatest military blunders of all time have resulted from juvenile evaluations in this department."[45] Knowing the enemy goes well beyond order of battle, to the source of strategic preference and military operational codes that are grounded in the social and cultural context of distinctive nations and regions.[46]

THE ASSAULT ON MUMBAI

Mumbai (formerly Bombay) is India's largest city, the country's financial hub, and home to the famous and lucrative "Bollywood" Hindi-language film industry. Its reputation is one of prosperous cosmopolitanism, and Western tourists are drawn to reputable hotels, an active nightlife, and rich cultural history. Unfortunately, in recent years, the port city has experienced a series of lethal terrorist attacks. These incidents include the detonation of two car bombs in August 2003 that killed approximately 50 people and seven bombs aboard passenger trains that killed more than 200 in July 2006.

On November 26–29, 2008, Mumbai was attacked by 10 determined terrorists who entered the city from the sea aboard dinghies. The attackers spread out to assault high-profile targets throughout Mumbai's urban center, firing at victims randomly and throwing explosives. Tourist sites, hotels, and a Jewish center were specifically selected for their symbolic value and to inflict maximum casualties. The ferocity of the assault is reflected in the following events:

- More than 50 people were killed at the Taj Mahal Palace and Tower hotel. During the initial assault on the night and early morning of November 26–27, terrorists seized and killed hostages. A large fire broke out as they fought National Security Guard commandos and police officers when the troops and officers conducted room-to-room searches. Dozens of hostages were rescued during the operation. Firefights continued for days as the terrorists evaded the security sweep, finally ending on the morning of November 29.
- More than 30 people were killed at the Oberoi Hotel, which was attacked at the same time and in a similar manner as the Taj Mahal Palace and Tower. Terrorists at the Oberoi seized and killed hostages on November 26–27 and began hide-and-seek gun battles with members of the National Security Guard. The Guard restored order during the afternoon of November 28.
- Eight people were killed at Nariman House, an ultra-orthodox Jewish Lubavitch-Chabad center. On the night of November 26–27, terrorists

attacked the center and seized hostages, including the center's rabbi and his wife. As gunshots were intermittently heard inside Nariman House, commandos assaulted the building on the morning of November 28 and secured the center by nighttime. Although many hostages were freed, others were killed by the terrorists. Victims included the rabbi and his wife.

- Members of the terrorist unit struck several other targets around the city, including the Chhatrapati Shivaji Terminus (where dozens were killed), the popular Leopald Café (frequented by tourists), and the Cama and GT Hospitals.

Indian security forces were caught off guard by the scope and violence of the assault. By the time order was restored, more than 160 people had been killed and hundreds more injured. Nine terrorists and approximately 20 police officers and soldiers were killed. The lone survivor among the terrorists signed a seven-page confession approximately 2 weeks after the attack, in which he confirmed that the men were members of Lashkar-e-Taiba (Army of the Pure), a Pakistan-based Islamist organisation. He described his weapons training at several Lashkar camps in Pakistan and his indoctrination on alleged Indian atrocities against Muslims. Training in Karachi, Pakistan, included how to operate fast boats. When he and nine others embarked on a ship in late November, each man was issued an AK-47 assault rifle, hand grenades, and ammunition. They were ordered to maximize casualties on their mission.

The involvement of Lashkar-e-Taiba resulted in an escalation in tensions between India and Pakistan. Distrust was exacerbated because of Lashkar's long affiliation with Pakistan's Directorate for Inter-Services Intelligence (ISI). This affiliation was instrumental in the group's rise to prominence and viability within the Islamist movement, largely because ISI allowed the group to engage in recruitment, training, logistical support, and networking. In fact, ISI patronage allowed the group to operate rather openly in Pakistan. Lashkar's initial role as a Pakistani proxy against India in Kashmir eventually grew into a sizable movement with wealthy patrons from Saudi Arabia and other countries. Their sophisticated use of the Internet permitted the group to communicate with fellow Islamists in Asia and the Middle East, thus enhancing its international image and contacts. Significantly, Lashkar operatives fought in Iraq against the American-led occupation.

Soft Power

One of the most important prerequisites for becoming a major soft power is to have "native ownership" of an ideology that can be used as a means of influence; that is, the ideology should be recognisable as a distinct and unique attribute of that particular country. During the Cold War, for example, the United States and Soviet Union represented the *de facto* embodiments of capitalist democracy and Marxist socialism, respectively. As mentioned earlier, Marxist-Leninist states emerged around the world during this period (including Cuba, Angola, and Vietnam, among others) and allied themselves with the USSR; likewise, newly-formed capitalist democracies like those of the three principal powers of the defeated Axis alliance (Germany, Japan, and Italy) came under the fold of American soft power in the post-WWII world and became close allies of the US On the other hand, it would be virtually impossible for a country like Pakistan to exercise any meaningful soft power based on ideology, since Pakistan's ideology is based on Islamic 'nationalism' where it views itself as part of a greater 'Ummah', but is certainly not recognised by the members of the 'Ummah' as its leader. **In other words, Pakistan does not have native ownership over its own ideology**, which inevitably leads to Pakistan associating itself with other, more influential members of the 'Ummah' like Saudi Arabia and Iran, at the obvious expense of its own subcontinental origins.[47]

In India idea of modernisation was strongly linked to urbanisation, industrialisation and to an accompanying rationalisation of previously 'irrational' views, such as religious beliefs and ethnic separatism. Loss of religious faith and secularisation dovetailed with the idea that technological development and the application of science to overcome perennial social problems of poverty, environmental degradation, hunger, and disease would result in long term human progress. However, with the decline in the belief in the efficacy of technological development to cure all human ills in India came a wave of popular religiosity with political ramifications.

> The Supreme Court established the "right to travel" as a fundamental right under the Indian constitution, following which the Indian parliament enacted the Passports Act of 1967. However, the act contains several provisions to refuse the issuance of a passport if the government thinks this would not be in "public interest."

India possesses considerable soft power resources arising from its Universalist culture, democratic political institutions and tradition of leadership among developing nations. Consequently, in the new millennium, Delhi began a concerted effort to channel these resources—including those of Indians living abroad—into generating soft power that might produce beneficial foreign policy outcomes.[48] However, for a country almost destined to provide significant moral leadership in the post-Cold War world, India's soft power resources have frequently proved not up to the task.[49] This basic fact presents an empirical puzzle: how is it that a nation such as India with a history of moral authority and leadership among developing nations, a tradition of statesmen highly regarded by interlocutors in the international sphere, and considerable cultural and domestic political resources to attract other nations to its cause could have failed to successfully wield soft power in order to achieve a favourable political environment for its foreign policy goals? Nowhere is this shortcoming more glaring than in India's own neighbourhood, where perceptions in almost every state range from ambiguous to openly hostile toward India's regional hegemony.[50]

India's shortcomings on this front are due to three factors:

(a) Lack of Resources.
(b) Lack of hard Power and No will to exercise hard power.
(c) Contested nature of its Identity.

First, its soft power resources are not as abundant as proponents of the idea might suggest. India's cultural influence abroad, while significant, pales in comparison to the cultures of the West already in circulation around the globe, and increasingly in comparison to Chinese culture in circulation in Asia and beyond. Official and semi-official Indian modes of cultural dissemination are also relatively few. Although Indian culture, which is based largely on universalist and assimilationist Hindu principles, is a potent source of attraction, India's domestic institutions and foreign policy have mitigated this effect on the perceptions of outsiders. In the domestic realm, India has done a much poorer job of lifting its population out of poverty when compared to China. India's public institutions are rife with corruption, inefficiency, patronage and nepotism. In Transparency International's 2015 Corruption Perceptions Index, India ranked 76 out of 174 countries, tied with Bosnia and Heregonvina, Brazil, Burkina Faso, Thailand, Tunisia and Zambia. In the words of one analyst,[51] "no amount of cultural promotion can undo the damage internationally caused by spectacular corruption scandals" of the sort that India has recently been witness to, and that have given rise to an anti-state social movement that made international front page news in 2011 to 2014. The rank has moved up from 94 in 2012.

On trade, India was held responsible to a great extent for blocking the efforts of the great powers to rescue the Doha Round in 2009.[52] On nuclear non-proliferation and testing, India continues to be a non-signatory to the Non-Proliferation Treaty (NPT) and the Comprehensive Test Ban Treaty (CTBT), despite having received official recognition as a nuclear power via the 2008 agreement with the US on civilian nuclear cooperation. On humanitarian intervention, India's approach to crises in Libya and Syria during its recent term on the UN Security Council invited much criticism from the West. As with China—which itself is struggling to increase its stock of soft power—Western observers are frequently heard asking if India can be a "responsible stakeholder" in the international system.

The second reason: India is not sufficiently far along in terms of hard power resources for its soft power to make a difference in its foreign policy. India's attractiveness following the end of the Cold War grew precisely because of its hard power resources, specifically economic growth, which made India a desirable international partner. It is no coincidence that references to India's soft power grew in frequency only after its economic gains were consolidated and the world could be optimistic about India's fortunes. Soft power is therefore not only generated by hard power (all else being equal, other countries are drawn to success), it also facilitates the smoother exercise of hard power by influencing the preferences of those who are the targets of a state's foreign policy.

The third and final cause of India's under performance with regard to soft power is the contested nature of India's own identity. India's ruling elites have yet to determine what kind of power their nation will be as it continues to rise, and this indecision contributes to a sense of incoherence in the portrayal of India's image to the world. On the one hand, India is the second largest contributor to the US-led UN Democracy Fund for the promotion of democracy around the world; on the other, it continually reiterates its unwillingness to become an exporter of democracy, i.e. to externalise its domestic political values.

India is increasingly a member of small groups of powerful states that determine the course of international bargaining over global issues such as trade, climate change, and international security; on the other, it clings to its identity as a developing and non-aligned country, remaining an active member of the Non-Aligned Movement and frequently arguing for special privileges due to its developing-nation status. Poorer countries in international organisations–such as the African nations and small island states in the climate change negotiations–are often frustrated by what they perceive to be India's pursuit of self-interest over the interests of developing nations, and rich countries decry India's unwillingness to compromise on issues that might cede some ground to the developed world.

At a more basic level, India's multiple social and political identities–Hindu, Islamic, economically liberal, protectionist, conscientious objector to nuclear treaties, responsible nuclear power, staunch supporter of human rights, opponent of humanitarian intervention–continue to conflict with each other both within Indian policymaking and in the messages and images that India portrays to the world. The end result is confusion at the receiving end, unpredictable policy shifts, and general distrust among India's interlocutors, none of which is conducive to the effective exercise of soft power.

Indian Diaspora

Diaspora, a Greek word composed of 'dia' and 'speirein', literally meaning 'to scatter' or 'to spread', refers in a generic sense to communities of migrants living or settled permanently in other countries, aware of their origins and identities and maintaining varying degrees of linkages with their mother countries.[53]

The term 'Indian diaspora' for emigrants from India, describes those people who have migrated from territories that are currently within the borders of the Republic of India, including their descendants who have gone to places outside the country as part of settlement or occupation. Currently, the Indian diaspora is composed of Non-Resident Indians (NRIs), Indian citizens not residing within India; People of Indian Origin (PIOs), who have acquired the citizenship of some other country.[54]

Modi and Soft Power

A favoured quote amongst Indians is that by Chinese ambassador and philosopher, Hu Shih: "India conquered and dominated China culturally for 20th centuries without ever having to send a single soldier across her border"; it was Indian Buddhism that helped shape Chinese civilisation. It is this age-old soft power that Modi started to tap into, whilst avoiding the hubris that comes with it. Humility in promoting Indian culture is particularly important in Asia where a lack of it has worked against India's diplomats in the past.

When introducing the concept of soft power, Nye[55] argued that "it is just as important to set the agenda and structure the situations in world politics as to get others to change in particular cases." Soft power can help a nation set the agenda and alter the preferences of other nations before they come to the bargaining table. Its main instrument–public diplomacy–aims for milieu goals, the creation of an enabling political environment for a state's foreign policy. However, as argued by Melissen,[56] "public diplomacy cannot achieve its aims if it is inconsistent with a country's foreign policy or military actions." To foreign policy and military actions one must add domestic values, politics, and institutions. In order for soft power to succeed, a country's message to the world cannot be at odds with the way it conducts itself at home and abroad. India, unfortunately, does not at this stage possess a coherent message or image. While this is partly a facet of the chaotic nature of India's democratic politics and the path it has taken toward great power until now, if soft power is truly to serve its interests India must take steps to address its domestic challenges and identity contradictions. In some respects, the issue is a matter of time. However, soft power has the potential to multiply the efforts of Indian diplomacy, and in this regard should be pursued as an important objective.

During his travels, Indian Prime Minister Narendra Modi makes a point of promoting India's soft power—including Bollywood, Sufi music and yoga as well as shared heritage in art, architecture, cuisine and democratic values. It's too early to assess if India's efforts are having any substantive impact in meeting the nation's foreign policy objectives, but for the first time a coherent effort is underway to raise India's brand value abroad. This is likely to have significant implications for the conduct of Indian diplomacy and the broader role of India in global politics in the coming years.

Under Modi, India is taking a strategic approach towards using its soft-power resources to enhance the nation's image abroad, even as soft power's role in global politics is under debate:

- Modi has affirmed: "democracy" makes India a valuable partner for the world. Modi has consistently emphasised the importance of Indian democracy. The NDA government under AB Vajpayee then offered support to the US initiative to develop a "community of democracies" at the global level. His successor, Manmohan Singh took a step forward by arguing that democracy is central to India's identity in the 21st century. But the Congress leadership remained ambivalent about lending such weight to Indian democracy and preferred 'non-alignment' and 'socialism' instead. Modi has stuck to that general line even as he highlights the global relevance of Indian democracy. In diplomatic engagements around the world, the Modi government consistently underscores India's democratic credentials. At a time when economic turmoil in the West is generating apprehensions about the value of democracy, India continues to signal the virtues of a democratic political order. The Modi government is unlike its predecessors, ambivalent about focusing on democracy, and instead the prime minister emphasises shared political values to strengthen ties with the West and democracies in Asia. Even when he visited Mongolia, Modi praised the nation as the "new bright light of democracy" in the world, thereby marking a distinction between the democratic values of India and Mongolia and those of authoritarian China.
- Modi underscored spiritual linkages between India and Central Asia, marking a contrast with growing extremism around the world, suggesting that "the Islamic heritage of both India and Central Asia is defined by the highest ideals of Islam–knowledge, piety, compassion and welfare." By emphasising India's ***multicultural heritage***, Modi undercut prevailing criticisms about his ideological leanings as a Hindu nationalist.
- External Affairs Minister Sushma Swaraj was keynote speaker for a June Sanskrit Conference in Bangkok. She spoke in Sanskrit to more than 600 experts from 60 nations, describing the language as "modern and universal," one the gathering should propagate. Underlining the contemporary relevance of the ancient language, Swaraj argued that proficiency in the language could "go a long way in finding solutions to contemporary problems like global warming, unsustainable consumption, civilisational clash, poverty, terrorism." It was the first time an Indian minister of Swaraj's rank attended the World Sanskrit Conference outside

the country since the group was organised in Delhi in 1972. Modi government is taking steps to promote the language internationally with a $20,000 International Sanskrit Award to scholars making significant contributions to the language, institution of fellowships for foreign scholars conducting research in India in Sanskrit language or literature, and opportunities for new learners to pursue courses or research in India.

- Yoga may be India's most successful and popular soft-power tool. Modi led thousands in a mass yoga programme in New Delhi on June 21, the first International Yoga Day. Modi had lobbied the United Nations and managed to win the support of 175 member states at the General Assembly for the resolution setting an international day of yoga. Yoga events were held in 251 cities across six continents with 192 countries participating.
- Under the banner of India's 'Look East'/'Act East' policy, Modi has used culture to appeal to the peoples of Asia. Much of this has been through Buddhism, which more than any other region or philosophy connects all of Asia. This year, India hosted the International Buddha Poornima Diwas, a global celebration of Buddha's birth, enlightenment and passing. The decision to host was initiated by Modi who led the prayers on the day. Modi stated "without Buddha this century cannot be Asia's century".
- India's soft power worked its magic before without much government support. This is most notable in the case of Bollywood – the world's largest film industry in terms of the number of films produced. Indian movies and music are watched and enjoyed in large parts of the world from the Middle East and North Africa to Central Asia. Yet Bollywood trails behind Hollywood in terms of its global reach.
- The new methodology he found includes changing India's global narrative i.e. drawing attention to India's sacrifices in WWI, its contribution to UN peacekeeping operations, and forcefully reiterating India's right for a permanent seat in the UN Security Council.
- Africa too has amazingly caught Modi's imagination. His Government unveiled India's Africa policy by gathering 54 African countries to the third India-Africa Forum Summit (IAFS) in October this year. He used no declarative words or the third world solidarity rhetoric; instead he focused on the partnership of pragmatism and potential as well as to confront global challenges together.

ENDNOTES

1. Huntington, Samuel P. (1997), *The Clash of Civilisations: Remaking of World Order* (New York: Simon and Schuster), p. 21.
2. Keegan, John (1993), *A History of Warfare* (New York: Vintage Books).
3. Wolfers, Arnold (1962), *Discord and Collaboration: Essays on International Politics* (Baltimore:

The Johns Hopkins Press).

4. Adler, E. (1997), "Seizing the middle ground: Constructivism in world politics," *European Journal of International Relations* 3(3), pp. 319-363.

   Fearon, James and Wendt, Alexander (2002), "Rationalism v. Constructivism: A Skeptical View," in Walter Carlsnaes, Thomas Risse, and Beth Simmons, Handbook of International Relations (Thousand Oaks, CA: Sage Publications), pp.52-72.

   Risse, T. (2003), *Beyond Iraq*: *Challenges* to the *Transatlantic Security Community*, AICGS/ *German-American Dialogue Working Paper Series* (Washington, DC: AICGS).

   Wendt, Alexander (1992), 'Anarchy is What States Make of It: The Social Construction of Power Politics', *International Organisation,* 46 (2): pp. 391-425.

   Wendt, Alexander (1995), 'Constructing International Politics,' *International Security* 20(1), pp. 71–81

   Wendt, Alexander (1999), *Social Theory of International Politics* (New York, NY: Cambridge University Press).

5. Wendt, Alexander (1992), 'Anarchy is What States Make of It: The Social Construction of Power Politics', *International Organisation,* 46 (2): pp. 391-425.

6. *Booth, Ken* (1987), 'New challenges and old *mind-sets*: ten rules for empirical realists', in Carl G. Jacobsen (ed.), *The Uncertain Course: New Weapons, Strategies and Mind-Sets,* (Oxford: Oxford University Press/SIPRI), pp. *39-66.*

7. Ehrlich, Paul (2000), *Human Natures* (Washington, D.C.: Island Press), p.260.

8. Giddens, A. (1990), *The consequences of modernity* (Stanford, CA: Stanford University Press).

9. Giddens, A. (1991), *Modernity and self-identity: Self and society in the late modern age* (Cambridge: Polity), p. 37.

10. **Hinduism** is in many ways a confusing and a nebulous term which relates to the manner in which Vedic Brahmanical values have influenced Indian Society. According to Dr. Radhakrishnan, *'The term* **'Hindu'** *had originally a territorial and not creedal significance. It implied residence in a well defined geographical area. Aboriginal tribes, savage and half-savage people, the cultured Dravidians and the Vedic Aryans were all Hindus as they were the sons of the same mother".* [Dr. Sarvepalli Radhakrishnan, *the Hindu View of Life* (London: Uncoin Books, 1927) p. 12.]. Others have said term **Hindu** is of non-Indian origin and was initially used by the Persians to denote the region of the Sindhu River (Sind); later Persians, Greeks and Arabs extended the region to include the whole of the Northern India. The term may even have referred to the people of the Area, but after the entry of Islam into the Sub-continent; it was distinctly used to distinguish people who practiced Hinduism from the followers of Islam.

    Jawaharlal Nehru declared it was *'incorrect and undesirable to use* **Hindu** *or* **Hinduism** *for Indian Culture, even with reference to distant past'.* Nehru suggested that, "the correct word for **'Indian'** as applied to country or culture or the historical continuity of varying traditions, is **'Hindi'**, from **'Hind'**, a shortened form of **"Hindustan"** [Land of Hindu's].

11. Indian civilisation is noted for its historical continuity and for the fact that elements of Indian tradition so firmly imbedded in the country's culture that they persists in influencing contemporary social and political behaviour. The vitality of Indian tradition lies in the **socio-religious** developments identified with the ideas and practices connected with **Hinduism.** India never developed a strong sense of political and social unity, and Indians are not homogeneous people, but Hinduism contributed to the making of a social system that has held together by the strength of religious philosophy. In India, even today like in many other parts of the world especially Africa separatist's tendencies are widely manifested in demands by several sections of the population for independent homelands.

12. Vishnu Purana, II. 3. 1. It would be wrong to think, as many do, that the conception of the fundamental unity of India is only of recent growth. This idea can be traced to ancient periods by the use of common name, **Bharatvarsha,** for the whole country, and the designation **Bharati Santati** applied to the people of India. Thus we read in the *Vishnu Purana* that *"the country lying to the north of the Ocean and to the south of* **himaadri** *(Himalaya) is called Bharata-varsha (land of Bharata), for there live the descendants of Bharat (Bharat santatih)."*
    Similarly the conception of political unity of India appears from references to *"thousand Yojanas of land that stretch from the Himalayas to the sea as the proper domain of a single universal emperor,"* and the conventional description in literature and epigraphic records of imperial domain stretching from Brahmaputra (on the Eastern Ocean) to the seven mouths of the Indus (or the Western Ocean). As regards cultural unity, the find-spots of Asoka's records prove that one language and one script were used, or at least understood; by common people all over India in the third century BC Since then the Sanskrit language and literature have throughout been a common bond of culture in addition to religious and social ideas and institutions.
13. Composed as primer for Kings, the **Arthashastra** is a masterpiece of tough minded real-politick. It makes no concessions to the gentler sensibilities in its understanding of how the business of government is to be conducted. Kautilya urges the King to use the sovereignty to its fullest: not only must he control his subjects by means of an intricate surveillance system, but he must constantly destabilize rival Kingdoms by means of intrigues and war. Kautilya was not in the least disturbed by the use of force, deception or conspiracy in the interest of the state. Indeed, he advocated extreme measures as routine policy.
14. According to Kautilya, the state striving for victory (*vijigsu*) would find itself to be at the Center of Circle (*mandala*), be its neighbours and national enemies. However, the next Circles of States, neighbours of the enemies would be the victor's natural friends and allies. Kautilya gives elaborate instructions as to how the aspiring state should strengthen itself internally and the means it should employ to systematically weaken its enemies. His main recommendations were that the rulers should use, one, danda (punitive), two, treat all neighbours as potential enemies.
15. Coomarswamy, the problem of governance was best described in terms of the relationship between the principles and *'Kshatra'* and *'Brahma'*: in the early Aryan Polity, *Kshatra* was the temporal power held by the King, while Brahma was the spiritual authority symbolised by the priest.
    Coomarswamy, invites attention to the coronation ritual, [found in the *Aitareya Brahmana,* vol. 27), during which the priest consecrates the King with the words:

    'I am that, you are This;
    I am sky; you are earth;
    I am harmony; you are the words;
    Let us two unite our houses'.

    The metaphor of idea marriage between king and the priest reflects the importance that the Vedic thinkers attached to governance, as against mere government; in this model, kingship is not an excuse for the indulgence of one's appetite for control, nor is it mechanical procedure for administration. Kingship is, rather, a sacred mandate to hold power and trust and use it responsibly for the general good, a mandate that king receives from priest.
    Coomarswamy illustrates this concept of regulated authority by appeal to the Vedic deity; Maitravarunau-Mitra, the Sun God, and Varuna the Sky God, conjoined in one presence. Maitravaravau incarnates the duality of perfect rule; the marriage of energy of restraint, power and wisdom, consciousness and life. In *Satpatha Brahmana,* (IV.1.4.) we read: **'Matra is counsel, Varuna the power, Mitra the priest, Varanu the King, Mitra the knower, Varuna**

the actor.... Whatever deed Varuna did that was not quickened by Mitra was unsuccessful.... Whatever deed the Varuna did, quickened by Mitra, came to fruition'.

Maitravarunan is an instruction in what a distinguished commentator has called, '**serene vitality**', a dynamic balance of opposites through which human possibilities can flower. The life of action demands stern will, alertness and moral flexibility: the life of contemplation calls for compassion, responsiveness and moral reflexivity.

16. Berger as quoted in Pathak, A. (1998), *Indian modernity: Contradictions, paradoxes, and possibilities.* (New Delhi: Gyan Publishing House).
17. Hanson, Victor Davis (1989), *The Western way of war: Infantry Battle in Classical Greece,* (New York: Knopf).
18. Smith, General Sir Rupert (2005), *The Utility of Force. The Art of War in the Modern World,* (London)
19. van Creveld, Martin (2008), The *Culture of War* (New York: Presidio Press).
20. Bates, D.G. abd Plog, F. (1990), *Cultural Anthropology* (New York).
21. Webster's Collegiate Dictionary, Springfield, *Mass: Merriam-Webster, 1977.*
22. DeBlij, H.J., and Muller, Peter (1985), *Geography Realms, Regions, and Concepts,* (New York, NY: Wiley and Sons Inc), p.19.
23 Ibid., p. 20.
24. Ibid.. p. 20.
25. Harris Mylonas in "Report of the Georgetown Symposium on Religion, Democracy and the Foreign Policy of the Obama Administration," Berkley Center for Religion, Peace, and World Affairs, June 7, 2010, pp. 16–17; as quoted in Aoun, Joy; Dannan, Liora; Hameed, Sadika; Lamb, Robert D., Mixon, Kathryn: St. Peter, Denis (2012) *Religious Movements, Militancy, and Conflict in South Asia, Cases from India, Pakistan, and Afghanistan,* (Center for Strategic and International Studies)
26. Chant, Colin (1999), Pre-Industrial Cities and Technology (London: Routledge), p. 60.
27. *Ibid,* p. 60.
28. *Ibid,* p. 72.
29. Gilbert Rozman, "China's Quest for Great Power Identity," *Orbis* 43, no. 3 (Summer 1999): 384.
30. Li, Rex (2009), *A Rising China and Security in East Asia: Identity Construction and Security Discourse* (Abingdon: Routledge).
31. Yu Xintian, "Zhongguo wenhua jiazhiguan de goujian yu chuanbo," *Guoji wenti yanjiu,* no. 6 (2011): 5-19, 126; Cai Tuo, "Dangdai Zhongguo guoji diwei zhong de jige wenti."
32. Campbell, David (1998), *Writing Security: United States Foreign Policy and the Politics of Identity* (Minneapolis: University of Minnesota Press).
33. Ayesha Siddiqa, "Terror's Training Ground," *Newsline,* September 9, 2009.
34. Zaidi, "A Profile of Baitullah Mehsud"; Hassan Abbas (2008), "A Profile of Tehrik-i-Taliban Pakistan," *Combating Terrorism Center (CTC) Sentinel* 1, no. 2 (January 2008): 1.
35. Smith, Anthony D. (1991), *National Identity* (Harmondsworth, Middlesex: Penguin Books, 1991), 17, 143.
36. Krasner, S.D. (1988), Sovereignty an Institutional Perspective, *Comparative Political Studies,* 21 (1), pp. 66-94.
37. Wallace, W. (1991), "Foreign Policy and national identity in the United Kingdom", *International Affairs,* 67 (1), pp.65-67.
38. Breuilly, John (1993), *Nationalism and the State,* (Oxford Road, Manchester, UK: Manchester University Press), p. 2.
39. Danielou, Alain, *A Brief History of India,* p. 106.

40. Alexander the Great, the Macedonian-Greek invader from the northwest, left important archaeological traces two millennia ago in the subcontinent, but apparently no deep socio-cultural imprints that manifest themselves in Indian society and culture today.
41. Cohen. Stephen P. (2001), *India: Emerging Power* (Washington, D.C.: The Brookings Institution), in Chapter 2, thoughtfully examines the shifts in strategic orientation and in the foreign and defence policies of India under Congress Party leaders from Nehru through his daughter, Indira Gandhi, and grandson, Rajiv Gandhi, to the rise of the more explicit promotion of Hindu culture under the Bharatiya Janata Party (BJP), led by Atal Behari Vajpayee. What is remarkable notwithstanding these *policy* shifts is the resilience of core values and premises of strategic culture.
42. "Strategic culture is that set of shared beliefs, assumptions, and modes of behaviour, derived from common experiences and accepted narratives (both oral and written), that shape collective identity and relationships to other groups, and which determine appropriate ends and means for achieving security objectives." *Note:* (1) This general definition seems to be a satisfactory working definition for strategic culture in the Indian case. However, it does not seem to cover rationales for acquisitive or imperialist behaviour, i.e., for "objectives" beyond security in the status quo sense, that may be present in other strategic cultures. (2) My understanding of Indian strategic culture is that it forms "loose" drivers (organic predispositions) that differentiate Indian approaches to the outside world—but not tight predictors of behaviour, specific policies, or outcomes of Indian diplomatic, military or security-related activity.

    Hindutva usually applies to Hindu revivalism in specifically religious and cultural forms, but the term is also used politically to connote traditional Indian civilisation and cultural consciousness in a broader sense. Many proponents regard their promotion of hindutva as inoffensive because Hinduism is multifaceted, rooted in natural forces and mythologies, does not require personal adherence to any narrow doctrine, has no centralized hierarchy of priesthood or catechism, and is by its polytheist nature diverse in rituals and forms of worship, is not oriented to proselytisation and is tolerant of many paths to understanding of the divine.
43. See more at: http://www.culturalsurvival.org/ourpublications/csq/article/ethnic-and-religious-conflicts-india#sthash.mhKgbzbN.dpuf.
44. Johnston, Alastair I. (1995), *Cultural Realism: Strategic Culture and Grand Strategy in Chinese History,* (Princeton, NJ: Princeton University Press).
45. Brodie, Bernard (1973), *War and Politics* (New York), p. 332. Colin Gray in his work *Modern Strategy* at p. 131, describes this remark as "one of the wisest observations in the entire history of strategic thought."
46. Jandora, John W. (1999), "War and Culture: A Neglected Relation," *Armed Forces and Society,* Vol. 24, No. 4, Summer, pp. 541-556.
47. Gartenstein-Ross, Daveed (2010), "Religious Militancy in Pakistan's Military and Inter-Services Intelligence Agency," in Gartenstein-Ross, Daveed and May, Clifford D. (eds.), *The Afghanistan-Pakistan Theater, Militant Islam, Security and Stability* (Washington, D.C.: Foundation for Defense of Democracies).
48. Hall, Ian (2012), "India's New Public Diplomacy: Soft Power and the Limits of Government Action," *Asian Survey* 52(6): 1089–1110.
49. Blarel, Nicolas (2012), "India's Soft Power: From Potential to Reality?", *IDEAS Reports – Special Reports,* Kitchen, Nicholas (ed.), SR010. *LSE IDEAS,* (London" London School of Economics and Political Science).
50. Gateway House (2012), *Neighbourhood Views of India,* Research Paper No. 7, December.
51. Malone, David (2011), "Soft Power in Indian Foreign Policy," *Economic and Political Weekly,* XLVI(36): 35–39.

52. Blustein, Paul (2009), *Misadventures of the Most Favoured Nations: Clashing Egos, Inflated Ambitions, and the Great Shambles of the World Trade System* (New York: Public Affairs).
53. Shamnad, N. (2009), *India and GCC Countries: Diaspora and Development* (available at http:// www.thescholar.kerala.gov.in/thescholar/.../downloadasf.php, accessed on 10 July 2016).
    Shamnad, N. (2011), 'Indian Diaspora in GCC Countries: The Case of Kerala', *Journal of Politics and Society*, Vol 6, no ½, pp. 78–85.
54. Shamnad, N. (2009), *India and GCC Countries: Diaspora and Development* (available at http:// www.thescholar.kerala.gov.in/thescholar/.../downloadasf.php, accessed on 10 July 2016).
55. Nye Jr, Joseph S. (1990), 'Soft Power', *Foreign Policy*, No. 80, Twentieth Anniversary, (Autumn), p. 164.
56. Melissen, Jan (ed.) (2005), *The New Public Diplomacy: Soft Power in International Relations*, (New York: Palgrave Macmillan), p. 14.

9

Technology and Security Policy of India

The industrial revolution also established the idea of military invention as a permanent and systematic feature of modern war. Not just the invention of new weapons which has happened through the ages but also the evolution of new means of destruction. The difference was the sustained conduct of military research with state support to take advantage of rapid technological change. One has only to remember early research in radar, aeronautics, space science, and atomic energy to see how war drove the state to support basic research. As a result the relationship between the state and industry, and between the state and research, became increasingly close, particularly during World War II and the Cold War. From the 1940s until the seventies military R&D led rather than followed the ideas of industry in critical sectors like electronics and aerospace. If not for this computers would probably have come some twelve to fifteen years later as also the first integrated circuits which led to the information revolution. After all the internet was first conceived in the sixties as a "post-apocalyptic command grid"—as a means of maintaining strategic military communication in the event of a surprise nuclear attack. India missed the industrial revolution.

India has been aspiring to be great power. It has been claimed that India's Defence industry is more than 200 years old. The history of DIB in India dates back to 1775 when British authorities accepted setting up of Board of Ordnance in Fort William, Kolkata. This was the official beginning of the Army Ordnance in India. In 1787 a gun powder factory was established at Ishapore which started production from 1791.

During the British rule some ordnance factories were established to produce some defence related goods, like manufacture of guns and ammunition at Cossipore. However, most of the defence related industries were rudimentary in nature. Since then the DIB in British ruled India grew to 7 Ordnance Factories (OFs) by the end of WWI and 18 OFs at the time of independence, generally catering to repair and overhaul and supplementing weapons and equipment produced in Britain. During this period India was never allowed to develop core competencies in industrial production.

Post-independence the Indian leadership aimed at attaining self-sufficiency in entire domain of defence production. To achieve this Industry Policy Resolution 1948 and The Industries (Development & Regulation) Act, 1951 emphasised 'core' industries (including defence sector) be taken care of by central government. Hence, eight Defence Public Sector Units (DPSUs) were established under aegis of Government, to undertake defence production. Defence Science Organisation (DSO), which was established to take up challenges of R&D, got amalgamated with technical development establishment (TDE) in 1958. Hence, DRDO was created which then comprised of 10 laboratories.

India has long harbored the goal of possessing an arms industry capable of supplying its military with advanced equipment. These ambitions go back more than 50 years, when the country attempted to design and build its own fighter aircraft, the HF-24 *Marut*. Today, India possesses one of the largest and most diversified defence industries in the developing world. At present, it consists of 39 Ordnance Factories (OFs) (with two more in the pipeline), nine Defence Public Sector Undertakings (DPSUs), and a small but emerging private sector. In addition, there are 50-odd defence research and development (R&D) laboratories under the umbrella Defence Research and Development Organisation (DRDO) which is responsible for designing and developing armaments for the armed forces. And yet, few nations have invested more time, effort, and capital in their defence industries and received so little in return.

Despite more than a half century of struggle, the history of India's (defence Industry)[1] is a nearly unbroken story of ambitious overreach and spectacular failures. While the rest of India appears to be racing into the 21st Century, powered by a dynamic, free-market-oriented economy, the defence sector seems mired in the country's Nehruvian socialist and protectionist past.[2] Consequently, the nation is still predominantly saddled with a bloated, non-competitive, non-responsive military-industrial complex—capable, it seems, of only producing technologically inferior military equipment, and even then, never on time and nearly always way over their original cost estimates. Given such longstanding deficiencies in its defence industrial base, it is little wonder why India's drive for great power status has been so fitful.

Currently, imports amount to nearly 70 per cent of India's total defence expenditure. While the country has been on a quest to become militarily self-reliant in producing equipment and systems that feature the indigenous "Made in India" tag, it has thus far failed to achieve strategic autonomy. A plethora of reasons have hampered the creation of a strong industrial base for the defence sector, not the least of which has been the half-hearted policies of the Indian government that have prevented private players from investing in this crucial sphere.

The list of failures and shocking delays in the country's defence sector is long. The cloak of secrecy under which research and development in defence operates causes even greater concern about inefficiencies, waste, questionable priorities, and failed or delayed projects the public is not yet aware of. Worse, many heads nod sagely at the mention of foreign direct investment in Indian defence public sector undertakings (DPSU) as if the solution to India's convoluted woes could be so easily imported. The question of what constitutes indigenisation is itself a tricky one. Would producing defence equipment under license be considered indigenisation? Would allowing foreign defence manufacturers to set up shop in India and procure locally be a sufficient condition?

Historical Background

Sir A.M. Eliot tells us that the Arabs learnt the manufacture of gunpowder from India, and that before their Indian connection they had used arrows of naptha. It is also argued that though Persia possessed saltpetre in abundance, the original home of gunpowder was India. It is said that the Turkish word top and the Persian tupang or tufang are derived from the Sanskrit word *dhupa*. The *dhupa* of the *Agni Purana* means a rocket, perhaps a corruption of the Kautaliyan term natadipika.[3] Heinrich Brunnhofer (1841-1917), German Indologist, also believed that the ancient Aryans of India knew about gunpowder.[4]

Throughout history, the evolution of war-fighting strategies has depended in large part on the level of technology available to warriors and leaders. Today, while basic human instincts remain much the same, technology has multiplied the human capacity to cause damage and destruction. Nations, like human beings, compete either by raising themselves to higher levels of techno-economic performance or by keeping others down, technologically and economically. Technology has been and remains the prime instrument for enhancing security and development, while maintaining superiority also by the denial of technology to others.

India inherited a rudimentary defence production infrastructure from the British at the time of gaining independence. Notwithstanding the fact that Indian army was fighting only the wars of the British—either within or outside the country—it was made to bear the costs of British imported weapons from India-

> Throughout history, **the evolution of war-fighting strategies has depended in large part on the level of technology available to warriors and leaders.** Today, while basic human instincts remain much the same, **technology has multiplied the human capacity to cause damage and destruction.** *Nations, like human beings, compete either by raising themselves to higher levels of techno-economic performance or by keeping others down, technologically and economically.* **Technology** has been and **remains the prime instrument for enhancing security and development,** while **maintaining superiority** also **by the denial of technology** to others.

generated revenue. It thus sustained the defence industry of UK. The indigenous industrial activity was confined to the lowest spectrum of defence production mainly comprising of repair and overhaul facilities of the imported weapon system. Notable pre-independence defence industries included: (a) Walchand Aircraft Factory in Bangalore which was engaged in repair and maintenance of the aircrafts. During the Second World War it was also employed by the US Air Force for servicing American Air Crafts; (b) Mazagaon Docks in Bombay that undertook repair of warships; (c) Garden Reach Shipyards in Calcutta which engaged in maintenance, repair and overhauling of Naval ships; (d) Gun and Shell Factory at Cossipore, Calcutta, established in 1801; (e) Ammunition Factory in Kirkee in Maharashtra established in 1889; (f) Rifle Factory at Ishapore established in 1901, and (g) Gun Carriage Factory at Jabalpur established in 1904. In all, there were 16 ordnance factories, the cumulative value of whose production in 1947-48 stood at $ 8 million.

During the Nehruvian era, India had no concept of forward strategic planning while expenditure on strengthening national security was seen as non-productive drain on scarce resources. Nehru thought that overall industrialisation of the country and establishing basic industries—the new temples of modern India—will automatically meet the defence requirements, a low priority item in his national agenda. While self sufficiency was the credo of those times, the basic approach was to develop self sufficiency in core industries completely neglecting either indigenous defence production or importing arms and equipment to keep the army in high state of defence preparedness. The first Industrial Policy Resolution adopted in 1948, divided the industries into four categories for the purpose of their allocation between private enterprise and a state enterprise. Defence sector Industries came under head Strategic and basic Industries. These groups of Industries were made the "exclusive monopoly" of the State. What was lost sight of was the fact that defence production was a highly specialised sector requiring heavy investments, a strong R&D back up and actual production, from design to production and eventual integration, had a long gestation period.

The model followed by Government had limited scope and was influenced by the 1948 report submitted by the British Nobel Prize winning scientist PMS Blackett, who was invited by Mr Jawaharlal Nehru to advice the government about how Indian State could leverage science for defence. Blackett had been at the Center of Allied war effort Research and Development Requirements. Blackett was privy to Ultra code breaking, the development of Nuclear Weapons, and other military program. Blackett's 1948 report went beyond the role of science in military affairs to address both India's strategic position and its military spending. Blackett recommended that India limit its military ambitions and pursue a policy of non-alignment. Blackett proposed defence spending should not be more than 2 per cent of GDP. He argued against India's acquisition of Nuclear and Chemical Weapons.[5] Blackett believed that given India's weak economy and low industrial base—the country did not have the wherewithal to produce complex weapons. Bulk production of simpler weapons would largely compensate the need for competitive weapons and provide 'an extremely valuable stimulus to the economy and present a very considerable step forward in industrialisation'.[6] Blackett's report resonated in the Indian Government especially with Nehru as it supported his view of reducing the Army. The India Government thus shifted its priorities from and pushed for infrastructure development over military readiness. Nehru appointed Daulat Singh Kothari a Blackett protégé, became the head of the Defence Service Organisation, the precursor to the Defence Research and Development Organisation (DRDO).[7] Whatever world may say, Nehru fell into a trap and ensure that Defence Forces were reduced to a state of incapability and Blackett ensured India would not rise.

Geneva Protocol on chemical and biological weapons, 1925

Outer Space Treaty, signed and entered into force 1967

Biological Weapons Convention, signed 1972, entered into force 1975

Missile Technology Control Regime (MTCR), 1987

Chemical Weapons Convention, signed 1993, entered into force 1997

Ottawa Treaty on anti-personnel land mines, signed 1997, entered into force 1999

New START Treaty, signed by Russia and the United States in April 2010, entered into force in February 2011

Arms Trade Treaty, concluded in 2013, entered into force on 24 December 2014

With the impending threat from China, though Defence Research and Development Organisation (DRDO) was created in 1958, it was but a half hearted exercise and the DRDO was starved of resources, quality technical manpower and lacked high level strategic direction. Reluctance of Western countries to transfer defence technologies or agree to industrial collaboration clubbed with bureaucratic controls—bereft both of expertise and security sensitivity—compounded the problem.

Following the 1962 Chinese debacle, the wisdom of expanding our defence production sector was realised, albeit at a heavy cost. New ideas were conceived and in course of time a number of new establishments and expansion of some existing units were undertaken.[8] These corporations, commonly known as Defence Public Sector Unit (DPSU), gave a quantum jump to India's defence industry. Working under the Ministry of Defence Production, eight DPSUs namely Hindustan Aeronautics Limited (HAL), Bharat Electronics Limited (BEL), Bharat Earth Movers Limited (BEML), Mazagaon Dockyard Limited (MDL), Garden Reach Shipbuilders and Engineers Limited, Goa Shipyard, Bharat Dynamics Limited (BDL), and Mishra Dhatu Nigam Limited (MDNL) became the mainstay of India's indigenisation programme. During 2009-10, Hindustan Shipyard Limited was transferred from the Ministry of Shipping to the Ministry of Defence.

A review by the US management firm of Arthur D. Little of the production infrastructure highlighted several deficiencies and a coordinated effort was mounted with the setting up of the Department of Defence Production. However the 'Supply' part of the Department was mainly to assist the Public Sector and the Services to source low value, unsophisticated stores or perhaps outsource some components or processes to the private (mainly small scale) industries, which were still not permitted to produce complete platforms or weapon systems.

In the post 1962 scenario, India's doctrine of self sufficiency in defence items, besides indigenous production, practically meant having reliable foreign sources for acquisition of weapons systems, access to technologies and un-interrupted supply of spares and components. India's first preference was to develop defence production relationship with the best European manufacturers—particularly Britain, France and Sweden. However, most of the Western countries, as also the United States refused to come forward and increasingly, a view started gaining ground in India for justifiable reasons, that the West for political reasons could not be a trusted and dependable long term partner. This led to the entry of the Soviet Union as a major supplier of defence equipment to India and, till today their share is estimated to be over 70 per cent. USSR decided not only to supply the MIG-21 and other weapons but also agreed to licensed production. This ushered India into an era of licensed production. This arrangement, though it served India well for two decades; after the breakup of the USSR and the changed profile of India's defence requirements, does not adequately address India's needs any longer. This licensing system also tied India to production stereotypes, thwarting India's indigenous growth and innovativeness to develop high-end weapon systems from design to production stage. The licence-manufacturing no doubt helped India strengthen its military capabilities but did little in strengthening its defence industrial and technological base.

In the history of India's defence production and R&D development acquisition of the Bofor's guns is an important landmark. The irregularities and briberies, whose trail reached right up to then Prime Minister Rajiv Gandhi's doors, rocked the nation. The nation has not yet been able to recover from its after effects. It continues to haunt India's defence acquisition programme seriously undermining India's combat readiness. Since the infamous deal in 1984, the Indian army has not been able to acquire any new artillery guns for more than quarter of a century leaving a big gap in our defence preparedness.

Technology today has become so intrinsic to human life that it is taken for granted. Its contribution is recognised more by its absence, when it is not available or denied. The pursuit of technology is thus very natural to human beings and nations: whether small or big, more developed or less developed; whether it be for survival, defence, development, or at times for more devious designs. Notwithstanding the negative implications, diffusion and proliferation of technology is unavoidable in today's interdependent world.

The importance of modern technology in security and world affairs has never been as convincingly demonstrated as in the military operation in Iraq of March–May 2003. The overwhelming techno-military dominance of the US-led coalition was vividly displayed on millions of television screens across the world, albeit against an enemy without even remotely comparable military capacity. The successful application of high-technology weapons and techniques was a demonstration of how, since the end of the cold war, the sole superpower has been sharpening its superior conventional military technological strength while much of the world was wishfully looking for a peace dividend. It was with the latest in technology that the US-led coalition was able to wage a high-precision war on a distant land to achieve its initial political aims with ease.

Arms Trade

The arms trade is interesting because it is where foreign policy concerns such as security, human rights, and international order interact most directly with economic concerns such as trade, jobs, and profits. Explanations of the trade that emphasise just economics or just politics must be unsatisfactory; both matter. Of course, actually calculating the economic and political benefits and costs of the arms trade is difficult.[9]

Top 10 Arm Exporters, for the Period 2010-14, percent of Global Share

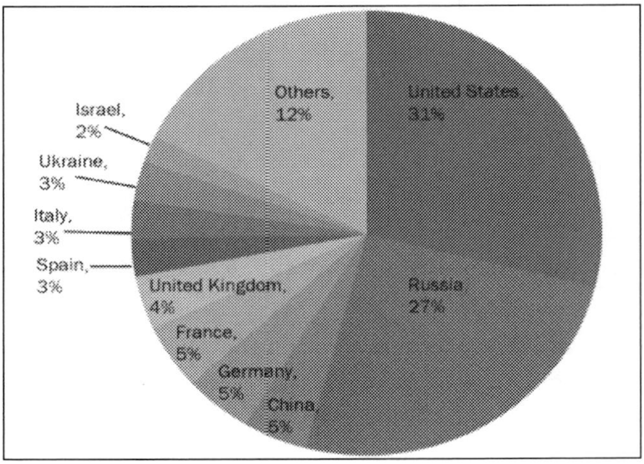

Source: www.sipri.org

Denial Regimes

Incidentally, each time a new technology arrives the human reaction has been very similar. When the Spartan king Archidamus saw for the first time a weapon that could shoot darts through the air he reacted with alarm. "O Hercules," he is said to have exclaimed; "the valour of man is at an end". As you know he was a bit premature. When the crossbow was reinvented in Europe in the 11th century, men marvelled at its murderousness. Attempts were made to have it banned and declared fit for use only against heathens! There is a deep root for the many technology control and denial regimes that we see in the modern world.

Technology export controls continue to be vital to US security and competitiveness, but also challenge the ability of industry, laboratories and academia to interact internationally. With limited exception, the transfer of a technology, computer code or even intangible information to a foreign destination or to a foreigner on US soil requires an approved export license. Travelling internationally with software or technical data on a laptop can even require a license. Virtually all technology exports require approval from one or more of over a dozen US Departments and Agencies that have jurisdiction over these licensing processes. Obtaining a license can be time-consuming, confusing, costly and frustrating, because of the complexity of and variations in the regulations across this diverse set of authorities.

The Wassenaar Arrangement

The Wassenaar Arrangement is a multilateral technology export control regime (MECR) with 40 participating states. The list of restricted technologies includes a "Munitions List", a Sensitive List and a Very Sensitive List. The Very Sensitive

List includes materials for stealth technology, equipment that can be used for submarine detection, advanced radar, and jet engine technologies. India is not a party to this arrangement, which is a successor to the COCOM, as group set up during the Cold War to prevent leakage of technology from the West to the East bloc.

US Technology Control Regime

The US, a leading country in terms of technology development, has put in place a system of controls to prevent sensitive technology from leaking into the hands of hostile entities. The Bureau of Industry and Security (BIS) of the Department of Commerce deals with issues involving national security and high technology. It regulates the export of sensitive goods and dual-use technologies; enforces export control, anti-boycott and public safety laws; cooperates with and assists other countries on export control and strategic trade issues; assists US industry to comply with international arms control agreements. Many sensitive goods and technologies (for example, encryption software) require a permit from the Department of Commerce before they can be exported. Recently, India and the US signed an end user verification agreement enabling the US to monitor high end defence and sensitive technology supplied to India.

Export Control Regimes

Historically, the industrialised nations have taken a variety of steps to keep dangerous weapons, as well as the means to develop such weapons, out of the hands of enemies, especially rogue states and terrorists. During the Cold War, the NATO countries, joined by the neutral countries in Western Europe, restricted the transfer of all conventional weapons and related technologies to the Soviet Union, China, and North Korea, through the Coordinating Committee for Multilateral Export Controls regime. In this case, the threat was unambiguous and extremely serious.

The *Wassenaar Arrangement on Export Controls for Conventional Arms and Dual-Use Goods and Technologies* establishes lists of items for which member countries are to apply export controls. Member governments implement these controls to ensure that transfers of the controlled items do not contribute to the development or enhancement of military capabilities that undermine the goals of the Arrangement, and are not diverted to support such capabilities. In addition, the Wassenaar Arrangement imposes some reporting requirements on its member governments,

The formation of the Australia Group (AG) in 1985 was prompted by Iraq's use of chemical weapons during the Iran-Iraq War (1980-1988). Australia concerned with Iraq's development of chemical weapons, recommended harmonisation of international export controls on chemical weapons precursor chemicals. As the AG membership grew, it expanded its focus to include chemical production equipment and technologies and measures to prevent the proliferation of biological weapons. Today the AG is composed of 40 member countries.

Missile Technology Control Regime (MTCR): The focus of the MTCR is to limit the proliferation of missiles capable of delivering weapons of mass destruction. Initially, the MTCR consisted of only seven members. The MTCR has grown to include 34 member countries that have agreed to coordinate their national export controls to stem missile proliferation. India has become full-fledged member of MTCR.

Nuclear Supplies Group (NSG): From India's point of view, it was formed to deny India access to sophisticated technology. The 48 members of the NSG include the five nuclear weapon states—the US, the UK, France, China and Russia. The other 43 are signatories to the Nuclear Non Proliferation Treaty (NPT).

Indigenous Production of Defence Equipment in India

As India is moving towards transformation from a regional power to a global power, the defence sector is increasingly occupying even bigger space in the country's long term strategic planning. As India is gaining power it is increasing its purchasing power as well with several high-end defence deals either in the pipeline or being envisioned to strengthen India's force structure. Estimates show that the Indian Air Force will have more than 1000 fighter jets and around 60 squadrons by 2030. India will be spending more than USD 80 billion on capital acquisitions in next five years.

The Indian government is very clear and focused in its vision for its defence sector—indigenisation of the industry and acquiring advanced technologies which will in turn help to reduce dependence on imports from other countries around the world. In nitty-gritty, it would create a ripple effect that the government is hoping to initiate in this sector. In this evolving Defence value chain it would be unfair to ignore the role that human resource skills, Research and Development (R&D) and the long standing Small and Medium Enterprises (SME) Defence Public Sector Units (DPSUs) suppliers and ordinance boards are going to play.

Modi and Technology

Shri Narendra Modi views technology as a major key to progress. He has infused five Es in governance: **Ease, Economy, Efficiency, Effectiveness** and **Ethics** and technology has been made an important tool of inculcating these five Es into governance!

Despite some recent stumbles, most economic and demographic metrics favor

India's growth for several more years. India's economic expansion is typical; it comes from its current low levels of physical, technological, and human capital deployed and its absorptive power for additional such capital. Although the Indian economy is fairly broad based, it does suffer from some imbalances: the export sector is small, manufacturing is underdeveloped, and there is little high technology industry.

India is in dire need of high technology industry. While there are several definitions, good examples of high technology are defence, telecom and networking, computing and automation, modern pharmaceuticals, commercial jet aircraft, and advanced instrumentation like MRI machines. Emerging high tech areas include genetic engineering and nanotechnology. High technology industries have some common elements, as they:

(a) need highly skilled scientific and engineering personnel;
(b) require high recurring R&D investments, typically a tenth to a third of annual sales;
(c) demand large initial investments that are often orders of magnitude of the unit sale price; and
(d) need very large global markets and are therefore often near monopolies.

All of this makes breaking into high tech industry very difficult. Recent examples from China have shown that it can be done with strong support of the national government and some preferential access to the domestic market. Qualcomm in wireless chips, Intel in computing, and Airbus for commercial jets all generally fit this model.

India is a big consumer of high tech, from cell phones and laptops, to jet travel and CAT scans. However, India adds negligible value in these high technology areas. It has fallen way behind China, Taiwan, South Korea, and Singapore to name a few of its Asian neighbours. It does not have an EDAS or even an Embraer for passenger jets, no Huawei for telecom equipment, no Qualcomm for wireless semiconductors and no TMSC in semiconductor fabrication. India does add value in high tech through design services undertaken by Wipro, Infosys, and Tata Elxsi among others.

Consider national security which includes any resource critical to the nation's well-being. For example, Information and Communications Technology (ICT) infrastructure is a good example as it is clearly crucial to banking, stock market, and air and rail networks. Protecting this infrastructure from cyber-attack is hard enough for countries like the US, which dominates in this technology. It is much harder for India which does not have an ICT capability.

With 60 per cent of India's defence requirements met through imports, local defence production is the heart of Make in India programme, Prime Minister Narendra Modi said at the inauguration of Aero India 2015 in Bengaluru.

> "We have the reputation of the largest importer of defence equipment.... We too need to increase our defence preparedness. We need to modernize our defence forces."

Modi went in for Make in India, Smart Cities, Digital India, The 12 technologies he identified are grouped as digitising life and work, smart physical systems, and energy technologies:

- **Digitising life and work**—the mobile Internet, the cloud, the automation of knowledge work, digital payments, and verifiable digital identity.
- **Smart physical systems**—the Internet of Things, intelligent transportation and distribution systems, advanced geographic information systems (GIS), and next-generation genomics.
- **Energy**—unconventional oil and gas (horizontal drilling and hydraulic fracturing), renewable energy, and advanced energy storage

'Make in India' model is not very different from previous models, focusing on achieving the goal of self-reliance in defence equipment manufacturing through greater participation of the private sector. But where it differs from the previous model is the greater degree of political and bureaucratic will to achieve the objective. It reposes greater trust in private sector.[10]

In less than two years of coming to power, the Modi government has already taken several broad reform measures pertaining to the defence industry, like industrial licensing, FDI cap, defence exports and level playing field between private and public sectors. The reform in licensing which came in the form of a series of government notifications issued between 26 June, 2014 and 22 September, 2014 is an attempt to codify and simplify the process of granting industrial licence (IL) and remove procedural hurdles and other complexities in the process. While identifying the items which are subject to IL, Government also made it clear that any item not included in the list is not subject to industrial licensing. It has also extended the validity of IL from the earlier three years to 18 years, removed the annual capacity norm as a condition for grant of IL and permitted sale of defence items to the government and public sector units and companies holding valid IL, without permission from MoD. The human interface involved in filling up the licence application has also been removed by putting it online.

Make in India also emphasises putting the private sector at the heart of the procurement process. The Modi government's first year itself saw the clearance of 39 acquisition proposals, of which 32 proposals worth Rs 88,900 crore (or 96 per cent of total value) were under the Buy (Indian) and Buy & Make (Indian) categories.

India is seeking to boost arms exports 20-fold in a decade to $3 billion, a push that if successful would transform one of the world's biggest importers into a major seller of defence equipment. Steps by Prime Minister Narendra Modi to spur defence manufacturing, if properly implemented, open up the possibility of hitting that figure by 2025, Defence Production Secretary A K Gupta said. The challenge is to boost private-sector investment and technological expertise, he said, "This will not only take us toward the goal of self-reliance in defense production, but will also create tremendous employment opportunities," Gupta, one of the top bureaucrats in India's Defence Ministry, said in the interview in New Delhi last month.

Modi's policy changes include fewer curbs on foreign investment in defence, looser export controls and a reworked procurement policy that's set to encourage domestic output. His government has authorised about $65 billion of arms purchases since taking power in May 2014 and is targeting a major naval expansion with locally made ships.

ENDNOTES

1. In the absence of a common definition and in the presence of a set of terms that almost denote the same meaning, like 'arms industry' and 'military-industrial complex' (MIC), a generally accepted term 'Defence Industry' is used here. Defence industry is referred to as an industrial unit or a set of units devoted to the production of military weapons and services for national security forces of the producing country. It also involves exports of such weapons and services for any buyer country or countries that (whose military forces) may intend to use them for national security purposes. Trade of these weapons and services involves state actors only.
2. Cohen, Stephen P. and Dasgupta, Sunil (2010), *Arming without Aiming: India's Military Modernization* (Washington, DC: Brookings Institution); Mohanty, Deba R. (2009), *Arming the Indian Arsenal* (New Delhi: Rupa); Singh, Ajay (2000), "Quest for Self-Reliance," in Jasit Singh, *India's Defense Spending* (New Delhi: Knowledge World); Mohanty, Deba R. (2004), *Changing Times? India's Defense Industry in the 21st Century* (Bonn: Bonn International Center for Conversion); Bedi, Rahul (2005), "Two-Way Stretch," *Jane's Defense Weekly*, February 2, 2005; Manjeet S. Pardesi and Ron Matthews, "India's Tortuous Road to Defense-Indus-trial Self-Reliance," *Defense and Security Analysis* 23, No. 4 (December 2007); Timothy D. Hoyt (2007), *Military Industry and Regional Defense Policy: India, Iraq, and Israel* (New York: Routledge).
3. Ray, Jagdesh Chandra, *Fire-Arms in Ancient India*, pp. 586-88.
4. Stache-Rosen, Valentine, *German Indologists: Biographies of Scholars in Indian Studies writing in German*, p.92.
5. Cohen, Stephen P. and Sunil Dasgupta (2010), *Arming without Aiming: India's Military Modernization,* Washington DC: The Brooking Institute), p. 6.
6. Blackett's Report.
7. Anderson, Robert S. (1999), 'Patrick Blackett in India: Military Consultant and Scientific Intervenor, 1947-72.' Part One, *Notes and Records of the Royal Society of London*, Vol. 53, No. 2 (May, 1999), pp. 253-273.

In 1967, Blackett reminisced, with characteristic confidence, about the experience of coming to India to try to influence the Defence establishment, and why he was selected:

Nehru spoke to all the scientists, but I was the only scientist there with professional military experience; five years at sea in the First War, and four years amidst the application of scientific methods to modem warfare. So it was not very accidental that Nehru chose me to advise him.' (1967 interview, Royal Society Archives, transcript, p. 4)

Five years later he said, with continuing satisfaction, 'On the whole I think that my views about the Indian armed forces expressed in 1948 have not proved too incorrect." (P.M.S. Blackett to B.R. Nanda, 8 February 1972, Royal Society Archives, Blackett Papers (PB), G.12) Blackett's memory in 1967 was consistent with his first report in 1948. After the Indian conflict with China in 1962 and Pakistan in 1965, Blackett said that his effort from the beginning had been to prevent the unnecessary and costly introduction of weapons and strategies which would not have practical value, and to focus attention on the military risks which India did face. The most pervasive problem he faced was, Blackett said, that:

Indian officials and advisers were thinking purely from a Whitehall angle. There was an appalling psychological dependence on every word that Whitehall speaks. I understand in the beginning, in 1948, there was very little time and experience to think for yourself. But a great many of your problems are due to imitative adoption of Whitehall habits. Actually a lot of that thinking should not be exported anywhere. Some of it is not even good here. (1967 interview, Royal Society Archives, transcript p. 7.)

8. See Ordnance Factory Board, *Annual Report* 2006-07, p. 12.
9. Hartley, Keith (2000), The benefits and costs of the UK arms trade, *Defence and Peace Economics,* Vol 11, Issue 3, pp. 445-459.
10. The trust factor with the private sector is perhaps best amplified in the government's recent decision to allow L&T to sign a Licensing Agreement for Transfer of Technology (LAToT) with DRDO for upgraded digital version of the Pilotless Target Aircraft (PTA), Lakshya. This is the first time that technology of a high-value product developed by DRDO was given to the private sector for licence production. Earlier, the public sector units had the exclusive rights on DRDO-developed items. All these developments mean that the private sector will now play an equally major role in India's defence production sector.

    PIB, 'One year of NDA: Ministry of Defence', http://pib.nic.in/nda/Achievements.aspx

10

INDIA'S DEFENCE FORCES

"We don't need a defence plan. Our policy is non-violence. We foresee no military threats. You can scrap the army. The police are good enough to meet our security needs." These were the words of India's first Prime Minister Jawaharlal Nehru in a response to Indian Armed Forces First Commander-in-Chief Gen Sir Robert Lockhart in 1946, on being briefed about the Paper on phased growth of the Armed Forces. What followed was downsizing the Army from its strength of over 2,80,000 to about 1,50,000. Pandit Nehru was not only of the opinion that the Armed Forces were not required in a peace loving country, but also reeled under the paranoia of a coup being transpired by the Army top Brass, as had happened in Pakistan a little later after independence. Hebeing pricky on the coup d'état issue was a nubbin of uneasiness that the Military would begrudgingly press by the sheer nature of its operations. India's conflict with Pakistan soon after Independence was one such instance that presented a Catch-22 for Nehru, requiring him to empower and embolden the Army yet be cautious of its operational powers so to prevent an onslaught on democracy. However, his paranoia took the best of him as Pakistan came under military rule in 1958.

> Nehru's legacy remains to be stabbing soldiers in the back when they stood guard at the borders, both financially and tactically.
> The Modi Government has been no better.

Nehru's idea of a functional democracy was an unending tenure to his rule, aided by submissive and pusillanimous administrative and military officials to facilitate that idea. Unfortunately for this Cambridge affiliate, meekness was not an adage in the Military, and thus set the Army out from Nehru's scheme of things. Pandit Nehru's administration brought about radical changes to the security infrastructure of the country. One of them was to have multiple Police agencies, and weaken his Army. His inward looking defence policy sought to counter the weight of the Army, and install 'Yes Men' in crucial places so as to place an untenable security infrastructure that would, in his own mind, help our democratic institutions. He raised multiple police agencies, lacking necessary training and discipline, and broadly functioning in a similar spectrum as the Army. The Central Armed Police Forces, as they are now known as, were constituted for specialised tasks, but were also tools to alleviate Nehru's paranoia of a possible coup. Nehru believed that the Police forces would quell any possible attempt by the Army to take over the government. As history came to realise in prospect, weakening the Army can have grave consequences, Nehru's legacy remains to be stabbing soldiers in the back when they stood guard at the borders, both financially and tactically.

India witnessed progress in many fields and public administration but inexplicably our Higher Defence Organisation has remained static. Ministry of Defence assumed full responsibility for the enunciation of the defence policy of the country and the administration of her Armed Forces. Lord Ismay was tasked to go into the restructuring of the Armed Forces at independence. Since then only three major changes have been introduced:

(a) Service Chiefs re-designated Chiefs of Staff in 1955, without change in any responsibilities;
(b) After 1962, the Defence Ministers Meeting was instituted. This is now held weekly;
(c) Committee for Defence Planning was set up in 1979 with the Cabinet Secretary as its Chairman—the Committee today exists only on paper.

As the Prime Minister, Pandit Nehru not only downsized the Army, but also went as far as downgrading the status of the Chief of Army by abolishing the Post of Commander-In-Chief of the Armed Forces that led to a huge dent in the Operational Efficacy of the functioning of the tri-services. He removed the Service Chiefs from all committees, thus depriving the Cabinet of their wisdom on matter of national security. The void created in the command structure was felt heavily in India's defeat in the India-China war of 1962. Nehru also went onto reallocate the official accommodation of the Army Chief, the Tri-Murti Bhawan to himself, and brought all the serving chiefs way down in the Official Order of Precedence. His sadism had much flare, and was the bright spark in the eye of Indian Bureaucracy. Subduing the Armed Forces allowed the Bureaucracy to attain much more power, however without similar checks and balances as maintained in the Armed Forces. Cuts in salaries, diminishing allowances and many other measures set a precedent to browbeat the Army into submission by laying financial constraints, apart from playing favourites in promotions to grow a crop of Generals who would bow down before their political masters, disregarding professional and personal ethos and honour while doing so. Modernisation of the Army had been forestalled by red tape and morale of the forces took a bad hit. The Civil administration came to subsume the military under its dominion of corruption and inaction to resonate its myopic view on National Security. Pandit Nehru facilitated a restructuring of the forces wherein the civilian services in place became de-facto masters of the Army. Even today, many of the appointment committees responsible for selecting appointments at higher levels in the army are constituted by Civil Servants, who are known to discourage tenancy of higher appointments by Generals of resolute and upright demeanour.

In order to comprehend the expanse of poor policies in play with regard to the Armed Forces, just take the case of the misadventure of 1962. The 1962 India-China War was an outcome of the hastily adopted Forward Policy that Nehru adopted in the face of the possibility of losing face as a leader. Nehru and his then Defence Minister, Krishna Menon (of the Jeep Scandal fame) at the onset of the growing power in the East were of the thought that an attack on the eastern front of India was an impossible event, and any discussion on investment militarily or otherwise was treated as an anathema to political discourse. Nehru was under the influence of Nobel Laureate PMS Blackett, a British scientist who never wanted India to grow strong. Nehru and Krishna Menon chose to assume that China and India shared bonhomie that could not never be marred by a military standoff. Krishna Menon was in fact a communist sympathiser, and his seemingly abject ignorance of the China issue was rather suspicious. The CIA too had noted his political views in its briefs over him in 1951, *"V K Krishna Menon is a member of the extreme left wing of the Congress Party and has associated with known Communists and fellow travelers. He is highly ambitious and would probably cooperate with and accept support from any group which might enhance his prospects for becoming Prime Minister".* From the Chinese build up in Aksai chin in 1959, to their continued excursion in NEFA (present day Arunachal Pradesh), Nehru and his leftist Defence Minister sat of the Chinese issue despite continued warning from the Military Intelligence on a possible war in early 1960s. While Chinese had been building a road inwards through Aksai Chin, Nehru was unrelenting in his attitude to accept the advice of the Army Commanders that redeploying troops from the western borders to the eastern was a necessity in the face of an impending disaster. However, Nehru would insult and brush away Officers for he had turpitude of humiliating Army Officers, and disregarding any of their advice while doing so. Many military strategists have noted that China was inching on the eastern sector, but till the last moment, Nehru was trying to pretend that any such action was not in the reckoning, and after the War, went onto show that it was not his political and personal misgivings that had cost India the War. Indian Army just wasn't ready to fight the Chinese with its diminished strength and poor equipment, but the reality was hardly anything that an egoistic Prime Minister could swell up to. Such was the situation that just before the war, Indian forces in the Ladakh sector were outnumbered six to one. Specifically in the Chushul Sector, India had strength of three companies (around 360 men) as against Chinese forces of the size of a brigade (around 2400 men). To aggravate issues, the Intelligence Bureau toed the official lines of appeasement and assuaged Nehru's ego by reiterating his views on China. In 1959, things came to such an extent that finding no room for National Interests, Gen Thimayya, and the then Army Chief sent out his resignation in protest over Nehru's short sightedness. However, he later withdrew his resignation on Nehru's reassurances of cooperation. Nehru though, being a political zealot went onto fashion the events in a different sense in his Parliament Speech by painting the General as a soldier wanting to run away in the midst of the impeding Indo-Sino hostility. In early 1960, Nehru adopted the "Forward Policy" as a means of countering China's buildup in Aksai Chin, thus, trying to consolidate Indian Positions in present day Arunachal and Ladakh areas. "I hope I am not leaving you as cannon fodder for the Chinese. God bless you all!" said, General KS Thimayya, India's Army Chief, to his fellow army-men in his farewell speech upon retirement in 1961.

However, with a poorly maintained Army, and regressive military policies, Army did not have the capability to fight a full-fledged war. Moreover, Krishna Menon and Nehru were of the impression that their prowess in political play gave made them well placed to give out directives to the Army. They reprimanded many senior Army officers for speaking out their mind, and subjugated the Army into the role of a Blind-Marching Infantry. In 1962, Nehru broke the chain of command, by maintaining direct contacts with local commanders, and bypassing the Chiefs and Army Headquarters in the process. As the Henderson Brooks-Bhagat report clearly showcases, many of the staff decisions were made in disregard to the ground situation of the army. As it has been uncovered by various findings by journalists across the globe, Nehru's taking on China had political considerations and thus gave no room for rational thinking. Pandit Nehru had no military or national thought and his handling of the Indian Army is a clear example in that regard. He was the 'Arm Chair General' that the Indian Army did not deserve and who shall be remembered in history for holding out as an example to this quote by Alexander the Great:

> I am not afraid of an army of lions led by a sheep; I am afraid of an army of sheep led by a lion.

In October 1962 when China attacked, "There was no overall political objective; no National Policy; no grand strategy and total unreadiness for military operations in the majestic Himalayan Mountains, against a first-class land power... We did not study the pattern of weapons and communications equipment that we may require. Army Schools of Instruction were oriented towards open warfare. There was little emphasis on mountain warfare despite the Army's deployment in Kashmir from 1947... The Army was forgotten; its equipment allowed to become obsolete, certainly obsolescent; and its training academic and outdated. We merely tried to maintain what we had inherited in 1947...The political assumptions of our defence policies were invalid and dangerous... In October 1962 Indians were shocked beyond words to discover that we had no modern rifle," Brigadier JP Dalvi in his book "Himalayan Blunder".

"Both the US and the USSR were willing to accommodate India as a Permanent Member of the UNSC (United Nations Security Council) in 1955, in lieu of Taiwan, or as a sixth member, after amending the UN charter. This Nehru refused! Nehru wanted the seat to be given to PRC (People's Republic of China), as Nehru did not want China to be marginalised! Even though not asked by China, India, of its own accord, had been vigorously advocating PRC for the Permanent Membership of the UNSC in lieu of Taiwan!" It was almost as if Nehru, for reasons one cannot fathom, totally ignored India's own strategic interests! Indian diplomats who have seen the files swear that at about the same time Jawaharlal also declined a US offer to take the permanent seat on the United Nations Security Council then held, with scant credibility, by Taiwan, urging that it be offered to Beijing instead...But it was one thing to fulminate against Great Power machinations, another to run a national foreign policy with little regard to the imperatives of power or the need of a country to bargain from a position of strength.[1]

Lal Bahadur Shastri (born 1904) succeeded Jawaharlal Nehru as Prime Minister of India in 1964. He had not been in power long before he had to attend to the difficult matter of Pakistani aggression, as represented by India, along the Rann of Kutch; and though a cease-fire under the auspices of the United Nations put a temporary halt to the fighting, the scene of conflict soon shifted to the more troubled spot of Kashmir. While Pakistan claimed that a spontaneous uprising against the Indian occupation of Kashmir had taken place, India charged Pakistan with fomenting sedition inside its territory and sending armed raiders into Jammu and Kashmir from Azad Kashmir. Shastri promised to meet force with force, and by early September the second Indo-Pakistan war had commenced.

The 1965 War remains memorable for two things. One was a monumental miscalculation by Pakistan. President Ayub Khan, egged on by his scheming and feckless Foreign Minister Zulfikar Ali Bhutto, sent a top-secret order to his army chief General Mohammed Musa: "As a general rule, Hindu morale would not stand for more than a couple of hard blows delivered at the right time and the right place. Such opportunities should therefore be sought and exploited."

Secondly, India's leadership—as it has done consistently over the past 2500 years—frittered away on the negotiating table what the soldiers won on the battlefield. Pradhan writes: "In a way, India's leadership, out of its sense of restraint, fair play and endeavour to seek enduring peace and goodwill with the neighbour, seems to have missed opportunities to solve the problem."

At the end of a bruising 22-day war, India held 1920 square kilometres of Pakistani territory while Pakistan only held 550 square kilometres of Indian land. The Haji Pir pass was also captured by Indian soldiers after an epic battle. And yet India surrendered everything at the Tashkent Declaration in January 1966.

He was decisive. But lived too short to impact the Defence Forces of the country.

Mrs Indira Gandhi followed her father's footsteps, demeaned the Army, she accepted the

(a) Firstly they abolished a separate Pay Commission for the Armed Forces and formulated equivalence between the Armed Forces and civilians,

(b) It was here that the Pay Commission considered that 'a trained infantry soldier with three years of service is below a skilled labour. Little do they know that it is the infantry soldier who does the actual fighting and charges the enemy with naked bayonet literally on the very front edge of the battle and makes eye and steel contact with the enemy? He is the one who bears the brunt of more than 90 per cent of casualty in all wars and yet he was considered the lowest strata to base their comparison. It also means that the infantry soldier with less than three years' service was considered a semi-skilled/unskilled labour? Just mark the irony of the sinister and ignorant move? Rest of the soldiers was equated based on these preposterous formulae?;

(c) Next step was to reduce the percentage of pension for the Armed Forces. The OROP that was effective till 1972 was annulled after the third pay commission. A soldier then served only for 15 years and went on pension at the ages ranging from 33 years to 36 years of age. In view of this, his pension was 70 per cent of his basic pay and an officer's pension was 50 per cent of his basic pay as the bulk of them retired at 50 years of age. The civilian counterparts were getting only 30 per cent of their basic pay as pension. Please note they served till they were 58 years of age (now 60 years) and the soldiers retired a quarter century earlier';

(d) Further the government put mandatory 33 years of service for full pension fully knowing that the soldier then retired after 15 years of service. They further as largesse made a seemingly generous gesture to the Armed Forces by pegging the mandatory service for full pension (50 per cent) to 25 years. Just look at the clever move; fully knowing that the soldier retired after 15 years of service. Thus the soldier in effect got only 30 per cent of pay after 15 years of service, as extrapolated from full pension of 50 per cent of pay with 25 years of service. Thus the Government ingeniously cut a soldiers pension from 70 per cent to 30 per cent of pay at the same time enhancing the civilian pension from 30 per cent to 50 per cent.

Mrs. Indira Gandhi like her father ensured that Army which brought glory was brought down a notch. Babus's had the last laugh.

Successive Prime Ministers just lowered the prestige and dignity of soldiers. Indian Defence Policies are in total disarray. With no strategic or political framework to address the challenges of the next century the services are procuring weapon systems and concepts that remain disconnected from future political or strategic realities. What the Indian Armed forces need is a real defence review that challenges the paradigms and assumptions of existing force and built in force structures that are connected in some ways to strategic realities. As the old saying goes, 'if you don't know where you are going, then any road will do'. Unfortunately, that aphorism sums up too much of the current direction of Indian strategic and military thinking about Indian Armed Forces... Regrettably, much of the recent debate on defence has paid little attention to history's lessons during periods of uncertainty and technological change. On the other hand attempts to redefine itself in a new era.

The Indian Army, besides being the world's third largest, enjoys a unique status of professional excellence. There is no other army in the world that is as battle hardened as the Indian Army that has fought and won in as treacherous terrain and climate as the world's highest glacial battlefield. Only the Indian troops are shifted across operational theatres as diverse as the sultry forests of the North East, torrid sands of Thar desert, reed infested riverine borderline of Punjab, mountainous J&K and the entire expanse of icy Himalayas from Siachen in north Kashmir to Along in eastern Arunachal Pradesh. Besides the LoC/LAC on both fronts—Pakistan and China respectively—being incessantly active, the Indian Army has been fighting terrorists and insurgents to keep the country together. Also, the Army's role in relief operations during natural calamities or other emergencies has been universally lauded all through. All this speaks very high of our officers and men at action level.

A growing recognition within the nation, however, of the sterility in our reactive approach to Indian Defence Forces needs and policy formulation should create increasing demands for more creative military thought and greater flexibility in force building. However, it does not appear that nation has the political will nor the defence establishments have the institutional inclination, nor the Ministry of Defence the bureaucratic restraint; to allow the integration of inter service thinking. To produce truly cohesive global and regional strategies—strategies that is realistically consistent with available resources.

(a) In India combat developments have been to reactive and are not being linked to a realistic, forward looking future strategy—a strategy that reflects the intellectual potential;
(b) Military force applications in future are likely to be significantly greater variety and complexity, and
(c) Have a cohesive recruitment and training of personnel.

The Officer Shortage

The net shortage of officers in the Army is said to be about 12000 at present. Surprisingly, all the shortage is at the 'teeth' level—the units required to fight and perform. There is no shortage at any Headquarters (from Brigade to Army Headquarters) or Establishments reputed for risk-free career advancing 'graded' tenures in peace locations. Infantry units—the ubiquitous performing arm of the Indian Army—are managing with 8-10 officers posted against an authorised scale of 21, which obviously means that the workload on officers is more than twice their legitimate share.

Conscious of these crucial deficiencies but unable to convince or get support from the Government on crucial military needs, the Army devised a quick-fix solution to 'solve' the problem of 'officer shortage'—post young officers on cross-attachment from the Services like ASC, AOC and so on to the infantry units deployed in field. Resultantly, it is common in units to find raw, untrained and unqualified lieutenants/captains officiating as Company Commanders. Often, more than one company/squadron is placed under command of a youngster even before he is mature and qualified enough to lead a platoon effectively in action.

Grooming of Officers

Not too long ago Army had systems to groom young officers under the care of seasoned field officers who would assign responsibilities, guide and educate youngsters to occupy their positions in due course. The luxury of having two officers—a company commander and his company officer—is no longer available to the commanding officers of today. The institution of Senior Subaltern also stands demolished. The youngster these days steps directly into the boots of his boss and flounders like an excited toddler in his father's shoes flaunting his large acquisition. Who would refute the imminent fall in such a situation?

Officer-Men Interaction gone Haywire

Overburdened officers always under pressure to meet deadlines in onerous tasking find little time to train, play or entertain with troops on a regular basis. Such a routine distances officers from the men. Being more educated, aware and conscious of his privileges, the modern jawan is quick to find/create alternative channels in such circumstances to seek remedies to his problems directly from the Commanding Officer who in most cases, readily obliges—often ignoring/overruling recommendations of the subordinate commanders thereby proving the sub-unit commanders ineffective and unnecessary in the eyes of JCOs and men in the unit. Unwittingly, this practice has evolved into a dangerous trend—hunger for cheap popularity—even as objectivity and sincerity is diminishing in today's Army. Crisis to crisis they move on, compromise and accomplish somehow.

Security of Men

Any Civil Servant posted to Assam or Jammu and Kashmir is allowed to retain accommodation at old duty station and new. This has created security for them. However, no such facility is provided to defence personnel. The old family system has been systematically broken by myriad of laws only meant for Hindus by the way of demolishing Hindu families. Men go home and return without even getting heard from the Civil Administration. This has set in a deep resentment and many want to quit prematurely. In years gone by the Civil Administration used to give a speedy hearing during the leave period of the soldier so he was free to carry out his duties to safeguard the nation.

Modi and Indian Defence Forces

BJP in their manifesto of 2014 on pages 37-39[2] had gone in great details on actions to be taken on Issues of Security and Defence in Case voted to power. Modi became the Prime Minister of BJP led Government and it is his responsibility to fulfill the promises so made. In more specific terms, the manifesto stated the party's commitment to "developing indigenous defense technologies and fast tracking of defense purchases" as well as making India "a global production platform for defense hardware manufacturing and software production." Another much observed clause was the pledge to "revise and update" India's nuclear doctrine, something which most commentators thought meant that India would give up its critical "No First Use" doctrine. Thus, both the image and material power of India were areas the BJP sought to redefine as it came to power.

Indian Armed Forces are different from all others organisations. The veterans remain in contact with the armed forces and play a dominant role in maintaining morale and well-being of the units to which they belonged. Prime Minister Modi took the ex-servicemen along during his campaign. He however failed to encash on the goodwill of the army and soon fell into trap of Bureaucracy. BJP using it as a political tool in its election campaign in 2014. As the Prime Ministerial candidate, Narendra Modi had expressed solidarity with the demand of OROP which won him confidence of ex-servicemen. But the promise remained unfulfilled and this brought war-veterans to roads again.

The first responsibility of government is the defence of the nation. Without sovereign authority within the nation government is irrelevant. Prime Minister Modi understood *realpolitik* but has failed to understand that nation gets respects and standing with the power it has.

NDA government has been slow in coming to grips with the problems of defence policy, in part due to the absence of a full-time minister in the initial months of the government. PM Modi initially gave Defence as an additional Charge to Mr Jaitley, who had no time for Defence. He then brought in Mr Parrikar. The appointment of Manohar Parrikar as Raksha Mantri injected a much-needed dose of dynamism to the defence ministry. Parrikar has on several occasions stated that he wants to expedite defence procurement even while adopting transparent processes. In his very first meeting of the Defence Acquisition Council, he gave the go-ahead for the long-stalled procurement of artillery systems. He has also been looking to revise the existing policies in order to give a boost to the indigenous defence industry in India. More recently, he has averred the need for institutional reforms and integration in the three services.[3]

The first test for the new government came in the field of border management. In July-August 2014, soon after the Modi government was sworn in, the Pakistan army and its border wing, the Rangers, decided to test its resolve and activated the LoC and the International Boundary (IB) in the Jammu-Samba sector. The government gave a free hand to the Army and the BSF to deal with the ceasefire violations. The Pakistani border troops were given a befitting response an order of magnitude harder than the provocation. They got the message and the guns soon fell silent.

In September 2014, even as President Xi Jinping of China was exchanging pleasantries with the Indian Prime Minister at Ahmedabad, the border guards of the People's Liberation Army (PLA), transgressed across the Line of Actual Control (LAC) at Chumar and Demchok in Ladakh. The Indian response was swift and of an appropriate scale to signal to the Chinese that they had no option but to withdraw. It took a while, but eventually the PLA decided that prudence was better than false bravado.

It is nearly a decade and a half since the Kargil Review Committee and the subsequent Group of Ministers (GoM) submitted their recommendations for national security reforms. About three years ago, another committee led by Naresh Chandra examined why the recommendations of the GoM were not fully implemented and suggested a new road map for reforms. Unless we want to perpetuate this practice of decennial enquiries into why the preceding decade was wasted, it is imperative that the government swiftly grasps the nettle and tackles the thorniest questions.

No question has been more controversial than the appointment of a Chief of the Defence Staff (CDS). The GoM's recommendation for the creation of a CDS reflected the lack of integrated planning and operations between the services during the Kargil War. In fact, this is a problem that has plagued the armed forces in almost every conflict since 1947. The appointment of a CDS as the single-point military advisor to the Raksha Mantri was expected to usher in top-down integration among the services and better coordination between the services and the government. The previous NDA government created a new joint headquarters of the Integrated Defence Staff (HQ IDS). But it baulked at appointing a CDS and instead appointed a Chief of Integrated Defence Staff (CIDS) who would run the HQ IDS until the CDS was appointed.

Procurements without policy are seen by several officers as a waste of resources as all answers do not lie in acquisitions. The Brookings report echoes this view when it stated, "India's three services have dramatically different views of what their role in India's security should be, and there is no political effort to ensure this coordination. Cold Start remains an iffy proposition, India's nuclear deterrent remains tethered to a single delivery system: fighter aircraft. Meanwhile the Indian Army's energies are dissipated with counter insurgency duties."

Furthermore, it constrains India's armed forces' ability to deal with regional security challenges more effectively, given that many are stationed along its disputed borders. Recent analyses have laid bare New Delhi's dysfunctional national security machinery, in which decision makers spend more time on internal procurement processes and battling bureaucracy than on developing foreign policy strategies, reducing India's capacity to pursue its strategic objectives effectively.

The Indian government never clearly articulated the strategic priorities that drive its military expansion and modernisation program or explained a coherent rationale for its costly investment in military hardware. It is surprising that there has been little public debate in India at this rise and for the country's ambitious military build-up plans.

Military violence and political consequences comprise two different currencies, and it is difficult to convert one into another by strategy/doctrine. There is a wide cultural divide between the two. Military and political professionals have different values, skills, perspectives and responsibilities. In addition, their personalities are different. Politicians, favour compromise as high virtue, regard expediency as a necessary mode of operation, are not economical with words, care little for truth.

Politicians career rise and fall with words. They hold to an honour code that would not pass muster in a military context. On the other hand, soldiers prefer who is decisive, determined, honest, loyal, and person of action. The conflict and tension in civil-military relations are aptly captured in pair of rival maxims: first, 'war is too important to be left to Generals'; and second, 'war is too important to be left to the politicians.' Soldiers believe that they alone represent the best interest of the country, and that they serve the state through the government of the day. Politicians and soldiers have to cooperate to generate positive strategic effectiveness. This need, and the hindrances to its efficient achievement, is a thread that runs through all of strategic history. It is here that Modi has not been able to make a mark in his doctrine.

ENDNOTES

1. Tharoor, Shashi (2003) *Nehru: The Invention of India* (Penguin Viking).
2. BJP in its manifesto of 2014 on pages 37-39 Extracts are given below:

Secure Indians—Zero Tolerance on Terrorism, Extremism and Crime

Comprehensive national security is not just about borders, but in its broad terms includes military security; economic security; cyber security; energy, food and water and health security; and social cohesion and harmony. To effectively address the issues of national security, we need to address the issues of—human resources, science and technology, system of governance and money.

National security cannot be compartmentalized based on one of issues but needs a clear roadmap to address it. Over the past decade, lack of a strong and visionary leadership, coupled with multiple power centres, has failed to address the issue of national security, leading to a chaotic situation and denting India's image in the international arena.

India has a sensitive neighbourhood and there are internal security issues. There have been intrusions inside the LAC (Line of actual control), loss of squadrons of combat aircraft by the air force, witnessing of a series of accidents by the Navy, leading to a loss in its combating capability built over many decades, communal riots, Maoist attacks, increase in incidence of Pakistan backed terror groups in India, illegal immigration across the eastern border, and racists' attacks in the national capital. All these are indications of surrendering of India's interest. This calls for a review and overhauling of the current system. With the financial situation worsening, the issue of national security can acquire a horrifying dimension.

BJP recognizes the importance of identifying a clear roadmap to address the issue head-on, with radical systemic changes.

Internal Security

BJP will:

- Revive the anti-terror mechanism that has been dismantled by the Congress, strengthen the role of NIA and put a system in place for swift and fair trial of terror related cases.
- Reform the National Security Council to make it the hub of all sector-related assessments. It will be accountable for real-time intelligence dissemination. Digital and Cyber security will be a thrust area.
- Insulate intelligence agencies from political intervention and interference.
- Completely revamp the intelligence gathering system by modernizing the intelligence department.

- Provide the State governments with all assistance to modernize their respective police forces and equip them with the latest technology. This will be taken up on a mission mode approach.
- Strengthen and expand the Civil Defence and Home Guards mechanism to create a group of citizens for community defence, self-defence and disaster management.
- Encourage and strengthen NCC training at the college and University level.
- Chalk a national plan in consultation and participation of the state Governments, to address the challenges posed by the Maoist's insurgency. Talks with the insurgent groups will be conditional and within the framework of the constitution.
- Take urgent steps for the safety of the migrant workers and communities from the Northeast and other states.

External Security—Its Boundary, Beauty and Bounty

BJP will:

- Address the issue of reforms with regards to defence equipment, support services, organisational reforms and other related matters.
- Address the increasing shortage of commissioned and non-commissioned staff in the defence forces on a priority basis, in a time bound manner.
- Implement one rank, one pension.
- Build a War Memorial to recognize and honour the gallantry of our soldiers.
- Take measures to make Short Service Commission more attractive.
- Set up the National Maritime Authority which will be equipped with the best of infrastructure, and will focus on coastal security.
- Modernize armed forces, and increase the R&D in defence, with a goal of developing indigenous defence technologies and fast tracking of defence purchases.
- Deal with cross border terrorism with a firm hand.
- Review and improve the border management. Punitive measures will be introduced to check illegal immigration.
- Set up four dedicated defence universities to meet the shortage of manpower.
- Appoint a Veterans Commission to address the grievances of veterans, including reforming ECHS and re-employment of ex-servicemen.
- Ensure greater participation of Armed Forces in the decision-making process of the Ministry of Defence.
- Implement measures to improve the efficiency of Armed Forces Tribunals, and minimize appeals by the Government.
- Ensure that servicemen can register and vote from their place of posting.
- Initiate the process of digitization of defence land in cantonment and in other places.

Defence Production

With its skilled human resources and technical talent, India can emerge as a global platform for defence hardware manufacture and software production. BJP will strengthen the Defence Research and Development Organisation (DRDO); encourage private sector participation and investment, including FDI in selected defence industries.

- Technology transfer in defence manufacturing will be encouraged to the maximum.
- We will find solutions to the problems hampering the growth of the defence sector.
- We will encourage domestic industry to have a larger share in design and production of military hardware and platforms for both domestic use and exports, in a competitive environment.

Independent Strategic Nuclear Programme

BJP believes that the strategic gains acquired by India during the Atal Bihari Vajpayee regime on the nuclear programme have been frittered away by the Congress. Our emphasis was, and remains on, beginning of a new thrust on framing policies that would serve India's national interest in the 21st century. We will follow a two-pronged independent nuclear programme, unencumbered by foreign pressure and influence, for civilian and military purposes, especially as nuclear power is a major contributor to India's energy sector.

BJP will:

- Study in detail India's nuclear doctrine, and revise and update it, to make it relevant to challenges of current times.
- Maintain a credible minimum deterrent that is in tune with changing geostatic realities.
- Invest in India's indigenous Thorium Technology Programme.

3. 'India may soon get a General no. 1 to boost tri-service integration', *Times of India*, 14 March 2015.

11

GEO-ECONOMICS AND INDIA'S STRATEGY

'From the strength of the treasury the army is born', said Kautilya. Traditionally the economy has entered into the national security debate through its impact on the nation's hard power: the funding of defence, the efficacy of the defence industrial base, and the use of economic sanctions and other instruments as non-kinetic tools of warfare. The long-term efficacy of hard power, however, depends greatly on the ability of a country to provide for it through an ever growing and innovative economy.

> **"..., economics is the continuation of war by other means."**[1]
>
> [1]Bell, Daniel (1990), 'Germany: The Enduring Fear,' *Dissent,* Vol. 37 (Fall).

Geo-economics may be defined in two different ways—as the relationship between economic policy and change on national power and geo-politics—in other words, the geopolitical consequences of economic phenomenon, or, as the economic consequences of geopolitical trends and national power. Both the notion of 'trade follows the flag', that there are economic consequences of the projection of national power, and the idea that 'the flag follows trade', that there are geo-political consequences of essentially economic phenomena, would constitute the subject matter of geo-economics.

The truth is that national security and economic strength are inextricably linked, and India needs to pursue both. In soloed government agencies, though, they are too often considered in isolation. India's economy is the foundation of its military and political power, and boosting growth helps relieve the downward pressure on defence and foreign-affairs budgets that reduces India's ability to shape international events. With the world aflame from Syria to Afghanistan, and tensions with China rising, international terrorism on the rise, the demand for India is higher than it has been in decades. The challenge today is supplying it.

As Kennedy put it: '... all of the major shifts in the world's military-power balances have followed alterations in the productive balances; and further, that the rising and falling of the various empires and states in the international system has been confirmed by the outcomes of the major Great Power wars, where victory has always gone to the side with the greatest material resources.'[1]

The second important articulation of the idea of 'geo-economics' was the 1990 essay of Edward Luttwak, '*From Geopolitics to Geo-economics: Logic of Conflict, Grammar of Commerce.*' Luttwak observed, "Everyone, it appears, now agrees that the methods of commerce are displacing military methods—with disposable capital in lieu of firepower, civilian innovation in lieu of military-technical advancement, and market penetration in lieu of garrisons and bases. States, as spatial entities structured to jealously delimit their own territories, will not disappear but reorient themselves toward geo-economics in order to compensate for their decaying geopolitical roles. ... 'geo-economics' is the best term I can think of to describe the admixture of the logic of conflict with the methods of commerce."[2]

> "...Economists are blind to the fact that economic activity is a source of power, as well as well-being. It is, indeed, probably the most important source of power and in a world in which military conflict between major states is unlikely economic power will be increasingly important in determining the primacy or subordination of states. ,In the realm of military competition, the instruments of power are missiles, planes, warships, bombs, tanks and divisions. In the realm of economic competition, the instruments of power are productive efficiency, market control, trade surplus, strong currency, foreign exchange reserves, and ownership of foreign companies, factories and technology."[1]
>
> [1]Huntington, Samuel P. (1993), 'Why international primacy matters', *International Security*, 18(4).

National security depends also on soft power, the ability of a country to generate and use its economic power and to project its national values. This, in turn, depends on long-term factors that contribute to economic growth and increase the total resource base available not only for defence but to provide economic security in the form of income and business opportunities for individuals. Economic growth depends on building human capital. It also depends on science, technology, and innovation. In addition, the increased integration of the India's economy into global markets means that India's security also depends on global economic stability, on a balanced international economy, the ability to coordinate key economic policies with other leading nations, and deterring threats to the international financial system. Soft power also enables the country to project Indian values through diplomacy, economic assistance, fostering democracy and human rights, and promoting sustainable development abroad.

The ends of India's international economic policy are to contribute to national economic growth and prosperity. Contributing to the prosperity of allies and friends and seeking global growth and development more generally support this goal. Rising standards of living have been an important policy goal of the India for generations. A strong economy is also necessary to pay for the implementation of foreign policy. Tax revenues are necessary to fund military, diplomatic, commercial, environmental, and humanitarian efforts. India's economic policy can influence the well-being of other nations, and thus the United States' global standing. The 2008 financial crisis was a major contributor to global recession, creating resentment in some countries and denting India's image. The growth of Indian economy outstrips every nation today, a commensurate gain in India's clout over international events and governance may follow soon.

India's rise constitutes one of the most fascinating and important stories of the past two decades, symbolising, along with China, the fundamental shift of power towards Asia. Yet while many acknowledge India's new found importance, the country remains one of the most misunderstood actors in the international community. During the Cold War, India was the only democratic regime that did not align with the West. After becoming a nuclear power in 1998, the country suffered international condemnation, only to become one of the United States' key strategic partners less than ten years later. While international analysts have traditionally looked at India primarily through the prism of the conflict with Pakistan, today it is routinely analysed in the context of a rising China. Neither viewpoint can do justice to India's much more important and complex role in the 21st century. The need to understand India's perspective has never been greater, and today no global challenge—be it climate change, nuclear proliferation or poverty reduction—can be tackled successfully without India's active contribution and engagement.

In the economic and financial realm, four large ideas or priorities will shape both India's domestic and international economic policy:

- Market capitalism was superior to socialism (high standards of living, vibrant entrepreneurs, and innovation were nourished best by free markets);
- Security considerations trumped economics (e.g., wars had to be won even at high economic cost; India going nuclear and US and Western Countries putting embargo on India).
- Economic growth and employment were best fostered by monetary and fiscal policy rather than by industrial policies that "picked winners and losers"; and
- Imbalances in trade and capital flows were largely self-correcting (foreign exchange rates determined by capital markets and appropriate government fiscal and monetary policy would bring balance into international accounts).

The current geo-economic environment threatens to undermine not only the future prospects of global agreements on trade and investment, but also the international rule-based system. One aspect of both the Transatlantic Trade and Investment Partnership (TTIP) and the Trans-Pacific Partnership (TPP) is essentially about trying to balance political relations and in turn alleviate any geopolitical and security dilemmas. The second characteristic concerns the creation of a market that's big enough to be able to continue to set the rules in the global economy.

It is important to mention at this point that both the TPP and TTIP don't include the BRICS economies in their negotiations. While their economies may be currently suffering some setbacks, as a result of the fast-shifting international order and the growing collaboration between these countries, the BRICS are fast becoming an organised political body. One such political entity that many observers believe should be better integrated into current international frameworks.

Given that the trade deals together would cover approximately 75 per cent of the world's GDP[3] operating under the current liberal economic order—the US and major Western economies could

ESSENTIAL ATTRIBUTES OF GEO-ECONOMIC POWER

1. Knowledge power and demographic transition; the empires of the future, observed Winston Churchill in 1946, will be the empires of the mind. Knowledge, that is human capability, is the single most important attribute of power in the modern world. Long term demographic shifts can alter the dynamics of knowledge power and have both geo-economic and geopolitical consequences
2. Agrarian transformation and search for resources; Agrarian transformation accelerates the pace of economic growth, facilitates industrial development, and helps ensure food security. Countries with assured access to natural resources have an advantage over those dependent on imports for vital resources, especially food and energy
3. Social and political transformation, especially the rise of a middle class and of entrepreneurial classes; the rise of an urban middle class and an entrepreneurial class is an important requirement of sustained and sustainable long term economic growth. Economic institutions and governance are critical determinants of these phenomena.
4. Fiscal capacity to fund military capability. The fiscal empowerment of the State, a consequence of high growth and improved governance, creates the fiscal resources required both for welfare and infrastructure spending and for building technological and military capability.[1]

[1]Kautilya wrote in his Arthasastra that, **'From the strength of the treasury the army is born'**. An idea that informs Kennedy's theory of ***'imperial overstretch'*** and Ferguson's hypothesis about the ***'square of power'*** in Ferguson, Niall (2001), *The Cash Nexus: Money and Power in the Modern World, 1700-2000* (Allen Lane: The Penguin Press).

maintain the ability to control influence over these emerging economies and others. According to this viewpoint, the intention is that China and other developing economies will ultimately have to decide whether they would rather be excluded from this market or agree to meet the standards on for example, complex issues such as agriculture, intellectual property and state owned enterprises.

Perhaps in response to the threat to exclude China and other developing economies in the above trade deals, and to what many see as an outdated system, China together with a number of emerging economies are starting to establish alternatives to the Bretton Woods institutions. These countries are starting to find new ways to cooperate economically. For years they have voiced their frustration over western dominance in global financial institutions and have recently advanced their challenge. Last year, China launched the Asia Infrastructure Investment Bank and we saw the launch of the New Development Bank (NDB) that includes Brazil, Russia, India, South Africa and China. These structures signify the first challenge to the current global economic order since World War II.

In light of the purported failure of the Bretton Woods institutions, we see countries, in particular emerging economies, disengaging from them and trying to create alternative regimes. The driving force behind this is as much geopolitical as it is economic. However, with the world facing challenges that respect no national borders and require multilateral responses, the effects of geo-economics on institutions of global governance could be to weaken our collective resilience to global risks and challenges. This could hamper the way we resolve conflict, address global terrorism and find a solution to climate change

India and Geo-Economics

India's role in today's international context abounds with paradox. At first sight, there are many reasons to be optimistic about India: it boasts one of the world's most dynamic economies, driven by a growing group of sophisticated entrepreneurs capable of competing globally. India has experienced unprecedented growth and stability since the end of the Cold War, and it is expected to turn into one of the world's five largest economies by the end of the decade. Given that the country finally seems to be capitalising on its potential, several analysts have proclaimed the 'Indian Century', and the government is ever more confident in its claim for a permanent seat on the UN Security Council and more responsibility in institutions such as the International Monetary Fund (IMF) and the World Bank. At the same time, India has become the world's largest arms importer, further boosting its profile and potential role in security affairs in the Indian Ocean. Due to its democratic credentials and reputation as a benign international actor, a consensus has emerged in the West that India is the world's best hope to balance a rising China both in the region and, at a later stage, in global affairs. Reflecting this, the United States' recognition of India as a nuclear power, a move that risked weakening the Non-Proliferation Treaty (NPT), was unprecedented and showed how important India has become in the view of foreign policy makers in Washington D.C. On top of all that, India boasts of considerable soft power—its vibrant democracy, millennia-old culture and benevolent standing help explain why the vast majority of international actors look kindly upon India's rise.

India continues to be among the top ten countries in terms of foreign direct investment (FDI) inflows globally and the fourth in developing Asia, as per the World Investment Report 2016 by the United Nations Conference for Trade and Development (UNCTAD).[4] India's Foreign Direct Investments inflows have increased to $44 billion in 2015 as compared to $35 billion in 2014, and the growth has been across the board, the report said. As an expected economic recovery gains ground, FDI inflows are likely to maintain an upward trend in 2015. In terms of sectoral composition, manufacturing is gaining strength, as policy efforts to revitalise the sector are sustained, including for instance the launch of the "Make in India" Initiative in mid-2014.[5]

A surge in investments in the first four months of 2016 is mainly on account of the Make in India initiative, alongside liberalisation measures and reforms initiated by the National Democratic Alliance, which make India an attractive investment decision, according to Nagesh Kumar, who heads the South, South-West Asia office of the United Nations Economic and Social Commission for Asia and the Pacific (UNESCAP). "The huge potential offered by India, the fastest growing major economy, is also one of the main reasons," he added.

To be sure, China with more than three times India's FDI at $136 billion in 2015 is ranked third in terms of FDI flows among all countries, as per the report.

However, India's global aspirations are starkly contrasted by the enormous difficulties it faces both at home and outside of its borders. With over 300 million Indians living below the poverty line and growing economic inequalities, India's rise has yet to translate into tangible benefits for the poor, most of whom live in rural areas that have benefitted little from recent economic growth. The Maoist Naxalite insurgency, affecting large swathes of the country, has rightly been identified by the government as India's most serious security concern. Violence saps the government's authority to take the country forward in these areas. Yet the insurgents' continued presence can be explained precisely because growth has not been sufficiently distributive. More importantly for India's foreign policy, Kashmir represents a bleeding wound that significantly diverts foreign policy makers' attention, reducing their capacity to focus on other urgent challenges.

Modi and Geo-Economics

Modi has underscored foreign policy as a priority from the beginning alongside a strong mandate to put India's economy in order. Modi aspires to re-invigorate India's emerging power status, which suffered in recent years due to poor economic growth. He has not only injected focus and ambition into India's foreign policy, but also linked it directly to his plan to transform India's economy. Modi's focus to a large extent has been on geo-economic and geopolitical engagement to further India's strategic interests.

Economics or to be precise geo-economics, has become the chief area of co-operation and engagement with major countries. Democracy promotion in multilateral organisations as well as other countries can now become another new aspect of the Indian foreign policy.

Modi has always been a man of trade and investment. Modi was one of the first Chief Ministers in India to organize events like 'Vibrant Gujarat' to invite businessmen from all over the world to attract investments. So after becoming the Prime Minister he is assiduously trying to build the image of India as a hub for manufacturing and businesses with his 'Make in India' campaign.

He wants to follow up his success in Gujarat on a larger National scale. No efficient foreign policy can be followed without strong economic clout and he knows it better than many of our contemporary politicians. It is for this reason that trade and investments has been a major area of discussion when dealing with major countries like China, Japan and the U.S.

Launched in September 2014, 'Make in India' has become Narendra Modi's signature programme as he aspires to convert India into a global manufacturing hub. His foreign policy mantra therefore is strongly driven by geo-economics—especially attracting foreign direct investment (FDI)—and at the same time seeks to consolidate India's leadership role in South Asia. While the previous Congress party-led governments prioritised relations with the US and the European Union (EU) (the Singh government negotiated the historic US-India nuclear energy agreement from 2005-2008 and launched free trade talks with the EU in 2007), Modi is shifting the focus to India's immediate neighbourhood and other major Asian countries like Japan, China and Australia, as well as the BRICS grouping.

He has managed to convince both China and Japan to invest heavily in India while re-establishing India's foothold in its precarious immediate neighbourhood. Reaffirming India's traditional non-aligned policy, Modi has employed a more muscular approach to asserting his country's independence while taking a very selective approach to multilateral cooperation. For example, India singularly vetoed the World Trade Organisation's (WTO) Trade Facilitation Agreement (TFA) in

July (a draft already agreed by the WTO's 160 members including the previous Congress-led Indian government at the Bali Ministerial Conference in 2013) over food security concerns. A breakthrough was reached in the fringes of the Asia Pacific Economic Cooperation (APEC) Summit in November, when the US agreed not to challenge India's food security policies at the WTO, removing the main impasse to the agreement. With the US, Modi has steered clear of joining any US grand strategy on Asia or the Islamic State (IS) in Iraq and Syria, but spoke during his visit there about trade, investment and bilateral security cooperation.

Economic power is the foundation of military power. The most important single indicator is GDP. Like defence budgets, however, GDP provides only a limited picture of power. It says little about the composition of the economy, such as whether it is spearheaded by leading sectors or dominated by old and declining ones. Other important variables include human capital and technology. The best readily available measure of human capital is the average year of educational attainment. For technology, the best indicator is per-capita expenditure on research and development.

ENDNOTES

1. Kennedy, Paul (1987), *The Rise and Fall of the Great Powers: Economic Change and Military Conflict From 1500 to 2000,* (New York :Random House), p. 439.
2. Luttwak, Edward (1990), 'From Geopolitical to Geo-economics, Logic of Conflict, Grammar of Commerce', *The National Interest,* no 20, p. 17-24.
3. Talking Trade with Congressmen Jim Costa and Erik Paulsen: *Why TPP and TTIP Advance U.S. Economic and Strategic Interests,* Miriam Sapiro, October 3, 2014, *Brooking,* see Cini, Jonathan (2015), 'Geo-economic competition: global disruptions from the new frontline,' *Strategic Security Analysis,* June 2015, No. 6 (Geneva Centre of Security Studies).
4. World Investment Report 2015, *Reforming International Investment Governance* (UNTACD) (Geneva: United Nations Publication).
5. World Investment Report 2015, *Reforming International Investment Governance* (UNTACD), (Geneva: United Nations Publication), p. 46.

12

THE MODI DOCTRINE

People eulogies Nehru for his expertise in international affairs, and credit him as the founder of India's foreign policy. Founder he was, but was the foundations solid? Or, were they rickety? Or, were there no foundations at all? Was it all airy ad-hocism, and one-man's-pontifications? Crucially, was it a foreign policy that benefited India? Or, was it merely a device for Nehru for self-posturing and to project himself internationally?

The policy of Non-alignment meant the acceptance of the inevitability of war but on the conviction that was could also be avoided. Non-Alignment stood for an independent policy conditioned and controlled by India's own strength. It meant not to entangle oneself with any kind of alliances or commitments that would lead to war and conflict.

> ***PANCHASHEELA***
>
> *Panchasheela*, a term derived from Buddhist scriptures, encapsulated the 'five principles of peaceful coexistence' as enshrined in the 1954 agreement between India and China, which were supposed to frame Sino-Indian relations as well as India's foreign policy more generally. The five principles referred to
>
> (1) Mutual respect for each other's territorial integrity and sovereignty;
> (2) Mutual non-aggression;
> (3) Mutual non-interference in each other's internal affairs;
> (4) Equality and mutual benefit; and
> (5) Peaceful coexistence.

Non-alignment implied a position to judge each issue without prejudice or bias. It enhanced the chances of effective mediation in bitter conflicts and thereby brightens the prospect of world peace.

Conceived as a struggle against colonialism and growing polarization of international relations resulting from military blocks and cold war, non-aligned

India has constantly struggled for all-round emancipation of the people of Asia, Africa, Latin America, the Caribbean and other parts of the world. Non-Alignment has achieved success and has continued to play a decisive role in efforts to promote world peace.

How come all our major neighbours became our enemies? And, a friendly neighbour, Tibet, disappeared as an independent nation? We lost Kashmir which was ceded by the then Maharaja Hari Singh to India under the legal Act which partitioned India in 1947...Nehru's foreign policy turned India into a country no one took seriously? Foreign Relations are evaluated by results not by its verbosity and pompousness.

Non-Alignment as policy did achieve some results but as far as India was concerned it was a total failure. Nehru never realised that foreign policy must be tied up with the immediate defence requirements in order to serve a useful purpose. The foreign policy needs economic and military power to back it.

Nehru continued to ignore military considerations in dealing with foreign policy issues. A story goes: The British General Sir Rob Lockhart, first Commander-in-Chief of free India's Armed Forces, was left in no doubt by his Prime Minister when he went to him with a Defence Paper, asking for a formal policy directive on defence. Nehru glanced through Lockhart's paper but was not in the least amused. 'Rubbish! Total rubbish!' the Prime Minister exploded (according to Lockhart). 'We don't 'We don't need a defence policy. Our policy is ahimsa (non-violence). We foresee no military threats. As far as I am concerned you can scrap the army – the police are good enough to meet our security needs'. It is thanks to the 'J&K war of 47-48' which brought home the harsh reality to our rulers.[1]

Nehru insisted on keeping the portfolio of external affairs for himself. It was a disadvantage to him that he did so, because, as head of the whole government of India, he had to deal with a range of internal problems already too much for one mind. And it was a disadvantage to the Indian foreign office and the Indian diplomatic service. In effect he did damage to both, and at a formative and impressionable stage of their growth...

BR Ambedkar criticised Nehru's foreign policy for trying to "solve the problems of other countries and not [exerting] to solve the problems of our own country!"[2]

Even after the disastrous 1962 India-China war, India showed a surprising level of complacency in national security affairs.[3]

In Brief, Nehru Foreign and Defence Policies were Total Failures

Nehru's successor both Lal Bahadur Shastri and Indira Gandhi did try to correct and bring Foreign Policy in tandem with military Power; In 1971 Mrs Indira Gandhi India signed the treaty of friendship with USSR in 1971. The **Indo–**

Soviet Treaty of Peace, Friendship and Cooperation signed between India and the Soviet Union in August 1971 specified mutual strategic cooperation.[4] The treaty was a significant deviation from India's previous position of alignment in the Cold War and in the prelude to the Bangladesh war; it was a key development in a situation of increasing Sino-American ties and American pressure.[5] The treaty was later adopted as a model for the Indo-Bangladesh Treaty of Friendship and Cooperation in 1972. India also carried out a peaceful nuclear explosion in 1974. There was a shift from Non-alignment to alignment during Mrs. Indira Gandhi's tenure as Prime Minister.

Mr Rajiv Gandhi committed Indian forces in Sri Lanka. India also prevented coup in Maldives in 1988. The 1988 Maldives coup d'état, was the attempt by a group of Maldivians led by Abdullah Luthufi and assisted by armed mercenaries of a Tamil secessionist organisation from Sri Lanka, the People's Liberation Organisation of Tamil Eelam (PLOTE), to overthrow the government in the island republic of Maldives. The coup d'état failed due to the intervention of the Indian Army, whose military operations efforts were code-named Operation Cactus by the Indian Armed Forces.

Only from the late 1980s did Nehruvian ideas of nonalignment, moral politik, and statist economic ideology begin coming under attack.[6] The year 1991 was a defining moment in the history of India's foreign and foreign and defence policies in the post-cold war scenario. The collapse and disintegration of the USSR at the one end and the acceleration in the processes of globalisation on the other, created a much larger space for India to manoeuvre at home and on global arena. India found itself automatically out of the perceived shadows of the "now former mighty USSR".

Nehru's economic model which was oriented towards Licence Raj, red tape and bureaucracy leading to large scale corruption had resulted in 2-3 per cent annual growth (which was mocked as "Hindu rate of growth" by economists) and the subsequent protection of such model by Indira Gandhi had led the nation into darkness and economic standstill.[7]

One of the more pronounced shifts in foreign policy came through the "Look East Policy" initiated in 1991. The other visible and tangible departure from the past was in the field of foreign economic policy as India decided to open its door for foreign investments and to deregulate and let its economy come out of insulation and face the challenges through globalisation and be part of the global market economy.

Rao energised the national nuclear security and ballistic missiles program, which ultimately resulted in the 1998 Pokhran nuclear tests. It is speculated that the tests were actually planned in 1995, during Rao's term in office, and that they were dropped under American pressure when the US intelligence got the whiff of it. Another view was that he purposefully leaked the information to gain time to develop and test thermonuclear device which was not yet ready. He increased military spending, and set the Indian Army on course to fight the emerging threat of terrorism and insurgencies, as well as Pakistan and China's nuclear potentials. It was during his term that terrorism in the Indian state of Punjab was finally defeated.

The whole discourse on hard power and military affairs was the exception not the norm, with change in discourse occurring visibly only after the nuclear tests of 1998. Several other important steps in the next two decades were made; these include for instance strategic partnerships with all major players such as USA, China, Russia and the EU.

In addition, India has forged some important regional links through grouping such as BRICS and IBSA. In the context of anti-piracy initiatives, India has emerged as a net security provider in for the small island countries in the Indian Ocean. These initiatives were, however, gradual, relatively subtle and/or a result of adjustments and adaptation to fast changing global geo-political realities and therefore can be treated as less pronounced. India also entered in a security treaty with Qatar.

India's vibrant political process effectively conveyed the democratic 'noise' of India's domestic politics to the international arena—much like the domestic opposition in the US or the UK to the Iraq policy espoused by government in those countries—there has been, in contrast, no corresponding deep "stateness", or residual reserve of basic national consensus about the core interests of the country. As such, while India joined large democracies like the US or the UK in terms of domestic dissent over national policy, unlike them, India's likely response to a crisis remains uncertain, whereas the American or British reaction in a similar situation was predictable to the outsider.

It was at this juncture Prime Minster Modi took over reigns of the Government. He understood *realpolitik* very well. Mr Modi was very clear that Foreign Policy has to be backed by a strong military which can only exist if nation became economically strong. He had no hang ups of idealism or past.Mr Modi had an elaborate Election manifesto. Modi belongs to Bhartiya Janta Party, its Election Manifesto of 2014,[8] in which salient tenants of the policy are clearly enunciated. These became guiding principles for the Modi Government. It is to Modi's credit that he has attempted to revive several good ideas of his predecessors and carry out their vision for India's security, while infusing his own vigour and enthusiasm and thereby adding his personal brand to these initiatives.[9]

In the 52-page election manifesto, only a little over one page accounted for foreign policy. Right at the outset, the party harks back to India's freedom movement and cites several leaders including B.G. Tilak, V. Patel, S.C. Bose and Mahatma Gandhi. Conspicuously absent was Jawaharlal Nehru in this group. Indeed, the manifesto complains that India's post-independence leadership (read Congress Party) discarded India's vision and instead adopted the British institutional framework, which was "alien to the Indian world-view." According to the BJP, India's leadership failed to "rekindle the spirit of India."[10]

The manifesto devoted attention to the need for more actively promoting its "soft power" through a Brand India campaign and civilisational values. It harked back to the first BJP government as having made it so India would begin to be "reckoned as an economic superpower." Thus, both the image and material power of India were areas the BJP sought to redefine as it came to power.

In the very first instance Prime Minister Narendra Modi challenged his senior diplomats "to help India position itself in a leading role, rather than [as] just a balancing force, globally".[11] Elaborating on this idea, the foreign secretary, Subrahmanyam Jaishankar, later noted that Modi's dramatic international initiatives reflected India's growing self-confidence, declaring that the country now "aspire[s] to be a leading power, rather than just a balancing power".[12]

Modi's clarion call for India to assume a leading, rather than merely a balancing, role signifies larger ambitions. Jaishankar summarised these aims succinctly when he stated, insofar "as larger international politics is concerned, India welcomes the growing reality of a multi-polar world, as it does, of a multi-polar Asia."[13]

In other words, India, by its choices at home and its actions abroad, would seek to create the distribution of capabilities at both the global and the continental levels that would accommodate its presence as an authentic great power. Although these aspirations are conveyed by the more modest locution "leading power," Modi's vision, strictly speaking, envisages India becoming a traditional great power—an inescapable conclusion if the desire for multi-polarity at the global level has any consequential meaning.

Realists correctly claim that wars are not won either by foot-tapping music or by mouth-watering food. They are referring to traditional forms of warfare and conflict that are largely determined by a state's military prowess. However, we live in an age where the nature of conflict is fast changing. States are competing for a share of the economic pie, scarce and finite resources, and influence, which often help determine the outcome of many bidding contests. It is these types of war that can be won or at least decisively influenced by a state's arsenal of soft power resources.

Modi's current foreign policy strategy can be termed '***universal engagement***'. Being the astute politician and champion of commerce that he is, Modi realises that India can advance only by selectively engaging foreign powers that hold the key to its future. Rising to power on a mandate of economic growth and development, he understands that India cannot grow without acquiring requisite raw materials and energy resources that remain in limited supply but high demand by other fast growing economies, such as neighbouring China as well as other BRICS (Brazil, Russia, India, China and South Africa) economies. His foreign trips are as much about securing access to crucial sources of energy and raw materials as about cementing India's long-ignored diplomatic and political ties within the region and beyond. If India hopes to be treated as a major power, then its outlook cannot be inward looking; it must embrace the responsibilities of its role as a major power state.

Neighbourhood First

"BJP believes that political stability, progress and peace in the region are essential for South Asia's growth and development. The Congress-led UPA [United Progressive Alliance] has failed to establish enduring friendly and cooperative relations with India's neighbours. India's relations with traditional allies have turned cold. India and its neighbours have drifted apart. The absence of statecraft has never been felt so acutely as today."

Narendra Modi and emphasised the centrality of India's neighborhood in its foreign policy. It asserted that "political stability, progress and peace in the region are essential for south Asia's growth and development" and promised that the government would "pursue friendly relations" in the neighborhood and "work towards strengthening Regional forums [original emphasis] like SAARC..."

At the 18th SAARC Summit in Kathmandu in November 2014, Modi pitched for "reinvigorating" and "revitalising" SAARC. He promised to help his neighbors on issues of trade, transit, visas, investments, education, health, communication and space technologies. Despite Modi's encouraging gestures the final outcome dashed any hope of reviving regionalism. Of the three connectivity agreements on road, rail and energy on the agenda, only one agreement—on establishing a regional energy grid—was ultimately concluded in a last-minute deal. There also no major breakthroughs on other important issues, such as fighting terrorism, flow of investments and financial agreements to deepen regional integration; the summit's ambitious theme of "Deeper Integration for Peace and Security" remained unrealised.

Partly due to the near failure of the SAARC summit and partly on account of the inability to address deep mistrust with some SAARC members Modi appears to have veered toward establishing stronger bilateral relations with other SAARC countries. Modi has been relatively more successful in pursuing bilateral relationship.

Pakistan remains a glaring challenge of Modi's "neighbourhood first" policy. While there was cause for celebration when Modi invited Sharif for his inauguration, relations soon deteriorated with India cancelling foreign secretaries' talks in July and the exchange of fire across the Line of Control.

India's Prime Minister Narendra Modi has taken a much tougher position on Pakistan than his predecessor did. India has intensified firing across the Line of Control in Kashmir and the international border, and has refused to resume the stalled bilateral dialogue until Pakistan takes action against anti-India militants based in Pakistani territory. Modi has also made two visits to Afghanistan, and supplied Kabul with offensive arms for the first time.

Act East Policy

The Act East Policy (AEP) was set in motion by Modi at the East Asia Summit in Myanmar in November 2014. Although some analysts dismiss the shift from the Look East Policy (LEP) launched by then Prime Minister Narasimha Rao in 1992 as merely a change in nomenclature, with both the AEP and LEP pursuing the same objectives, this is not an accurate assessment. While it is true that there is considerable continuity between the two, in several significant areas the AEP has gone well beyond what LEP could achieve in 20-plus years.

This is partly because India today is not the India of 1992. At that time, the country was facing an uncertain future on the international policy front, due to factors such as the disintegration of the Soviet Union, and a sharp fall in India's foreign exchange reserves, such that the country had enough to provide an import cover for merely 10 days.

With AEP, India's multi-dimensional ties with ASEAN have been given greater vigour and dynamism. This is especially important in a context of rapidly-changing geopolitical realities, defined by the assertive rise of China. The renewed focus and new direction of the AEP are evident in the extensive high-level visits—by India's president, Vice President, and Prime Minister to nine of the 10 ASEAN states—over the last 23 months. One outcome is that bilateral and multilateral relations, some of which were stagnating, have assumed renewed energy and focus, as have projects—for example, the India-Myanmar-Thailand trilateral highway. Modi allocated $1 billion to promote connectivity, and signalled the primacy of '**connectivity, culture and commerce**'.[14] Recognising that the AEP's success will be measured by its contribution to the security and economic development of India's North East, these states have been drawn in as active partners in the AEP.

India's relations with ASEAN have broadened to encompass security, strategic, political and counter-terrorism realms, as well as defence collaboration. This is in addition to furthering economic ties, which were the primary focus of the LEP.

Collaboration to curb terrorism has become a priority, especially considering the rising strength and influence of the Islamic State. Defence partnerships with several ASEAN states, particularly Singapore[15] and Vietnam,[16,17] have progressed, after high-level bilateral visits in the last two years. The AEP has sought to significantly expand its geographical coverage to include other countries in East Asia, like Japan, Australia, Fiji and other Pacific Island nations, South Korea, and Mongolia.

India's strategic engagement with its Asia-Pacific partners reflects both its competition with China, and its ambitions for a greater global role. It is in India's interest to see a multipolar order in Asia, but India's motivation for engaging with the region exists independently of its relationship with China. India has shown a desire for a greater role in Asia, including as a security provider.

India under Prime Minister Modi has established a Special Strategic Partnership with Japan and strategic partnerships with South Korea and the Philippines. India also has a strong and traditional Strategic Partnership with Vietnam where defence and security relationships are being substantially being reinforced.

Of these, India's partnership with Japan has witnessed the most dynamic growth. Several path-breaking and historic steps have been taken to energise bilateral ties, particularly the decision taken by Japan—the only country in the world to have suffered a nuclear attack—to sign a civilian nuclear deal for commerce in nuclear technology and equipment with India on 14 December 2015.

Modi has sought to establish or rejuvenate ties with countries that India has not focused on in recent years. For example, he visited Australia in November 2014, the first visit by an Indian Prime Minister to that country after 28 years; his visit to Fiji in the same month was the first in 33 years; and his visit to Mongolia in May 2015 marked the first ever by an Indian Prime Minister.

Modi has also worked on developing normal ties with China by hosting President Xi Jinping in September 2014 and paying a reciprocal visit in May 2015. It is a matter of some satisfaction that no cross-border incursions by Chinese forces have taken place after September 2014, when Modi delivered a strong message to Xi during his visit to India.

On China's disputatious claim of a large track of the South China Sea, India has firmly articulated its principled position of freedom of navigation, maritime security, and expeditious resolution of disputes according to provisions of international law (the UN Convention on Law of the Seas, 1982), developing a Code of Conduct, and settlement through dialogue and peaceful means. India is especially concerned because more than 40 per cent of its trade traverses through the South China Sea[18] and it also has interests in harnessing the fossil resources in this region. India participated in a naval exercise in South China Sea.

US and 11 other Pacific Rim Nations concluded negotiations on the Trans-Pacific Partnership Agreement.[19] India has expressed its interest in concluding the talks on the Regional Comprehensive Economic Partnership (RCEP)[20] Agreement during 2016. The RCEP, along with the implementation of the free trade agreement on investment and services between ASEAN and India, will boost the economic development of all member countries.

According to Bruce Riedel at Brookings, a long time South Asia expert, "This past January, when President Barack Obama traveled to India to watch the Republic Day parade in New Delhi with Prime Minister Narendra Modi, the Pakistani Chief of Army Staff General Raheel Sharif, the country's strong man, was in China meeting his counterparts. The geopolitics of Asia was on vivid display. The region's dual axes and their evolving relationships—India and America on the one hand, and Pakistan and China on the other—will be central to the global order in our times."

During US President Barack Obama's visit to India as the chief guest at the Republic Day celebrations in January 2015, Modi said, "For too long India and the US have looked at each other across Europe and the Atlantic. When I look towards the East, I see the Western shores of the United States."[21] By aligning India's Act East Policy with the US's 'pivot' to Asia through a Joint Strategic Vision, India seeks to expand its manoeuvrability and geo-strategic space. This will help India to counter the growing assertiveness of, as well as foster balanced relations with, China.

Link West

"Look west", a new invention by Modi, explains much about India's new approach of flexing its muscle and showing to the world that recognising India as a great power in the region, and in the world, has become inevitable. India's stakes are rising and, like all other great powers, it should also have legitimate interests in all parts of the world. In this regard, India is now focusing on the Middle East. It is important to mention that India has always referred to itself as a country of "West Asia", even if it does not exist there.

No country can disregard the strategic importance of the Middle East, including India. However, previous regimes in India showed their unwillingness to attach importance to the region. India's relations with South East Asia and the Middle East were never symmetrical. In the case of the former, India could easily take new initiatives supported by domestic politics. On the contrary, India's relations with Middle Eastern countries have never been too warm because of the ideological affiliation of the Middle East towards Islam and its closer link with Pakistan. Also, India's warmer relations with Israel were an obstacle while engaging closely with that part of the world.

Modi has signalled that India is willing to expand its ties with Israel. In this regard, he met US Jewish leaders and Israeli Prime Minister Benjamin Netanyahu during his visit to the US. If no obstacles are seen, he may become the first Indian prime minister to visit Israel. Here is the complication. Arab history shows that having a closer relationship with Israel means increased hostility with Arab countries. Modi is aware of such complications and, at the same time, he knows India's stakes in the Middle East that range from energy security to counterterrorism. It is the understanding of this complication that translates into Modi focusing more on the Middle East while adopting an independent policy vis-à-vis Israel and the Arab countries. On the other hand, both Israel and the Arab countries also want to build a stronger and deeper relationship with India.

Modi's invention of the "link west" policy is aimed at addressing India's legitimate interests in the region. At the same time, it needs to be cautious about the new sectarian divide in the region—a deep cleavage between the Sunnis and Shias, particularly after the Syrian civil war and the rise of the Islamic State of Iraq and Syria (ISIS).

India's 'Connect Central Asia' Policy

A significant reason for India's move to engage more closely with the Central Asian region is geostrategic. The need to boost India's energy security in the backdrop of abundance of natural resources like hydrocarbons and uranium in the region and the growing threat of extremist outfits like the ISIS too has prompted India to seek deeper engagement with the five "Stans". **India was able to counter** China's "One Belt, One Road" initiative that envisages connectivity via rail, road and sea. India was worried with the "belt" taking within its swathe Central Asia too. Modi pushed for "North South Transport Corridor". The proposed "corridor" aims to reduce the cargo transportation time and transactions cost among India, Central Asia and Russia. And also bypass Gwadar Port in Pakistan. The North South Corridor reduces the distance to sea port for the countries of the region for trade.

Indian Ocean Outreach

Unlike the rhetoric of the past, the Modi government truly perceives the Indian Ocean as India's "immediate and extended neighbourhood", vital for its security and for which India must assume a degree of responsibility in shaping its future. Modi's four-pronged vision for the region was unveiled during his visit to Mauritius last month. This focuses on defending India's maritime territory and interests; deepening economic and security cooperation with maritime neighbours and island states; promoting collective action for peace and security; and seeking a more integrated and cooperative future for sustainable development.

Prime Minister Modi's vision for Indian Ocean, as captured in acronym SAGAR, or security and growth of all in the region, encapsulates India's approach to broader Indo-Pacific region. We are not only committed to safeguard India's land and maritime territories and interest but will also make our capabilities available to other regional countries. Humanitarian assistance and disaster relief, or HADR, is a major focus of our efforts. The evacuation of citizens of a number of countries from Yemen, post-earthquake efforts in Nepal and the assistance provided to Sri Lanka as the first responder following recent floods are a few examples.

Collective action and cooperation is the way forward to deal with maritime threats like terrorism, piracy and natural disasters. This will also improve trust and confidence and reduce the scope for military competition. India is contributing actively to the Regional Cooperation Agreement on Combating Piracy and Armed Robbery against Ships in Asia. In Singapore, India has also projects on safety and security of navigation as a part of Strait of Malacca mechanism.

Economic Diplomacy

Reading between the lines, the manifesto clearly prioritised economic development: "Comprehensive national security is not just about borders, but in its broad terms includes military security; economic security; cyber security; energy, food and water and health security; and social cohesion and harmony. To effectively address the issues of national security, we need to address the issues of human resources, science and technology, system of governance and money."

A hallmark of Mr Modi's foreign policy is his stress on economic diplomacy, which he does through actively promoting his government's 'Make in India' initiative, and assuring the foreign governments and the top corporates of ease of doing business in India.

Modi's signature economic initiatives are projects: "Smart cities" embody the dream of India's economy surging to an electronically powered boom. "Make in India" captures the vision of a resurgent Indian manufacturing sector, propelled more by capacity building and incentives than by fresh import restrictions. Infrastructure is very concrete—and creates things made of concrete, capable of being photographed. As part of the 'Make in India' initiative, the Prime Minister has urged foreign governments to participate in India's railways sector, in manufacturing, infrastructure, defence, smart cities, urban planning and other sectors. He has also been seeking active participation of foreign countries in his government's other initiatives like Digital India, Skill India, Clean Ganga Mission, Swachch Bharat Mission and Renewable Energy.

Soft Power

Modi speaks of India's vibrant democracy, its "unity in diversity" ethos, not only as the indispensable ingredient for governing its remarkably complex society, but as the necessary path toward greater peace and coexistence in the world; a world which would allow his country to achieve sustainable levels of development and prosperity. Its traditional style of democracy promotion emphasises leading by example, not preaching to others; listening to local demands and waiting to be asked for assistance; avoiding the appearance of bullying its smaller neighbours.

Under the banner of India's 'Look East'/'Act East' policy, Modi has used culture to appeal to the peoples of Asia. Much of this has been through Buddhism, which more than any other region or philosophy connects all of Asia. This year, India hosted the International Buddha Poornima Diwas, a global celebration of Buddha's birth, enlightenment and passing. The decision to host was initiated by Modi who led the prayers on the day. Modi stated "without Buddha, this century cannot be Asia's century".

As a devout Hindu, Modi is not shy about preaching the virtues of what he considers not a religion but a way of life that encompasses all societies, a philosophy that teaches, "all should be happy, all should be healthy, all should live life to the fullest," as quoted by Modi in his May 8, TIME Magazine interview. As India succeeds at home, "we increase our ability to help our friends," he told the Mongolian parliament in his address on May 17. "This is the urge of the land of Buddha and Gandhi. This is the instinct born from our ancient belief in the world as one family." He proceeded to connect Buddha's message of kindness and compassion for all to the foundational principles of democracy and human rights as an ancient common heritage that will unite Asia around peace and cooperation.

Prime Minister Narendra Modi has invented a new concept in diplomacy, 'spiritual neighbourhood'. Addressing the Great Hural, the Mongolian Parliament, the Prime Minister affirmed, "I bring the greetings of your 1.25 billion spiritual neighbours. There is no higher form of a relationship; no bonds more sacred than this."

Internal Security

In the Arthashastra, Kautilya wrote that a state could be at risk from four types of threats—internal, external, externally-aided internal and internally-aided external. He advised that of these four types, internal threats should be taken care of immediately, which are far more serious than external threats. The most dangerous enemy is the enemy within.

Indian Prime Minister defined the largest challenges facing India at the beginning of 2010—"Terrorism, Naxalism, Communalism, Corruption and

Regionalism", which can also be attributed as the various internal threats haunting the country. India is experiencing internal security problems due to insurgency movements, ethnic conflicts, religious fundamentalism or cussed political polarisation.

Nation cannot be secured unless its internal security is also ensured. A nation in chaos cannot be secured from external threats. Internal strife and disorder can damage national interests, endanger the lives of citizens, lead to breakdown of law and order, make enforcement of laws difficult and the country more vulnerable to external threats. In such a state, society cannot progress smoothly nor can citizens feel secured.

India's stability is gravely impinging on her internal law and order situation. Manifestations of threat range from communal/sectarian violence to Jihadi terrorism, separatist insurgencies in northeast and Naxalite extremist militancy. A new report from US has revealed that besides persistent and significant external threats from groups like Pakistan's Lashkar-e-Taeba and Jaish-e-Mohammad and Bangladesh's Harakat-ul-Jihad-i-Islami-Bangladesh, India faces numerous attacks from domestic terror outfits. Naxalism, synonymous with Left Wing Extremism, has come to pose the single biggest threat to India's internal security.

Islamist fundamentalist organisations rooted in religious obscurantism have long been prone to sudden bursts of irrational violence at the slightest provocation. The Kashmir conflict and upsurge of the groups like Student Islamic Movement of India (SIMI), Harkat-ul-Jihad-ul-Islami Bangladesh (HUJBI), Jama'at-ul-Mujahideen Bangladesh (JMB), and Jama'at-e-Islami Bangladesh (JIB) is a glaring representation of a similar 'fundamentalist religious empowerment'. Such communal conflicts have resulted in tragic traumas and an intolerant atmosphere of hostility and hatred created by the terrorists, who bluff themselves as Jihadi—in the name of almighty Allah.

A disturbing factor is the ability of these hidden groups to mobilize resources, international linkages, up-gradation of weaponry, interlinking with different violent groups, access to sophisticated weapons and modern communication which make it difficult for the existing infrastructure of State's national security apparatus to match it.

Modi Government has taken a different course from previous Government, it decided to take punitive action on any action by terrorists in India. At first blush, deterrence would appear to offer the solution to this problem. A robust deterrent policy would make launching attacks against India prohibitively costly. As a result, terrorists and their sponsors would stop attempting to do so. Deterrence formed the bedrock of United States grand strategy during the Cold War. Could it offer a solution to one of the central problems facing contemporary Indian security policy? Only time will tell. But it has started taking effect.

Defence

The Parliamentary Standing Committee on Defence in 1997 requested that the government of India "examine the feasibility of preparing a formal National Defense Policy document for being placed before the government." In its second report (1996-97) it stated that "the committee was informed that there is no formal written document called India's Defense Policy...in the absence of any documents explaining articulated policy with stated national objectives and national interests, it was not possible for the policy to be analysed and modified." Outside the government, many independent analysts have written extensively on the need for a long-term national security strategy.[22] The Kargil Review Committee established in the aftermath of the Kargil War in 1999 also highlighted this issue.[23]

As long as there has been war, there have been efforts to deter actions a nation considers threatening. A logical approach is for the government to set out the aims of its external policies and to state unambiguously the political direction and commitments which it expects the armed forces to support. The defence planners would then process these together with appropriate intelligence inputs to determine the shape and size of the armed forces, which could meet these commitments.

Modi at very first instance brought in Mr M Parikkar to head the Defence Ministry. Indian Defence Forces were highly demotivated, the major issue involved (i) *corruption*—Agusta helicopter deal—there was a deal of 12 Agusta Westland-101 helicopters for a price of Rs. 4,600 crore. An Italian investigation found out that bribes amounting to Rs. 427 Crore could have been paid to middlemen. General VK Singh then COAS alleged that massive bribes have been paid to some politicians for procuring Tatra army trucks. (ii) *Mishaps/Accidents*: IAF had over 100 accidents in the Indian Air Force took place in last 8 years. A mishap took place INS Sindhuratna—which claimed the lives of two officers. It was primarily due lack of availability of batteries. (iii) Foreign Aggression: Numerous cease fire violations Pakistan, beheading of Indian soldiers, unprovoked aggression had taken place. However these were not being retaliated. Chinese People's Liberation Army (PLA) troops encroached 19 km into Indian Territory and stayed in India for three whole weeks. This was a very embarrassing situation for India. (iv) Unceremonious dumping of Head of the Defence forces: Gen VK Singh was not given his due as he targeted A K Antony and his people in corruption cases. Antony's ministry came up with some records that suggested that Singh was born in 1950. However, Gen VK Singh matriculation certificate suggested that he was born on 10 May 1951. The tussle turned ugly, reached no amicable solution and Singh was denied a graceful exit as also the Supreme Court ruling that for Government Jobs only date as per matriculation certificates was denied to him by the Government. Navy Chief Admiral DK Joshi took the onus of responsibility of the accident on board INS *Sindhuratna.* No one in the Ministry of Defence was taken to task. (v) The modernisation had suffered during the last decade and no Gun for artillery was procured for over 30 years.

India's lethargy in the defence sector had been noted in a report by the Brookings Institution that stated, "what suffices for a military modernisation plan is a wish list of weapon systems amounting to as much as $100 billion from the three services and hollow announcements of coming breakthroughs from the Defence Research and Development Organisation (DRDO), the premier agency for military research in India. The process is illustrative. The armed forces propose to acquire certain weapon systems. The political leadership and the civilian bureaucracy, especially the Ministry of Finance, react to these requests, agreeing on some and rejecting others. A number of dysfunctions ensue".

Another important issue of getting Parikkar must be the failure of DRDO to deliver. The DRDO has not been able to deliver anything in time. In spite of the fact that crores of Rupees have been spent nothing tangible is there to show. The Akash missile system for the army and navy is the case. It is total disaster.

The Modi government went in earnest to meet the demands of the Defence Forces, especially equipment. In more specific terms, the manifesto stated the party's commitment to "developing indigenous defense technologies and fast tracking of defense purchases" as well as making India "a global production platform for defense hardware manufacturing and software production". It welcomed foreign firms to establish production facilities in India.

Another much observed clause was the pledge to "revise and update" India's nuclear doctrine, something which most commentators thought meant that India would give up its critical "No First Use" doctrine.

Modi's biggest failure in Management of Defence is the failure of personnel policies. The Army has been demotivated. This is not the place to discuss in detail, but needless to say, the soldier has been cheated the maximum. He is compelled to retire at the age of 35-40 years after putting in 15 years of service. He was paid 70 percent of pay to compensate for his early exit. But Modi failed to rectify this although he promised to resolve the issue. Army has to keep its profile young if it has to fight in harsh conditions. The pay was protected, but Nehru and Indira destroyed the structure of pay by raising bureaucrat's pay and allowances. The bureaucrat's never are hauled up for failure to provide governance and the defence forces are compelled to retrieve situation. Kashmir and North East is burning and no bureaucrat ever gets hit by stone for his failures. Modi has proved that he is not a person who can be taken on his words as far national security is concerned. He is Nehru in disguise.

Conclusion

Modi changed the very concept and brought in ***Deterrence*** in Security policy. The concept of deterrence is deceptively simple. Deterrence is the use of conditional threats to convince an adversary not to take particular proscribed action. It seeks to preserve the status quo. It differs in this respect from compellence, which uses conditional threats to convince an adversary to take particular desired action, thereby altering the status quo. Both deterrence and compellence are subsets of coercion. Coercion uses conditional threats to convince an adversary to behave in a desired fashion, either continuing its current behaviour (deterrence), or altering its behaviour in some way (compellence).

Two types of deterrence exist: deterrence by denial and deterrence by punishment. Deterrence by denial prevents the enemy from achieving the benefit that he seeks, or makes doing so excessively costly and difficult. In essence, deterrence by denial threatens the enemy with a very good defence, and convinces him that successful attainment of his objective at a reasonable cost is extremely unlikely. Pakistan is feeling the heat of Deterrence by denial.

When dealing with Islamist militants, India lacks a number of the advantages that the US enjoyed during the Cold War. A successful terrorist attack requires only a handful of operatives to slip through India's security cordon. It is easy and cheap for terror organisations to continually deploy small numbers of personnel until they eventually succeed in doing so. Even repeated failure at the hands of Indian security services is unlikely to be prohibitively costly for terror groups. Thus, deterrence by denial is difficult for the Indians to achieve.

Deterrence by punishment, in contrast, does not seek to prevent the enemy from achieving his goals. Rather, it threatens to harm something that the enemy values in the event that he engages in particular proscribed behaviour, thereby making that behaviour prohibitively costly.

Deterrence succeeds when the adversary's expected cost from engaging in the proscribed activity (cost of deterrent threat ′ the likelihood of suffering that cost) exceeds the activity's expected benefit (benefit of proscribed activity ′ the likelihood of realizing that benefit). Simply put, deterrence will succeed if the adversary believes that engaging in the proscribed activity 'is not worth it.'

Deterrence by punishment is problematic as well. India does not generally know in advance the terrorists' identity and location, and thus cannot easily target them. In addition, since the terrorists are stateless actors and are willing to die for their cause, it is difficult to inflict high costs on them in retaliation for their attacks. What homeland can India threaten to devastate?

One potentially viable option would be for India to threaten to punish third-party supporters of the terrorists, rather than the terrorists themselves. Specifically, the Indians could warn the Pakistani government that if it allows any further attacks on India to be launched from its soil, India will retaliate directly against Pakistan. In theory, this would solve the problems of identity and location discussed above; India can be confident that the Pakistani government highly values its territory, and the Indians know precisely where that territory is located. Attacks on terrorist training camps in PoK, or pinprick strikes across the international border, are unlikely to be sufficient; even if India succeeds in hitting these targets, they are not sufficiently valuable to impose serious costs on Pakistan.

Recent Indian doctrinal innovation has attempted to operationalize this 'limited war' logic. For example, India's 'Cold Start' doctrine seeks to drive Indian armoured, infantry, and artillery forces into Pakistan within 72 to 96 hours of a mobilization order. The Indians' objective would be to attack Pakistani forces and to seize a long, shallow swathe of Pakistani territory—a swathe sufficiently large to seriously harm Pakistan, but not so large as to threaten the state's survival and trigger a nuclear response. The ability to threaten to inflict such costs could, in theory, help India to deter Pakistan from supporting further anti-Indian militancy.

Modi seems to be redefining the terms on which India is likely to engage with the world in the coming years. Pragmatism coupled with a more confident assertion of Indian interests is likely to be the hallmark. He is not shy about reaching out directly to new constituencies such as the Non-Resident Indian (NRI) and business communities in other states. For India's friends, a new outreach is in the offing. For India's adversaries, new red lines are being drawn.

On the security front, there is a new purposeful response against China with a focus on more efficient border management and defence acquisitions. Modi has reached out to the US, despite his personal grievances over a visa denial by Washington when he was the chief minister of Gujarat, and there is a refreshing focus on immediate neighbors. The manner in which evacuations from Iraq were handled earlier this year as the threat from the Islamic State gathered pace showed a government that is operationally well-prepared. The Modi government has been more hard-nosed about Pakistan and is not backing down in face of Pakistan's escalatory tactics. So the larger picture that is emerging is of a government that is not as risk averse as previous governments and will be willing to take risks should the need arise.

The bedrock of a nation's strength in contemporary global politics remains its economic strength. By putting the Indian story back into reckoning after callous mismanagement by its predecessor, the Modi government has shored up India's previously dwindling credibility. The fact that it has been able to do this despite an obstructionist opposition is even more remarkable. For all the disruption of the Parliament by the Congress Party, the image of a business-minded Modi government remains intact for the outside world.

Modi is following the Realist international discourse built on the principle of give and take and, as the adage goes, there are no free lunches. Each country ruthlessly pursues its national interest and if other states get in the way, they find ways of winning them over, neutralising them or punishing them. Kautilyan injunctions call for pitilessly using *saam* (suasion), *daam* (purchase), *dand* (punishment) and *bhed* (division) as the ways of getting on in the real world.

Modi is perusing a rational choice: in which social actors, in seeking to realise their value-derived interests, will choose whatever means are made available by the prevailing democratic order. If thwarted, they will rethink their values, redefine their interests, and choose new means to realise them ... The ontology is not materialistic: values shape interests, and values include many nonmaterial elements.

ENDNOTES

1. Thpliyal, Maj Gen Sheru (2009), 'India's Foreign Policy: A Muddle for Sixty Two Years,' *Indian Defence Review.*
2. Crocker, Walter (2009), *Nehru: A Contemporary Estimate,* (Random House India).
3. It could be described as underbalancing in realist terms. For a discussion of this concept, see Randall L. Schweller, *Unanswered Threats: Political Constraints on the Balance of Power* (Princeton, NJ: Princeton University Press, 2006).
4. Hanhimaki, Jussi M. (2004), *The Flawed Architect: Henry Kissinger and American Foreign Policy* (Oxford University Press).
5. Cashman, G., Robinson, L.C. (2007), *An Introduction to the Causes of War: Patterns of Interstate Conflict from World War I to Iraq,* (Rowman & Littlefield).
   Rao, RVR Chandrashekhar (1973), Indo-Soviet Economic Relations: *Asian Survey,* Vol. 13, No. 8. (Aug., 1973), pp. 793-801, University of California Press,
6. Ollapally, Deepa and Rajesh Rajagopalan (2011), "The Pragmatic Challenge to Indian Foreign Policy," *The Washington Quarterly* 34, Issue 2 (Spring 2011).
7. http://en.wikipedia.org/wiki/Hindu_rate_of_growth
8. Bhartiya Janta Party, its Election Manifesto of 2014, extracts of Policy on Foreign Relations. Foreign Relations—Nation First, Universal Brotherhood.

   BJP believes a resurgent India must get its rightful place in the comity of nations and international institutions. The vision is to fundamentally reboot and reorient the foreign policy goals, content and process, in a manner that locates India's global strategic engagement in a new paradigm and on a wider canvass, that is not just limited to political diplomacy, but also includes our economic, scientific, cultural, political and security interests, both regional and global, on the principles of equality and mutuality, so that it leads to an economically stronger India, and its voice is heard in the international fora.

   BJP believes that political stability, progress and peace in the region are essential for south Asia's growth and development. The Congress-led UPA has failed to establish enduring friendly and cooperative Foreign Relations—relations with India's neighbours. India's relations with traditional allies have turned cold. India and its neighbours have drifted apart. Instead of clarity, we have seen confusion. The absence of statecraft has never been felt so acutely as today. India is seen to be floundering, whereas it should have been engaging with the world with confidence. The collapse of the Indian economy has contributed to the sorry state of foreign affairs in no small measure.

We will build a strong, self-reliant and self-confident India, regaining its rightful place in the comity of nations. In this, we will be firstly guided by our centuries old tradition of ***Vasudeva Kuttamba***. At the same time, our foreign policy will be based on best National interests. We will create a web of allies to mutually further our interests. We will leverage all our resources and people to play a greater role on the international high table.

India has long failed to duly appreciate the full extent and gamut of its ***soft power*** potential. There is a need to integrate our soft power avenues into our external interchange, particularly, harnessing and focusing on the spiritual, cultural and philosophical dimensions of it. India has always played a major role in world affairs, offering a lot to the World. This has been its tradition since time immemorial. The magnetic power of India has always been in its ancient **wisdom** and **heritage**, elucidating principles like **harmony** and **equity**. This continues to be equally relevant to the world today in today's times of Soft power. We will adopt ***Proactive Diplomacy*** to spread the same. India was reckoned not only as Vishwaguru but also a vibrant trading society. Our ancestors used to trade with foreign nations through the routes of sea, centuries ago. This was based on the strength of our business acumen and integrity, our products and crafts. The symbols of our ancient civilisations stand as a testimony to our architectural and urban planning excellence. We will revive **Brand India** with the help of our strengths of **5-T's: Tradition, Talent, Tourism, Trade and Technology**.

Guiding Principles of our Foreign Policy will be:

- Equations will be mended through pragmatism and a doctrine of mutually beneficial and interlocking relationships, based on enlightened national interest.
- We will champion uniform international opinion on issues like Terrorism and Global Warming.
- Instead of being led by big power interests, we will engage proactively on our own with countries in the neighbourhood and beyond.
- In our neighbourhood we will pursue friendly relations. However, where required we will not hesitate from taking strong stand and steps.
- We will work towards strengthening Regional forums like SAARC and ASEAN.
- We will continue our dialogue, engagement and cooperation, with global forums like BRICS, G20. IBSA, SCO and ASEM. States will be encouraged to play a greater role in diplomacy; actively building relations with foreign countries to harness their mutual cultural and commercial strengths.

Also,

- We will expand and empower our pool of diplomats, ensuring our message is taken to the world and our great nation represented on the whole in a befitting manner.
- The NRIs, PIOs and professionals settled abroad are a vast reservoir to articulate the national interests and affairs globally. This resource will be harnessed for strengthening Brand India.
- India shall remain a natural home for persecuted Hindus and they shall be welcome to seek refuge here.

9. Maioran, Diego (2015), 'Early Trends and Prospects for Modi's Prime Ministership', *The International Spector,* Vol 50, No 2.
10. Ibid.
11. Indian Press Information Bureau, Prime Minister's Office "*PM to Heads of Indian Missions,*" press release, February 7, 2015, http://pib.nic.in/newsite/PrintRelease.aspx?relid=115241.

12. Subrahmanyam Jaishankar, "IISS Fullerton Lecture by Dr. S. Jaishankar, Foreign Secretary in Singapore" (speech presented at the International Institute for Strategic Studies, (Singapore, July 20, 2015).
13. Subrahmanyam Jaishankar, "IISS Fullerton Lecture."
14. Chand, Manish, *Act East: India's ASEAN Journey*, Ministry of External Affairs, Government of India, 10 November 2014, http://www.mea.gov.in/in-focus-article.htm?24216/Act+East+Indias+ASEAN+Journey
15. Ministry of External Affairs, Government of India, *Joint Statement on a Strategic Partnership between India and Singapore*, 24 November 2015, http://www.mea.gov.in/bilateral-documents.htm?dtl/26060/Joint+Statement+on+a+Strategic+Partnership+between+ India+ and+Singapore+Renewed+Spirit+New+Energy+++++November+24+2015
16. Ministry of External Affairs, Government of India, *Joint Statement on the State Visit of Prime Minister of the Socialist Republic of Vietnam to India*, 28 October 2014, http://mea.gov.in/incoming-visit-detail.htm?24142/Joint+Statement+on+the+State+Visit+of+Prime+Minister+of+the+ Socialist+Republic+of+Vietnam+to+India+October+2728+2014
17. President of India, Government of India, *Joint Communiqué Between The Socialist Republic Of Vietnam And The Republic Of India*, 15 September 2014, http://www.presidentofindia.nic.in/press-release-detail.htm?1105
18. Ministry of External Affairs, Government of India, speech by Foreign Secretary at National Maritime Foundation on *'India as a Consensual Stakeholder in the Indian Ocean: Policy Contours'*, 19 November 2010, http://www.mea.gov.in/Speeches-Statements.htm?dtl/816/
19. The twelve nations that negotiated the TPP are the U.S., Japan, Australia, Peru, Malaysia, Vietnam, New Zealand, Chile, Singapore, Canada, Mexico, and Brunei Darussalam.
    What Is the Trans-Pacific Partnership Agreement (TPP)?
    The Trans-Pacific Partnership (TPP) is a secretive, multinational trade agreement that threatens to extend restrictive intellectual property (IP) laws across the globe and rewrite international rules on its enforcement. The main problems are two-fold:
    (1) **Digital Policies that Benefit Big Corporations at the Expense of the Public:** The IP chapter would have extensive negative ramifications for users' freedom of expression, right to privacy and due process, as well as hindering peoples' abilities to innovate. Other chapters of the agreement encourage your personal data to be sent borders with limited protection for your privacy, and allow foreign corporations to sue countries for laws or regulations that promote the public interest,
    (2) **Lack of Transparency**: The entire process has shut out multi-stakeholder participation and is shrouded in secrecy.
    The TPP contains a chapter on intellectual property covering copyright, trademarks, and patents. The official release of the final TPP text confirmed what we had long feared: that U.S. negotiators pushed for the adoption of copyright measures far more restrictive than currently required by international treaties, including the controversial Anti-Counterfeiting Trade Agreement (ACTA).
20. It will bring ten ASEAN countries and other six countries (China, Japan, South Korea, India, Australia and New Zealand) together. These six members have FTAs with the ASEAN currently. If it materializes, it is supposed to be one of the most vital free-trade blocs in the world; the combined geo-political resources would put the grouping into a totally different league, making it the most important economic grouping of the world.
21. Press Information Bureau, Government of India, *Text of Remarks by Prime Minister at the India-U.S. Business Summit*, 26 January 2015, http://pib.nic.in/newsite/PrintRelease.aspx?relid=114960

22. See Brahma Chellaney, "Challenges to India's National Security in the New Millennium," in Brahma Chellaney (ed.), *Securing India's Future in the New Millennium* (New Delhi: Orient Longman, 1999) pp.583-588; Kapil Kak, "Directions of Higher Defence-II," *Strategic Analysis,* July 1998; Gurmeet Kanwal, "India's National Security Strategy in a Nuclear Environment," *Strategic Analysis,* December 2000, pp.1591-1628.
23. See *From Surprise to Reckoning: The Kargil Review Committee Report* (New Delhi: Sage, 2000).

BIBLIOGRAPHY

Abbinski, Henry (1997), *'Australia and The Indian Ocean'*, International Conference on Indian Ocean Studies, held in August 1977 at Perth.

Adler, E. (1997), "Seizing the middle ground: Constructivism in world politics," *European Journal of International Relations* 3(3).

Adler, E., Nad Barnett, M. (1998), 'Security Communities in Theoretical Perspective', in Adler and Barnett (Eds.) *Security Communities* (Cambridge: Cambridge University Press).

Adler, E., Nad Barnett, M. (Eds.) (1998), *Security Communities* (Cambridge: Cambridge University Press).

Agnew, J. (1987), *Place and Politics: the geographical mediation of state and society* (London: Allen and Unwin)

____ (1993), Representing space: space, scale and culture in social science. In Duncan J. and Ley, D., *Place/culture/representation* (London and New York: Routledge).

____ (1994), "The territorial trap: the geographical assumptions of international relations theory." *Review of International Political Economy*, 1, pp. 53-80.

Agnew, John A, and Duncan James S. (Eds) (1989), *The Power of Place* (Boston: Unwin Hyman).

Allison, Graham and Gregory F. Treverton (eds.), (1992), *Rethinking America's Security: Beyond Cold War to New World Order* (New York).

Amnesty International (1998), A Human Rights Crisis in Kosovo Province: The Protection of Kosovo's Displaced and Refugees, http://www.amnesty.org.

____, (2000), Kosovo: 'Collateral Damage' or Unlawful Killings? http://www.amnesty.org.

Anonymous (2004), *Imperial Hubris: Why the West is Losing the War on Terror* (Washington, DC: Brassey's).

Archer, C. (1983), *International Organizations* (Routledge)

Arif, K. (Ed.) (1984), *Documents on China-Pakistan Relations* (Lahore: Vanguard Books).

Aron, Raymond (1958), *War and Industrial Society* (Oxford: Oxford University Press).

Atlantic Council, (2009), *Needed: A Comprehensive U.S. Policy Toward Pakistan*, Report of Task Force co-chaired by former Senator Chuck Hagel of Nebraska and Senator John Kerry of Massachusetts (Washington, DC: The Atlantic Council, February 2009).

Auspitz, Josiah Lee (1976), "Individuality, Civility, and Theory: The Philosophical Imagination of Michael Oakeshott," *Political Theory* 4 (August), pp. 261-352

Ayesha Siddiqa, "Terror's Training Ground," *Newsline*, September 9, 2009

Ayoob, Mohammed (2000/2001), "*Nuclear India and Indian-American ... US Policy and Asian Security*," *Survival* 42:4 (Winter 2000/2001), pp. *51-71*

Azar, E. and Chung in Moon (eds.), (1988), 'National Security in the Third World: The Management of Internal and External Threats' (University Press, Cambridge)

Baev, Pavel K. (2008), Sad Wisdom of Hindsight: Soviet intervention in Afghanistan (1979-89), in: Bernard, Cheryl et al. (ed.), *Afghanistan: State and Society, Great Power, Politics and the Way Ahead* (Santa Monica: RAND), pp. 37-45

Bailer, Seweryn (1986), *The Soviet paradox: External Expansion, Internal Decline* (London: I.B. Tauris & Co Ltd.)

Bajpai, Kanti and Stephen P. Cohen (1994), 'Cooperative Security and South Asian Insecurity', in Janne E. Nolan (ed.), *'Global Engagement: Cooperation and Security in the 21st Century'*, (Washington D.C.: The Brookings Institute).

Baldwin, D.A. (1995), 'Security Studies and the End of the Cold War', *World Politics*, vol. 48, no. 1, pp. 117-41.

Banerjee, Sumanta (1995), "Mao and the Indian Communist Movement," *China Report* 31 (1), pp. 37-66

Barnett, Michael N., and Martha Finnemore (1999). The politics, power, and pathologies of international organizations. *International Organization* 53(4): pp. 699–732

Bateman, S. and Bergin, A. (2010), *Our Western Front: Australia and the Indian Ocean*, Barton, ACT: ASPI.

Bates, D.G. abdPlog, F. (1990), *Cultural Anthropology* (New York).

Bauman, Zygmunt (1990), *Modernity and the Holocaust* (Cambridge: Polity).

Bercher, Micheal (1993), *The New States of Asia* (London: Oxford).

Berger, Thomas (2000), 'Set for stability? Prospects for conflict and cooperation in East Asia', *Review of International Studies*, 26, 3, 2000, 405-28,

Behuria, Ashok, Smruti Pattakaik & Arvind Gupta (2012), 'Does India have a Neighbourhood Policy' *Strategic Analysis*, Vol. 12, No. 3 (July-September), pp 233-240.

Bellany, I. (1981), Towards a Theory of International Security', *Political Studies,* vol. 29, no. 1.

Berridge G.R. and James, Alan (2003), *A Dictionary of Diplomacy* (Hampshire, UK: Palgrave Macmillan), p. 180.

Bernard, Cheryl (2008), The next Afghanistan, in: Bernard, Cheryl et al., (ed.), *Afghanistan: State and Society, Great Power, Politics and the Way Ahead* (Santa Monica: RAND), pp. 47-53.

Bhagwatiu, Jagdish (2004), *In Defence of Globalization* (New York: Oxford University Press), p. 204.

Bhargava, Rajeev (Ed.) (1999), *Secularism and Its Critics* (New Delhi: Oxford University Press).

Bhalla, Abhishek (2016), 'Pathankot attack: Drug Cartels – India officials' nexus under scanner *Mail Today* (January 6, 2016) (New Delhi)

Bhola, P.L. (1986), *Pakistan-China Relations* (Jaipur: R.B.S.A. Publishers).

Bhutto, Zulfiquar Ali (1969), *The Myth of Independence* (Lahore: Oxford University Press)

Blank, S. (2005), *Natural Allies, Regional Security in Asia and Prospects for Indo-American Strategic Cooperation* (Carlisle: Strategic Studies Institute),

Blarel, Nicolas (2012), "India's Soft Power: From Potential to Reality?", *IDEAS Reports – Special Reports,* Kitchen, Nicholas (ed.), SR010. *LSE IDEAS* (London: London School of Economics and Political Science)

Blechman, Barry M. and Stephen S. Kaplan (1978), *'Force Without War: United States Armed Forces as a Political Instrument'* (Washington DC: The Brookings Institution).

Blustein, Paul (2009). *Misadventures of the Most Favored Nations: Clashing Egos, Inflated Ambitions, and the Great Shambles of the World Trade System* (New York: Public Affairs)

Bock, P.G. and Berkowitz, Morton (1966), 'The Emerging Field of National Security', *World Politics,* 19..

Booth, Ken (1987), 'New challenges and old *mind-sets*: ten rules for empirical realists', in Carl G. Jacobsen (ed.), *The Uncertain Course: New Weapons, Strategies and Mind-Sets* (Oxford: Oxford University Press/SIPRI), pp. *39-66.*

____ (1991), 'Security and Emancipation', *Review of International Studies,* 17, pp. 313–26

____ (2007), *Theory of World Security* (Cambridge: Cambridge University Press).

Booth, K., and Wheeler, N. (2008), *The Security Dilemma – Fear, Cooperation and Trust in World Politics* (New York: Palgrave Macmillan),

Brodie, Bernard (1973), *War and Politics* (New York)

Boyd, R.G. 'The Strategic Significance of the Malacca Straits: Report of the

Department of National Defense Canada', reproduced in *'Strategic Digest',* September 1977 (New Delhi: IDSA)

Brown, Judith (1999), *Nehru* (New York: Longman), p. 268

Brown, Lester (1977), *Redefining National Security,* Worldwatch Paper No. 14 (Washington, DC, 1977).

Banerjee, Sumanta (1995), "Mao and the Indian Communist Movement," *China Report* 31 (1) 1995, pp. 37-66

Basrur (ed.) Rajesh M. (2001), *South Asian Security, Security in the New Millennium: Views from South Asia* (Colombo: Regional Center for Strategic Studies).

Bull, Hedley (1971), *"The Anarchical Society: A Study of Order in World Politics"* (Macmillan Press, Melbourne), p.18.

Bull, Hedley (1995), *The Anarchical Society. A Study of Order in World Politics.* 2nd edn. (Houndsmills: Macmillan);

Buncombe, A. (2008): India lashes out at old enemy, in: The Independent, http://www.independent.co.uk/news/world/asia/india-lashes-out-at-old-enemy-1042720.html

Bureau of International Narcotics and Law Enforcement Affairs, "2011 INCSR: Countries Reports: Afghanistan through Costa Rica," March 3, 2011, *www.state.gov/j/inl/rls/nrcrpt/2011/vol1/156359.htm*

Burke, Jason (2003), *Al-Qaeda: Casting a Shadow of Terror* (London: I. B. Tauris).

Buzan, Barry (1983), *'People, States and Fear: The National Security Problem in International Relations',* (Sussex: Wheatsheaf Books)

____ (1991), *People, States and Fear: An Agenda for International Security Studies in the Post-Cold War Era, 2nd Edition* (Boulder, CO)

____ (1996), "International Society and International Security", in Rick Fawn & Jeremy Larkins (eds.) *International Society after the Cold War. Anarchy and Order Reconsidered* (Houndsmills: Macmillan), pp. 261-287

Buzan, Barry and Weaver Ole (2003), *Regions and Power: The Structure of International Security* Cambridge: Cambridge University Press)

Callard, Keith (1957), Pakistan: A Political Study (New York)

Campbell, David (1998), *Writing Security: United States Foreign Policy and the Politics of Identity* (Minneapolis: University of Minnesota Press).

Carlsnaes, Walter, Thomas Risse, and Beth Simmons (Ed.) (2002), *Handbook of International Relations* (Thousand Oaks, CA: Sage Publications)

Cerny, P.G. (1990), *The Changing Architecture of Politics: Structure, Agency, and the Future of the State* (London: Sage Publications.

Chamling, Dhiraj R. (1978), *India and United Nations'* (New Delhi: Associated Publishing House).

Chandershekar Rao, PVR (1985), 'Regional Co-Operation in South Asia', *The Round Table,* No. 293, January 1985, pp. 53-65

Chant, Colin (1999), Pre-Industrial Cities and Technology (London: Routledge)

Chadda, Maya (1997), *Ethnicity, Security, and Separatism in India* (New York: Columbia University Press).

Chandershekar Rao, PVR (1985), *'Regional Co-operation in South Asia',* The Round Table, No. 293, pp. 53-65,

Chatterjee, P. (1972), The Classical Balance of Power Theory, *Journal of Peace Research*, March 9:51-61

Chapman, D. and N. Khanna (2004), *The Persian Gulf, Global Oil Resources, and International Security* (Working Paper no 419), (Binghamton, NY: Department of Economics, Binghamton University)

Chinmaya, R. Gharekhan (20070 'India and The United Nations', in Atish Sinha and Madhup Mohta eds., *Indian Foreign policy: Challenges and Opportunities* (New Delhi: academic Foundation).

Chipman, John (1991), 'Third World Politics and Security in the 1990's: The World Forgetting. By the World Forgot'. *The Washington Quarterly*, No 14 (Winter 1991)

Chritopher, Warren (1993), "The CSCE Vission: European Security Rooted in Shared values," Statement to the Plenary Session of Conference on Security and Cooperation in Europe, Rome, Novemeber 30, 1993, as quoted in Mearsheimer, John J. (1994/95), 'The False Promise of International Institutions', *International Security,* Winter 1994/95, Vol 19, No 3, pp. 5-49

CIRS (Center for International and Regional Studies) (2009), *International Relations of the Gulf* (Report of Working Group 1), (Doha: CIRS)

Cohen, Saul Bernard (1964), *'Geography and Politics in The Divided World'* (London: Methun).

Cohen, Stephen P. (2001), *India: Emerging Power* (Washington, D.C.: Brookings Institution Press).

Collins, A. (ed.) (2007), *Contemporary Security Studies* (New York: Oxford University Press).

Condoleezza Rice, 'A balance of power that favors freedom', 1 October 2002, http://www.manhattaninstitute.org/html/w12002.htm, accessed 17 Jun 2012.

Constituent Assembly Debates, Vol. 2, Part II, 8 March 1949.

Cordner, L. (2011). "Progressing Maritime Security Cooperation in the Indian Ocean Region," *Naval College War Review* 64(4), pp. 68-88.

Cornell, Svante E. (2002), *Small Nations and Great Powers: A Study of Ethnopolitical Conflict in the Caucasus* (Richmond: Curzon Caucasus World).

Craig, Mary (1992), *Tears of Blood: A Cry of Tibet* (Harper Collins)

CSIS (Center for Strategic and International Studies) (2007), *The United States, India, and the Gulf: Convergence or Divergence in a Post-Iraq World* (Report of the Persian Gulf Initiative Workshop), (Washington, DC: CSIS.)

Curcio, Karly, "Corruption in India Stifles Economic Growth, Fosters Violence Against Whistleblowers," September 13, 2010, www.financialtaskforce.org/2010/09/13/corruption-in-india-stifles-economic-growthfosters-violence-against-whistleblowers/

Curnings, Bruce (1995), *Divided Korea: United Future??* (New York: Foreign Policy Association).

Curtis, L. et al (2011), *Shared Goals, Converging Interests: A Plan for US-Australia-India Cooperation in the Indo-Pacific*, Washington DC: Heritage Foundation, Department of Defense (2009).

Danielou, Alain (2003), *A Brief History of India* (Rochester, Vermont: Inner Traditions).

Datta-Ray, Sunanda K (2002), *Waiting for America: India and the United States in the New Millennium* (New Delhi: HarperCollins,).

DeBlij, H.J., and Muller, Peter (1985), *Geography Realms, Regions, and Concepts* (New York, NY: Wiley and Sons INC

Desai, Morarji (1974), *The Story of My Life*, Vol. II (New Delhi: S. Chand), pp. 171-72

Deutsch, K. W., D. Singer (1964), "Multipolar Power Systems and International Stability" *World Politics,* Vol. 16, No. 3 (April), pp. 390-406.

Deese, David A. (1994), *'The New Politics of American Foreign Policy'* (New York: St. Martin's Press).

Diehl, Paul F. (1991), "Geography and War: A Review and Assessment of the Empirical Literature," *International Interactions* 17: pp. 11-27

____ (1999), *A Road Map to War* (Nashville: Vanderbilt University Press).

Dikshit, R.D. (2006), *Political Geography: The Spirituality of Politics,* 9th Edition (new Delhi: Tata McGraw-Hill Publishing Company Ltd).

Dixit, J.N. (2002), *India-Pakistan in War and Peace* (London: Routledge).

D'Souza, Shanthie Mariet and Jetley Rajshree (Eds.) (2013), *Perspectives on South Asian Security* (London: World Scientific Publishing Co. Pvt. Ltd.)

Downs, George W. (ed.) *Collective Security Beyond the Cold War* (Ann Arbor: University of Michigan Press).

Doyle, T. (2011), 'Building Indian Ocean regionalisms: an agenda for IORG research', in V. Sakhuja (ed.), *Reinvigorating IOR-ARC,* New Delhi: Pentagon Press, pp. 1-17.

Dossani, Rafiq, Daniel Sneider and Vikram Sood (2009), *Does South Asia Exist?* (Washington D.C.: Brookings Institute).

Durkheim, Emile, *'The Rules of Sociological Method',* translated and edited by W.D. Halls and Steven Lukes (New York: The Free Press, 1982).

Ehrlich, Paul (2000), *Human Natures* (Washington, D.C.: Island Press)

Emmott, Bill (2008), *Rivals: Hoe the Power Struggle Between China, India and Japan Will Shape Our Next Decade* (Barnes and Nobel).

Evans, Graham and Newnham, Jeffrey (1988), *The Penguin Dictionary of International Relations,* London: Penguin Books), p. 43

Fairgrieve, James (1927), *Geography and World Power* (London: University of London Press Ltd).

Fawcett, Louise (1995/1997), "Regionalism in Historical Perspective", in Louis Fawcett and Andrew Hurrell (eds.), *Regionalism in World Politics: Regional Organization and International Order* (Oxford University Press)

Fawcett, Louise and Andrew Hurrell (eds.), (1995), *Regionalism in World Politics: Regional Organization and International Order* (Oxford University Press)

Fawn, Rick & Larkins, Jeremy (eds.) (1996), *International Society after the Cold War. Anarchy and Order Reconsidered* (Houndsmills: Macmillan)

Fearon, James and Wendt, Alexander (2002), "Rationalism v. Constructivism: A Skeptical View," in Walter Carlsnaes, Thomas Risse, and Beth Simmons, Handbook of International Relations (Thousand Oaks, CA: Sage Publications

Fisher, Fritz (1967), *Germany's Aims in First World War* (New York: W.W. Norton)

Flak, Richard (1993), *'The Challenge of Globalization and Emergence of Global Civil Society',* Rajiv Gandhi Institute of Contemporary Studies Paper No. 5 (New Delhi: Rajiv Gandhi Institute of Contemporary Studies, Rajiv Gandhi Foundation)

Freedman, Lawrence (1989), *The Evolution of Nuclear Strategy* (New York).

____ (2000), Victims and victors: reflections on the Kosovo war', *Review of International Studies*, 26, 3, pp. 350-53.

Fulbright, J. William (1996), *'The Arrogance of Power'* (New York: Random House).

Fox, W.T.R. (1949), 'Interwar International Relations Research: The American Experience', *World Politics*, 2, pp. 67-79.

Gaikwad, Sanjay (1990), *Dynamics of Indo-Soviet Relations: The Era of Indira Gandhi* (New Delhi: Deep & Deep Publications)

Ganguly, Sumit (2001), *Conflict Unending: India-Pakistan Tension since 1947* (New Delhi: Oxford University Press)

____ (2002), Back to Brinkmanship – How India and Pakistan arrived at a nuclear standoff, in: CERI/CNRS Sciences-Po, p.2. http://www.cerisciencespo.com/archive/july02/artsg.pdf (accessed on 12 Jun 2016)

Ganguly, S., and Hagerty, D.T. (2006), *Fearful Symmetry: India-Pakistan Crises in the Shadow of Nuclear Weapons* (Washington: Washington University Press).

Gartenstein-Ross, Daveed (2010), "Religious Militancy in Pakistan's Military and Inter-Services Intelligence Agency," in (ed.) Gartenstein-Ross, Daveed and May, Clifford D. *The Afghanistan-Pakistan Theater, Militant Islam, Security and Stability* (Washington, D.C.: Foundation for Defense of Democracies)

Gartenstein-Ross, Daveed and May, Clifford D. (Ed.) (2010), *The Afghanistan-Pakistan Theater, Militant Islam, Security and Stability* (Washington, D.C.: Foundation for Defense of Democracies)

Garth, Evans (1993), *'Cooperating For Peace 3: The Global Agenda for the 1990's and Beyond'* (St Leonard's, NSW: Allen & Unwin)

Garver, John W. (2016), *China's Quest: The History of The Foreign Relations of The People's Republic of China*, (NewYork, NY: Oxford University Press)

Gateway House (2012), *Neighbourhood Views of India*, Research Paper No. 7, December

Green, M.J. and A. Shearer (2012), "Defining US Indian Ocean Strategy." *The Washington Quarterly* 35(2), pp. 175-189.

Geyer, M. (1989), 'The militarization of Europe, 1914–1945' in Gillis J. (ed.) *The Militarization of the Western World* (New Brunswick, NJ: Rutgers University Press), pp 65-102.

Giddens, A. (1990), *The consequences of modernity* (Stanford, CA: Stanford University Press).

Giddens, A. (1991), *Modernity and self-identity: Self and society in the late modern age* (Cambridge: Polity), p. 37.

Gilbert Rozman, "China's Quest for Great Power Identity," *Orbis* 43, no. 3 (Summer 1999)

Glaser, Charles L. (1971), "The Security Dilemma Revisited," *World Politics*, Vol. 50, No. 1 (October 1997), pp. 171–201

Gleditsch, N.P. & Njølstad, O. (Eds.), (1990), *Arms race: Technological and Political Dynamics* (London: Sage Publications).

Glennon, Michael J. (2003), "Why the Security Council Failed," *Foreign Affairs* 82, No. 3.

Goldstein, Judith (1996), 'International law and Domestic Institutions: Reconciling North America "Unfair" trade laws', *International Organization*, 50, pp. 531-564

Guo, Xuetang and Mehdi P. Amineh (2007). "The 'Great Game' Continued: Central Eurasia and Caspian Region Fossil Fuels, *International Institute for Asian Studies* (IIAS) Newsletter, No. 45, Autumn.

Goswami, B.N. (1971), *Pakistan and China: A Study of Their Relations* (New York: Allied Publishers);

Graham Allison (2004), *Nuclear Terrorism: The Ultimate Preventable Catastrophe* (New York: Times Books).

Gray, Colin S. (1998), *Modern Strategy* (Oxford, UK: Oxford University Press).

Greenstein, Fred I. and Nelson W. Polsby (eds.), (1975), *Handbook of Political Science, Vol. 8: International Politics* (Reading, MA,)

Griffiths, Martin and O'Callaghan, Terry (2002), *International Relations: The Key Concepts* (London)

Grunfeld, A. Tom (2015), *The Making of Modern Tibet* (Routledge)

Gupta, Bhabani (1983), "Regional Security: The Indian Doctrine," *India Today*, August 31, 1983, p. 20.

Haas, Earnest B. (1953), The Balance of Power: Prescription, Concept, or Propaganda, *World Politics*, Vol. 5, No. 4 (Jul., 1953), pp. 442-477

Haass, Richard N. (2008), "The Age of Nonpolarity: What will follow US Dominance", *Foreign Affairs*, May–June

Haftendorn, H. (1991), 'The Security Puzzle: Theory-Building and Discipline-Building in International Security', *International Studies Quarterly*, vol. 35, no. 1.

Hall, Ian (2012), "India's New Public Diplomacy: Soft Power and the Limits of Government Action," *Asian Survey* 52(6): 1089–1110

Halliday, Fred (1994), *'Rethinking International Relations'* (London: Macmillan).

Hammond, Grant T. (1993), *Plowshares Into Swords: Arms Races in International Politics, 1840-1991* (Columbia, SC: University of South Carolina Press).

Hanson, Victor Davis (1989), *The Western way of war: Infantry Battle in Classical Greece* (New York: Knopf).

Harris Mylonas in "Report of the Georgetown Symposium on Religion, Democracy and the Foreign Policy of the Obama Administration," Berkley Center for Religion, Peace, and World Affairs, June 7, 2010, pp. 16–17; as quoted in Aoun, Joy; Dannan, Liora; Hameed, Sadika; Lamb, Robert D., Mixon, Kathryn: St. Peter, Denis (2012), *Religious Movements, Militancy, and Conflict in South Asia, Cases from India, Pakistan, and Afghanistan* (Center for Strategic and International Studies)

Harris, Lyndsey (2006), 'Introducing the Strategic Approach: An Examination of Loyalist Paramilitaries in Northern Ireland', *British Journal of Politics and International Relations*', Vol. 8, No. 4

Hashimoto, Ryutaro (1994), 'Vision of Japan: A Realistic Direction for the 21st Century' (Tokyo: K K Best Sellers)

Hastings, J. (2011), 'The fractured geopolitics of the United States in the Indian Ocean Region', *Journal of the Indian Ocean Region*, Vol. 7 (2), in press.

Healy, Brian, and Arthur Stein. "The Balance of Power in International History Theory and Reality" *Journal of Conflict Resolution* 17.1 (1973): 33-61.

Hechter, Michael (1999), *Containing Nationalism* (New York: Oxford University Press)

Heinz Gärtner, Adrian Hyde-Price, and Erich Reiter (eds.) (2001), *Europe's New Security Challenges* (Boulder: Lynne Rienner Pub)

Herz, J.H. (1950), "Idealist Internationalism and the Security Dilemma", in *World Politics,* Vol. 2, No.2 (Cambridge University Press), pp. 171-201.

Hilali, A.Z. (2001), 'India's Strategic Thinking and its national Security Policy', *Asian Survey,* 41, pp. 737-764.

Hinton, Harold C. (ed.), (1980), *The People's Republic of China, 1949-1979: A Documentary Survey*, vol. 1, 1949-1957 (Wilmington: Scholarly Resources), pp. 165-166.

____ (1980), The People's Republic of China 1949-79, A Documentary Survey volume 2 (Delaware: Scholarly Resource Inc.)

Holloway, David (1994), *Stalin and the Bomb: The Soviet Union and Atomic Energy, 1939-1956* (New Haven: Yale University Press),

Hopkirk, Peter (1994), *The Great Game: The Struggle for Empire in Central Asia* (New York: Kodansha America).

Hosokawa, Morihiro (1993), "New Japan Party: Responsible Reform' (Tokyo: Tokyo Keizai Shinposha).

Hough, Peter (2004), *Understanding Global Security* (London: Routledge)

Howard, Michael (1964), 'Military Power and International Order', *International Affairs,* Vol. 40, No. 3,

Huntington, Samuel P. (1996), 'Democracy for the Long Haul' *Journal of Democracy,* Vol 7. No 2. April 1996.

Huntington, Samuel P. (1997), *The Clash of Civilizations: Remaking of World Order* (New York: Simon and Schuster),

Hyde-Price, Adrian (2001), "'Beware the Jabberwock!' Security Studies in the Twenty-First Century," in. Heinz Gärtner, Adrian Hyde-Price, and Erich Reiter (eds.) *Europe's New Security Challenges* (Boulder: Lynne Rienner Pub, 2001), pp 27-54 (p.38).

Ichiro Ozawa (1994), *'Blueprint for A New Japan: The Rethinking of A Nation'* (Tokyo: Kodansha International).

Ikenberry, G. John (2001), *After victory: Institutions, strategic restraint and the rebuilding of order after major wars* (Princeton: Princeton University Press).

____ (ed.) (2002). *America unrivaled: The future of the balance of power* (Ithaca: Cornell University Press).

____ (2003a), Is American multilateralism in decline? *Perspectives on Politics* 1 (3), pp. 533–50.

____ (2003b), State power and the institutional bargain: America's ambivalent economic and security multilateralism. In *U.S. Hegemony and international organizations: The United States and multilateral institutions* (ed.) Rosemary Foot, S. Neil MacFarlane and Michael Mastanduno, 49-72 (Oxford: Oxford University Press).

Indian Annual Register: July-December 1946 (Clacutta: N.N.Mitra 1947)

Indian Council of World Affairs, *India and the United Nations* (New York: Manhattan, 1957).

INSEC [Informal Sector Service Centre] (2010), *Nepal Human Rights Yearbook 2010* (Kathmandu: INSEC).

Jablonsky, David (1992), 'National Power', *In the United States Army War College Selected Readings AY 93, Course 2, War, National Policy and Strategy',* Vol. 3 (Carlisle Barracks, PA: US Army War College,)

Jacobsen, Carl G. (ed.), *The Uncertain Course: New Weapons, Strategies and Mind-Sets* (Oxford: Oxford University Press/SIPRI),

Jacobson, H.K. (1979), *Networks of interdependence: International Organizations and Global Political System* (New York: Alfred A. Knopf)

Jackson, Robert and Sorensen, George (1999), Introduction to International Relations (New York: Oxford University Press).

Jandora, John W. (1999), "War and Culture: A Neglected Relation," *Armed Forces and Society*, Vol. 24, No. 4, Summer, pp. 541-556.

Jay P. (1979), Regionalism as geopolitics. *Foreign Affairs 58,* pp. 485-514.

Jervis, Robert (1976), *Perception and Misperception in International Politics (*Princeton, NJ: Princeton University Press).

Jervis, Robert, "Deterrence theory revisited," *World Politics* 31(2) (1979): 289-324.

Jeshurun, Chandram (1993), "South East Asia", in Jayanth Dhanapala (ed.), *Regional Approaches to Disarmament Security and Stability* (Aldershot, U.K. Dartmouth for the Institute for Disarmament Research.), p. 51.

Jha, Nalini Kant (1988), "Indo-US Pakistan Triangle: Illusion and Reality", *Link* (New Delhi), Vol. 30, No.23, January 10, 1988, pp.26-28

____ (1998), "Understanding Conflict and Cooperation between Two Democracies of the World," *Third Concept* (New Delhi), vol. 2, no. 14, April 1988.

Joeck, Neil (1985), "Pakistani Security and Nuclear Proliferation in South Asia," *Journal of Strategic Studies,* Vol. 8, No. 4, December, 1985.

Johnson, H.C. and Niemeyer (1954), 'Collective Security: The Validity of an Ideal', *International Organization,* 8

Johnston, Alastair I. (1995), *Cultural Realism: Strategic Culture and Grand Strategy in Chinese History* (Princeton, NJ: Princeton University Press).

Josiah Lee Auspitz, "Individuality, Civility, and Theory: The Philosophical Imagination of Michael Oakeshott," *Political Theory* 4 (August 1976), pp. 261-352

Kaplan, R.D. (2009), "Center Stage for the Twenty-First Century: Power Plays in the Indian Ocean." *Foreign Affairs* 88(2) pp. 16-32.

Kaplan, Stephen S. (1981), *'Diplomacy of Power, Soviet Armed Forces as a political Instrument'* (Washington DC: The Brookings Institution).

Kapur, Ashok (2006), *Indian from Regional to World Power* (New York: Routledge)

____ (2011), *India and the South Asian Strategic Triangle* (Abingdon, Oxon, OX14 4RN)

Kapur, P.S. (2005): India and Pakistan's Unstable Peace: Why Nuclear South Asia is Not Like Cold War Europe, in *InternationalSecurity* volume 30, issue 2 (Fall 2005), pp. 127-152

Karan, P.P. (1973), "The Changing Geography of Tibet," *Asian Profile: Asia's International Journal Devoted Excl. to Asian Affairs* 1.1

Kautilya. *"Kautilya: The Arthashastra."* Ed. Rangarajan (1992) (L.N. Penguine Books), p. 498

Keane, A.H., FRGS, *'Encyclopedia of Asia: Compendium of Geography with Maps and Illustrations'*, Vol. II (New Delhi: Discovery Publishing House, 1997).

Keegan, John (1993), *A History of Warfare* (New York: Vintage Books).

Kelly, Philip (1986), "Escalation of Regional Conflict: Testing the Shatterbelt Concept," *Political Geography Quarterly*, Vol. 5, No. 2, pp. 161-180

Kelly, Robert E. (2007), "Security Theory in the 'New Regionalism.'" *International Studies Review* 9), p. 197–229.

Kennan, George (1947), 'The Sources of Soviet Conduct', *Foreign Affairs*, 25(4), 566-582.

Kennedy, Paul (1988), *'The Rise and Fall of The Great Powers: Economic Changes and Military Conflict'* (New York: Random House).

Kenneth H. Keller (1997), 'Unpackaging the Environment', in *'Environment Change and Security Project Report'* (Washington D.C.: Woodrow Wilson Centre), Issue 3, Spring 1997.

Keohane, Robert O. (1984), *After hegemony: Cooperation and Discord in the World Political Economy* (Princeton, N.J.: Princeton University Press)

____ (1988), 'International Institutions: Two Approaches," *international Studies Quarterly*, Vol. 32, No. 4 (December), pp. 379-396.

____ (1989), *International Institutions and State Powers: Essays on International relations Theory* (Boulder, Colo.: Westview Press)

Khalilzad, Zalmay (1995), "Losing the Moment? The United States and the World After the Cold War," *The Washington Quarterly*, Spring 1995, pp. 87–107.

Khurram Murad (ed.), (2002), *Fundamentals of Islam* (New Delhi: Markazi Maktaba Islami Publishers)

Kissinger, Henry (1994), *Diplomacy* (New York: Simon & Schuster)

____ (2002), "Pre-emption and the End of Westphalia," *New Perspectives Quarterly* 19, no. 4 (Fall 2002).

Koshy, Ninan (2006), Under The Empire: India's new Foreign Policy (New Delhi: Left Wood)

Knorr, Klaus (1973), 'National Security Studies: Scope and Structure of the Field', in Frank N. Trager and Philip S.

Kronenberg (eds.), *National Security and American Society: Theory, Process and Policy* (Lawrence, KS.)

Krasner, Stephen D. (ed.) *International Regimes,* Special Issue of *International Organization,* Vol. 36, No. 2 (Spring),

Krauthammer, Charles, "The Unipolar Moment," *Foreign Affairs, America and the World 1990/91,* Vol. 70, No. 1, available from Lexis/Nexis Academic Universe, accessed Dec 16, 2013.

Khrushchev, Nikita S (1974), *Khrushchev Remembers: The Last Testament* (Boston: Little, Brown)

Lake, David A., and Morgan, Patrick M. (1997), "The New Regionalism in Security Affairs," in David A. Lake and Patrick M. Morgan, eds., *Regional Orders: Building Security in a New World* (University Park, PA: The Pennsylvania State University Press)

Lake, David A., and Patrick M. Morgan, eds., *Regional Orders: Building Security in a New World* (University Park, PA: The Pennsylvania State University Press)

Lakshmi, Rama (2011), "U.S. Firms Lose Out On Indian Fighter Jet Contract," *The Washington Post* (28 April 2011), http://www.washingtonpost.com/world/us-companies-bypassedin-india-fighter-jet-deal/2011/04/28/AFPVwC5E_story.html

Lamont, James and Girija Shivakumar, "US groups look for answers on jet snub," *Financial Times* (29 April 2011), http://www.ft.com/cms/s/0/08f82c52-7277-11e0-96bf-00144feabdc0.html#axzz1M3CrKutz

Landes, David S. (1998), *'The Wealth and Poverty of Nations: Why some Are So Rich and Some so Poor'* (New York: W.W. Norton).

Lane, Charles (1996), "The Satellite Revolution," *The New Republic*, Vol. 215, No. 7, August 12, 1996, p. 22.

Lavoy, Peter R. (2009), Asymmetric *Warfare in South Asia: The Causes and the Consequences of Kargil Conflict* (Delhi: Cambridge University Press)

Lemke, Douglas (2002), *Regions of War and Peace* (Cambridge, UK: Cambridge University Press).

Lengxi, Wu (1999), *Shinianlunzhan, 1956-1966: Zhong Suguanxihuiyulu, 1956–1966* [*Ten Years of Debate, 1956-1966: Recollections of Sino-Soviet Relations*] (Beijing: Zhongyangwenxian), p. 152

Levy, Marc A. (1995), "Is the Environment a National Security Issue?" *International Security* 20(2): 35-62. Web.

Li, Rex *(2009), A Rising China and Security in East Asia: Identity Construction and Security Discourse* (Abingdon: Routledge).

Lipschutz, R. (Ed.) (1995), *On Security* (New York: Columbia University Press)

Lipson, Charles (1994), "Is the Future of Collective Security Like the Past?", in Downs, George W. (ed.) *Collective Security Beyond the Cold War* (Ann Arbor: University of Michigan Press).

Liu, Xuecheng (1994), *Sino-Indian Border Dispute and Sino-Indian Relations* (Lanham, MD: University Press of America)

Lopez-Alvez, F. (1989), "Political Crises, Strategic Choices and Terrorism: The Rise and Fall of the Uruguayan Tupamaros', *Terrorism and Political Violence*, Vol. 1, No. 2

Lüthi, Lorenz (2008). *The Sino-Soviet Split: Cold War in the Communist World* (Princeton: Princeton University Press), pp, 82-84.

Lüthi, Lorenz M. (2011), "Chinese Foreign Policy, 1960-1979," in Tsuyoshi Hasegawa (ed.), *The Cold War in East Asia, 1945-1991* (Washington, D.C.: Woodrow Wilson Center Press)

Luttwak, Edward N. (1990) 'From Geo-politics to Geo-economics: Logic of Conflict, Grammar of Commerce', *The National Interest, 20, Summer*

____ (1993), *'The Endangered American Dream'* (New York: Simon and Schuster)

Lyon, Peter (1968), "The Foreign Policy of India" in F. S. Northedge (ed.), *The Foreign Policies of the Powers* (London, 1968), pp. 260-261.

Mackinder, H.J. (1904), The geographical pivot of history. *The Geographical Journal*, 1904, 23, pp. 421–37

Malik, J. Mohan (1989), 'Hands across the Himalayas', *Pacic Defence Reporter*, March, pp. 43–45;

____ (1995), 'China–India Relations in the Post-Soviet Era: The Continuing Rivalry', *China Quarterly*, 142, pp. 317–355

Malone, David (2011), "Soft Power in Indian Foreign Policy," *Economic and Political Weekly*, XLVI(36): 35–39

Mansfield Edward D., and Helen V. Milner (1999), "The New Wave of Regionalism", *International Organization* Vol. 53, No.3, Summer

Mao Zedong, "Problems of War and Strategy," November 6, 1938, *Selected Works of Mao Tse-tung*, vol. 2 (1967) (Beijing: Foreign Languages Press), pp. 219-235

Mao Zedong, "Talk with the American Correspondent Anna Louise Strong," August 1946, *Selected Works of Mao Tse-tung*, vol. 4 (1967), (Beijing: Foreign Languages Press), pp. 97-101

Mao Zedong (1969), "On The Tibet question and Taiwan Question", *JYMG*, Vol. 8, pp. 247-49.

Margolis, E. (2005), "India Rules the Waves," Proceedings. *U.S Naval Institute*, 131.3, March 2005, pp, 66–70, 70.

Masayoshi, Takemura, 'A Small but Shinning Country: Japan' (Tokyo: Tokyo Keizai Shinposha, 1994 (in Japanese).

Matthews, Lloyd J. (Ed.) (1998), *Challenging the United States Symmetrically and Asymmetrically: Can America Be Defeated* (Carlisle Barracks, Pennsylvania: US Army War College Strategic Studies Institute)

Matthews, Jessica Tuchman (1989), 'Redefining Security', *Foreign Affairs*, 68 (1989), pp. 162–77

Mattoo, Aaditya and Arvind Subramanian (2004). 'The WTO and poorest countries: The stark reality.' *IMF Working paper* 04/81.

Maxwell, Neville (1970), *India's China War* (London: Cape)

Mearsheimer, John J. (1994/95), 'The False Promise of International Institutions', *International Security*, Winter 1994/95, Vol. 19, No 3, pp. 5-49

____ (2001): *The Tragedy of Great Power Politics* (New York: W.W. Norton).

McCormick, John (1999), *The European Union: Politics and Policies* (Boulder Colo.: Westview Press)

McGillivray, Fiona and Alastair Smith (2000), 'Trust and Cooperation through agent specific punishments,' *International Organization* 54(40, pp. 809-24.

McMahon, Robert (1994), *Cold War on the Periphery: The United States, India, and Pakistan* (New York: Columbia University Press).

Medcalf, R., Heinrichs, R. and Jones, J. (2011), *Crisis and Confidence: Major Powers and Maritime Security in Indo-Pacific Asia*, Sydney: Lowy.

Medcalf, R. (2012), 'Unselfish giants? Understanding China and India as security providers', *Australian Journal of International Affairs*, Vol. 66 (1), pp. 1-13.

Melissen, Jan (Ed.) (2005), *The New Public Diplomacy: Soft Power in International Relations* (New York: Palgrave Macmillan)

Menon, K.P.S. (1963), *The Flying Troika: Extracts from a Diary* (London: Oxford University Press)

Minh-ha, T.T. (1996), An acoustic journey. In Welchman, J.C. (ed.) *Rethinking Borders* (Minneapolis, MN: University of Minnesota Press).

Modelski, George and Tompson, William R. (1996), *'Leading Sectors and World Power's: The Co-evaluation of Global Economics and Politics'* (Columbia: University of South Carolina Press)

Modi, Narendra "Address to the Joint Session of Australian Parliament," (speech, Parliament of Australia, Canberra, 18 November 2014). http://www.narendramodi.in/prime-minister-narendra-modis-address-to-the-joint-session-of-the-australian-parliament-6909 accessed June 18, 2016

Modi, Narendra, Speech at the International Fleet Review 2016 at Vishakhapatnam, India

Modi, Narendra "Media Statements by Prime Minister of India and Prime Minister of Vietnam in New Delhi," media statement, 28 October 2014, http://www.mea.gov.in/incomingvisitdetail.htm?24143/Media+Statements+by+Prime+Minister+of+India+and+Prime+ Minister+of+Vietnam+in+New+Delhi+October+28+2014;

Modi, Narendra "Opening Statement by Prime Minister at the 12th India-ASEAN Summit," (speech, India-ASEAN Summit, Nay Pyi Taw, Myanmar, 12 November 2014), http://www.mea.gov.in/incomingvisitdetail.htm?24143/Media+Statements+by+Prime+Minister+of+India+and+Prime+ Minister+of+Vietnam+in+New+Delhi+October+28+2014

Mohan, C. Rajah (2004), *Crossing the Rubicon: The Shaping of India's Foreign Policy* (New York: Palgrave)

Molander, Roger C., and Wilson, Peter A. (1993), '*The Nuclear Asymptote: On Containing Nuclear Proliferation*' (Santa Monica, Calif.: RAND)

Moon, Chung in (eds.), (1988), '*National Security in The Third World: The Management of Internal and External Threats*' (University Press, Cambridge).

Morgan, P. (2007), 'Security in International Politics: Traditional Approaches', in Collins, A. (ed.) *Contemporary Security Studies* (New York: Oxford University Press).

Morley, David, Robins, Kevin (1995), *Spaces and Identity: Global Media, Electronic Landscapes and Cultural Boundaries* (Routledge)

Muni, S.D., and Muni, Anuradha (1984), '*Regional Co-operation in South Asia*' (Delhi: National Publishing House).

Murray, Williamson and Allan R. Millett (2000), *A War to be Won: Fighting the Second World War* (Cambridge, Mass.: Harvard University Press 2000).

Myrdal, Gunnar (1968), *Asian Drama: An Inquiry Into the Poverty of Nations* (New York: Pantheon)

Narendra Modi, "Address to the Joint Session of Australian Parliament," (speech, Parliament of Australia, Canberra, 18 November 2014). http://www.narendramodi.in/prime-minister-narendra-modis-address-to-the-joint-session-of-the-australian-parliament-6909 accessed June 18

Narasimha Murthy, P.A. (1986), *India and Japan: Dimensions of Their Relations* (New Delhi: ABC Publishing House).

NeguN, Silviu (2005), "Introducere în Geopolitica," *The Romanian Economic Journal Tempus* 15, no. 1, p.3.

Nepali, R.K. (2009), Democracy in South Asia, *International Institute for Democracy and Electoral Assistance* (Stockholm, Sweden)

Ness, G.D., and Brechin, S.R. (1988), "Bridging the Gap: International Organizations as Organizations," *International Organization*, 42(2), p. 270)

New China News Agency (1954), *"Agreement between India and China on Trade and Intercourse Between Tibet Region of China and India,"* April 29, 1954

Nincic, D. (1970), *The Problem of Sovereignty in the Charter and in the Practice of the United Nations* (Leiden: Nijhof),

Niou, Emerson MS, and Peter C. Ordeshook (1987), "Preventive War and the Balance of Power A Game-Theoretic Approach," *Journal of Conflict Resolution* 31(3) pp.387-419.

'*North South: A Programme For Survival*', Report of the Brandt Commission (London: Pan, 1980).

Norbu, Dawa (2001), *China's Tibet Policy* (Richmond: Curzon)

North, Douglas C., and Thomas, Robert P. (1970), 'An Economic Theory of the Growth of the Western World," *The Economic History Review*, 2nd series, Vol. 23, No. 1 (April),

Notes on Mikoyan-Nehru Conversations, 26–28 March 1956, in SDC, Subject File 19, 1956, NMML. Extracts of the conversations are reproduced in *Selected Works of Jawaharlal Nehru,* Vol. 32,

Nye Jr, Joseph S. (1968), *International Regionalism: Readings* (Boston: Little, Brown.)

____ (1990), 'Soft Power', *Foreign Policy,* No. 80, Twentieth Anniversary (Autumn)

____ (2002), *The Paradox of American Power: Why the World's Only Superpower Can't Go it Alone* (New York: Oxford University Press)

____ (2004), *Soft Power: The Means to Success in World Politics* (New York: Public Affairs).

Nye, J.S., and S.M. Lynn-Jones (1988), 'International Security Studies: A Report of the Conference on the State of the Field', *International Security,* 12 (4), pp. 5-27

Nye, Joseph S., and William A. Owens, 'America's Information Edge', *Foreign Affairs,* vol. 75, no. 2, March/April 1996

Obama, Barack (2010), "National Security Strategy." Available at http://www.whitehouse.gov/sites/default/files/rss_viewer/national_security_ strategy.pdf

Osgood, Robert, Cited in E. Azar and Chung in Moon (eds.), *'National Security in The Third World: The Management of Internal and External Threats'* (University Press, Cambridge 1988)

Pacione, Michael Ed. (1988), *The Geography of the Third World: Progress and Prospects* (London: Routledge)

Palme, Olof (1982), "Common Security: A Programme For Disarmament", Report of the Independent Commission on Disarmament and Security Issues under the Chairmanship of Olof Palme (London: Pan Books), pp. 138-39.

Palmer, Jr., Bruce (1978), 'Strategic Guidelines for thew United States in the 1980s', in Palmer, Jr., Bruce (ed.), *Grand Strategy for the 1980s* (Washington DC.: American Enterprise Institute for Public Policy Research).

Pathak, A. (1998), *Indian modernity: Contradictions, paradoxes, and possibilities* (New Delhi: Gyan Publishing House).

Pathak, Bishnu and Uprety, Devendra (2009), *Terai–Madhes Searching for Identity Based Security* (Kathmandu: Conflict Study Center), pp. 1-17.

Paul, T.V., James Wirtz, and Michel Fortmann (eds.) (2004), *Balance of power theory and practice in the twenty-first century* (Stanford: Stanford University Press).

Paul, T.V., and Nayar, Baldev Raj (2003), *India in the World Order: Searching for Major Power Status* (Cambridge: Cambridge University Press),

Perle, Richard (2003), "United They Fall," *The Spectator* (22 March 2003).

Petersen, Alexandros and Barysch, Katinka, *Russia, China and the Geopolitics of Energy in Central Asia,* The Center for European Reform, p. 1 available at http://www.cer.org.uk/sites/defaults/files/publications/attachments/pdf/2011/rp_010-4118.pdf

Peterson, John and Hugh Ward (1995), 'Coalitional Instability and the New Multidimensional Politics of Security: A Rational Choice Argument for US–EU Cooperation', *European Journal of International Relations*, 1 (1995), pp. 131–56

Powell, C. (2001), "U.S. Looks to its Allies for Stability in Asia and the Pacific," *International Herald Tribune*, 27 January 2001.

Prozumenshikov, M.Y. "The Sino-Indian Conflict, the Cuban Missile Crisis, and the Sino-Soviet Split, October 1962: New Evidence from the Russian Archives," *CWIHP Bulletin* 8-9 (Winter 1996/97)

Pyakuryal, Kailash; March, Kathryn and Bipin Acharya (eds.) (2007), *Nepal in Conflict: Theoretical underpinnings, conflict resolution, conflict transformation, and Peace-building.* Pyakural, Kailash *et al. Nepal in Conflict* (Kathmandu: Sociological/ Anthropological Society of Nepal).

Quinlan, Michael (1997), *Thinking About Nuclear Weapons* (London: Royal United Services Institution).

Radhakrishnan, Dr. Sarvepalli (1927), The Hindu View of Life (London: Uncoin Books)

Raghavan, Srinath (2010), *War and Peace in Modern India: A Strategic History of Nehru Years* (London: Palgrave Macmillan)

Raghavan, V.R. (2007), Working Paper, The Stanley Foundation's Conference: After the Unipolar Moment: Asia and Regional and Global Order, May 31, http://www.stanleyfoundation.org/publications/working_papers/RAGHAVAN_working_paper_May_conference_FINAL.doc

Rahul Roy-Chaudhry, 'The Indian Coast Guard in the 1990's', *Indian Defence Review* (New Delhi: Lancers, October 1993),

Raja Mohan, C. (2006), 'India and the Balance of Power', *Foreign Affairs,* July-August, pp.17-32

_____ (2011), 'India and Australia: maritime partners in the Indo-Pacific', *The Asialink Essays*, Vol. 3 (7), November, pp. 1-4.

Rasmussen, Mikkel Vedby (2008), Afghanistan and the Boomerang Effect, in: Bernard, Cheryl et al. (ed.), *Afghanistan: State and Society, Great Power, Politics and the Way Ahead* (Santa Monica: RAND), pp. 17-35

Rashid, Ahmed (2011), "The Way Out of Afghanistan," *The New York Review of Books* (11 January 2011).

Rathjens, G.W. (1974), "Flexible Response Options," *Orbits,* Fall 1974.

Raustiala, Kal, and Anne-Marie Slaughter (2002), "International Law, International Relations and Compliance." *Handbook of International Relations* (Sage Publications). 28 Feb. 2011.

Reddy, T. Ramakrishna (1968), *India's Policy in the United Nations* (Cranbury, NJ: Associated University Presses)

Reid, James J. (1992), 'Total war, the annihilation ethic, and the Armenian genocide, 1870-19182 in Richard G. Hovanissian, *The Armenian Genocide: History, Politics, Ethics* (Basingstoke: Macmillan).

Risse, T. (2003), *Beyond Iraq: Challenges* to the *Transatlantic Security Community,* AICGS/ *German-American Dialogue Working Paper Series* (*Washington, DC:* AICGS).

Romm, Joseph J. (1993), *Defining National Security* (New York)

Rose, Leo E. (1989), in Robinson, F. (ed.), *Cambridge Encyclopedia of India, Pakistan, Bangladesh and Sri Lanka* (Cambridge: California University Press)

Robinson, F. (ed.), *Cambridge Encyclopedia of India, Pakistan, Bangladesh and Sri Lanka* (Cambridge: California University Press)

Rosecrance, R. (1966). Bipolarity, Multipolarity, and the Future. *The Journal of Conflict Resolution, 10*(3), 314-327. Retrieved from http://www.jstor.org/stable/173003

Rostow, W.W. (1972), *The Diffusion of Power: An Essay in Recent History* (New York: Macmillan).

Roy-Chaudhary, Rahul (1993), 'The Indian Coast Guard in the 1990's', *Indian Defence Review* (New Delhi: Lancers), October 1993.

Rubin, Barnett R. (2007), Saving Afghanistan, in: *Foreign Affairs* 86(1), pp. 57-78.

Ruggie, John Gerard (1992), "Multilateralism: The Anatomy of an Institution," *International Organization,* Vol. 46, No. 3 (Summer)

____ (2003), "The United Nations and Globalization: Patterns and Limits of Institutional Adaptation." *Global Governance* 9.3 (2003): 301-321.

Rumley, D. (2005), 'The geopolitics of Asia-Pacific regionalism in the 21st century', *The Otemon Journal of Australian Studies*, Vol. 31 (1), pp. 3-25.

Rumley, D. (2007), 'Australia's regional security challenges: a geopolitical perspective', in D. Rumley and D. Gopal, eds., *Globalisation and Regional Security: India and Australia*, Delhi: Shipra, pp. 133-157.

Rumley, D. (2012), 'Refloating IOR-ARC: Australian perspectives', in V. Sakhuja (ed.), *Reinvigorating IOR-ARC*, New Delhi: Pentagon Press, pp. 87-105.

Russett, Bruce (1967), *International Regions and International Systems* (Chicago, IL: Rand McNally)

Russett, B., Oneal, J.R., and Davis, D.R. (1998): "The Third Leg of the Kantian Tripod for Peace: International Organizations and Militarized Disputes, 1950–85," *International Organization, 52*(2), pp. 441–6

Sakhuja, Vijay (2016), "Forecast 2016: Indian Ocean Politics and Security", IPCS, accessed on June 28, 2016

Sali, M.L. (1998), *India-China Border Dispute: A Case Study of the Eastern Sector* (New Delhi: A.P.H. Publishing Corporation),

Simes, Dimitri K. (2003), America's Imperial Dilemma', *Foreign Affairs,* vol 82, no. 6, November/ December 2003

Syed, Anwar Hussain (1974), *China & Pakistan: Diplomacy of an Entente Cordiale* (Amherst: The University of Massachusetts Press,)

Schaffer, Howard B. (1993), *Chester Bowles: New Dealer in the Cold War* (Cambridge: Harvard University Press).

Schelling, Thomas *(1980), The Strategy of Conflict* (Cambridge, MA: Harvard University Press)

____ (1984), *Choice and Consequence: Perspectives of an Errant Economist* (Cambridge, MA: Harvard University Press)

Schireider, Gerald and Patricia A. Weitsman (ed.), (1997), *'Enforcing Cooperation: Risky States and Inter-Governmental Management of Conflict'* (London: Macmillan Press Ltd.).

Semmel, Bernard (1981), *Marxism and the Science of War* (Oxford: Oxford University Press).

Shah, Saubhagaya (2002), 'From Evil State to Civil Society', in Dixit, K & Ramachandran, S (Eds.) *State of Nepal* (Lalitpur: Himal Books), pp.137-160

Shakya, Tsering W. (1999), *The Dragon in the Land of Snows: A History of Modern Tibet Since 1947* (London: Pimlico)

Shanks, Cherly, Jacobson, Harold K., and Kaplan, Jefery H. (1996), 'Inertia and Change in the Constellation of International Governmental Organizations, 1982-2992', *International Organization,* 50(4), pp. 593-626.

Shapiro, I. (2007), *Containment: Rebuilding a Strategy against Global Terror* (Princeton).

Shapiro, M.J. and Alker H.R. (eds.), (1996), *Challenging boundaries: global flows, territorial identities* (Minneapolis, MN: University of Minneapolis Press).

Shaw, Martin (1990), 'Strategy and social process: lessons from strategic studies', *Sociology*, 24, 3, pp.465-73.

____ (1993), 'There Is No Such Thing as Society: Beyond Individualism and Statism in International Security Studies', *Review of International Studies*, 19, pp. 159–7

____ (2000), Theory of the Global State: Globality as Unfinished Revolution (Cambridge: Cambridge University Press)

Sheridan, G. (2011), 'New Australia-US push deals India in to Pacific', *The Australian* newspaper, 17 September and available at: http://www.theaustralian.com.au/news/opinion/new-australia-us-push-deals-india-in-to-pacific/story-e6frg76f-1226139302534

Sigal, L.V. (1979), "Rethinking the Unthinkable," *Foreign Policy,* no. 34 (Spring 1979).

Silviu Negu Ñ. (2005), "Introducere în Geopolitica" *The Romanian Economic Journal Tempus* 15, no. 1.

Simes, Dimitri K. (2003), America's Imperial Dilemma', *Foreign Affairs,* vol 82, no. 6, November/December 2003

Singh, Jaswant (1998), 'Against Nuclear Apartheid', *Foreign Affairs,* September/ October 1998, Vol. 77, No. 5, pp. 41-52.

Singh, Major Narendar (1982), *Terrorism*, Dissertation for MSc, Madras University, at Defence Services Staff College Wellington (Unpublished).

Singh, Colonel Narendar (1997), Landmines Ban: Another Convention on Disarmament, *Free Press*, Vol. XV, No. 134, November 17

_____ (1997), "India's Maritime Strategy', *Free Press,* Vol. XV: No. 142, November 26, 1997.

_____ (1997), Dominance Through Technology, *Free Press,* Vol. XV, No. 145, November 29.

_____ (1997), The Battle of Islamgarh, *Free Press,* Vol. XV, No. 150, December 5.

_____ (1998), India's Deadly Strategic Gambles, *Garha Chronicle*, Vol. V, No. 10, January 5.

_____ (1998), US Opposition to India's Ambition's, *Garha Chronicle*, Vol. V, No. 33, February 28.

_____ (1998), Pakistan: A Failed State, *Garha Chronicle*, Vol. V, No. 53, March 21.

_____ (1998), Our failure in Strategic Planning, *Garha Chronicle*, Vol. V, No. 98, May 5.

_____ (1998), Chemical and Biological Weapons Conventions *Garha Chronicle*, Vol. V, No. 102, May 9.

_____ (1998), 'India Should Ignore Japanese Rhetoric', *Garha Chronicle,* Vol. V, No. 139 (Indore City Edition, June 15.

_____ (1998), Exports Mandatory to Sustain Defence Plans, *Garha Chronicle*, Vol. V, No. 160, July 6.

_____ (1998), Tibet's Dilemma: India Need's to Review her Policy, *Garha Chronicle*, Vol. V, No. 175,, July 21.

_____ (1998), NAM and India: Need to have more pragmatic look, *Garha Chronicle*, Vol. V, No. 218, September 3.

_____ (1998), The Great Game Being Replayed, *Garha Chronicle*, Vol. V, No. 258, October 14.

_____ (1998), Rationale for Maritime Forces, *Garha Chronicle*, Vol. V, No. 312, December 8.

Singh, Col (Retd) Narendar (2006), *Conduct of War* (New Delhi: Manas Publications).

Singh, Swaran (2003), *China—South Asian: issues, equations, policies* (New Delhi: Lancer's Books).

Sinha, Mira (1979), "China: the Making and Unmaking of Nehru's Foreign Policy," *China Report* 15/2, p. 60.

Smith, Anthony D. (1991), *National Identity* (Harmondsworth, Middlesex: Penguin Books, 1991)

Smith, Donald Eugene (1963), *India as a Secular State* (Princeton: Princeton University Press)

Smith, Jeff (2013), "Frontier Tension: Is China Provoking India at Disputed Border?" *Defense News*, May 5, 2013, accessed May 5, 2016, http://www.defensenews.com/article/20130505/DEFREG/305050007/Frontier-Tension

Smith, M.L.R. (1995), *Fighting For Ireland? The Military Strategy of the Irish Republican Movement* (London: Routledge)

____ (2008), 'William of Ockham, Where Are You When We Need You? Reviewing Modern Terrorism Studies', *Journal of Contemporary History*, Vol. 44, No. 2

Smith, General Sir Rupert (2005), *The Utility of Force. The Art of War in the Modern World* (London)

Smoke, Richard (1975), 'National Security Affairs', in Fred I. Greenstein and Nelson W. Polsby (eds.), *Handbook of Political Science, Vol. 8: International Politics* (Reading, MA).

Snyder, Glenn H. "The security dilemma in alliance politics." *World Politics*, 36.04 (1984): 461-495.

Solingen, Etel. (1998), *Regional Orders at Century's Dawn: Global and Domestic Influences on Grand Strategy*. (Princeton, NJ: Princeton University Press).

Starr, S. Frederick (2008), A Regional Approach to Afghanistan and Its Neighbors, in: Tellis, Ashley J et al., (ed.), *Challenges and Choices* (Strategic Asia 2008-09), (Seattle: National Bureau of Asian Research), pp. 333-362.

Starr, Richard F. (1998), "Russia's Blue Print for National Strategy', in Schemer, Benjamin F. (ed.) *'Strategic Review'* (Boston: US Strategic Institute, Spring 1998).

Stiglitz, Joseph E. (2002), *Globalization and its Discontents* (New York, NY: W.W. Norton), Chap 3.

Subimal Dutt Papers, Subject Files, File #32, p.48

Swamy, Subramanian (2001), *India's China Perspective* (New Delhi: Konark)

Tang, Chritopher (2012), Beyond India: The Utility of Sino-Pakistan Relations in Chinese Foreign Policy, 1962-65, *Cold War International History Project* No. 64 (Washington D.C.: Woodrow Wilson International Center for Scholars)

Tankel, Stephen "Lashkar-e-Taiba: From 9/11 to Mumbai," *The International*

Center for the Study of Radicalization and Political Violence (April/May 2009), http://icsr.info/news/attachments/1240846916ICSRTankelReport.pdf.

Tetlock, Philip E. and Aaron Belkin (Eds.) (1996), *Counterfactual Thought Experiments in World Politics: Logical Methodological and Psychological Perspectives* (Princeton: Princeton University Press).

Thakur, Ramesh and Van langenhove Luk (2006), 'Enhancing Global governance Through regional Integration', *Global Governance,* Vol 12, No 3 (July-September 2006).

The Hindu, "Time to demonstrate an 'Act East' Policy". *The Hindu, 12 November 2014.* Retrieved 12 November 2014

The Times of India, "PM Modi meets Myanmar President U Thein Sein". *The Times of India.* 12 November 2014. Retrieved 12 November 2014

Tickner, J. Ann (1995), 'Re-visioning Security', in Ken Booth and Steve Smith (eds.), *International Relations Theory Today* (Oxford), pp. 175–97

Trager, Frank N. and Philip S. Kronenberg (eds.), (1973), *National Security and American Society: Theory, Process and Policy* (Lawrence, KS.)

Tuathail, G.Ó. (1992), 'The Bush Administration and the 'End' of the Cold War: A Critical Geopolitics of US Foreign Policy in 1989,' *Geoforum* 23: 437-452.

Ullman, Richard. H. (1983), 'Redefining Security', *International Security,* 8 (1), pp. 129-153

United Nations Official Records, 2nd Session of General Assembly 1947, 1.138

United Nations Office on Drugs and Crime, "The Global Afghan Opium Trade: A Threat Assessment, 2011," July, 2011: 7, www.unodc.org/documents/data-and-analysis/Studies/Global_Afghan_Opium _Trade_2011-web.pdf.

United Nations Office on Drugs and Crime, "Opium Production in Afghanistan shows increase, prices set to rise," October 11, 2011, http://unama.unmissions.org/Portals/UNAMA/Documents/October11_UNODC_Opium_ Survey_ Press_Release_ENG.pdf.

United Nations, *Yearbook of the United Nations,* Office of Public Information, 1947, United Nations

U.S. Atomic Energy Commission, "An Interim Report of British Work on Joe," 22 September 1949, Top Secret; Source: Harry S. Truman Library, President's Secretary's Files, box 199, NSC-Atomic

US National Defense University's Institute for National Strategic Studies in their 1998 Strategic Assessment available at http://www.ndu.edu/inss/ sa98/ sa98ch11.html

vanCreveld, Martin (2008), *The Culture of War* (New York: Presidio Press

Vázquez-Gómez, José de J. (1993), "Modelling multidomain security." *Proceedings on the 1992-1993 workshop on New security paradigms.* ACM, 1993.

Vohra, Ranbir (1977), *'The Making of India: A Historical Survey'* (New York 10504: ME Sharpe. Inc.).

Waver, O. (1995), "Securitization and Desecuritization" in R. Lipschutz (Ed.) *On Security* (New York: Columbia University Press)

Wagner, R. Harrison, "The theory of games and the balance of power," *World Politics* 38(4) (1986): 546-576

Walt, Stephen M. (1987), *The origins of alliances* (Ithaca: Cornell University Press).

____ (1991), 'The Renaissance of Security Studies', *International Studies Quarterly*, 35, no. 2, pp. 211–39

____ (2002), Keeping the world "off balance": Self restraint in U.S. foreign policy. In *America unrivaled: The future of the balance of power* (ed.), G.J. Ikenberry (Ithaca: Cornell University Press), pp. 121–54.

____ (2004). Can the United States be balanced? If so, how? American Political Science Association Annual Convention, Chicago, September 2–4, 2004.

Waltz, Kenneth N. (1979), *Theory of International Politics* (Reading, MA)

____ (1993), 'The Emerging Structure of International Politics', *International Security*, 18, pp. 44–79

Webster's Collegiate Dictionary, Springfield, *Mass: Merriam-Webster*

Weiss, Stanley A. (2008), "India, the Incredible and the Vulnerable", *International Herald Tribune*, April 23, 2008.

Weitsman, Patricia A. (ed.), (1997), 'Enforcing Cooperation: Risky States and Inter-governmental Management of Conflict" (London: Macmillan Press Ltd.)

____ (1997), "Intimate Enemies: The Politics of Peacetime Alliances," *Security Studies* 7 (1), pp. 156 192.

____ (2003), "Alliance Cohesion and Coalition Warfare: The Central Powers and the Triple Entente," *Security Studies* 12 (3), pp. 79 113.

____ (2004), *Dangerous Alliances: Proponents of Peace, Weapons of War* (Palo Alto.: Stanford University Press).

____ (2006), "The High Price of Friendship," *The New York Times*, August 31.

____ (2009), "With a Little Help from our Friends? The Costs of Coalition Warfare," *Origins: Current Events in Historical Perspective* 3 (1), p.113.

Wendt, Alexander (1992), "Anarchy is What States Make of It: The Social Construction of Power Politics", *International Organization*, vol. 46, no. 2 (Spring), pp. 391-425.

____ (1995), 'Constructing International Politics' *International Security* 20(1), pp. 71-81

____ (1999), *Social Theory of International Politics* (New York, NY: Cambridge University Press).

Westad, O. Arne (1998), "The Sino-Soviet Alliance and the United States," in: O. Arne Westad (ed.), *Brothers in Arms: The Rise and Fall of the Sino-Soviet Alliance, 1945-1963* (Washington, D.C.: Woodrow Wilson Center)

Whittlessey, Derwent S., P.E. James and C.F. Jones, *'American Geography – Inventory and Prospect'* (Syracuse University, 1954).

Wiseman, Geoffrey (1989), 'Common Security in The Asia Pacific Region', *The Pacific Review,* Vol. 5, No. 1.

Wesley, M. (2011), 'Irresistible rise of the Indo-Pacific', *The Australian* newspaper, 4 May – accessible at: http://www.theaustralian.com.au/news/arts/irresistible-rise-of-the-indo-pacific/story-e6frg8nf-1226047014015. 8

Williams, M.C. (1997), "The Institutions of Security Elements of a Theory of Security Organizations." *Cooperation and Conflict* 32 (3), pp. 287 307.

Wolfers, Arnold (1952), "National Security as an Ambiguous Symbol', *Political Science Quarterly,* Vol. LXVII, No. 4, December 1952, p. 481

_____ (1962), *Discord and Collaboration: Essays on International Politics* (Baltimore: John Hopkins Press)

Wolpert, Stanley (1984), *Jinnah of Pakistan* (New York: Oxford University Press)

Woosang, Kim, and Hyun, In-Taek (2004), "Toward new concept of security: Human security in world politics" in 2008 World Policy Conference at http://www.worldpolicyconference.com/

William T. Tow, Ramesh Thakur, and In-Taek Hyun (eds.) *Asia's Emerging Regional Order, Reconsidering Traditional and Human Security* (New Delhi: Manas Publications).

Wu, Lengxi (1994), *Yi Mao zhuxi* (Recalling Chairman Mao), (Beijing: Xinhua)

Wu Lengxi (1999), *Shinianlunzhan, 1956-1966: Zhong Suguanxihuiyulu, 1956–1966* [*Ten Years of Debate, 1956-1966: Recollections of Sino-Soviet Relations*] (Beijing: Zhongyangwenxian),

Wyatt-Walter, Andrew (1995/1997), "Regionalism, Globalization, and World Economic Order", in Fawcett and Hurrell (eds), *Regionalism in World Politics: Regional Organization and International Order* (Oxford University Press),

Xuecheng, Liu (1994), *The Sino-Indian Border Dispute* (New York: Lanham)

Xuetang, Guo and Mehdi P. Amineh (2007). ˉThe Great Game' Continued: Central Eurasia and Caspian Region Fossil Fuels, *International Institute for Asian Studies (IIAS),* Newsletter, No. 45, Autumn.

Young, Oran R. (1982), 'Regime Dynamics: The Rise and Fall of International Regimes', in Krasner, Stephen D. (ed.) *International Regimes,* Special Issue of *International Organization,* Vol. 36, No. 2 (Spring)

_____ (1989), *International Cooperation: Building Regimes for Natural Resources and Environment* (Ithaca, N.Y.: Cornell University Press)

Yu Xintian, "Zhongguowenhuajiazhiguan de goujianyuchuanbo," *Guojiwentiyanjiu,* no. 6 (2011): 5-19, 126; CaiTuo, "Dangdai Zhongguoguojidiweizhong de jigewenti."

Zafar Imam (1975), *Ideology and Reality in Soviet Policy in Asia: Indo-Soviet Relations, 1947-1960* (Delhi: Klyani).

Zaidi, "A Profile of Baitullah Mehsud"; Hassan Abbas (2008), "A Profile of Tehrik-i-Taliban Pakistan," *Combating Terrorism Center (CTC) Sentinel* 1, no. 2 (January 2008).

Zakaria, Fareed (2012), "The World has changed, Mr. Romney", *The Washington Post*, 1 February 2012, at http://www.washingtonpost.com/opinions/the-post-american-worlddemands-a-new-approach-from-the-us/2012/02/01/gIQAba5ziQ_story.html

Zeitourn, Mark and Jeroen Warner (2006), "Hydro-Hegemony: A Framework for Analysis of Trans-boundary Water Conflict', *Water Policy*, Vol. 8, No. 5, pp.435-60.

Zemanek, K. (1984), 'Interdependence', In Bernhardt, R (ed.) *Encyclopedia of Public International Law* (New York: Elsevier).

Zipf, G.K. (1949), *Human Behaviour and Principle of Least Effort* (Cambridge, M.A.: Addison-Wsley).

Ziring, Lawrence (1971), *The Ayub Kahn Era: Politics' in Pakistan 1958-1969* (Syracuse: Syracuse University Press).

Ziring, Lawrence, Robert E. Riggs, and *Jack C. Plano* (2005), *The United Nations: International Organization and World Politics*. Fourth Edition (*Belmont, CA*: Thomson *Wadswort*).

INDEX